ABOUT ISLAND PRESS

Island Press is the only nonprofit organization in the United States whose principal purpose is the publication of books on environmental issues and natural resource management. We provide solutions-oriented information to professionals, public officials, business and community leaders, and concerned citizens who are shaping responses to environmental problems.

In 1998, Island Press celebrates its fourteenth anniversary as the leading provider of timely and practical books that take a multidisciplinary approach to critical environmental concerns. Our growing list of titles reflects our commitment to bringing the best of an expanding body of literature to the environmental community throughout North America and the world.

Support for Island Press is provided by The Jenifer Altman Foundation, The Bullitt Foundation, The Mary Flagler Cary Charitable Trust, The Nathan Cummings Foundation, The Geraldine R. Dodge Foundation, The Ford Foundation, The Vira I. Heinz Endowment, The W. Alton Jones Foundation, The John D. and Catherine T. MacArthur Foundation, The Andrew W. Mellon Foundation, The Charles Stewart Mott Foundation, The Curtis and Edith Munson Foundation, The National Fish and Wildlife Foundation, The National Science Foundation, The New-Land Foundation, The David and Lucile Packard Foundation, The Surdna Foundation, The Winslow Foundation, The Pew Charitable Trusts, and individual donors.

Stewardship Across Boundaries

STEWARDSHIP ACROSS BOUNDARIES

Edited by

Richard L. Knight and Peter B. Landres

ISLAND PRESS

Washington, D.C. • Covelo, California

Cover photos: A portion of the upper Swan Valley in western Montana. A 1989 SPOT image is on the left, and on the right is the ownership of this area overlaid on the SPOT image. Each square is one mile on a side. Ownership is as follows: horizontal lines are Montana state lands; vertical lines are Plum Creek (a timber company) lands; diagonal lines running from the upper left to the lower right are private lands; diagonal lines running from the upper right to the lower left are USDA Forest Service lands; and cross-hatched lines are Confederated Salish-Kootenai Tribal lands. These images show the variety of ownership in a relatively small area, the legacy of checkerboard ownership, and the mixed ownership of land that appears relatively contiguous on the SPOT image. Many thanks to Don Krogstad, Flathead National Forest, for his time and expertise in providing and helping to prepare these images.

Library of Congress Cataloging-in-Publication Data
Stewardship across boundaries / [edited by] Richard L. Knight and
    Peter B. Landres
        p.   cm.
    Includes bibliographical references and index.
    ISBN 1-55963-515-0(cloth). — ISBN 1-55963-516-9 (pbk.)
    1. Land use—Management. 2. Boundaries—Environmental aspects.
3. Conservation of natural resources—United States. 4. Natural
resources—United States—Management.   I. Knight, Richard L.
II. Landres, Peter B.
HD205.S74   1998   98–10505
333.73'0973—dc21   CIP

Printed on recycled, acid-free paper

Manufactured in the United States of America
10 9 8 7 6 5 4 3 2 1

We dedicate this work to Aldo Leopold.
By his writings and through his intellectual descendants, a
land is being made where barriers are dimmed and lands are connected.

"It is a fact, patent both to my dog and myself, that at daybreak I am the sole owner of all the acres I can walk over. It is not only boundaries that disappear, but also the thought of being bounded."

—Aldo Leopold, *Great Possessions*

Contents

Acknowledgments

We are indebted to the chapter authors. The issue of cross-boundary stewardship is certainly not new, yet remarkably little is written about the topic. Accordingly, our authors struggled in covering familiar natural resource issues, but from the startlingly fresh perspective of peering over human-constructed lines on the land. Although the authors' services were voluntary, their sense of cooperation and dedication to this project made our work seem part of a family effort. By their actions, they reflect a new generation of those who view boundaries as opportunities rather than barriers.

Those who know Island Press and its staff will understand our debt to them for their contribution to stewardship and natural resources. Barbara Dean has been a friend and willing partner to our ideas from the inception, and Barbara Youngblood offered calm sureness with all the ten thousand details. The arduous task of copyediting was adroitly handled by Christine Paige.

Richard Knight wishes to thank the many individuals at Colorado State University and elsewhere who have shaped his thoughts through discussion and disagreement. In particular, he feels indebted to Heather Knight, George Wallace, Curt Meine, Gary Meffe, and his parents and siblings for days spent outdoors and discussions over the years regarding land and people.

Peter Landres wishes to thank Madeline Mazurski for her patience and understanding, as well as her sharp wit and perceptive editing. David J. Parsons, director of the USDA Forest Service's Aldo Leopold Wilderness Research Institute, graciously and generously gave his time and the full support of the Institute to allow work on this book. Special thanks are due to many others who contributed in often subtle ways to some of the ideas expressed in this book, especially Tim Hogan with his relentless, keen, and cheerful intellect; Alan Watson with his fresh and energetic thoughts on wilderness social science; and Dave Parsons with his deep and broad experience in Sequoia and Kings Canyon National Parks. Curt Meine suggested the wonderful example of the "boundary fishing place" Chabanakongkomuk.

Introduction

Every piece of land, no matter how remote or untrammeled, has a boundary. Imposed on a landscape usually for administrative purposes, boundaries are lines demarcating and dividing an area into units. These lines may follow topographic and biological features, such as mountain ridges or rivers, or, more often, boundaries follow the straight lines of political dictate and compromise. Administrative boundaries almost always fragment a landscape, disrupting the ebb and flow of individuals and ecosystem processes. Alternatively, boundaries often serve important roles, such as marking the line protecting wilderness from mechanized contrivances. Cronon (1983) cites an example of the Native American "boundary fishing place" Chabanakongkomuk near present-day Worcester, Massachusetts, whose name could be interpreted as "You fish on your side, I fish on my side, nobody fish in the middle—no trouble."

Although there are several recent syntheses on ecological boundaries as ecotones and edges (Hudson 1991, Hansen and di Castri 1992, Risser 1995), remarkably little has been written on the impact of administrative boundaries and adjacent lands on natural resources and their management. For example, biological impacts of administrative boundaries and adjacent lands on national parks were first described in the scientific literature a little more than a decade ago (Newmark 1985) and were recently identified as one of the greatest threats to designated wilderness (Cole and Landres 1996), regardless of the form of activity (e.g., whether livestock grazing or subdivisions) occurring on adjacent lands (Knight and Mitchell 1997). Even more telling, boundaries are seldom listed in the indexes of contemporary books on management issues concerning the conservation of biological diversity. Forman (1995) is a notable exception to this trend, offering in-depth discussion of ecological boundaries and their policy and management implications.

How did we get to where we are today, with so many different state, federal, and local agencies and private organizations, each with differing and sometimes conflicting mandates, policies, and regulations, all searching for ways to coexist on a shared landscape? The reasons for today's fragmented management are many, but we focus on two. First, ecologically, boundaries were a necessary part of traditional vegetation descrip-

1

tions developed by the pioneers of ecology in the early 1900s. One of the tenets of this pioneering ecology, embodied in the phrase "a balance of nature," was that ecosystems were internally regulated and in equilibrium with climate, inexorably moving toward a single climax or stable condition. These early concepts fostered the belief that ecosystem boundaries were tangible, rather than arbitrary constructs of our intellect and desire to understand a complex world. Second, managerially, boundaries were necessary to define administrative jurisdiction and responsibility, so it was desirable for natural resource agencies to accept the notion of relatively fixed ecosystem boundaries. This combination of ecological and managerial factors led to a belief that lands managed by an agency were separate and independent from other lands, that what happened on one side of a border didn't necessarily affect what happened on the other.

The consequences of this belief were several, including managers making land-use decisions in isolation from managers on adjoining lands, loss of species that must disperse or migrate across administrative borders, increased likelihood of threats such as alien species or pollutants moving into and compromising natural systems, and disruption of natural processes such as fire that flow across large areas of land. Ultimately, these impacts reduce the biological and social values of public and private lands. Furthermore, as noted by Forman (1995), "It is simply inept or poor-quality work to consider a patch as isolated from its surroundings in the mosaic. Designs, plans, management proposals, and policies based on drawing an absolute boundary around a piece of the mosaic should be discarded. Moreover, because we know it is wrong, i.e., we know ecological context is as important as content, the practice is unethical. Ethics impel us to consider an area in its broadest spatial and temporal perspectives."

It is time for a change in the way U.S. natural resources are managed. Today managers recognize the importance of focusing beyond as well as within their boundaries, and ecologists recognize that the 1900s view of ecosystems does not capture their spatial and temporal dynamism (Landres 1992, Pickett et al. 1992, Christensen 1995). Both managers and scientists now see that administrative and ecosystem borders are arbitrarily defined and delineated; they are not closed but leaky and experience inputs and fluxes from things as diverse as water and pollutants to migrating species and humans crossing borders to hunt, cut firewood, or picnic. Refreshingly, with this shift from the belief in "a balance of nature" to a new more realistic view embodied in the phrase "the flux of nature" (Pickett et al. 1992), there is reason to believe that natural resource managers can be more responsive to the dynamic nature of human-dominated landscapes (Pickett and Ostfeld 1995). This new land perspective emphasizes that managers are involved with users and individuals beyond the boundaries they are responsible for because what occurs beyond their borders directly and indirectly affects what occurs within their borders.

The complex biological, socioeconomic, and managerial impacts of boundaries are a significant component of land-use decisions and practices today. Managers now face the difficult task of sustaining biological diversity while providing amenity and commodity uses from landscapes that have been delineated and affected by boundaries established in the past (Gunderson et al. 1995, Smith et al. 1995). These impacts affect lands spanning a continuum of management goals, from designated wilderness to lands devoted solely to commodity production. Boundary impacts are perhaps most difficult to manage on multiple-use lands, which lie between the ends of the management continuum, where ecosystem management strives to provide goods and services while maintaining native biological diversity, and where managers strive to balance both amenity and commodity values (Yaffee et al. 1996).

Our goals for this book are many. First and foremost we wish to draw attention to boundary impacts and stewardship across boundaries to spur open discussion between students, scientists, managers, and activists on this emerging topic. Second, we would like to provide a forum for people with legal, social, and ecological perspectives to develop their ideas on boundary impacts and cross-boundary management. Our third goal is to show how legal, social, and ecological conditions interact in causing boundary impacts and how their integration is necessary for improving land management. Our fourth aim is to promote critical thinking about boundary impacts to inspire new research that could then be used in improving management across boundaries. And the fifth goal is to provide diverse case studies illustrating a range of approaches to cross-boundary stewardship.

Part I develops a framework for understanding administrative boundaries and their effects. This section includes chapters on the ecological, social, legal, and institutional dimensions of administrative lines. The four chapters in Part II examine issues related to the type of boundary, from wilderness, to recreation, private forestry, and private–public boundaries. Part III presents a series of case studies illustrating the efforts of those who have attempted to cross boundaries and find ways to cooperate that promote land stewardship. The case studies range from New

York to Florida, from Arizona to the Rocky Mountain states. Part IV examines what it takes to build bridges across boundaries. Accordingly, there is a chapter on cooperation, a speculative chapter that explores a future where lines on the land are vanishing, and a concluding chapter integrating the book's various themes.

This book examines the complex and important issues surrounding both public and private land boundaries in the United States. We chose to restrict our topic to the United States because we wished to cover a broad and complicated topic well. We hope that the book also applies elsewhere as the subject of cross-boundary stewardship is a general one, applicable to every part of the globe.

We hope that this book will be useful in both the classroom and the meeting room and that it will be used by all those diverse individuals and entities who share concern for the land that nurtures us.

REFERENCES

Christensen, N.L. 1995. Fire and wilderness. *International Journal of Wilderness* 1:30–34.

Cole, D.N., and P.B. Landres. 1996. Threats to wilderness ecosystems: impacts and research needs. *Ecological Applications* 6:168–184.

Cronon, W. 1983. *Changes in the land: Indians, colonists, and the ecology of New England*. Hill and Wang, New York.

Forman, R.T.T. 1995. *Land mosaics: the ecology of landscapes and regions*. Cambridge University Press, Cambridge, England.

Gunderson, L.H., C.S. Holling, and S.S. Light, editors. 1995. *Barriers and bridges to the renewal of ecosystems and institutions*. Columbia University Press, New York.

Hansen, A.J., and F. di Castri, editors. 1992. *Landscape boundaries: consequences for biotic diversity and ecological flows*. Springer-Verlag, New York.

Hudson, W.E., editor. 1991. *Landscape linkages and biodiversity*. Island Press, Washington, DC.

Knight, R.L., and J. Mitchell. 1997. Subdividing the West. Pages 272–274 in *Principles of conservation biology* (G.K. Meffe and C.R. Carroll, editors). Second edition. Sinauer Associates, Sunderland, MA.

Landres, P.B. 1992. Temporal scale perspectives in managing biological diversity. *Transactions of the North American Wildlife and Natural Resources Conference* 57:292–307.

Newmark, W.D. 1985. Legal and biotic boundaries of western North American national parks: a problem of congruence. *Biological Conservation* 33:197–208.

Pickett, S.T.A., and R.S. Ostfeld. 1995. The shifting paradigm in ecology. Pages 261–278 in *A new century for natural resources management* (R.L. Knight and S.F. Bates, editors). Island Press, Washington, DC.

Pickett, S.T.A., V.T. Parker, and P.L. Fiedler. 1992. The new paradigm in ecology: implications for conservation biology above the species level. Pages 65–88 in *Conservation biology: the theory and practice of nature conservation preservation and management* (P.L. Fiedler and S.K. Jain, editors). Chapman and Hall, New York.

Risser, P.G. 1995. The status of the science examining ecotones. *BioScience* 45:318–325.

Smith, G., C. Robinson, and M. Shannon. 1995. *Crossing over the lines: multi-jurisdictional, multi-ownership, multi-party, multi-problem landscape management strategies*. Report of the Eastside Ecosystem Management Strategy Project, Columbia River Basin Assessment, USDA Forest Service, Pacific Northwest Research Station, Portland, OR.

Yaffee, S.L., A.F. Philips, I.C. Frentz, P.W. Hardy, S.M. Maleki, and B.E. Thorpe. 1996. *Ecosystem management in the United States: an assessment of current experience*. Island Press, Washington, DC.

Understanding Administrative Boundaries and Their Effects

A broad perspective is needed to comprehend how boundaries delineate landscapes that, in turn, define humans and societies. Our introductory section takes this approach with chapters that address the human, ecological, and legal and institutional aspects of boundaries. We begin with an insightful chapter by Eric Freyfogle titled "Bounded People, Boundless Land." This chapter explores the seeming contradictions within our society that impose boundaries on our lives and our affairs, yet at the same time require cooperation across boundaries for individuals and communities to flourish.

Using Robert Frost's poem "Mending Wall" and Wendell Berry's short story "The Boundary," Freyfogle explores the contradictions created by walls and fences. With "Mending Wall" Freyfogle reflects on our culture's fascination with walls. Yet, using Frost's poem as a metaphor, Freyfogle suggests that nature has a different view, "The frozen-groundswell spills the upper boulders in the sun and makes gaps even two can pass abreast." "Something there is, that doesn't love a wall . . . that wants it down." The singular beauty of this powerful poem, however, is how it illustrates that the stone wall, the boundary between two neighbors, also unites them in community. It requires them to cooperate each year, to walk the wall, each on his own side, and to put back the stones that nature has spilled during the winter, with one neighbor commenting that "Good fences make good neighbors."

Freyfogle concludes his evocative chapter with an examination of Wendell Berry's short story "The Boundary." Here, an aging farmer, Mat Feltner, is taking one last walk along his farm's fenced boundary. Freyfogle writes, "The fence, he worries, might have fallen into disrepair and gone unnoticed. The younger men, rushing to get the harvest done, perhaps have been too busy to check the fence and mend it. So cane in hand Mat sets out to inspect his physical boundary, with a weariness in his bones that, for the moment, he seems to shake." Mat finds the fence in good repair, a reminder that he had no reason to fear, for those who will remain on the farm after he has died are imbued with the same love and responsibility for the farm that he has. Freyfogle uses this story to illustrate the positive values of boundaries. Berry, Freyfogle argues, speaks highly of private land ownership carefully bounded. Berry says that "land cannot be properly cared for by people who do not know it intimately, who do not know how to care for it, who are not strongly motivated to care for it, and who cannot afford to care for it." And so, Freyfogle suggests, bounded people may feel a responsibility for land within fences that, in time, allows them to feel responsibility for people and land across their own borders.

By reaching to the humanities and drawing forth writings by those as thoughtful and gifted as Frost and Berry, Freyfogle introduces the often contradictory nature of boundaries. Initially one might think that boundaries are bad, that they blur and distort the real lines across the land that nature bestows, those created by watersheds and vegetation. But Freyfogle sees the uncertainty inherent in this thinking as humans also inhabit these lands and inevitably draw their own lines. Freyfogle offers questions that later chapters address in greater detail. Are artificial lines bad? Do bounded lands also delineate levels of responsibility for people that might, in turn, foster stewardship and responsibility? Can people promote community by working together along their shared edges?

───

The three chapters that follow Freyfogle's chapter explore boundaries from ecological, social, and legal and institutional views. Collectively these chapters address the natural and human constructs that comprise our book. Peter Landres and his coauthors begin with a chapter titled "Ecological Effects of Administrative Boundaries." Intentionally or otherwise, "When different land-use practices are imposed on either side of the thin line of the administrative border, a distinct ecological boundary zone is inevitably created that can filter, block, or concentrate the movement of such diverse things as animals, plant seeds, fire, wind, water, and nutrients."

This chapter introduces a conceptual model that examines the boundary zone and its structural and functional attributes. Structural attributes describe the physical aspects of a boundary and include such things as the width, height, and length of the boundary zone. Functional attributes describe the flows that occur across or along a boundary and include such things as animal movements as well as nutrients, seeds, spores, and soil that are transported in air or water. Because the boundary zone differs from the area further away from the line, these flows and movements may be impeded or accelerated, but in any case, the boundary usually acts as a selective filter.

Initially boundaries do little more than delineate responsibilities and ownership. Over time, however, the effects of different land-use practices produce different ecological effects on either side of the line. Landres et al.'s model stresses that (1) management goals and actions are the primary cause of these boundary effects, (2) altered flows either into or out of an area will likely be detrimental to that area, (3) boundary effects follow a distinct temporal sequence, and (4) once established, these effects may have long-term consequences.

These long-term consequences can affect the land along the boundary (called "boundary habitat"), as well as the area away from the line (called "isolation impacts"). For example, differing land-use practices on either side of a boundary delineating a forest multiple-use area from a wilderness area may result in quite different species composition, soil erosion levels, and microclimatic conditions on either side of the line. In addition to changes in this boundary habitat, isolation impacts occur far from the administrative border. These changes may alter the overall size of the core area, affect ecological processes, and also have an impact on plant and animal populations. Changes in fire management illustrate how administrative lines can have impacts far beyond the borders. By stopping fires at administrative boundaries, plant succession, species composition, and other ecological processes are altered far from where the fires are suppressed.

The chapter offers an agenda for boundary-related research that focuses on four topics: boundary structures, fluxes and gradients along and cross these structures, filtering mechanisms affecting these fluxes, and the ecological effects both along and away from the borders. The chapter concludes with an appeal to land-use planners to be aware of the ecological effects of administrative borders and the need to develop a landscape-scale perspective when formulating policy.

In his chapter titled "Social Dimensions of Boundaries: Balancing Cooperation and Self-Interest," Mark Brunson addresses the nature of boundaries from a social perspective and describes the behavioral and attitudinal aspects of cross-boundary relationships. Just as administrative lines
are human constructs to delineate ownership and jurisdictional responsibility, so too norms and mores are human constructs that dictate human
behaviors across and within areas formed by borders. Boundaries exist
because they achieve societal ends, yet societies also promote relationships that transcend boundaries. Brunson argues that "we can sustain
ecosystems across boundaries only if we understand how humans behave
with respect to places they claim as territory."

Brunson begins with an examination of the social functions of boundaries. In this light he explores the concept of human territories and how
their boundaries are maintained. Territorial boundaries may reflect more
than ownership or administrative responsibility. For example, some
groups or individuals consider portions of the public lands to be their territories and they may defend them as such. Accordingly, camping parties
may send one member of their group a day early to secure a favored
campsite. Ranchers who have grazed cows on public lands for decades
may evidence a proprietary feeling for portions of a national forest or
rangeland. Perhaps not surprisingly, agency employees themselves may
form territorial attachments that may impede cross-boundary management. Because natural resource managers devote their careers to land
stewardship, they, too, may develop an attachment to particular land settings or, almost as likely, cultivate an agency loyalty that makes working
with other agencies or individuals difficult.

Surprisingly, the same social structures and institutions that serve to
maintain territories also serve to encourage cooperation between territorial entities. Although a federal land management agency may post and
patrol a wilderness boundary against certain activities, the agency also
promotes access and compatible land management activities within the
wilderness boundary. But Brunson believes that adherence to social
norms is more important for compliance of acceptable activities within
administrative boundaries than the maintenance of formal legal structures. Accordingly, birdwatchers who enjoy watching nesting falcons
along a cliff may be more effective in censuring rock climbers from disturbing the birds during the nesting season than an agency-enforced ban
against climbing.

It is along these lines that Brunson next discusses the role of attitudes toward boundaries. Attitudes are important because they influence whether agencies or individuals enter into partnerships that transcend jurisdictional boundaries, as well as how they behave within these partnerships. Because attitudes are strongly influenced by people's values, the likelihood of cooperation in cross-boundary stewardship is enhanced if people share values.

Brunson discusses three types of cross-boundary relationships: (1) between public agencies and private property owners, (2) between two or more public agencies, and (3) between departments within agencies. When cross-boundary stewardship involves private property owners adjacent to public lands, the issue of private property rights becomes especially important. Yet cooperation among adjoining landowners is possible only if both public and private entities are willing to cede some control over their defended territories to the larger partnership. Brunson goes on to explain that the degree to which this will occur depends on attitudes toward stewardship objectives and toward the public and private entities that constitute the partnership.

Boundaries between agencies are almost as common as those among private landowners and agencies. Brunson argues that because approaches to management differ greatly among agencies, cross-boundary cooperation is challenging. Not only do agency mandates differ, but also agency cultures may place differing emphases on loyalty to the agency, as well as responsibility to visitors and surrounding communities. Brunson believes that, although agencies may have problems working together in practice, their policies are geared toward cooperation. Cross-agency cooperation is enhanced, Brunson believes, if agency representatives attempt to understand partner agencies' viewpoints and constraints. This is particularly important when the agencies involved are state and federal and disputes are framed as federal domination versus states' rights.

Similar pressures that operate between agencies also operate within them. Whereas historically natural resource agencies had relatively few missions, today they are being asked to address an increasing number of goals. Accordingly, different groups within agencies tend to show loyalty to their professions and resource uses that can lead to intra-agency friction. Can a silviculturist and wilderness manager find common ground when discussing a logging operation adjacent to a wilderness boundary? Will recreational planners and wildlife and fishery biologists find a way to ensure the protection of biological diversity across multiple-use landscapes that are increasingly gridded with administrative lines? Brunson has no easy answers to this conundrum but stresses the importance of maintaining permeable intra-agency boundaries by ensuring that all partners in a collaborative project understand and discuss relevant differences that may exist within an agency.

To be successful, Brunson concludes, cross-boundary stewardship should be designed to acknowledge the existence of territories, to recognize the various mechanisms of defense that territorial claimants employ, and to accommodate the need for these claimants to maintain an acceptable level of territorial control. One way to do this, he argues, is for agencies and individuals to yield rather than impose control, thereby taking advantage of humans' tendency to behave in ways that can resolve potential conflicts between territorial self-interest and community cooperation.

━━━

To conclude this section, Errol Meidinger in his chapter titled "Laws and Institutions in Cross-Boundary Stewardship" examines how laws and institutions contribute to cross-boundary issues. Both the ecological aspects and the social dimensions of cross-boundary management have their underpinnings in law and institutions. Laws determine a society's response to an issue and institutions carry out laws and contribute to public policy. Meidinger examines first the social actors in cross-boundary issues, then the rules and institutions affecting the issues.

Private, corporate, and government landowners are important players whose mandates and practices vary enormously. Only some government and a few private and corporate landowners have mandates to practice cross-boundary stewardship, but most probably have the capacity to do so. Whether they do depends largely on laws and institutions structuring landowner relationships with each other and society.

Under laws pertaining to cross-boundary management, Meidinger examines common law, environmental law, and nonenvironmental law. Aspects of common law, such as trespass, nuisance law, and the plethora of laws pertaining to easements and covenants all have the potential to contribute to cross-boundary management, although presently they have done little to promote it. Regarding environmental law, most federal statutes on air pollution, water pollution, hazardous chemical production, and endangered species management, as well as laws targeting coastal zones, wild and scenic rivers, and wetlands, are efforts to control cross-boundary problems through rules. Finally, nonenvironmental laws can contribute, either positively or negatively, to cross-boundary issues. For example, high federal estate taxes and local property taxes that reflect the development potential of land can encourage rapid resource liquidation, sale, or development that can, in turn, create new cross-boundary problems.

Meidinger next visits institutions and fundamental changes taking place within them. These changes embody a variety of goals and consequences to cross-boundary cooperation. Among these, recent judicial interpretations of uncompensated "takings" of private property and laws defining acceptable public participation in formulation of government policy both support growing private involvement in policy formulation. Conversely, Meidinger states that the most important change in public–private relationships is the growing amount of "public" policy making occurring almost entirely outside of government processes. Recent watershed and landscape planning efforts involving multiple landowners and agencies working to develop cross-boundary stewardship plans certainly support the concept of cross-boundary stewardship. As Meidinger states, these developments are "creating new local, national, and international environmental programs because they shift policy making outside governmental processes. Thus, like it or not, governments are placed in the role of being participants in local, national, and global policy networks, rather than near-exclusive makers and enforcers of public policy."

Meidinger concludes with the suggestion that laws and institutions cannot be expected to make cross-boundary stewardship mandatory. Indeed, because cross-boundary stewardship cannot be defined with sufficient clarity, it is probably best not to attempt to legislate it. Meidinger believes that rules cannot be written precisely enough to produce appropriate outcomes in every real-world situation. Accordingly, he concludes that the trend for government institutions to show increasing discretion according to appropriate principles in a network of accountability is more functional than rules, for, after all, cross-boundary stewardship is a social ideal, not a legal standard.

C h a p t e r   1

Bounded People, Boundless Land

Eric T. Freyfogle

Like many of Robert Frost's poems, "Mending Wall" is a study in contradiction (Frost 1969). Set in rural New England, it is a narrative poem about boundaries and walls in nature, culture, and the human mind. As the poem opens, spring has arrived in the rocky farm country, and with it has come an annual ritual: the mending of the stone wall that divides the narrator's farm from his neighbor's. Choosing a date as they have done before, the adjacent farmers together walk their shared wall, each replacing the stones on his side. As the work proceeds, the narrator engages us with various musings, about the rocky wall, about his stern neighbor, and about the jumbled ways that people and land fit together. From the neighboring farmer directly we hear only a single sentence. Twice repeated, it is the line of the poem that has become best known: "Good fences make good neighbors."

Our culture has latched on to this proverb, no doubt because it captures so well a number of our foundational tendencies and assumptions. We like fences and erect them often, routinely separating mine from yours. We like to divide land and instinctively think of land as parceled and bounded. Frost, however, did not mean to endorse this adage outright, and the narrator in "Mending Wall" is intent on challenging it. "Something there is," the narrator tells us, "that doesn't love a wall, That wants it down." "The frozen-ground-swell" of winter "spills the upper boulders in the sun, And makes gaps even two can pass abreast." Nature, it seems, dislikes this stone wall. Freezing and thawing work against it, and so does gravity. Wandering hunters also play a role, knocking down stones to "have the rabbit out of hiding." Then there are the more mysterious forces that seem secretly to pull at stone walls. Elves at work, the narrator speculates, "but it's not elves exactly." However caused, the

15

wall's gaps appear yearly: "No one has seen them made or heard them made, But at spring mending-time we find them there."

"Something there is that doesn't love a wall, That wants it down. Good fences make good neighbors."

As Frost's narrator relates his tale of labor shared, he argues for his side of this age-old issue. The stone wall has no purpose, he points out. The neighbor's farm "is all pine and I am apple orchard. My apple trees will never get across, And eat the cones under his pines. . . ." Walls make sense when there are cows, "but here there are no cows." So why do fences make good neighbors? the narrator demands to know—asking of himself and of us, but not, importantly, of his neighbor. "Before I built a wall I'd ask to know What I was walling in or walling out, And to whom I was like to give offence." As the poem continues the narrator presses on, to the point of questioning his neighbor's intellect and modernity. The stodgy neighbor, he contends, appears like "an old-stone savage armed" as he approaches the wall, stone in each hand. "He moves in darkness as it seems to me, Not of woods only and the shade of trees."

Until poem's end, Frost seems tilted toward the narrator's view of things, yet it is the tradition-tied neighbor who has the last say, the neighbor who "will not go behind his father's saying" and apparently has no appetite for spring-time challenges. "Good fences make good neighbors," the neighbor says again, proud that he has thought of the idea. There the poem ends, and the mending work goes on.

Following the Ripples

"Mending Wall" is a useful place to begin an inquiry into stewardship across land boundaries. The poem sets up the central conflict, leaves it unresolved, and in doing so provokes us to dwell on the subject, to consider how boundaries have arisen out of our culture, how they influence us in thought and deed, and how we have used them, for good and ill, to shape the land and our lives. "A good poem," Robert Penn Warren once said (1989), "drop[s] a stone into the pool of our being, and the ripples spread." In the case of "Mending Wall" the ripples set loose are many, and they spread in varied ways—outward across the land, backward into our history, and inward, to our nature as cranky, proudful, and yet hopeful human beings.

In "Mending Wall" Frost is clear only on one point: nature has no need for walls, stone or otherwise. To build a wall is to rearrange the land in a way that nature begins at once to resist. When it comes to the needs of humans, Frost's story is more complex and he does no more than frame the problem suggestively. Cows have a habit of wandering; for cattle owners, at least, walls are a positive good. For hunters, walls are a nuisance, if not a danger; game animals do not respect them, so hunters will not either. Orchard owners, needing no walls, think of them mostly as aimless work, although Frost's narrator can view his enterprise with light heart, as "just another kind of outdoor game."

With these points made, Frost has covered the practical aspects of walls: They are useful for some purposes, bothersome for others. As readers we are left with the issues of human character, cognition, and yearning; we are left to consider why we like walls so much and how they reflect and shape who we are. For Frost's narrator, his neighbor's love of walls has an unnaturalness to it. There is a darkness, a lack of enlightenment, to the neighbor's desire for distinct boundaries, a territorial longing with roots that reach back to the stone age. So vigorous is this tradition that the narrator has trouble even questioning his neighbor's wisdom in conversation. In the end, despite his speculations, he bows to tradition and never makes his points aloud.

Frost leaves us to reflect on all of this, to follow the ripples set in motion by his fictional farmers. Why do good fences make good neighbors, if no animals need control? Is there something within us that makes boundaries essential? Is there something in our ability to witness the land, to grasp it in our minds, to sink our roots into it and take responsibility for it that somehow drives us to divide the land into distinct pieces? Nature may need no boundaries, but what about us?

"Mending Wall" achieves as much as it does because it brings together so provocatively the several traditions that underlie our talk on landscape-scale issues. There is the obvious tradition of building walls, marking off territory, and protecting turf, a tradition summed up in the neighbor's "good fences" adage. In this strand of thought, land parcels are discrete things, managed separately, and connected to one another only at the edge. Frost's narrator, in contrast, identifies himself with an alternative tradition, one that has to do with practical judgment, questioning inherited wisdom, and adhering to old ways only when they make sense. Less interested in the human psyche, this pragmatic tradition pays closer attention to the land and searches for better ways to get things done.

Implicit in Frost's poem, unspoken of by either farmer, is a third tradition—the equally vital tradition of communal cooperation, of neighbors identifying a shared need and stepping forward to labor for the common good. We see this tradition in the spring ritual of mending the wall, which carries on for yet another year. We do not quite know why Frost's narrator never questions aloud the good-fences proverb, but his reticence likely has more to do with this third tradition, with the maintenance of communal bonds, than it does any pleasure he gets from his "outdoor game."

As Frost brings together these three traditions, he heightens the contradictions, giving shape to an especially fine poem: Inherited ways versus questioning and novelty. Independence versus neighborly cooperation. Liberty versus solidarity. Boundedness, of land and people, versus the unboundedness of the organic whole.

Ecology and the Old Grid

Particularly in landscapes controlled by private landowners, the old grid mentality of separate land parcels retains a firm grip in American culture. Activities in one place, we know, do not stay within boundary lines: flowing water pays little attention to land deeds, which means pollution does not either. Wandering animals are no more heedful, so that their survival depends on many land managers. We have recognized this blurring of boundaries and long talked about the challenges posed by land-use externalities. But externalities always were viewed as the exception, particularly in economic models. If they were not modest enough to ignore, they were things that we could halt by appropriate technology or "internalize" through regulations or financial arrangements. They posed no threat to the regime of separate land management.

Whatever else ecology has done, it is causing us to rethink this heritage of discrete land parcels. It pushes us to consider new visions of private ownership and to think seriously about community-based land management (Freyfogle 1995). The cardinal rule of popular ecology, that everything in nature is connected to everything else, contains a measure of exaggeration, but the links in nature nonetheless are pervasive, cumulative, and illusive. The closer one looks, the less separation ones sees in land parcels and land uses. Connections simply are too ubiquitous for us to treat them as lightly as we have. To start from the opposite side, to assume the interconnection of land parcels is to think of the land as a unified whole rather than as a collection of distinct pieces. It is to conceive of landowners and land managers not as independent operators coincidentally working nearby, but as co-workers in a larger single enterprise, dependent for their success on a common goal and in continuing need of shared guidance.

As ecologists have talked about the land in organic terms, they have danced around the idea of land health as an overall management goal (Costanza et al. 1992). Many scientists see intellectual sense and practical utility in this idea, and they have begun articulating what land health might mean in practice, in particular settings. Landscapes can be more or less healthy, in terms of the many elements essential to bountiful life, even as their resident species change over time. Aldo Leopold believed this when he wrote A Sand County Almanac (1949); in essence, it is Leopold's meditation on the subject. When Leopold talked about land health, he focused on the basics: conserving soil, maintaining water flows and water quality, and mitigating significant, human-caused changes in species populations. Land health was not a purely scientific concept for Leopold. It reached beyond that to include his seasoned intuitions and his long-maturing ethical values. For Leopold and others, land health became a way of referring to a more sensitive, more humble means of interacting with that mysterious organic unity that he called "the land."

Today we know more than Leopold did, but land health as a purely scientific term remains imprecise and hence, for many scientists, suspicious. Ecology now appears dominated by population biologists and other scientists trained to look at nature from the bottom up, beginning with individual species (Pickett and Ostfield 1995). As often as not, scientists with this perspective find more chaos and change in nature than do scientists trained to look from the ecosystem level down, at energy and nutrient flows, at soil and biomass retention, and at hydrologic flows (Worster 1993). To the outside observer, recent shifts in ecology suggest a dialectical interaction between top-down and bottom-up approaches to the study of the land community; between talking about the coherence of communities as a whole and focusing instead on the sometimes radical incoherence of their constituent members. Academic fields often progress by precisely this type of indirection: swinging one way, then another, with direction best seen by stepping back for the long view. Dialectical shifts are particularly common when our knowledge is radically incomplete, as it is in the case of natural functioning. Over the long term, one might predict, both top-down and bottom-up approaches will retain value in our continuing effort to make sense of nature's ways. More certainly, the land community will retain mysteries that we cannot solve.

Observers from outside ecology have had less trouble embracing land health as a management goal, largely because they have felt more comfortable using ethics and practical reasoning to shore up science's gaps (Westra 1994). The elements of a land community typically interact in ways that are exceedingly complex and well beyond our full comprehension. To deal sensibly with such a community requires us to acknowledge and embrace both of these realities—nature's complexity on the one hand, and the vastness of our ignorance on the other. Science alone cannot bring these realities together, for science proceeds solely from the known and speaks only about the known. To deal with ignorance we need to mix science's lessons with a heavy dose of ethical reasoning and include a strong sense of caution and humility.

Land health has become the most common way today of talking about this mix. It draws on the best of our science and blends it with our ethical sentiments and conclusions (Callicott 1996). To give land health greater clarity, then, particularly in the field, we need to keep working on our science, making it as good and as pertinent as we can. Yet we also need to keep working on the ethical side of things, deciding what we value in nature and what it means to live virtuously on the land. In general terms, land health is our shorthand way of describing what the land would look like if we stopped degrading it. It is our way of bringing together and acting on our senses of moral value, particularly the moral value we perceive in other species. It also has become our way of talking about our duties, perhaps profound, to future generations. The process going on here, it needs to be clear, is not a simple matter of proceeding from the "is" of nature to the "ought" of ethical norms. It is something more complex. We simply do not know the "is," and we continue to struggle with the "ought" as a matter of widely shared, maturely considered ethical values. Land health combines these two elements. It is ethically guided science; it is scientifically informed ethics. And we must recognize that it is a vision that will keep changing as we continue to move toward it, learning more, talking more, and striving to become better than we have been (Lee 1993).

As environmental thought has focused on land health it has assumed an increasingly communitarian tone in language and reasoning (Freyfogle 1996). Environmental writers now speak more confidently about the moral value that resides in the collective whole, even as they acknowledge the moral value of individual pieces, particularly the human pieces. Environmental thought places greater weight on the preservation and enhancement of natural ecosystem processes, both because they sustain the land community as such and because they are useful (or more) to the long-term prospering of humankind.

As a vision of what the land ought to look like, land health pushes us to transcend our grid mentality. It asks us to center our sights on nature's organic wholeness and to downplay or eliminate artificial boundaries. It pushes us to side with Frost's iconoclastic narrator and to ask hard questions about human-drawn lines on the land, whether they be ownership lines or the limits of political jurisdictions. Restoring the integrity of large river systems, for instance, is a kind of work that cannot be done, or even envisioned, in disjointed pieces. Biodiversity issues are similar: We cannot talk about protecting species, particularly wandering ones, without looking beyond the horizon (Noss and Cooperrider 1994). On these issues and other matters of land health, a wide view seems essential.

Yet, despite the value of this organic vision, despite the organizing unity of land health, we have good reason to go slow. However confident we are in our ability to combine science and ethics, we need to pause before pulling out our erasers and getting rid of old lines. Land health as vision may have no need for boundaries, but the *practice* of land health raises different concerns, ones that we cannot wisely ignore. Land management is an activity engaged in by people—people who inevitably possess limited abilities, people with ingrained values and attitudes, people who usually can know well only a few places and whose love of the land can stretch too thin. Before erasing boundaries, we need to think about these people and about the alternative traditions identified in Frost's poem. To look only to land health is to ignore Frost's persistent, tradition-driven neighbor and to ignore, too, the potential benefits of the cooperative spirit that he helps sustain. Bounding the land, whatever its costs, has long had something to do with focusing and encouraging a landowner's care. It has had something to do, also, with the promotion of local community, which in turn has helped foster land health.

And so the question remains: Might we still have good reasons for bounding the land, despite our embrace of an organic view of it? Might we, paradoxically, still best serve the whole by first breaking it into parts?

Mat Feltner's World

Robert Frost's inquiry into boundedness in "Mending Wall" is usefully carried forward in another fine piece of literature, a short story, "The Boundary," by the Kentucky farmer and writer Wendell Berry (1986).

For many readers, Berry has become our preeminent writer of place. In an era of mobility, Berry has written about staying put and sinking roots. In a time when critics have blamed problems on big business and corrupted politics, Berry has looked inward to the human soul, to probe our flaws and our possibilities. As concerned as anyone about sagging land health, he has never considered the issue apart from the long-term health of humans. Attentive to the land community, he has never separated it from the human community and from the ways that peoples have succeeded and failed in their efforts to live sensibly at home. Berry is much admired for his essays and poetry, yet many readers find his thoughts displayed most lucidly in his several novels and stories (Freyfogle 1994). All are set in a fictionalized version of Berry's home country, along the Kentucky River just south of the Ohio. In his fiction, Berry recounts the lives of several interconnected farm families over the course of the past century. In the process, he probes many of the challenges of twentieth-century life, including the central challenge of using the land without abusing it. In the failings of Berry's characters we recognize the failings of our culture, made clear by specific illustration. In their successes, we see our possibilities of hope.

In "The Boundary" Berry returns the reader to the life of one of his favorite characters, Mat Feltner. A dependable, honorable man, Mat has enjoyed a long and successful marriage to his hilly, demanding farm and to the community of people who have surrounded him all his life. Mat has been one of the good ones in this community, a man who shunned darkness, lived in the light, and helped others stay on the right path. On the day of the story, Mat's life is nearing its end. Knowingly, willingly, he approaches the boundary that separates him and those who will continue after him from the many acquaintances he has among the dead. On this day, weak though he is, Mat gets the urge to inspect the barbed-wire fence that surrounds his rugged farm. The fence, he worries, might have fallen into disrepair and gone unnoticed. The younger men, rushing to get the harvest done, perhaps have been too busy to check the fence and mend it. So cane in hand Mat sets out to inspect his physical boundary, with a weariness in his bones that, for the moment, he seems to shake.

Crossing his field, Mat travels into the woods and down the ravine. As he walks and inspects, Mat considers what this farm has meant to him for eight decades, and to the people who have come before him and those who will follow. He reminds himself, fondly and easily, of the endless fascination that the land has provided him. As his memory takes over, Mat recalls the day seventy-five years earlier when, as a boy, he accompanied his father and a work crew that installed the fence. It is a warm memory, and Mat lingers on it. Soon the scene shifts: It is forty years later now and Mat has taken charge, leading to the same place a work crew that includes his own son. The two scenes, we note, are remarkably similar; the ways of living and enjoying the land have changed little over the decades; the continuities of manners and means roll on with the years. Time continues to swirl in Mat's mind and he is reminded, again and again, of the work that has been done on the farm and of the people who have mixed their lives with the place. They are largely dead now, at rest on a hill not far away, yet Mat senses their presence beside him. Transcending death, they have retained their memberships in the local community—they remain present in the enduring memories of the living and in the communal wisdom that they nourished and passed down.

Checking the fence, Mat soon realizes that he has feared without cause. The younger men have not been too busy. The needed work has been done and done well, just as Mat would have done it years earlier and just as Mat's father, Ben, would have done it before him, the generations securely linked in a tradition of good work and attentive devotion. Warmed by these thoughts, Mat struggles on, his strength ebbing as the terrain becomes more rugged. Mat's path has taken him, he realizes, to a place where he has trouble continuing on. Yet he refuses to give in. His life has not been about giving in. "He chooses," as he always has, "the difficult familiar way."

As the day wears on, Mat knows that his wife, Margaret, has missed him and will be worried. He thinks, too, of the younger men at work in the hayfield a ridge or two away—what they will be doing at that time of day, how they will be doing it, and the feelings that will inhabit them. So familiar are their lives, so intertwined are their ways, that the members of this community give rise to something greater than what they are as individuals. The land is part of them, and they are part of it. There is a unity here, and we feel it powerfully, a wholeness that radiates in health, contentment, and beauty.

Tired though he is, Mat strains to mount the long hill, once again giving all that he has to his place. Echoing scripture, he recalls instinctively what he has known all along: that he must "give up his life in order to have it." Slowly, wearily, he carries on:

A shadowless love moves him now, not his, but a love that he belongs to, as he belongs to the place and to the light over it. He is thinking of Margaret and of all that his plighting with her has led to. He is thinking of the membership of the fields that he has belonged to all his life, and will belong to while he breathes, and afterward. He is thinking of the living ones of that member-ship—at work in the fields that the dead were at work in before them.

Reaching the crest, Mat rests against a large walnut tree that "stands alone outside the woods." There he will soon be found and helped home by younger members who partake of this same love. As we watch Mat lean against the tree, we sense how like the tree he has become. They are kindred spirits, the two of them, equal enough in age and coming, finally, to the same spot. By the life he has led, standing erect in the light, Mat, too, has stood "outside the woods." Just as the walnut has relinquished its nuts, so Mat has given freely of himself, nourishing the land and giving rise to new life. Like the tree, Mat has sunk deep and lasting roots.

Owning, Caring, and Belonging

"The Boundary" is a lyrical, moving tale, a love story of an elevated kind. The story has to do with the mending of a fence, as Frost's poem does, yet the fence again supplies merely the stage for human drama. The tradition of neighborly cooperation, present in "Mending Wall," runs much deeper in Berry's homeland. No talk is needed here for the mending work to get done. Mat's taut fence, we sense, yields direct benefits by containing the farm's stock, yet its chief value is intangible. As Mat walks the bounds of his chosen farm, probably for the last time, he recalls to his mind and identifies for us the exact terrain that has been the focus of his life. He has mixed his labor with this place, hard labor and plenty of it. The boundary of his farm has been the boundary of his particularized love. Attentive to its many limits—its slopes, its fragile soils, its vital springs—he has wooed the farm with care. Married to it, he has forsaken all oth-ers; mixing his manhood with it, he has made it yield.

In "The Boundary" Berry gives a far different, more favorable view of land division than we commonly see in environmental writing. Mat Felt-ner, we quickly realize, is an extraordinary farmer. We cannot assume that another owner would have tended his farm so well. Still, Mat is a believable character, based no doubt on a real-life farmer whom Berry has known. For Mat Feltner and others, perhaps many others, boundaries offer positive virtues. They mark out lines of responsibility. They allow for a special love between owner and soil. They nourish a special sense of continuity across generations and thereby foster greater attention to the generations who will inherit the land and depend on its productivity. A vital element of this continuity, Berry reveals, is the preserving and enhancing of special knowledge about a given place, the kind of local, practical knowledge that so often separates the sensitive land use from the unintentionally abusive. Mat Feltner learned how to respect his farm from his father and others. By watching and listening he learned what could be done on it and where. Mat, we sense, has preserved that vital fund of knowledge and added to it. He has fulfilled his stewardship duties to the human community as well as to the land, conveying freely to younger members the wisdom that he knows is not just his.

In "The Boundary" and elsewhere, Berry speaks highly of private landownership. It supplies, he notes, an incentive to care and furnishes us with some of our most useful metaphors of stewardship and attachment to place. Tenant farmers in Berry's fictional landscape rarely have Mat Feltner's type of devotion, for they lack the indispensable tenure and security that foster lasting devotion. The word property, as Berry sees it, "always implies the intimate involvement of a proprietary mind—not the mind of ownership, as that term is necessarily defined by the industrial economy, but a mind possessed of the knowledge, affection, and skill appropriate to the keeping and use of its property" (1984). The essential point, Berry cautions, is that "land cannot be properly cared for by people who do not know it intimately, who do not know how to care for it, who are not strongly motivated to care for it, and who cannot afford to care for it" (1993). Given these constraints, proper landownership can only occur when land is divided into human-size pieces, when it is owned and used on such a scale that all work is the product of a "proprietary mind." Mat Feltner succeeded because his farm was small enough for him to know intimately. Had he taken on more acres, had he hired tenants to work on his behalf, his land surely would have suffered.

Berry's portrait of the Feltner farm is an especially alluring one, but before embracing it we need to ask questions. Mat Feltner, we see, is a responsible land steward; he knows his land and how it ought to be used, and he stays within its natural limits. But we must wonder, does the land management of even such a sensitive steward take into account the needs of the larger landscape? Is consideration given to the ecosystem processes that compose and sustain the larger region of which his land is a part? Does he provide adequate room for resident plant and animal species? Are his drainage practices consistent with the prevention of downstream flooding? However noble Mat's motives, does he really know enough to use his land so as to foster the health of the surrounding whole? To generalize and cut to the bottom line: is it possible to conceive of private ownership, of discrete land parcels, in such a way that the needs of the encompassing natural community are fully met?

By turning to the larger corpus of Berry's fiction it becomes possible to answer these questions in the special case of Mat Feltner. Feltner, we see, is tightly woven into the fabric of a larger community. He belongs to something much bigger than his land and his family, and he devotes time and energy to that larger being. Mat, plainly, is a community leader, the kind of man who steps forward to deal with shared problems as they arrive. Knowing that, we might predict that he would help lead his community in addressing landscape-scale environmental problems. He is the kind of farmer, who, living today, would promote and guide cooperative farm measures. He would help organize a community-supported agriculture project, for the mutual benefit of farmers and urban food buyers. Having the chance, he would step forward to talk about such things as watershed planning and encourage his neighbors to join him in studying regional problems and searching for fair, cooperative ways of dealing with them.

What makes us have faith in Mat Feltner as private landowner is precisely his deviation from the ownership model that holds such sway today, and it is because of that deviation that we need to embrace Berry's vision with caution. Guided by senses of responsibility and community, Mat Feltner exhibits little of the libertarian fervor that has so infected modern understandings of private property rights. The land for Feltner is not an economic asset, and farming is not principally a money-making activity. The main goal each year, for Feltner and for Berry, is the maintenance or enhancement of the land's fertility. To own farm land, then, is less a matter of liberty than of lasting responsibilities—to the land, to the local community, and to the generations before and after. Without all of this, particularly without the community to help sustain and direct him, Mat Feltner would not succeed.

In the end, Berry's support for private landownership and distinct land boundaries is a highly qualified one. Private ownership is essential as he sees it, for without secure ties a land manager simply will not take good care of the land, particularly land as challenging as Mat Feltner's hilly farm. Unless land is divided into small pieces that humans can understand and know and love, sloppy work will follow, and with sloppiness comes declining land health. Yet private ownership is plainly not enough, and we misread Berry by thinking otherwise. The community must be there for guidance and inspiration. The ethic of care and coop-

eration must be there, too, an ethic not unlike Aldo Leopold's land ethic
to temper and leaven all that is done. And that ethic must lead to a sense
of vigilant alertness, an attentiveness to the land's health and a commitment to learn and do whatever becomes needed to sustain that health.

When all of these elements are present, as they are in "The Boundary,"
we can expect the land to flourish. But what are we to do, we must ask,
when they are not? What are we to do when a landscape is populated by
land tenants and not owners? What happens when the community is
simply not there to provide the support and local wisdom? How can we
respond when economic forces drive farm prices down to the point where
stewardship brings not simple living as with the Feltners, but economic
hardship or bankruptcy? What happens when the problems facing local
communities are simply beyond their capacity to mend—when a distant
polluter poisons their water or drops acid rain on their trees? And how,
one wonders, does outside scientific expertise fit into Berry's tight-knit
local town? Mat Feltner loves his family and works well with his neighbors, but what about the university experts who one day will knock on
his door, bearers of disruptive news?

Exalting the Individual

Land boundaries in American thought cannot be talked about apart from
their larger intellectual context: the context of American liberalism,
which in various forms dominates our thought. To bound land is to give
rise to a parcel that is separate from the larger landscape. Once bounded,
a parcel shifts from being an indistinct piece of a whole to being an independent element. Bounding a parcel immediately gives rise to tension, a
particular kind of tension that is so well known to us: the tension
between the individual and the community, between a value scheme that
exalts the pieces and one that honors the collective whole.

As Louis Hartz (1955) observed decades ago, the story of America has
been preeminently a story of ascending liberalism. By liberalism Hartz
meant not a partisan political view, but a social and moral view that promoted the individual human and sought to liberate the individual from
restraint. By focusing on the individual, liberalism departed from older
European views of society, which wove humans more tightly into social
and economic systems and spoke of them in collective, status-bound
terms, as members of tribes or villages or feudal orders. American liberalism first cropped up chiefly in the economic realm; we liberated the
individual largely to promote more vigorous, unrestrained economic

enterprise. From the economic realm liberalism spread to political rights, to religion, and to morality, leading ultimately to the fragmented, atomistic social view of our age.

So dominant has liberalism been and become that we breathe it in our country unawares (Gaylin and Jennings 1996). In its right-wing form liberalism exalts pure liberty, employing today the new rhetoric of libertarianism and free-market economics. On the political left, greater emphasis is placed on substantive equality among individuals and on the involvement of the state to enhance the flourishing of individuals who might otherwise be ground down. Across the political spectrum it is the individual who counts. A dissenting, minority tradition exists, as it always has, yet our left–right political spectrum hardly notices it. The dissenting tradition pops up on issues of social morality, pushed often by the so-called Christian political right. In intellectual circles the dissenting tradition flourishes in communitarianism, a strand of thought that criticizes our excessive individualism and seeks to return us to a more balanced position between the autonomous individual and the social whole (Etzioni 1995).

The dominance of liberalism in America has had many causes that require only brief note. The nation was founded at a time when the rhetoric of individual rights flourished as an antidote to political and economic oppressions in Europe. By 1800 those oppressions were largely gone in America, which meant that individualism could flourish here nearly unchecked. Among English philosophers, John Locke proved particularly attractive for America's budding liberals. In Locke's political scheme, people possessed individual natural rights that arose in advance of, and hence trumped, the powers of collective governance. Chief among those rights for Locke was the right to private property, which he presented in novel terms, as a presocial right that checked monarchical power. Locke's reasoning about private property—his labor theory of ownership—makes little sense to us today, and philosophers have long abandoned it (Freyfogle 1996). But it was not Locke's reasoning that people cared about, then or now. It was Locke's implied conclusion, that private property created an enclave for the individual apart from the state, a place of privacy and escape, and a counterbalance to state power. Locke's natural-rights reasoning held particular appeal on the frontier, where land and private property often arose before any formal mechanisms of governance.

Economic liberalism gained ground during the first half of the nineteenth century, to the point, indeed, where the state of Maine in 1843 dropped all educational requirements for admission to the practice of law! During the century's middle decades, abolitionism and the Civil War heightened attention to civil liberties and fueled the rhetoric of individual rights, a rhetoric that, after the war, shifted easily from the voting rights of former slaves to the economic liberties and laissez-faire rhetoric of big business. Since the late nineteenth century, civil rights campaigns have helped liberalism remain ascendant, from the push for voting rights for women to the minority-focused rhetoric of late century. Only times of collective hardship, such as war and economic depression, brought setbacks for this dominant political ideology. Most recently, liberalism in its right-wing form has gained ground by the failings of collectivist policies in the former Soviet Union and Eastern Europe.

Arising out of and fueling this shift toward individualism has been the influence of free-market economics and economic theory. In the worldview of the market, only individuals count, monied individuals whose preferences the market can aggregate and satisfy. As it combines the wants of individual purchasers, the market competes directly with other forms of collective action, and it has done exceedingly well in that competition. Market proponents largely oppose measures that disrupt market actions, including citizen-led measures that interfere with what the market can do and how. The more atomized and isolated purchasers are, the more the market can stimulate their wants and appeal to their base instincts. In the mentality of the market, everyone and everything is a commodity with a price tag. Moral worth counts for nothing.

When the market deals with nature it begins by dividing it into transferable parts—acres of land, barrels of oil, tons of ore, board-feet of lumber. Parts of nature that have no market value are worthless, and today those parts are many. As an organic whole the land community can have no market value, for the whole as such cannot be bought and sold. Only discrete parts have value, natural resources we call them, preferably resources with predictable bounds that the market can shift to their higher economic uses. The market, to put it simply, stands opposed to any form of organic vision, whether of society or of the land. As it does this, it sustains and strengthens our liberal tradition. It encourages us to divide and bound the land, and, indeed, insists that we do so. It blinds us to all connections.

The upshot of all of these factors and forces—cultural, political, and economic—has been a pronounced tendency for us to think of problems in terms of the individual human, whether as market participant, as voter, or as private property owner (Ehrenfeld 1978). Two centuries ago, the leaders of the French Revolution proclaimed their guiding values as liberty, equality, and fraternity (Spragens 1995). Here in America, fraternity (or solidarity, as sometimes phrased) has become a distinctly suspicious goal, deriving as it does from a moral vision that sees worth in communities and other collectives. Equality, of course, remains important for us, but today it often lacks the substantive element that supplied its original core meaning. It has become mere equality of opportunity, reduced, that is, to a mere subset of liberty. Hands down, liberty has become our central political value, and we define it usually in negative terms, such as freedom from interference in the pursuit of individual wishes, particularly (if not exclusively) freedom from collective governmental interference (Gaylin and Jennings 1996).

The Burdens of Autonomy

With this cultural background it is easy to see why environmental problems have been so awkward to remedy, particularly problems that stem from poor land-use practices. In a culture of individualism, collective action becomes suspect, and so, too, does any concept of the common good. When we view the world as a collection of pieces, it becomes easy to talk of tolerance and individual respect as the sole virtues and to forget about words such as cooperation, sharing, community, trust, and citizenship. As Daniel Kemmis has put it, "To the extent that our language of individualism keeps us from naming and building upon what we have in common, we are impoverished, not only in language, but in many other ways as well" (1990).

Given our embrace of individualism we have trouble talking about private ownership in anything like the way that Wendell Berry does, as membership in a larger whole with responsibilities as well as opportunities. Landowners, we know, cannot simply do what they want; they need to respect the equal rights of their neighbors. But when we speak now of the limits on property rights, we do so chiefly in terms of an owner's duty to avoid overtly harming an individual neighbor. Our talk has not been in terms of duties to a larger collective whole, whether to the social community or the natural landscape. Nor have we yet said much about duties to care for the land itself, even land that we own, whether because of the land's inherent moral value or because its conservation is a duty we owe to future generations (Freyfogle 1996).

When we return in this light to the case of fictional Mat Feltner, considering what he has achieved, we become aware just how far Mat stands apart from modern culture. Feltner embraces that strand of liberalism that dignifies the individual, but he would reject, if not despise, today's free-market libertarianism. Were we to assign Feltner to an intellectual tradition, we might best place him in the little-remembered tradition of Southern conservatism, a tradition that honored the community as well as individual liberty, that favored limits on the market, and that fit all human enterprises into a constraining moral order. Whatever its defects, Southern conservatism aimed at far more than the avoidance of harm to individuals (Genovese 1994). It called people to live honorably. It encouraged them to elevate their moral faculties. It promoted, in its fashion, the well-being of the whole.

In the realm of land use, American liberalism has fueled an implicit separation of the public realm from the private, and in doing so has added to the many challenges of stewardship across boundaries (Freyfogle 1995). Land use, we assume, is a private matter, as long as the use does not overtly harm others. Individual liberty prevails here, unless a landowner disrupts the liberty of another individual. Private land in this tradition stands starkly apart from publicly owned land, which is properly managed for public rather than private aims. By embracing this public–private distinction American culture deviates from the European view, which has long blurred the public and private in important respects. In the European tradition, land use has remained what it was centuries ago—a public matter as well as a private one, without regard to ownership (Cribbet 1967). Private property in that tradition is more a creation of the community than an individual natural right. Given this intellectual base, the community has an important, expected say in how private lands are used, not to the exclusion of the private owner's wishes, but in partnership with that owner. In the case of publicly owned property the European tradition has also blurred the public–private line. Private users, individually and collectively, often hold use rights in public lands, in grazing lots, forests, beaches, and wet meadows. These rights are clearly private property, yet they are defined, regulated, and protected by law.

When we peer into Mat Feltner's world we see that landownership there largely adheres to a tradition that is no longer fully ours. As landowner, Mat has internalized his community's norms aimed at fostering the common good. Mat needs no policeman or land-use regulator to watch his work. He loves his land; he respects his community. He shoulders his duties willingly, and in doing so encourages others to follow his lead. Because enough of Mat's neighbors are like him, little need exists for formal land-use controls. Feltner's world, as best we can tell, remains unburdened by contentious zoning hearings. It includes no lawsuits challenging regulatory action. No land parcels are owned by distant corporations, led by faceless officers heedless of local expectations. What Feltner's world amounts to, it appears—and we need to recognize it as such—is local governance of the most efficient and respectful kind, governance that guides the individual without overtly telling him what to do. It is, plainly, an ideal.

The problem with this ideal, of course, is that we have trouble recognizing it as something that might exist in our time. We cannot reproduce Feltner's agrarian world, however much we might want to. Still, Mat Feltner's world offers lessons to us, ones that we ought not to overlook. Embedded within this world are features and virtues on which we might draw, perhaps in some fashion even mimic.

In Mat Feltner's world the public and private realms are hard to pull apart. Mat's home is his castle, and he enjoys there substantial privacy, but his farming decisions draw very much on communal norms. Mat the farmer is aware of the larger community and is constantly guided by it. That community, we note, exercises its guidance indirectly, by creating and sustaining social norms, and here, too, as observers we can learn. Social norms can wield great power; when they work, they cost little and interfere less with a person's self-respect. As he farms Mat is guided by ethics as much as economics: No one tells him to farm that way, he simply sees it as the right way. His ethics include a concern for future generations, a concern that, if he thought about it, would doubtless be a central element of his land ethic. Mixed with Mat's ethics is an equal concern for aesthetics, for the simple beauty of the land when its soil is rich and its resident life healthy and abundant. Mat's ethical and aesthetic concerns are related to the small size of his farm and his ownership of it; the farm is something he can know intimately, care for well, and invest with his dreams. Finally, there is Mat's commitment to neighborly cooperation. Mat's character inclines him in that direction; were his character otherwise, he might well have spent more time in the dark woods. Yet Mat's pride in his locale has something to do with his honored status in it. He is more than just one of the governed: He is a person who helps lead.

Respecting the Parts, Respecting the Whole

Since the mid-1970s environmental thought has taken an intellectual turn, particularly in the discourse that lies behind the public scenes. In the political realm, talk still goes on about the individual's right to a clean environment and about the direct impact of environmental ills on individual well-being. At a deeper level, though, environmental thought has shifted away from the liberal tradition, allying itself now with the communitarian dissent. Our land will not become healthy, many now believe, unless we temper substantially our enthusiasm for the autonomous individual and our embrace of liberty as prime political goal (Ehrenfeld 1978; Jackson 1994). We need to shift back toward the middle, toward a ground where both the individual and the community count in moral terms. Humans are not and never have been isolated individuals. They flourish now, as they have in the past, in social settings, in families, villages, churches, neighborhoods, and other social groups. They flourish, too, when they are parts of healthy landscapes. For these various collectives to thrive, our culture needs to attach more value to them (Hannum 1997). Our social norms need to afford them greater weight. In our legal discourse they need to count. The communitarian aim, it should be emphasized, is not to make the community all important and give the individual moral value only by way of his membership in it. The aim is for balance, to rectify our dangerous and damaging swing far to one side (Etzioni 1995).

It is in this context—in the need for more healthy communities—that we can most profitably collect and discuss our ideas about land stewardship across boundaries. In most parts of our country, the land community is not a wilderness empty of people. Our lands are inhabited by people who live there and work there. To talk of the health of such a land community is to include necessarily the health of the resident people and their social and economic enterprises. For the land community to survive, local people simply must find ways to rise above the radical individualism of our day. They have to gain the sense that, living where they do, they necessarily form and participate in a land community, along with their neighbors and the other life forms that surround them (Freyfogle 1993, Sale 1985). Once this first, hard step is taken, there then comes the need to get people to care more about the health of that community, in addition to the well-being of their human neighbors. They need to gain about their lands and their social communities the kinds of feelings that we see in Mat Feltner and other members of Wendell Berry's fictional world (Mills 1995). To have those feelings, people themselves must feel valued and respected, which means that communal governance needs to occur chiefly at the local level (Western and Wright 1994). Local governance also is needed because good land use is such an intensely practical endeavor, aided by, if not dependent on, the wisdom of those who know the land best.

Stewardship across boundaries aims to promote a communitarian goal, some version of land health, however phrased. The challenges of achieving that goal will be many, as "Mending Wall" and "The Boundary" make clear to us. As Frost reminds us, nature does not need the boundaries that we draw and the walls that we build. Boundaries and walls are for people, and like Frost's narrator, before adding them to the landscape we ought to ask why we are doing so. Once this question is before us, we quickly see reasons for boundaries, or rather we quickly see the single encompassing reason for boundaries: we bound the land because we are bounded people; a flawed, proudful people, as the religious tradition might put it. We bound the land because of the limits that we face, in our characters and our abilities and our visions. So deeply embedded are some of our limits that we have little choice but to recognize them and work within them. But in other cases our limits are self-imposed. And they are new enough, and weak enough, that we can reduce their considerable ill effects.

In Frost's neighbor and in Mat Feltner's community, we see some of the character traits and tendencies that justify our continued use of certain boundaries: our ability to know and love only a human-size piece of land; our need to feel attached to the land and hence connected to our labor; our ingrained love of territory and our firm attachment to private property; our need to feel a part of a community; our desire for engagement with others in dignified ways. Landscape-scale planning inevitably and quickly encounters these realities about people. Together they make a difficult job even more difficult. Respecting the land requires that we respect the people. Promoting land health requires that we promote social well-being. To succeed, stewardship efforts need to accept and work within these limits, even while pushing people to rise higher, to think more ethically, to concern themselves more with future generations, and to imagine the beauty that would come from a healthier local land. For any of this to happen, new institutional arrangements must arise, ones that engage people in self-government not through their narrow, interest-group representatives, but in person, as true, civic-minded republicans (Kemmis 1990, John 1994).

Beyond these limits, though, are other limits that now constrain us, and many of these limits we would do well to unbind and discard. Our individualism and love of liberty have simply become too strong, so much so that they constrain our ability even to talk seriously about the common good. We are similarly hampered by our infatuation with the free market, with market-set valuations of things, and with the market's tendency to view nature as merely a collection of discrete resources. Intellectual limits like these have prompted us to bound the land needlessly and to make our boundaries more important than they ought to be. We somehow have to get away from them. Then there is our institution of private property—so valuable with its incentives for stewardship and care, so harmful in its tendency to undercut community and to downplay or cover up the links among land parcels. Private property is a cultural institution, created by us and changeable by us. We can do much to improve this institution and need soon to get at it (Freyfogle 1996). In rethinking private property, we also need to rethink our undue tendency to separate the public and the private. Land use is inevitably the kind of activity that mixes these two realms. Once we see that, we can move toward new visions of the landscape, visions that draw on older traditions of the shared commons where public ownership and guidance, blended with private use rights, are crafted to serve both common and individual aims.

And so our challenges are many, as we endeavor collectively to tend a land that is so much bigger than we are and so much beyond our ability to understand. We are, we must confess, bounded people in a boundless land, a paradox and a reality that sets the stage for our work. To nourish the land's health, we must make ourselves better than we are and improve our institutions along with ourselves. To make the land better for us, we must make ourselves more worthy of it.

REFERENCES

Berry, W. 1984. Whose head is the farmer using? Whose head is using the farmer? Pages 19–30 in *Meeting the expectations of the land* (W. Jackson, W. Berry, and B. Colman, editors). North Point Press, San Francisco.

Berry, W. 1986. The boundary. Pages 75–98 in *The wild birds: six stories of the Port William Membership* (W. Berry, editor). North Point Press, San Francisco.

Berry, W. 1993. *Sex, economy, freedom and community*. Pantheon, New York.

Callicott, J.B. 1996. Do deconstructive ecology and sociobiology undermine Leopold's land ethic? *Environmental Ethics* 18:353–372.

Costanza, R., B.G. Norton, and B.J. Haskell, editors. 1992. *Ecosystem health: new goals for environmental management*. Island Press, Washington, DC.

Cribbet, J. 1967. Some reflections on the law of the land—a view from Scandinavia. *Northwestern University Law Review* 62:277–313.

Ehrenfeld, D. 1978. *The arrogance of humanism*. Oxford University Press, New York.

Etzioni, A., editor. 1995. *New communitarian thinking: persons, virtues, institutions, and communities*. University Press of Virginia, Charlottesville.

Freyfogle. E. 1993. *Justice and the earth: images for our planetary survival*. The Free Press, New York.

Freyfogle, E. 1994. The dilemma of Wendell Berry. *University of Illinois Law Review* 1994:363–385.

Freyfogle, E. 1995. The owning and taking of sensitive lands. *UCLA Law Review* 43:77–138.

Freyfogle, E. 1996. Ethics, community, and private land. *Ecology Law Quarterly* 23:631–661.

Frost, R. 1969. Mending wall. Pages 33–34 in *The poetry of Robert Frost*. Holt, Rinehart and Winston, New York.

Gaylin, W., and B. Jennings. 1996. *The perversion of autonomy*. The Free Press, New York.

Genovese, E.D. 1994. *The southern tradition: the achievement and limitations of an American conservatism*. Harvard University Press, Cambridge, MA.

Hannum, H., editor. 1997. *People, land, and community*. Yale University Press, New Haven.

Hartz, L. 1955. *The liberal tradition in America*. Harcourt, Brace & World, New York.

Jackson, W. 1994. *Becoming native to this place*. University Press of Kentucky, Lexington.

John, D. 1994. *Civic environmentalism: alternatives to regulation in states and communities*. Congressional Quarterly Press, Washington, DC.

Kemmis, D. 1990. *Community and the politics of place*. University of Oklahoma Press, Norman.

Lee, K. 1993. *Compass and gyroscope: integrating science and politics for the environment*. Island Press, Washington, DC.

Leopold, A. 1949. *A Sand County almanac and sketches here and there*. Oxford University Press, New York.

Mills, S. 1995. *In service of the wild: restoring and reinhabiting damaged land*. Beacon Press, Boston.

Noss, R., and A.Y. Cooperrider. 1994. *Saving nature's legacy: protecting and restoring biodiversity*. Island Press, Washington, DC.

Pickett, S.T.A., and R.S. Ostfield. 1995. The shifting paradigm in ecology. Pages 261–278 in *A new century for natural resources management* (R.L. Knight and S.F. Bates, editors). Island Press, Washington, DC.

Sale, K. 1985. *Dwellers in the land: the bioregional vision*. Sierra Club, San Francisco.

Spragens, T.A., Jr. 1995. Communitarian liberalism. Pages 37–52 in *New communitarian thinking* (A. Etzioni, editor). University Press of Virginia, Charlottesville.

Warren, R.P. 1989. The themes of Robert Frost. Pages 285–301 in *New and selected essays* (R.P. Warren, editor). Random House, New York.

Western, D., and R.M. Wright. 1994. *Natural connections: perspectives in community-based conservation*. Island Press, Washington, DC.

Westra, L. 1994. *An environmental proposal for ethics: the principle of integrity*. Rowman & Littlefield, Lanham, MD.

Worster, D. 1993. *The wealth of nature*. Oxford University Press, New York.

Chapter 2

Ecological Effects of Administrative Boundaries

Peter B. Landres, Richard L. Knight,
Steward T. A. Pickett, and M. L. Cadenasso

All lands, no matter how large or small, remote or near, pristine or modified, are delineated by administrative boundaries. As Forman (1995) noted, "The history of civilization is a saga of linearization or geometrization of the land. The soft curves of nature have been replaced by the hard lines of humans. What are the ecological gains and losses from this seemingly inevitable process?" Imposed for a variety of purposes, boundaries have many intentional and unintentional effects on the surrounding lands. When different land-use practices are imposed on either side of the thin line of the administrative border, a distinct ecological boundary zone is inevitably created that can filter, block, or concentrate the movement of such diverse things as animals, seeds, fire, wind, water, and nutrients. These effects isolate areas from one another, with long-term and far-reaching effects on the lands on either side of the boundary.

To understand the effects of administrative boundaries we first define borders and the boundary zone surrounding borders, discuss structural and functional attributes of boundaries, and last develop a conceptual model of the major ecological effects caused by boundaries. Although it is simple, the model provides a structured framework for understanding potential boundary effects that may be useful in planning and mitigating the adverse ecological effects of administrative boundaries. We conclude that administrative boundaries may have profound effects on ecological systems: Understanding these effects and the larger cultural and ecological context of landscapes is fundamental to improving the long-term stewardship of the natural resources that provide benefits and services valued by society.

Administrative Boundaries

Administrative borders or boundaries are lines that separate different ownerships, jurisdictions, or responsibilities, and often different management philosophies, goals, and practices. Private property boundaries, for example, are usually clearly defined by surveys, whereas federal, state, and local governments confer jurisdiction to management agencies through acts or statutes. Boundary lines are typically placed for historical, political, economic, or social reasons, forming a complex mosaic of lands owned by different parties and used for different purposes. The Greater Yellowstone area, for example, occupies more than 7.3 million hectares and is administered by three states, two national parks, three national wildlife refuges, four federal agencies, as well as numerous private owners, all with different management goals (see Chapter 11). The administrative boundaries separating diverse private and public lands are usually well known by those who have jurisdiction over the land, as are the borders between areas designating different management actions on land owned by a single entity. The USDA Forest Service, for example, has many different management designations and goals for its land.

Administrative boundaries are often placed on the landscape without regard to natural discontinuities or transitions, such as between forest and grassland or along topographic changes. When viewed on a map, these boundaries typically exhibit the rectalinearity of political, social, and economic compromise. When viewed from the ground, borders may be marked or not, obvious or subtle. Some boundaries are marked with fences or other structures and signs denoting ownership and use. Other boundaries are not marked or obvious, such as between a designated wilderness and adjacent multiple-use forest or along the middle of a stream. An administrative border is like a glass wall that may not be readily apparent, but because nearly all terrestrial and aquatic ecosystems are open systems requiring continual flows or fluxes of energy and matter, differences in management goals and land-use practices on either side of the border inevitably disrupt these flows, causing changes in ecological conditions and processes.

Conceptual models of natural ecological boundaries, their attributes, and their effects have been developed for terrestrial systems (Wiens et al. 1985, Forman and Godron 1986, Gosz 1991, Forman and Moore 1992, Wiens 1992, and Forman 1995), and for riverine systems (Naiman et al. 1988). Schonewald-Cox and Bayless (1986) and Buechner (1987) developed boundary models for the specific case of nature reserves. Although our focus on administrative boundaries is more restrictive than the models developed generally to understand ecological boundaries and more expansive than for one specific type of administrative boundary, we do draw extensively from these substantial and important efforts in developing a conceptual model to describe administrative boundaries and their ecological effects.

Attributes of Administrative Boundaries

Administrative boundaries exhibit two general types of attributes: structural and functional. Structural attributes describe the physical aspects of a boundary and the changes that occur across or along it; functional attributes describe the flows that occur across or along a boundary. In-depth discussion and examples of boundary attributes may be found in Holland et al. (1991), Hansen and di Castri (1992), and Forman (1995); we selectively discuss those attributes and impacts that are especially relevant to administrative boundaries. Even though they are discussed separately, structural and functional attributes strongly interact with one another to determine the ecological effects caused by administrative boundaries. In addition, these attributes change over time because of natural ecological change, as management outcomes take effect or as management goals change.

Structural Attributes

Initially an administrative boundary simply is a line on a map, but over time a three-dimensional boundary structure develops that includes its width, height, and length (Figure 2.1). Width is the perpendicular distance from the administrative border that is occupied by altered habitat caused by the penetration of different ecological conditions, such as temperature, moisture, plants, animals, or seeds from one area into an adjacent area. This area of altered habitat has been called the induced or generated edge (Schonewald-Cox and Bayless 1986) because it is an artificial area produced by the different management actions on either side of the administrative border. The generated edge is similar to an ecotone where elements from distinct adjacent areas intermix. Height is the vertical profile or structure at the boundary, as well as the difference in vertical structure across the generated edge. With markedly different management actions occurring on either side of a boundary, differences

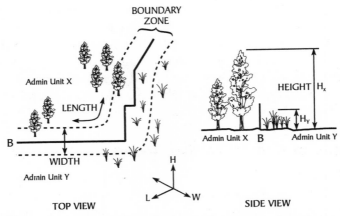

Figure 2.1. Primary structural attributes of administrative boundaries, illustrating width, height, and length attributes. The boundary zone includes the administrative border (B) between two administrative units (denoted X and Y) as well as the area influenced by the reciprocal actions of the adjacent ecological systems on each other. (Modified from Forman and Moore 1992.)

in vertical structure can be pronounced, as between clear-cut and uncut forest or between pasture and forest.

Length is the linear distance along an administrative boundary (Figure 2.1) and can be derived in several ways: actual length, straight-line length, or curvilinearity (actual divided by straight-line length). Length also can be combined with other features of a site, such as the area enclosed by the boundary, to yield insightful analyses. For example, the perimeter-to-area ratio is an important component of the filtering function of boundaries (see later). In addition, a boundary can be divided into distinct segments based on different criteria, such as patterns of ownership or vegetation types. Boundary segmentation may then be used to analyze potential impacts on different portions of a boundary or to derive a general estimate of potential impacts by examining segment variability along a boundary's length. In Organ Pipe Cactus National Monument, for example, Schonewald-Cox and Bayless (1986) analyzed boundary segments to track human-caused threats to vegetation.

Additional structural attributes include contrast and porosity. Contrast is the amount of change across the generated edge (Figure 2.2). Any variable, such as temperature or humidity, or the density of a plant or animal species, or the concentration of a soil nutrient, can vary across a generated edge, forming a gradient of change. Lower contrast presents less of a barrier to fluxes across a boundary, and discrete areas of lower contrast along a boundary may represent a "pore" allowing easier flow across a boundary. Disturbances that run perpendicular to a border, whether natural (such as a fire or a wind storm) or anthropogenic (such as a road), may create pores by obliterating the differences on adjacent sides of a border, thereby decreasing contrast. Recreational trails, for example, are small-scale disturbances that cross administrative borders and allow access to exotic plants that otherwise may not have been able to enter an area (Tyser and Worley 1992), and fires may allow exotic plants to penetrate widely across a protected area (Floyd-Hanna et al. 1993). Segmenting a boundary into categories of low, intermediate, or high contrast may yield estimates of boundary porosity, or the degree to which a given length of boundary impedes or facilitates a specific type of flow across it. Because different types of flows are impeded or facilitated by a boundary differently, boundary porosity must be clearly identified in reference to a specific type of flow.

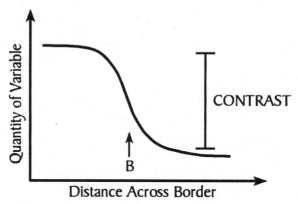

Figure 2.2. Gradient of change in any ecological variable across an administrative boundary zone. The vertical axis represents the state of any ecological variable of interest, for example population density of a particular species, concentration of a soil nutrient, ambient temperature or humidity, reproductive rate of a plant species, or predation rate on ground-nesting birds. The horizontal axis represents the distance or width across a boundary zone, and B denotes the location of the administrative border. Contrast is the amount of change in the variable of interest across the boundary zone or across a predetermined unit of distance.

The amount of change per unit distance across a boundary (Figure 2.3) can vary independently of contrast, also affecting flows across a boundary area. Areas with high contrast and a high rate of change likely pose the greatest barriers to natural fluxes across a boundary, whereas areas with lower rates of change likely pose less of a barrier to cross-boundary fluxes because the contrast per unit area is reduced. Buffer zones often are suggested for reducing the negative effects of administrative borders, and this proposed benefit may largely result from the increased width of the boundary zone, thereby reducing the rate of change and contrast across the boundary. In other instances, areas with high contrast may allow certain species access to habitats that they otherwise may not have entered. Brown-headed cowbirds (*Molothrus ater*), for example, are nest parasites that live in open fields where water is available, yet they fly up to seven kilometers into adjacent forest to lay their eggs in the nests of forest interior migratory songbirds (Rothstein et al. 1984).

Functional Attributes

There are two primary functional attributes of boundaries: a conduit function affecting flow along the length of a boundary, and a filtering function affecting flow across the boundary.

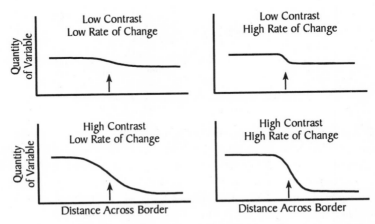

Figure 2.3. Four possible combinations in the amount of contrast and the rate of change in the variable of interest across a boundary zone. The small vertical arrow denotes the location of the administrative border.

Conduit Function

The creation of a boundary can markedly affect fluxes along this edge. Mule deer (*Odocoileus hemionus*), for example, move along certain forest edges in New Mexico (Forman and Moore 1992), shifting the population from one area to another. In human-dominated landscapes, roads often are placed close to administrative boundaries, so that vehicular or foot traffic is a common flux along the boundary, affecting many of the plants and animals in this area. Pollutants from motor vehicles also "splash" through the boundary along the road, affecting the ecosystem beyond in a linear strip along the border (Smith 1990). Convolution, or curvilinearity of the edge as seen on a map, can influence how the administrative boundary affects fluxes along it. Forman (1995), for instance, found that boundary curvilinearity affected the use and movement patterns of elk (*Cervus canadensis*) and mule deer: as curvilinearity increased, movement along the border decreased and movement across the border increased. Although administrative boundaries have been shown to affect some fluxes along them, this conduit function has received little attention from ecologists, and there is little understanding of the fluxes that are affected and of the mechanisms driving them.

Filtering Function

Flows of matter or energy occur within the ground, along the surface, and in the air (Figure 2.4). Virtually everything moves across a landscape by one of two modes (Forman 1995): locomotion (e.g., animals), or as part of the mass flow of air or water (e.g., nutrients, seeds, spores, soil, tree leaves). Because the boundary zone is different from the surrounding area, these flows may be impeded, accelerated, or not affected as they encounter this zone (Figure 2.5). Like the selective permeability of a cellular membrane the boundary thus acts like a selective filter altering flows across it. Ambrose (1987) applied this analogy in discussing the impact of the administrative boundary on Great Smokey Mountains National Park. Forman and Moore (1992) review how the thermodynamics and molecular phenomena of membranes provide "a highly informative analogy" and "a solid foundation for understanding landscape boundary structure and function."

The filtering function regulates the flow of energy and matter across a boundary, influencing not only what moves across the boundary, but also how fast and how much. Filtering is one of the most important effects of

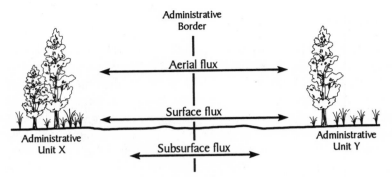

Figure 2.4. Three types of ecological fluxes affected by an administrative border and boundary zone. Aerial and surface fluxes generally move greater distances than subsurface fluxes.

boundaries, and administrative boundaries often are intentionally established to provide this filtering function. For example, during a timber-harvesting operation, water and soil nutrients are allowed to flow in while recreationists are excluded; in designated wilderness, recreationists are allowed in while motorized and mechanized vehicles are not. Unintentional ecological effects of boundary filtering are likely greater than the intentional effects and are discussed under Ecological Effects of Administrative Boundaries.

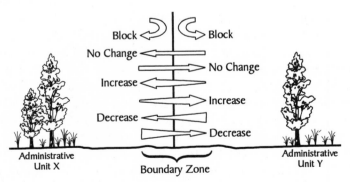

Figure 2.5. Possible changes in fluxes and flux rates across an administrative border and boundary zone. Either administrative unit may act as the "focal" side from which fluxes may increase, decrease, or not change; either side may therefore be a source or a sink for a resource, contaminant, influence, or organism. The boundary zone functions as a semipermeable membrane profoundly affecting ecological flows across a landscape.

Filtering Mechanisms

Inferences derived from natural ecological boundaries provide an organizational structure for discussing filtering mechanisms of administrative boundaries. Boundary filtering may be largely influenced by two interacting factors: the probability of encountering a boundary, and the probability of crossing a boundary (Wiens 1992). Both probabilities are strongly influenced by multiple factors, especially landform physiography, structural attributes of the boundary, and characteristics of the abiotic or biotic vector (e.g., wind or water, or animals, respectively). Landscapes with steep elevational gradients and topographic complexity exhibit greater potential energy of gravity and differential heating and cooling (causing airflow), increasing the likelihood that both types of vectors encounter and cross an administrative boundary. For example, Swanson et al. (1992) found that landform complexity strongly influenced the pattern of water movement and disturbances, thereby affecting the pattern and density of plant association ecotones. Alternatively, topographic complexity may hinder the movement of small and slow-moving animals because of the greater distances involved, as well as the different microclimates and other factors found in complex terrain.

Perimeter-to-area ratio is an important structural attribute of administrative boundaries that influences filtering. A large perimeter-to-area ratio indicates that most vectors, whether abiotic or biotic, have a higher probability of encountering the boundary. For example, Stamps et al. (1987) found that insect emigration and immigration rates were higher in areas with higher perimeter-to-area ratios, and Buechner (1987), using simulation models, found that patch perimeter-to-area ratio was the major factor influencing animal movement across patch edges.

Several characteristics of biotic vectors, including mobility, size, demographics, and behavior, also influence the likelihood of encountering and crossing an administrative boundary. Great mobility, whether because of flight (e.g., bats, insects, and birds), small size that allows individuals to be carried by wind or water across land (e.g., spores, or small seeds), or large size that allows individuals to travel large distances (e.g., large ungulates and large predators), increases the chances of encountering and crossing a boundary. Large size also confers physiological buffering against changes in external conditions, allowing large animals to cross high-contrast areas where there may be large differences in ecological conditions. A large population density in one area may force individuals to disperse into adjacent areas, increasing the likelihood of contact with a boundary. Alternatively, high population densities in an adjoining area may create a "social fence" that prevents dispersal into that area, as Hestbeck (1982) hypothesized for certain rodents. The habitat-selection preferences and behaviors of species also can strongly influence the probability of boundary crossing.

Boundary filtering is influenced by the probabilities of a vector encountering and crossing a boundary. The likelihood of any vector crossing a boundary is highest when both probabilities are high. Conversely, when both probabilities are low, it is not likely that a vector will cross a boundary. When one probability is low and the other is high, the outcome of boundary filtering is uncertain. For example, although a single low-contrast segment may allow most abiotic and biotic vectors to cross a border easily, if the vector never encounters this segment, no boundary crossing will occur. By contrast, large-scale disturbances, such as wind storms or fire, are more likely to decrease contrast over a greater length of administrative border, allowing cross-boundary movement of abiotic and biotic vectors over this larger area. Boundary filtering is therefore a vector-specific and context-specific process.

Ecological Effects of Administrative Boundaries

An administrative boundary has no ecological effect when first established as merely a line drawn on a map. Shortly thereafter, different goals for the land on either side of the boundary drive different management and land-use actions, often creating ecological differences on either side of the boundary (Figure 2.6). These ecological differences, especially in microclimate, soil, plants, and animals, establish most of the structural and functional attributes of the boundary (Forman 1995), in turn augmenting the ecological differences in a positive feedback cycle. This conceptual model of the development of boundary effects stresses that (1) management goals and actions are the primary cause of boundary effects; (2) altered flows either into or out of an area will likely be detrimental to that area; (3) boundary effects follow a distinct temporal sequence; and (4) once established, these effects may have long-term and far-reaching consequences that are difficult or impossible to overcome. Administrative boundaries fragment ecological systems in diverse ways with diverse consequences (review in Saunders et al. 1991; see also Angelstam 1992). We organize these many boundary effects into two broad groups: boundary habitat and isolation impacts.

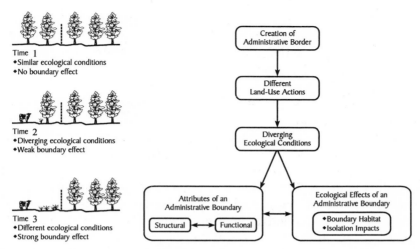

Figure 2.6. Right: Conceptual model of the development of ecological impacts caused by administrative borders. The boxes represent fairly discrete stages in the development of ecological impacts. Different land-use goals and actions on either side of the border cause ecological conditions on either side of the border to diverge. Diverging ecological conditions simultaneously both create the structural and functional attributes of the boundary zone, and cause immediate boundary habitat and isolation impacts. Structural and functional boundary attributes amplify the boundary habitat and isolation impacts, and these ecological impacts reinforce the boundary attributes in a positive feedback cycle. Left: Temporal sequence of the development of ecological impacts caused by administrative borders, corresponding to the stages of the conceptual model. Initially there is no ecological effect of the administrative border because it is simply a line drawn on a map and there are no land-use differences on either side of the border. At time 2 differences in land-use goals and actions begin to create different ecological conditions and to establish the structural and functional attributes of the boundary. At time 3 there is a strong boundary effect with self-perpetuating feedback between boundary attributes and ecological impacts.

Boundary Habitat

Boundary habitat is the distinct area or zone and set of ecological conditions surrounding an administrative border created by the reciprocal influence of the ecological systems on either side of that border. This distinct ecological boundary zone thus overlaps with and extends beyond the administrative border. Boundary habitat generally differs from the adjoining interior area in three major respects: microclimate, soil conditions, and species composition (Forman 1995). Microclimatic differences in temperature and humidity occur because differing vegetation structures alter solar gain and flux. For example, light, soil moisture, humidity, and wind momentum all varied across the boundary zone from a clear-cut to an old-growth Douglas fir (*Pseudotsuga menziesii*) forest (Chen et al. 1995; see also Matlack 1993). Similar microclimate and soil effects were observed across boundary edges in tropical forests (Williams-Linera 1990, Camargo and Kapos 1995). Numerous examples of microclimate and soil gradients across boundary zones are discussed by Forman (1995).

The boundary zone may be used more intensively or heighten change in ecological fluxes. When administrative boundaries abut heavily used transportation corridors or densely settled land-use areas, they may be exposed to increased pollution loading, runoff, vandalism and human disturbance, or entry by organisms such as domestic animals, pests, or exotic plant species. Likewise, when administrative boundaries coincide with abrupt structural changes in a landscape, as between a closed canopy forest and a meadow, flux rates of important ecological materials may change. For example, Weathers and Cadenasso (1996) found that atmospheric deposition of sulfate, calcium, and nitrate, and subsequent nutrient input to the forest floor, were all higher in forest edges than in forest interiors. Higher flux rates also are driven by broad-scale patterns of land use; the greatest change in landscape heterogeneity, including patch size and density, occurs closest to the border of Great Smokey Mountain National Park (Ambrose and Bratton 1990). Therefore, boundary habitat may be a site of intensification of ecological fluxes in landscapes.

Differences in species composition between interior areas and boundary habitat have long been observed. The boundary area may have different species because of different land-use practices, microclimate and soil conditions, or a mix of species from areas adjacent to the border. Vegetation gradients across boundaries have been documented in many different ecosystems (e.g., Ranney et al. 1981, de Casenave et al. 1995, Murcia 1995, Jose et al. 1996). Management practices on one side of a border that disturb soil increase the chance that exotic plants may grow there. These plants may then invade other portions within the boundary area or beyond (Murcia 1995). By contrast, Brothers and Spingarn (1992) found that the wall of forest vegetation at the edge of a clearing effectively repelled most exotic plants, pointing to the need for more research and understanding about the movement of biotic vectors across a boundary zone.

Animals, often habitat generalists that thrive at the interface of different plant communities or seral stages, readily colonize and establish new populations in the boundary zone. Bird communities along City of Boulder Open Space borders, for example, are substantially different from those in core areas in the open space lands (Bock et al. in press). Bird communities along these open space borders are dominated by the American robin (*Turdus migratorius*), house sparrow (*Passer domesticus*), and common grackle (*Quiscalus quiscula*). Away from these borders the bird communities include species that are often less common, such as pygmy nuthatches (*Sitta pygmaea*), western tanagers (*Piranga ludoviciana*), and solitary vireos (*Vireo solitarius*).

Altered species composition in the boundary area also results from management actions on one side of a border that create favorable conditions for species that are aggressive competitors, predators, or parasites. These species then move into adjoining boundary areas or beyond, typically reducing the density of existing native species. European starlings (*Sturnus vulgaris*), for example, are highly aggressive nest competitors that displace native species both in boundary and interior areas (Weitzel 1988, Kerpez and Smith 1990). As discussed, parasitic brown-headed cowbirds invade nests in nearby forested areas. In general, the rates of nest predation among forest birds are much higher closer to borders with open land. Andren and Angelstam (1988), for example, found that predation rates were significantly higher on artificial nests within 50 meters of forest edge.

Isolation Impacts

A variety of impacts may occur far from the generated edge, primarily caused by the altered flux of species, seeds or other propagules, and disturbance processes across the boundary area. Collectively these may be called isolation impacts because the effects do not occur within the boundary area itself but within the interior of the administrative unit. Three general types of isolation impacts are particularly relevant to the administrative borders: impacts on interior or core areas, impacts on ecological processes, and impacts on populations.

Impacts on Interior or Core Areas

Away from the generated edge, habitat conditions in the interior of an administrative unit, or core area, can still be affected by conditions in the boundary area. First, the overall size of the interior or core area is reduced with consequent impacts on populations (see Impacts on Populations). The extent to which the core area is reduced depends on many factors, principally the vegetation structure that buffers temperature and moisture conditions and the flux of abiotic and biotic vectors. A wide range of reduction in core area is reported in the literature, varying from one or two meters, to tens or hundreds of meters from the border (Forman 1995). Second, if large-scale flows are altered (see Impacts on Ecological Processes), vegetation in core areas may be drastically altered. For example, Habeck (1985) found that fire suppression on lands adjacent to the Selway-Bitterroot Wilderness increased fuel loads and the probability of fires spreading into remote parts of the wilderness and burning western red cedar (*Thuja plicata*) forests that typically burn infrequently. Third, impacts from wide-ranging exotic species can significantly alter interior areas far from administrative borders. Feral pigs, for example, have had a devastating impact on native vegetation throughout Hawaiian national parks (Stone and Loope 1987).

Impacts on Ecological Processes

Adjacent land practices and boundaries may block or disrupt vital ecological flows across large portions of a landscape. For example, irrigation diversions and power generation outside Everglades National Park and Grand Canyon National Park, respectively, altered hydrological flow regimes within these parks, severely altering vegetation and wildlife communities (Kushlan 1987, Stevens et al. 1995). In contrast to disrupted fluxes, different management goals on one side of the border may promote or enhance the spread of certain ecological flows that are detrimental to the other side of the border. Fire management illustrates the problems of both disrupted and enhanced fluxes across borders. In the first case, fires that initiated in lower elevation areas and subsequently spread up into higher vegetation types are now largely suppressed, thereby also stopping the fires that would naturally have burned up into higher elevations (Kilgore and Heinselman 1990). In the second case, the example of the Selway-Bitterroot Wilderness shows how different management actions on one side of a border result in fires spreading into areas that they typically would not reach. These changes in fire regimes extend far beyond the administrative border and most likely affect these ecosystems well into the future.

Natural ecological succession results in changes in species composition, the architecture of ecological systems, and system function over time. Nearly all ecological systems change over time, because of internal interactions or as responses to changes in the larger physical environment. Exotic species common in adjacent lands and boundary areas can fundamentally alter the course of ecological succession, causing different species composition and altered ecological functions. For example, successional pathways following a hot fire were significantly altered by the exotic musk thistle (*Carduus macrocephalus*) in Mesa Verde National Park (Floyd-Hanna et al. 1993).

Impacts on Populations

Administrative boundaries affect populations in several ways, especially by disrupting dispersal, decreasing the overall size of an area, and surrounding the isolated area with conditions and threats that are detrimental to survival. Plant and animal populations often consist of spatially separate subpopulations connected through movement from one population to another, forming a metapopulation. Dispersal is key to maintaining recruitment among the subpopulations of a metapopulation, and boundaries and intervening areas that disrupt this flow of individuals across the landscape isolate subpopulations, reduce metapopulation viability, and increase the probability of extinction. In many cases, dispersal and recolonization among fragmented populations is critical for regional survival of a species (Fahrig and Merriam 1994).

An isolated area is a fragment of a former larger area and may now be a "sink" area that loses individuals from a population as they emigrate from the area (Pulliam and Danielson 1991), an effect recognized long ago by Wright et al. (1933) for wildlife in national parks. For species that occupy large home ranges and disperse widely, such as top trophic level carnivores and omnivores like the grizzly bear (*Ursus arctos horribilis*) or wolverine (*Gulo luscus*), these impacts may be especially acute (Newmark 1985). In Algonquin Provincial Park, Ontario, Canada, a yearly average of 11 percent of the Park gray wolf (*Canis lupus*) population was killed by humans from 1988 through 1993 when the wolves left the Park (Forbes and Theberge 1996). Similarly, for large herbivores such as elk that migrate seasonally, boundary areas and adjacent land activities may prevent the seasonal migrations necessary for survival (Lyon and Ward 1982). Bison (*Bison bison*) leaving Yellowstone National Park are killed because they may be vectors for brucellosis, a disease causing higher abortion rates in livestock (Meagher 1989, Keiter 1997).

Isolated populations are more susceptible to extirpation from many causes (reviewed by Lande 1993), including disease, predation, competition, disturbances. Isolated populations also suffer a variety of genetic problems associated with a smaller effective population size, including reduced heterozygosity, inbreeding depression, and genetic drift (reviewed by Brussard and Gilpin 1989). For example, reduced fertility in fewer than fifty remaining Florida panthers (*Felis concolor coryi*) caused by inbreeding depression now contributes to an even smaller population size (Ballou et al. 1989). Dispersal among relatively isolated subpopulations is essential to maintaining species' genetic integrity and variability, but boundary habitats may restrict or prevent dispersal. Based on genetic theory, the notion that one individual per generation moving into a population could maintain the population's genetic integrity has been applied as a rule of thumb in designing conservation programs for many different species. Mills and Allendorf (1996) reviewed these uses and the assumptions behind this rule of thumb, concluding that for genetic purposes only this rule provides an adequate minimum floor for immigration rates.

Both boundary habitat and isolation impacts may persist long after the boundary has served its intended purpose. The species composition on two sides of a tumbledown fence that once separated a pasture from a row crop field is one example; an ancient Anasazi village boundary in the Colorado Plateau is another. The use and ecological significance of such contrasting patches may differ because of contrasting nutrient concentrations or vegetation composition and structure that have persisted into the present. Therefore, how these contrasting patches are used now may well depend on what people did there long ago. Altered species composition and ecological processes, such as fire and succession, also may fundamentally change the ecological system, moving it to a new ecological state (Sprugel 1991).

Research Needs

Current understanding of administrative boundaries and their ecological effects is insufficient for effective landscape-scale stewardship. Compounding the problems of meager understanding, there is little or no strategic planning to integrate research on multiple causal factors. For example, data do exist on plant and animal species composition across boundaries, but most other factors contributing to the structure of the boundary zone have been neglected. In cases where the physical environment has been measured, those measurements have neglected soil processes and structures or have been taken independently of detailed quantification of the vegetation gradients across edges. In this section we offer an agenda for boundary-related research, focusing on four topics: boundary structures, fluxes and gradients along and across these structures, filtering mechanisms affecting fluxes across boundaries, and the ecological effects within and beyond the boundary zone.

Boundary Structures

To understand the ecological implications of different administrative borders, one of the first research priorities is to develop better knowledge about the three-dimensional ecological structure of the boundary zone. What are these structures? Where do they occur? How do they develop? How do they influence the boundary zone? Ultimately, the purpose of describing the three-dimensional structure of a boundary is to relate this structure to important ecological functions or management goals. To date, however, relatively few of the structures that contribute to boundaries have been quantified and described, either along the length of a boundary or how these structures change over time due to natural succession or other changes brought about by land-use decisions. For example, the conditions that contribute to contrast, porosity, boundary segmentation and segment variability are known basically from conceptual models that have received little confirmation from empirical studies. Even though geographic information systems based on remotely sensed data offer much promise for detecting and quantifying landscape-level boundaries (Johnston et al. 1992) and administrative borders, techniques for delineating natural ecological boundaries are still in their relative infancy (McCoy et al. 1986, Fortin and Drapeau 1995). Because the administrative boundary zone also is an ecological boundary, a better understanding of natural ecological boundary structures and fluxes across them may greatly improve how we understand and manage administrative boundaries.

Fluxes and Gradients

One of the most significant impacts of administrative boundaries is how they alter ecological fluxes across a landscape. What are these abiotic and biotic fluxes? How did they move across the landscape before the border was in place? How do they move across the landscape now? What are the effects of these altered fluxes on the valued attributes that occur on both sides of the boundary? How do these fluxes change over time and along the length of a boundary? Most studies have focused on the static state of a variable at fixed points across the boundary. It is also important to begin measuring actual fluxes of materials and energy across boundaries, especially the movement and behavior of nutrients, organisms, and disturbance processes. For instance, the movement of exotic seeds through the boundary zone and into the interior needs to be quantified so that the potential impact and strategies for managing these species can be determined. The movement patterns and behavioral responses of animals, especially insects, birds, and predatory and herbivorous mammals, must be better understood to manage and restore fragmented forests in today's cultural landscapes.

Research also can describe the many ecological gradients and trends across boundary zones, ranging from plant and animal population densities, vegetation architecture and microclimate, and soil nutrient and organic matter concentrations, to rates of soil nutrient turnover, primary productivity, and decomposition. Quantifying gradients across boundaries requires an arbitrary starting or zero point through which the gradients run. However, the specific location of this arbitrary point is rarely stated. Furthermore, researchers may assume that this point defines one end of the gradient of factors that change across the boundary, but these gradients can extend well beyond the usual structural anchors. For example, changes in environmental factors to levels characteristic of the forest can actually occur outside the wall of understory vegetation defining the structural edge of the forest (Cadenasso et al. 1997). Researchers need to examine entire ranges of environmental gradients at boundaries, and not assume that a structural anchor is necessarily the ecological end point of the gradient.

Filtering Mechanisms

Although it is well known that boundaries act as semipermeable membranes blocking, increasing, or decreasing flows into and out of areas on either side of the border, there is little understanding of filtering mechanisms. How do boundary structures, such as width, contrast, segmentation, or convolution, affect flows? Which flows are affected, and how much are they affected? What are the temporal dynamics of filtering? For instance, are some flows affected only during some seasons? What are the spatial dynamics of filtering? For instance, are some flows affected only in some places? What are the primary drivers influencing the probability of different abiotic and biotic vectors encountering and crossing a boundary area? There is a plethora of questions related to filtering mechanisms. The answers will provide the grist for improving both basic knowledge about natural ecological boundaries and management frameworks for reducing the ecological impacts of administrative boundaries.

Ecological Effects

As with filtering mechanisms, the research needs for understanding the ecological effects of administrative boundaries are vast. Three basic questions can help structure this discussion of research needs: What are the short-term, small spatial-scale effects? What are the long-term, large spatial-scale effects? And, what are the cumulative effects of multiple factors?

Short-term effects are the changes within the boundary area resulting from different management and land-use actions on either side of the border, as well as changes in fluxes across the boundary. What components, such as species or vegetation types, are affected? Do certain boundary attributes have a greater or lesser effect on certain components? Substantial information on game species in ecotones provides some answers, but short-term effects on other species and on most processes, and on the mechanisms of these impacts, are largely unknown.

Long-term, large-area effects are poorly understood, yet these effects may have the greatest impact on the long-term productivity of ecological systems, including those systems that produce goods and services valued by society. Important research questions abound. How does the boundary area, as well as the structural and functional attributes of boundaries, change over time? Will a different species milieu in boundary and interior areas alter successional pathways and lead to entirely different ecosystems? How far away from a boundary will species composition, population demographics, and ecological flows be affected? How long will these effects persist? Administrative boundaries and adjacent interior areas provide an opportunity, and reason, to test basic ecological concepts on community invasibility, resilience, and multiple stable states.

Ecological impacts from administrative boundaries come in suites, not singly as described in this chapter. For example, a boundary would simultaneously affect a population in several ways: disrupted dispersal of individuals; exposure to new biotic vectors such as exotic species; exposure to new microclimatic conditions; altered flow of disturbance processes such as fire; and reduction in the genetic integrity of the population due to isolation effects. These impacts have both short- and long-term consequences. In addition, they most likely are synergistic, resulting in even greater impacts. Cumulative effects from multiple factors form the milieu of boundary impacts, but research tends to look at isolated factors, thereby improving the likelihood of successful research, but at the cost of ecological reality and management applicability. Although certainly difficult, research on multiple factors and cumulative effects would help fill the current information vacuum on methods for ameliorating boundary impacts and improving ecological stewardship across boundaries.

Conclusions

Administrative borders are not simply lines on maps. They have profound effects on the ecological systems immediately surrounding the border and far from it and may change these ecological systems in fundamental, long-lasting ways. Some of these changes are intentional, but most are not. The conceptual model of boundaries and of their effects developed here has far-reaching implications for policy, planning, and management to improve landscape-level stewardship.

First, landowners and managers need to recognize and accept responsibility for the ecological effects of their boundaries, direct and indirect, short-term and long-term, rather than treating the boundary area as an expendable commons.

Second, the boundary model developed here suggests that incongruent management goals and actions on either side of the boundary are more important in causing the disruption of ecological fluxes across administrative borders than the usually reported incongruency between administrative and ecological borders. For example, even if administrative and ecological boundaries coincided perfectly, different management goals on either side of the boundary would still cause boundary effects, including isolation impacts to the interior of the administrative units. If this supposition is correct, then in addition to striving for ecologically placed boundaries (see Theberge 1989 for guidelines), more effort is needed to make management goals and actions compatible across administrative borders. In some cases it is possible to conform management with natural ecological boundaries, such as the use of ridge lines or rock outcrops as natural fire breaks by fire management officers in defining fire management zones. Even though most administrative borders are fixed, such as borders between agencies, borders defining management zones *within* an agency have a much better chance of conforming with ecological boundaries. Therefore, reducing ecological impacts will likely require two approaches: striving to make management goals and actions compatible across administrative borders, and making internal management borders and ecological boundaries coincide.

Third, buffer zones may alleviate some, but not all, of the ecological impacts caused by administrative boundaries. By reducing the contrast or the rate of change between adjacent areas, buffer zones may permit more natural ecological flows across a boundary. However, creating buffer zones also increases the width of the generated edge, potentially exacerbating or causing additional ecological impacts. In general, the greater the difference in management goals on either side of a border, the greater the need for, and width of, a buffer zone. Clear-cutting up to the edge of a wilderness, for example, has the greatest ecological impact; a buffer zone within the timber management area would temper some of these impacts.

Finally, landscape-scale stewardship requires landscape-scale planning and management. A management style that focuses solely on particular isolated parcels of land is likely to fail to produce desired long-term outcomes because the health and productivity of all ecosystems are contingent on the larger cultural and ecological landscape of which they are a part (Pickett and Ostfeld 1995). Even interior or core areas are embedded in a larger environmental context and are affected by management goals and actions on surrounding lands. Petit et al. (1995) offer a detailed example of landscape-level planning and management for neotropical birds. The information in this chapter strongly points to the critical need for explicitly taking into account the ecological effects of administrative boundaries and for developing a landscape-scale perspective that takes into consideration larger areas and longer time frames, and fosters coordinated planning and setting of land-use goals.

ACKNOWLEDGMENTS

We thank Tim Hogan, Madeline Mazurski, David Parsons, and Christine Schonewald for valuable and needed discussion, and comments that significantly clarified a draft of this chapter.

REFERENCES

Ambrose, J.P. 1987. Dynamics of ecological boundary phenomena along the borders of Great Smokey Mountains National Park. Ph.D. thesis. University of Georgia, Athens, GA.

Ambrose, J.P., and S.P. Bratton. 1990. Trends in landscape heterogeneity along the borders of Great Smoky Mountains National Park. *Conservation Biology* 4:135–143.

Andren, H., and P. Angelstam. 1988. Elevated predation rates as an edge effect in habitat islands: experimental evidence. *Ecology* 69:544–547.

Angelstam, P. 1992. Conservation of communities—the importance of edges, surroundings, and landscape mosaic structure. Pages 9–70 in *Ecological principles of nature conservation* (L. Hansson, editor). Elsevier Applied Science, New York.

Ballou, J.D., T.J. Foose, R.C. Lacy, and U.S. Seal. 1989. *Florida panther* (Felis concolor coryi) *population viability analysis and recommendations.* Captive Breeding Specialist Group, Species Survival Commission, IUCN, Apple Valley, MN.

Bock, C.E., J.H. Bock, and B.C. Bennett. In press. Songbird abundance in grasslands at a suburban interface on the Colorado High Plains. In *Ecology and conservation of grassland birds in the Western Hemisphere* (J. Herkert, editor).

Brothers, T.S., and A. Spingarn. 1992. Forest fragmentation and alien plant invasion of Central Indiana old-growth forests (P. Vickery and J. Herkert, editors). *Studies in Avian Biology* 6:91–100.

Brussard, P.F., and M.E. Gilpin. 1989. Demographic and genetic problems of small populations. Pages 37–48 in *Conservation biology and the black-footed ferret* (U.S. Seal, E.T. Thorne, M.A. Bogan, and S.H. Anderson, editors). Yale University Press, New Haven.

Buechner, M. 1987. Conservation in insular parks: simulation models of factors affecting the movement of animals across park boundaries. *Biological Conservation* 41:57–76.

Cadenasso, M.L., M.M. Traynor, and S.T.A. Pickett. 1997. Functional location of forest edges: gradients of multiple physical factors. *Canadian Journal of Forest Research* 27:774–782.

Camargo, J.L.C., and V. Kapos. 1995. Complex edge effects on soil moisture and microclimate in central Amazonian forest. *Journal of Tropical Ecology* 11:205–221.

Chen, J., J.F. Franklin, and T.A. Spies. 1995. Growing-season microclimate gradients from clearcut edges into old-growth douglas-fir forests. *Ecological Applications* 5:74–86.

de Casenave, J.L., J.P. Pelotto, and J. Protomastro. 1995. Edge-interior differences in vegetation structure and composition in a Chaco semi-arid forest, Argentina. *Forest Ecology and Management* 72:61–69.

Fahrig, L., and G. Merriam. 1994. Conservation of fragmented populations. *Conservation Biology* 8:50–59.

Floyd-Hanna, L., W. Romme, D. Kendall, A. Loy, and M. Colyer. 1993. Succession and biological invasion at Mesa Verde National Park. *Park Science* 9:16–18.

Forbes, G.J., and J.B. Theberge. 1996. Cross-boundary management of Algonquin Park wolves. *Conservation Biology* 10:1091–1097.

Forman, R.T.T. 1995. *Land mosaics: The ecology of landscapes and regions*. Cambridge University Press, Cambridge.

Forman, R.T.T., and M. Godron. 1986. *Landscape Ecology*. John Wiley, New York.

Forman, R.T.T., and P.N. Moore. 1992. Theoretical foundations for understanding boundaries in landscape mosaics. Pages 236–258 in *Landscape boundaries: consequences for biotic diversity and ecological flows* (A.J. Hansen and F. di Castri, editors). Springer-Verlag, New York.

Fortin, M.-J., and P. Drapeau. 1995. Delineation of ecological boundaries: comparison of approaches and significance tests. *Oikos* 72:323–332.

Gosz, J.R. 1991. Fundamental ecological characteristics of landscape boundaries. Pages 8–30 in *Ecotones: the role of landscape boundaries in the management and restoration of changing environments* (M.M. Holland, P.G. Risser, R.J. Naiman, editors). Chapman and Hall, New York.

Habeck, J.R. 1985. Impact of fire suppression on forest succession and fuel accumulations in long-fire-interval wilderness habitat types. Pages 110–118 in *Proceedings—symposium and workshop on wilderness fire* (J.E. Lotan, B.M. Kilgore, W.C. Fischer, and R.W. Mutch, technical coordinators). USDA Forest Service, General Technical Report INT-182. Intermountain Research Station, Ogden, UT.

Hansen, A.J., and F. di Castri, editors. 1992. *Landscape boundaries: consequences for biotic diversity and ecological flows*. Springer-Verlag, New York.

Hestbeck, J.B. 1982. Population regulation of cyclic mammals: the social fence hypothesis. *Oikos* 39:157–163.

Holland, M.M., P.G. Risser, R.J. Naiman, editors. 1991. *Ecotones: the role of landscape boundaries in the management and restoration of changing environments*. Chapman and Hall, New York.

Johnston, C.A., J. Pastor, and G. Pinay. 1992. Quantitative methods for studying landscape boundaries. Pages 107–125 in *Landscape boundaries: consequences for biotic diversity and ecological flows* (A.J. Hansen and F. di Castri, editors). Springer-Verlag, New York.

Jose, S., A.R. Gillespie, S.J. George, and G.M. Kumar. 1996. Vegetation responses along edge-to-interior gradients in a high altitude tropical forest in peninsular India. *Forest Ecology and Management* 87:51–62.

Keiter, R.B. 1997. Greater Yellowstone's bison: unraveling of an early American wildlife conservation achievement. *Journal of Wildlife Management* 61:1–11.

Kerpez, T.A., N.S. Smith. 1990. Competition between European starlings and native woodpeckers for nest cavities in saguaros. *Auk* 107:367–375.

Kilgore, B.M., and M.L. Heinselman. 1990. Fire in wilderness ecosystems. Pages 297–335 in *Wilderness management*, 2nd edition (J.C. Hendee, G.H. Stankey, and R.C. Lucas, editors). North American Press, Golden, CO.

Kushlan, J.A. 1987. External threats and internal management: the hydrologic regulation of the Everglades, Florida, U.S.A. *Environmental Management* 11:109–119.

Lande, R. 1993. Risks of population extinction from demographic and environmental stochasticity and random catastrophes. *American Naturalist* 142:911–927.

Lyon, L.J., and A.L. Ward. 1982. Elk and land management. Pages 443–477 in *Elk of North America: ecology and management* (J.W. Thomas and D.E. Toweill, editors). Stackpole Books, Harrisburg, PA.

Matlack, G.R. 1993. Microenvironment variation within and among forest edge sites in the eastern United States. *Biological Conservation* 66:185–194.

McCoy, E.D., S.S. Bell, and K. Walters. 1986. Identifying biotic boundaries along environmental gradients. *Ecology* 67:749–759.

Meagher, M. 1989. Evaluation of boundary control for bison of Yellowstone National Park. *Wildlife Society Bulletin* 17:15–19.

Mills, L.S., and F.W. Allendorf. 1996. The one-migrant-per-generation rule in conservation and management. *Conservation Biology* 10:1509–1518.

Murcia, C. 1995. Edge effects in fragmented forests: implications for conservation. *Trends in Ecology and Evolution* 10:58–62.

Naiman, R.J., H. Decamps, J. Pastor, and C.A. Johnston. 1988. The potential importance of boundaries to fluvial ecosystems. *Journal of the North American Benthological Society* 7:289–306.

Newmark, W.D. 1985. Legal and biotic boundaries of western North American national parks: a problem of congruence. *Biological Conservation* 33:197–208.

Petit, L.J., D.R. Petit, and T.E. Martin. 1995. Landscape-level management of migratory birds: looking past the trees to the forest. *Wildlife Society Bulletin* 23:420–429.

Pickett, S.T.A., and R.S. Ostfeld. 1995. The shifting paradigm in ecology. Pages 261–278 in *A new century for natural resources management* (R.L. Knight and S.F. Bates, editors). Island Press, Washington, DC.

Pulliam, H.R., and B.J. Danielson. 1991. Sources, sinks, and habitat selection: a landscape perspective on population dynamics. *American Naturalist* 137 (suppl.):S50.

Ranney, J.W., M.C. Bruner, and J.B. Levenson. 1981. The importance of edge in the structure and dynamics of forest islands. Pages 67–96 in *Forest island dynamics in man-dominated landscapes* (R. L. Burgess and D. M. Sharpe, editors). Springer-Verlag, New York.

Rothstein, S.I., J. Verner, and E. Stevens. 1984. Radio-tracking confirms a unique diurnal pattern of spatial occurrence in the parasitic brown-headed cowbird. *Ecology* 65:77–88.

Saunders, D. A., R. J. Hobbs, and C. R. Margules. 1991. Biological consequences of ecosystem fragmentation: a review. *Conservation Biology* 5:18–32.

Schonewald-Cox, C.M., and J.W. Bayless. 1986. The boundary model: a geographical analysis of design and conservation of nature reserves. *Biological Conservation* 38:305–322.

Smith, W.H. 1990. *Air pollution and forests: interaction between air contaminants and forest ecosystems*, 2nd edition. Springer-Verlag, New York.

Sprugel, D.G. 1991. Disturbance, equilibrium, and environmental variability: what is "natural" vegetation in a changing environment? *Biological Conservation* 58:1–18.

Stamps, J.A., M. Buechner, and V.V. Krishnan. 1987. The effects of edge-permeability and habitat geometry on emigration from patches of habitat. *American Naturalist* 129:533–552.

Stevens, L.E., J.C. Schmidt, T.J. Ayers, and B.T. Brown. 1995. Flow regulation, geomorphology, and Colorado River marsh development in the Grand Canyon, Arizona. *Ecological Applications* 5:1025–1039.

Stone, C.P., and L.L. Loope. 1987. Reducing negative effects of introduced animals on native biotas in Hawaii: what is being done, what needs doing, and the role of National Parks. *Environmental Conservation* 14:245–258.

Swanson, F.J., S.M. Wondzell, and G.E. Grant. 1992. Landforms, disturbance, and ecotones. Pages 304–323 in *Landscape boundaries: consequences for biotic diversity and ecological flows* (A.J. Hansen and F. di Castri, editors). Springer-Verlag, New York.

Theberge, J.B. 1989. Guidelines to drawing ecologically sound boundaries for national parks and nature reserves. *Environmental Management* 13:695–702.

Tyser, R.W., and C.A. Worley. 1992. Alien flora in grasslands adjacent to road and trail corridors in Glacier National Park, Montana (U.S.A.). *Conservation Biology* 6:253–262.

Weathers, K.C., and M.L. Cadenasso. 1996. Function of forest edges: nutrient inputs. *Bulletin of the Ecological Society of America* 77:471.

Weitzel, N.H. 1988. Nest-site competition between the European Starling and native breeding birds in northwestern Nevada. *Condor* 90:515–517.

Wiens, J.A. 1992. Ecological flows across landscape boundaries: a conceptual overview. Pages 217–235 in *Landscape boundaries: consequences for biotic diversity and ecological flows* (A.J. Hansen and F. di Castri, editors). Springer-Verlag, New York.

Wiens, J.A., C.S. Crawford, and J.R. Gosz. 1985. Boundary dynamics: a conceptual framework for studying landscape ecosystems. *Oikos* 45:421–427.

Williams-Linera, G. 1990. Vegetation structure and environmental conditions of forest edges in Panama. *Journal of Ecology* 78:356–373.

Wright, G.M., J.S. Dixon, and B.H. Thompson. 1933. *Fauna of the national parks of the United States: a preliminary survey of faunal relations in national parks.* Fauna Series No. 1, U.S. Government Printing Office, Washington, DC.

Chapter 3

Social Dimensions of Boundaries: Balancing Cooperation and Self-Interest

Mark W. Brunson

This book exists because scientists, resource managers, and policy makers have come to understand that ecological entities cannot be protected or sustainably managed within the bounds of existing administrative units. Other authors discuss why cross-boundary stewardship is necessary, why administrative boundaries create circumstances harmful to ecosystems, and how political structures and management strategies might be devised to effectively promote cross-boundary stewardship. This chapter establishes some of the context for that discussion by examining the nature of boundaries themselves from a social science perspective and by describing some of the behavioral and attitudinal aspects of cross-boundary relationships.

Boundaries can take many forms. In this discussion the term *boundary* refers to physical demarcations, including not only the mapped boundaries of nations, states, public agency jurisdictions, and private landholdings, but also the often-invisible, but nonetheless real, boundaries that groups or individuals may establish to define their "turf." All boundaries are social constructs, marking human-perceived differences in the nature and identity of places. They may follow natural contours in a landscape, such as a state border that follows a river or a wildlife refuge boundary that traces the outline of a prairie marsh, or they may be derived solely from artificial systems of organization such as the township-and-range grid established over most of the western half of the United States. Even ecosystem boundaries are social constructs in that they reflect the spatial extent of natural conditions that characterize a human-defined categorization within the continuous range of actual and potential conditions.

Boundaries exist because they achieve societal ends. Yet societies also promote relationships that transcend boundaries. Stewardship across boundaries can be achieved only if we find a balance between basic, but contrasting, human needs: (1) to protect a space in which one can achieve both personal and group well-being; and (2) to cooperate with others to achieve a harmonious society and a healthy environment. Human societies have, in fact, developed in such a way that these seemingly contradictory motives and outcomes actually can be complementary. As the proverb goes, "Good fences make good neighbors." A key to successful cross-boundary stewardship lies in accommodating motivations for both territorial self-interest and community cooperation. To borrow a term from the natural sciences, ecological stewards must safeguard the *permeability* of boundaries, maintaining the integrity of discrete territories while allowing the free passage of ideas and information as well as organisms and ecosystem fluxes.

This chapter first describes territorial defense and collaborative action in terms of their cultural, social, and psychological bases and their relationships to boundaries. These ideas are then applied specifically to issues pertaining to cross-boundary stewardship of natural systems, using examples drawn mainly from the Intermountain West. Three types of cross-boundary relationship are considered: between public agencies and private property owners, between two or more public agencies, and among departments within agencies. The chapter concludes by considering what further social science research might reveal about the characteristics and sustainability of permeable, stewardship-enhancing boundaries.

The central idea of this chapter is that we can sustain ecosystems across boundaries only if we understand how humans behave with respect to the places they claim as territory. The discussion is guided by two models of human behavior. The first model holds that human behaviors can be explained as a combination of biological, cultural, social, and psychological influences. Although there is some debate among social and behavioral scientists about the relative influence of biological and social factors (Wrong 1961, Wilson 1978), it is possible to explain virtually everything we do—from our religious rituals to the ways we clean our teeth—as the result of some combination of heredity, physiology, cultural tradition, childhood socialization, and enduring or momentary personal preference. Some behaviors may be governed chiefly by biological factors—for instance, a fright response to a charging grizzly bear or an instinctive slap at a biting mosquito. Yet park rangers devote considerable effort to teaching hikers what to do if a bear attacks (a social influence), while the Jains of India strive to adhere to their belief that it is wrong to kill any insect, even mosquitos (a cultural influence). Conversely, it may be hard to see a biological basis for behaviors that display personal tastes, such as choosing a bedtime novel or a poster for an office wall. Yet psychologists say humans may be predisposed to seek visual or cognitive stimuli that offer moderate levels of incongruence (Berlyne 1960, Deci 1975), such as escapist fiction or posters of faraway places. There is even evidence that the presence of wall art showing outdoor scenes is associated with reduced stress and improved surgical recovery rates (Ulrich 1993).

Such a model of human behavior acknowledges the contributions to understanding made by a wide range of academic disciplines, from evolutionary biology to anthropology to sociology to environmental psychology, and this chapter draws on all of these. However, the discussion draws most heavily on ideas in social psychology, and it is that discipline that provides the second model of human behavior guiding the chapter: that human behaviors, whether they occur in an individual or group context, are guided largely by attitudes (i.e., moderately enduring tendencies to evaluate persons and situations in certain ways and to act in accordance with those evaluations). Although the expression of an attitude as behavior may be blocked by intermediary influences (peer group pressures; circumstances that make the behavior difficult to perform; masking of the attitude by a different, more salient attitude; and so on), attitudes nonetheless can predict the likelihood of behaviors (Ajzen and Fishbein 1980, Manfredo 1992). By seeking to understand attitudes toward property, boundaries, and various natural resource constituencies, we can better predict participation in cross-boundary stewardship efforts.

Social Functions of Boundaries

Most boundaries, whether of a nation or a city lot, mark the limits of a defended territory. To understand the nature and necessity of boundaries, it is helpful first to examine how and why humans establish and maintain territories. Ethologists argue that there is an obvious evolutionary advantage for individuals and groups to control a defensible space that can provide basic biological needs such as food and shelter (Tinbergen 1953, Lorenz 1967). Anthropologists have observed that, even though virtually all societies defend territories, defense behaviors intensify as cultures shift from a foraging strategy to a collector strategy, whereby groups no longer move from place to place as food supplies are exhausted but instead develop specially organized task groups to gather and store resources (Dyson-Hudson and Alden-Smith 1978, Binford 1980, Mandryk 1993). Modern American society is, in essence, a highly developed collector system.

Just as territorial behaviors vary within the human species, such behaviors may vary within groups or individuals. For example, temporal variation is common. Groups might defend a space at times when resources are scarce, but at other times share a predictable and bountiful resource such as a fruit crop or spawning run. More frequent temporal cycles also occur; for example, in a study of city parks, Lee (1972) found that territories shifted in ownership throughout the day, such as when park benches frequented by senior citizens in the morning "belonged" to drug dealers at dusk.

Not only do communities maintain territories, but nested within those spaces are many smaller territories. Environmental psychologist Irwin Altman (1975) distinguished between three types of territories in communities: *primary* territories owned and used exclusively by individuals or groups, identified as theirs by others, controlled on a relatively permanent basis, and central to the day-to-day lives of the occupants (e.g., houses, apartments); *secondary* territories that are less exclusive but may be differentially accessible and subject to more or less mild forms of defense (e.g., neighborhood bar, office waiting room); and *public* territories that are not occupied permanently and are intended to be open to all (e.g., streets, parks). Just as a community contains many group territories, the latter may be subdivided into territories for individuals. For example, a family will defend its home as a primary territory with respect to others outside the family group, but that home also contains primary (bedrooms, closets), secondary (kitchen, garage), and public territories (backyard, family room). Finally, at shifting locations within any of these spaces there also can be found the well-defended territories known as "personal space," that is, the invisibly bounded area around a person's body into which intrusion is discouraged (Sommer 1969).

How Territory Is Maintained

Once a claim is staked to a territory, its boundaries must be maintained. Because humans maintain several territories simultaneously, at any given time they may be engaged in several maintenance behaviors, from giving body language cues that keep interlopers out of personal space to lobbying for a stronger military. These behaviors fall into the general category called "territoriality." A useful definition of territoriality was offered by

geographer Robert Sack (1983): "the attempt to affect, influence, or control actions, interactions, or access by asserting and attempting to enforce
control over a specific geographic area." Defense of a socially maintained
territory rarely means forcibly expelling intruders; rather it is exhibited
through defenders' efforts to *control* what happens within "their" space.
Control may be exercised through codified state and federal laws, in
jurisdiction-specific regulations such as subdivision covenants, or in the
unwritten rules that guide interpersonal relationships.

Most of the rules common to any territory cannot be found in any
written code, but instead take the form of social norms. These norms are
standards of behavior that members of a distinguishable group are
expected to follow, often but not always simply within the boundaries of
a given territory, and that are enforced by positive and negative sanctions
(Loomis 1960, Cancian 1975). Because territories are nested within
other territories, we learn to abide by the rules of several territorial entities simultaneously. For example, in a state park we know we should obey
not only state and federal laws but also park regulations and social norms.
Moreover, we have repertoires of place-specific behaviors; for instance,
we learn that standards of posture, language, personal grooming, and
other behavioral aspects are different on an athletic field from what they
are in the personnel office of a prospective employer, and we behave
accordingly or pay the consequences.

Recognizing Boundaries

If behavioral standards are enforced within territories, people must be
able quickly to identify which territories they currently occupy. Thus territories need a boundary that is not only known to the maintainers, but
can also be identified by the persons or groups with whom they interact.
Whereas other species mark their territories by olfactory or auditory cues,
humans most often do so using easily learned and recognized visual cues:
fences and hedges, "No Trespassing" signs, border guards with subma-
chine guns, or the tenseness of posture that tells us we have stepped
within someone's personal space.

Boundaries are usually respected, but if they are not easily recognizable, mistakes about behavior can occur. If a territory is not strongly
defended, such mistakes have only minor consequences. For example,
unwitting territorial intrusions are common in the West, where the cost
of erecting fences or signs can be prohibitive along boundaries that can
stretch for many miles between human habitations. Most such intrusions

are greeted with a friendly correction or mild reprimand, yet every year there are incidents where campers are ordered off private property by shotgun-wielding landowners, or hunters are fined for unwittingly shooting animals in a national park. The consequences of territorial violation depend in large part on whether society determines that the defender or the violator has a greater burden of determining ownership, as well as on whether responsibility for violation can be easily assigned. Much of the work of attorneys concerns the fine details of boundary violation and its consequences, which may range from criminal sanction for trespass to assuming liability for accidents on one's property to identifying parties responsible for cleanup of Superfund sites.

Cooperation Between Territorial Entities

Even though boundaries mark the limits of defensible territories, thousands of human activities require people to transcend territorial limits. These activities range from marriages between residents of neighboring communities to treaties between nations. Like territorial behaviors, cooperative behaviors are determined in part by basic biology (e.g., mating instincts), as well as personal preference (e.g., joining a club whose members share hobby ideas). However, the principal influence occurs at the level of the culture or society. Indeed, the entire idea of "society," a system of structures and institutions that outlines relationships between individuals and groups, rests on the idea that it is beneficial to share resources lying within others' defended territories. More than four centuries ago, English philosopher Thomas Hobbes (1651) wondered how social order was possible among biological beings and why human society was not a war of all against all. Hobbes's question has become a central focus in the academic disciplines of sociology and political science, and the literature addressing it is voluminous in size and sweeping in scope. Even the most cursory examination of that literature reveals something interesting about territories and boundaries: the same social structures and institutions that serve to maintain territories also serve to encourage cooperation among territorial entities.

Society's mechanisms to encourage cooperation between individuals and groups can be formal or informal, global or interpersonal. Formal legal systems that help landowners maintain their territories also serve to encourage cooperation through the establishment and enforcement of contracts that are, in effect, mechanisms for the signatories to outline exactly how much control of a relationship they'll retain and how much they'll cede to the other parties. More often, however, it is social norms that set the rules for cooperation by setting expectations for justice and equity in relationships.

Adherence to social norms almost certainly is more important to the functioning of society than maintenance of formal legal structures. This idea is expressed in the popular literature (Fulgham 1988, Bennett 1993) and is borne out by research on the sociology of law. A helpful analysis of this phenomenon was offered by law professor Robert Ellickson (1991), who studied cattle trespass and open-range disputes in Shasta County, California, to understand why disputants do not invoke the law when theories of rational choice suggest that they should. What Ellickson found was that informal norms for maintaining community well-being overrode immediate self-interest. If shared fences or other facilities needed repairs, ranchers did minor work themselves as needed and invoked a norm of proportionality to handle larger projects. To resolve trespass disputes, injured parties generally put up with minor damage or, if damage was heavy or persistent, used informal controls such as negative gossip or a tit-for-tat "borrowing" of the offending party's property to maintain control. So rarely were legal channels invoked that Ellickson believes laws function in relatively cohesive rural societies largely to "invigorate" social control or fill in gaps where informal control mechanisms may fail. Conversely one could argue that the loss of cohesion associated with an urbanized, highly mobile society is responsible for the continued growth of conflict and litigation in the United States.

Another line of research in legal sociology has found that norms of procedural justice can override norms of distributive justice (Thibault 1975, Tyler 1989). Cooperators tend to be more willing to accept decisions that result in reduced territorial control if they believe that the adverse decision resulted from a fair process. This is why critics of natural resource planning processes often point to agencies' overemphasis on meeting legal stipulations of the National Environmental Policy Act (NEPA) and other laws and a consequent lack of attention to the affected publics' need to feel that their concerns have been truly heard (Blahna and Yonts-Shepard 1989, Krannich et al. 1994). Increasingly advocates of ecosystem management call for abandoning traditional decision-making processes in favor of collaborative partnerships between territorial entities and other affected parties. The design of such groups invariably emphasizes norms of procedural justice (Crowfoot and Wondolleck 1990). This issue is discussed further in Chapter 14.

Values and Attitudes About Boundaries

In issues of public policy it is often as important to know what people *want* to occur as it is to know what actually *is* occurring. This is true because public agencies are said to represent a larger constituency whose needs, values, and desires are supposed to help guide a democratic society. It also is true because people's interactions with others are guided in part by their expectations about how those others will behave. For those reasons it is important for persons seeking to achieve cross-boundary stewardship to understand the attitudes of relevant others toward territory, boundaries, and cooperation.

Attitudes have various antecedents: social influences from childhood onward, personal experiences, beliefs about what is true, and basic underlying values. Only individuals can have attitudes; groups cannot. However, certain attitudes are likely to be prevalent within groups whose members share experiences, beliefs, and values. Some attitudes are long-held and deeply rooted, but others are transitory and shallow, susceptible to normative pressures or information that changes beliefs about reality (i.e., education or propaganda). Deeply rooted attitudes are likely to arise from frequent exposure to others' expressions of that attitude, and from deeply held values.

The term *value* is overused in discussions of natural resources. In a single article one might see the term used to describe the worth of a resource traded in a market, the various goods and services that society desires from natural places (called "social values" in the ecosystem management literature), and deeper beliefs about what is right. It is this last kind of value that influences attitudes. A person typically has hundreds of attitudes but relatively few values. "Value" in this context was defined by Rokeach (1973) as "an enduring belief that a specific mode of conduct or end-state of existence is personally or socially preferable to an opposite or converse mode of conduct or end-state of existence."

Rokeach identified eighteen basic core values ranging from individual traits (happiness, wisdom) to societal characteristics (equality, national security). One of the latter, which Rokeach called "world of beauty," is said to be a key influence on environmental attitudes. Several of these core values are sustained through some level of territorial defense, including a comfortable life, family security, national security, and freedom. Others must be sustained through cooperation: a world at peace, equality, and social recognition. Rokeach argues that everyone holds all eighteen values, but people act according to a *value system*, that is, the way those values are organized along a continuum of relative importance.

Attitudes toward territory, boundaries, and cross-boundary cooperation are important determinants of the success or failure of cross-boundary stewardship efforts because they influence whether agencies or individuals will enter into partnerships that transcend jurisdictional boundaries, as well as how they behave within those partnerships. Such attitudes are strongly influenced by the holders' value systems; people are more likely to participate in cross-boundary stewardship if they feel cooperation and a "world of beauty" are more important than defensive values. Other likely attitudinal influences are persons' beliefs about the need for such stewardship, their past exposure to stewardship ideas, their beliefs about how significant others will react to stewardship initiatives, previous personal experiences (their own or significant others') with stewardship activities, and the strength of potentially conflicting attitudes toward territorial control.

Boundaries, Territoriality, and Western Public Lands

This section applies the basic concepts of territory, cooperation, and boundaries to the specific issues of encouraging cross-boundary stewardship in the public-lands states of the West. General influences are discussed first, followed by specific examples of effects on relationships between agencies and private citizens, between different land-management agencies, and between entities in multiple-use agencies.

One of the most important steps toward achieving cooperative cross-boundary stewardship is to identify who holds territorial claims to the landscape. This may be more difficult than it seems because natural-resource managers are trained primarily to recognize the importance of a landscape for nonhuman ecosystem components (e.g., that it serves as summer range for one species, contains critical mating or rearing habitat for other species, and provides conditions necessary for seedling establishment in still others), but may be less able to recognize the full range of human territorial claims.

Although public lands are theoretically held in common by all citizens, not everyone sees them as "public territories." Invariably some groups or individuals consider portions of the public lands to be secondary or even primary territories, and they defend them as such. Depending on the type of perceived threat, defense may be made via formal institutional structures such as public hearings and lawsuits or through such less formal means as when camping parties send one member into the woods a day early to claim a preferred campsite.

Among the groups that form primary or secondary territorial attachments are agency employees themselves. Natural resource managers devote their careers to shaping the future of the landscapes they manage. It is not surprising that they may develop emotional or practical attachment to certain settings within those landscapes. A second class of obvious territorial claimants are those who have obtained a legal right to exercise some degree of control over a public place, such as grazing permittees, oil and gas leaseholders, ski resort operators, and so on. These entities have long been consulted on management decisions because they were obvious stakeholders and because they define and defend their territories through formal legal structures that have obvious standing in courts of law.

Managers have been less successful in accommodating stakeholders whose territories are marked and defended through extralegal means but are no less important to the claimants. These may include rural residents who have hunted, fished, gathered firewood, or otherwise held a usufructuary claim to a public setting (Fortmann 1990); residents and visitors who value a landscape for its scenic qualities; and recreationists who form an enduring attachment to a public setting through repeated use. These claimants are increasingly successful at defending their claims through such formal means as agency appeals, lawsuits, and legislative action.

Researchers have begun to pay closer attention to the issue of place attachment in natural resources, especially in the context of outdoor recreation, because such attachments can lead to conflict between user groups and increase the negative consequences of changes in management (Williams et al. 1992, Schroeder 1996). Analyses of place attachment can yield surprising information about how affected communities define territories. Brandenburg and Carroll (1995) interviewed residents of three forest-dependent communities about management options for a heavily forested valley in western Washington. Residents of two communities favored multiple-use management that included new roads and extensive timber harvest. However, those in the community closest to the valley preferred that it be left pretty much alone. Even though they had recently felt the pain of a sawmill closure and otherwise were staunch supporters of the timber industry, community members had always used that valley as a recreation setting and were willing to forgo economic gain to protect their territory in its present form.

To understand the complexity of territorial relationships, consider the example of Pineview Reservoir, one of Utah's most popular recreation areas. Territorial claimants include agency personnel; the operator of the campground and marina concession; lakeshore property owners; other residents of the immediate local area, who value the reservoir as an environmental amenity but not necessarily as a recreation setting; and recreation visitors, most of whom come from more heavily populated suburbs farther west and south. Reservoir visitors tend to segregate themselves based on recreation activity needs (swimmers at one beach, jet-skiers at another) as well as sociodemographic characteristics, such as age or ethnicity. However, their territories overlap, and only portions of those territories are defended, such as when anglers defend prime fish habitat or managers establish no-wake zones for safer swimming. This territorial overlap is sometimes spatial, sometimes temporal. One beach is visited on weekday afternoons by young people from lakeview communities who come to socialize with friends and ride personal watercraft, but on weekends the same beach is used almost exclusively by Hispanic families from larger towns in the area. Weekend visitors to the adjacent beach also are mostly Hispanic, but there the visitors are teens and young single adults who maintain their territory with loud stereos, nuisance behaviors, and even gang-style graffiti. When USDA Forest Service managers began an ecosystem management assessment at the reservoir in 1996, they knew they would not only have to account for the needs of fish, wildlife, and traditional stakeholders, they would also have to develop stewardship efforts that reach out to ethnic minorities who might have had little or no positive interaction with federal officials.

Cross-boundary stewardship of the western public lands is complicated by the greater difficulty of marking and recognizing boundaries. Agencies vary in their attention to boundary marking. The U.S. Fish and Wildlife Service, with its relatively small refuges (outside Alaska) and its particular sensitivity to human intrusions, probably does the best job among federal agencies of marking boundaries with fences and signs. Conversely, boundary identification is a particular problem for wilderness managers who may hesitate to erect fences or signs that might impinge on the wilderness experience, and consequently find their jurisdictions illegally entered by motorized recreationists or logging crews.

Boundaries are marked only if they are legally defined, so it can be difficult for managers to recognize less formal territories that are claimed within a particular landscape. Knowing about such territories can be important for cross-boundary stewardship. For example, managers may be able to protect against recreation use impacts by distributing information about ecological impacts, but only if they can effectively target that information at the groups using the setting of concern. Or they might be able to identify appropriate recreation clubs (e.g., local and regional snowmobile, angling, or climbing organizations) that can represent recreational users in stewardship discussions. Often within agencies the people who are best able to recognize territorial boundaries are not included routinely in stewardship planning. Law enforcement specialists, recreation technicians, visitor center receptionists, and others who have frequent contact with the public may be useful sources of information about groups or individuals who may be likely to identify certain land-scapes as claimed territories.

Boundary Issues Between Public and Private Lands

When cross-boundary stewardship involves landscapes owned by both public and private entities—as it most often does, even in the West—the issue of property rights becomes especially important. Increasingly, water-shed-level partnerships of public and private owners are advocated as solutions to stewardship problems. Yet cooperation among adjoining landowners is possible only if private landowners are willing to cede some control over their defended territories to the larger partnership. Individuals' willingness to cede that control will depend on their attitudes toward the stewardship objectives and toward the public entities in the partnership, as well as on the importance they place on cooperative, defensive, and environmental values.

Americans seem to emphasize private property more than any other culture. Partly this is because so many emigrants to North America were escaping an economic system that concentrated land and wealth in the hands of a small minority. In the New World, anyone who plowed a plot of ground could lay claim to a tiny fiefdom where the settler alone was in strict control. As the new nation expanded westward, Thomas Jefferson practically deified the farmer-settlers: "Those who labor in the earth are the chosen people of God, if ever He had a chosen people, whose breasts He has made His peculiar deposit for substantial and genuine virtue" (Abernethy 1964). Agrarian virtue became religious duty as the Mormons settled the Great Basin and set about to "make the desert bloom." Agricultural landowners in the West were raised to a favored status, and to maintain that status they had to protect their fiefdoms against any sort of incursion—even that of the government that had made it possible for the homesteader to acquire the property in the first place.

This cultural legacy of agrarian virtue and self-made nobility remains strong in the contemporary West. It can be seen in the immaculate, well-watered lawns of suburbs where chronic drought long ago should have made obsolete a form of landscape design with origins in the ostentatious country estates of eighteenth-century England and France. It also can be seen in the adherence, especially by rural westerners, to a myth of frontier independence that belies the reality of railroad land grants, huge water projects, mining incentives, below-cost timber sales, and other taxpayer subsidies that made western settlement feasible. Even with such assistance it was hard to make a living from the arid land. Nowadays many rural westerners feel they must maintain continuity of control over family farm and ranch operations because to do otherwise might render meaningless the struggles of one's parents and grandparents to prosper on the land (Jorgensen 1984). If cross-boundary stewardship appears to threaten that control, agricultural landowners may see it as a threat to their lifestyles as well as to their livelihoods.

Other important stakeholders also may be wary of stewardship efforts. The region's largest private landowners are timber, railroad, mining, and energy companies that may perceive disincentives to join stewardship efforts because environmental protection potentially threatens the natural resource uses that built their fortunes. Because those same resources also built most western economies, rural community leaders who are crucial to the success of stewardship programs may hesitate to support them for fear of antagonizing natural resource industry interests (McBeth and Foster 1994).

Yet other influences on western attitudes tend to reinforce communitarian values. It would have been impossible to settle the Interior West without a great deal of cooperation among settlers. Early Mormon settlements, in particular, functioned as communal societies whose members had well-defined and strongly enforced roles of mutual support, and there remains a norm of seeking assistance within the community before turning to government for support (Nelson 1952, Arrington 1958, Stegner 1970). To the extent that agency managers are seen as part of the community—a circumstance that until recently was deliberately discouraged in some agencies (Colfer and Colfer 1978)—this emphasis on communitarian values in the rural West may make participation in cross-boundary partnerships more likely. The "world of beauty" value also is strong in the West, and the cultural construction of land among private landowners tends to incorporate not only its economic potential but also its open vistas, wildlife, clean air and water, and other environmental amenities (Jorgensen 1984).

Given these contrasting influences, we might expect landowners to express ambivalent attitudes toward cross-boundary stewardship. Indeed, recent studies suggest that forest and rangeland owners are wary about cooperating with public agencies in cross-boundary efforts, but not opposed to the idea outright. A recent survey (Brunson et al. 1996b) found that three in four private forest owners would give some consideration to joining a multi-owner partnership, even though nearly half reported being concerned about the loss of private property rights in recent years. However, fewer than 25 percent were ready to join a partnership right away; the rest would join only after the process had been tested elsewhere or if certain conditions were imposed (e.g., the federal government were not involved, or if the protection of commodity uses were an expressed goal of the partnership). Owners of large properties most critical to ecosystem protection were less likely to reject the idea of cooperation outright, but more likely to impose conditions on participation. Similarly Utah ranchers and rural leaders interviewed in early 1995 (Brunson et al. 1996a), generally were not ready to trust federal agency officials, but felt that partnerships with those agencies might be the only way to stave off legislative or judicial solutions imposed by outsiders. As predicted by the studies in legal sociology by Tyler (1989), interviewees were more likely to express positive attitudes toward cross-boundary cooperation if they felt they would be given a chance to design a "fair" collaborative process.

There is hope for the future in the increasing evidence that cross-boundary cooperation between public and private landowners, although administratively "messy," does indeed work (e.g., Cannon 1996). In a survey of participants in eight collaborative partnerships for range management (Brunson and Richardson 1997), most respondents rated the partnerships as fair and effective, resulting in benefits to both land and landowners. The Nature Conservancy began in the early 1990s to purchase and operate large working ranches in an effort to sustain rangeland biodiversity as well as ranch economies. The idea behind this approach to conservation is that biodiversity can be protected more easily if ranches remain economically viable rather than being converted to subdivisions and if neighboring ranchers can learn about and use sustainable grazing practices. Preliminary observations of two such operations suggest that, despite initial skepticism, local residents have quickly become willing partners of the Conservancy and have even begun to try some of the grazing practices that the group advocates.

Boundaries Between Agencies

Many public agencies have responsibility for aspects of natural ecosystems, and the people within those various agencies don't always cooperate easily. Approaches to management differ greatly between multiple-use agencies such as the Forest Service and USDI Bureau of Land Management and single- or dominant-use agencies, such as the National Park Service or USDI Fish and Wildlife Service. The latter agency has sometimes clashed with other agencies since it was granted authority under the Endangered Species Act to veto government projects that could jeopardize a threatened or endangered species. Also common are tensions between state fish and wildlife agencies, which are responsible for managing wild animal populations, and the federal and state agencies that manage those animals' habitats. Relationships between agency officials can be difficult because their mandates differ and also because their "agency cultures" may place differing emphases on loyalty to the agency, responsibility to visitors and surrounding communities, and proper deference paid to employees trained in various academic disciplines (Kennedy 1985, 1988).

Although agencies may have problems working together in practice, their policies are geared toward cooperation. Care generally is taken not to tread on another agency's "turf" (Kunioka and Rothenberg 1993). Thus, when a national monument was proposed at Mono Lake, California, in the early 1980s and the Forest Service argued that it should retain jurisdiction, the Park Service chose not to push its case. In 1986 when Great Basin National Park was created from lands managed by both agencies, there was tension among the agencies' personnel in Nevada, but their concerns were not reflected in public statements by superiors in Washington, DC. The Park Service has openly criticized other agencies when it feels that activities on adjacent lands threaten park resources, but analysis of one such case in Glacier National Park found that norms of cooperation overrode the Service's legal authority fully to protect its resources (Sax and Keiter 1987).

On the whole, then, we might expect to find that natural resource agencies will be publicly committed to cooperating in cross-boundary efforts, but relationships between representatives of various agencies within the partnerships themselves might sometimes be strained. Their "territorial defense" may not be directed toward maintenance of agency jurisdictional boundaries per se, but rather toward adopting an approach to management that is most consistent with each agency's "culture."

Cross-agency cooperation may be fostered if agency representatives take pains to try to understand partner agencies' viewpoints and constraints. Too often this is not the case, however, especially when state and federal agencies must work together. Often state and federal agency disputes are described in terms of power, as state officials accuse federal counterparts of trying to "usurp" authority that under the U.S. Constitution is delegated to states, and federal officials deride state agencies as "hook-and-bullet" biologists or obstructionists. The state of Montana, for example, for years maintained a very limited hunting season on grizzly bears, largely because the state wildlife agency was funded by license fees and could spend money on grizzly research only if the species was hunted. Federal biologists in Montana understood the constraints faced by their state counterparts, but their bosses in Washington, pressured by environmentalists who chose to ignore the political realities in western states, saw the situation as state-agency provincialism and eventually forced the abandonment of the grizzly season. Although clearly an alternative to hunting was needed, federal officials' failure to understand state needs led to inter-agency tensions that threatened subsequent cooperation.

Boundaries Within Agencies

The same sorts of pressures also operate within agencies. Fifty years ago natural resource agencies had straightforward objectives: the Grazing Service wrung AUMs from arid rangelands, the Forest Service safeguarded reliable flows of timber and water, the Fish and Wildlife Service preserved game habitat, and so on. But in the 1970s and 1980s agencies expanded their staffs in response to environmental laws and a new recognition of the interconnectedness of natural systems. Different occupational groups within agencies tended to be bound together by shared interests and experiences, and natural loyalties to professions and resource uses led to intra-agency friction. That friction was reinforced by administrative procedures that called for interdisciplinary teams of experts who would debate among themselves about solutions to multiple-use conflicts (Brunson and Kennedy 1995). Agencies trying to manage for a fuller range of products and services sometimes sought to produce multiple resources at the same places, but at other times they set aside places where a particular resource would be emphasized, thereby erecting boundaries *within* agencies.

Some intra-agency boundaries are marked on maps, but others are not. National forest plans designate which lands are to be managed as big game winter range and which will furnish timber above all else. Occasionally the boundaries are set by Congress, most notably in the case of wildernesses and wild and scenic rivers. Such boundaries are usually respected by everyone in an agency, although there are occasional examples of entry into wilderness by loggers or road-builders, usually due to mistakes in identifying unmarked boundaries on-site. However, other intra-agency boundaries are invisible, maintained largely by agency cultures that dictate which resource is seen as more "worthy" of protection or which branch of the agency will suffer the brunt of budget cuts. Stewardship across these boundaries can be especially difficult because nonagency partners may not understand that there are internal differences in agencies, and because top agency administrators may be blind to their effects or may pretend they don't exist.

This can lead to misunderstandings harmful to collaborative processes. For example, members of a watershed-level partnership might be dismayed to learn that federal funds they'd agreed would go to habitat restoration suddenly had been diverted to firefighting elsewhere in an agency's jurisdiction. Fire protection is a revered activity within forestry agencies, and it is easy to justify firefighting as a wildlife expenditure because fires consume vegetation that provides habitat. But to a wildlife advocate who has waited years for a favorite restoration effort, the sudden shift of plans represents a betrayal of trust. As with inter-agency boundaries, a critical step toward maintaining permeable intra-agency boundaries may be to ensure that all partners in a collaborative project understand and discuss relevant differences that may exist within the agencies in their partnership.

Conclusions and Future Directions

We live in a territorial society. Our territories form an infinitely complex network that is variable in time, space, and defensive intensity. Humans maintain many boundaries at once, seeking to control the spaces within those boundaries and to defend claims based on legal authority, emotional attachment, and biological inclination. The existence of these territories complicates the task of protecting ecosystems that invariably transcend human boundaries, but they exist because society cannot function without them. Cross-boundary stewardship efforts will be futile if they seek to eliminate such boundaries.

Instead stewardship projects should be designed to acknowledge the existence of territories, to recognize the various mechanisms of defense that territorial claimants employ, and to accommodate the need for those claimants to maintain an acceptable level of territorial control. In other words, we must strive for a viable level of permeability, maintaining the integrity of discrete territories while allowing the free passage of information as well as ecosystem components.

When conservation advocates discuss information in the context of cross-boundary stewardship, they generally mean a one-way flow of environmental education that can reduce public concerns and misinformation about target species. But the flow must be two-way. Just as landowners and local officials need to learn the scientific basis for biologically based solutions, conservation advocates must seek to understand economic and social factors that lead to local opposition. Forbes and Theberge (1996) describe a cross-boundary stewardship attempt that demonstrates the perils of unidirectional communication strategies. Canadian authorities tried to use public education to ease fears about a newly imposed ban on killing wolves near an Ontario provincial park, but local opposition to the ban actually reduced the flow of information to conservation authorities as many landowners stopped voluntarily reporting dead wolves and withheld permission for researchers to travel on their property.

As human populations grow and natural systems undergo greater stress, conservation advocates often seek regulatory approaches to stewardship that would "transcend" boundaries by imposing uniform restrictions to nonuniform territories. Examples of this might include early attempts at restricting timber harvests to minimize loss of spotted owl habitat or the environmentalist-sponsored 1996 ballot initiative in Oregon that would have required cattle to be fenced out of riparian areas on private land. Yet, as Holling and Meffe (1996) have pointed out, the "command-and-control" approach to managing resource uses is really no different from our attempts to control nature by suppressing all fires in national parks, building levees along the Mississippi River, or stabilizing the wildly flooding streams of the Colorado River Basin with dams. Such attempts to harness nature have had unforeseen consequences as the loss of flexibility reduces the system's ability to respond to external perturbations. Social systems, too, must be flexible enough to withstand unexpected shocks and stresses. One way to do that is by *yielding* rather than *imposing* control, thereby taking advantage of humans' tendency to behave in ways that can resolve potential conflicts between territorial self-interest and community cooperation.

Attitude research suggests that Americans are ready to give collaborative cross-boundary partnerships a chance, but they also are wary about losing the right to reserve options—to be flexible in the face of uncertainty about the consequences of shared decision making. Partners in stewardship efforts must be sensitive to the defensive instincts of all participants. This means following norms of procedural justice and sharing authority even when one is politically or legally empowered to impose one's will on others. It requires considerable effort devoted to identifying all those who may hold claims to an ecologically relevant landscape. And it calls for full, open discussion of boundaries and defensive strategies, especially among and within agencies, so that all participants understand the social terrain as well as the biophysical terrain.

This chapter has described research in a variety of academic disciplines aimed at understanding the roles that territory and cooperation play in human interactions. Almost none of it examined these issues in the context of cross-boundary stewardship of ecosystems. As the first wave of stewardship projects begins, it is important to evaluate those efforts in light of what we've learned so far and don't yet know. For example, we can benefit by knowing which social and psychological influences (e.g., values, norms, education) are most influential on attitudes of stewardship partners and which form barriers to successful participation. Which kinds of territorial claims are most difficult to recognize? Which claimants have the greatest resistance to losing current levels of control? Can education and ecological literacy offset barriers to participation that arise from deeply rooted values and norms? Answers to questions such as these can prove crucial if we are to sustain a natural balance between cooperation and self-interest among cross-boundary stewards.

REFERENCES

Abernethy, T.P., editor. 1964. *Thomas Jefferson's "Notes on the state of Virginia."* Harper & Row, New York.

Ajzen, I., and M. Fishbein. 1980. *Understanding attitudes and predicting social behavior.* Prentice Hall, Englewood Cliffs, NJ.

Altman, I. 1975. *The environment and social behavior: privacy, personal space, territory, crowding.* Brooks/Cole, Monterey, CA.

Arrington, L.J. 1958. *Great Basin kingdom: economic history of the Latter-Day Saints, 1830–1900.* Harvard University Press, Cambridge, MA.

Bennett, W. 1993. *The book of virtues*. Simon and Schuster, New York.

Berlyne, D.E. 1960. Conflict, arousal, and curiosity. McGraw-Hill, New York.

Binford, L.R. 1980. Willow smoke and dogs' tails: hunter-gatherer settlement systems and archaeological site formation. *American Antiquity* 45:1–17.

Blahna, D.J., and S. Yonts-Shepard. 1989. Public involvement in resource planning: toward bridging the gap between policy and implementation. *Society and Natural Resources* 2:209–227.

Brandenburg, A., and M.S. Carroll. 1995. Your place or mine? The effect of place creation on environmental values and landscape meanings. *Society and Natural Resources* 8:381–398.

Brunson, M.W., and J.J. Kennedy. 1995. Redefining "multiple use": agency responses to changing social values. Pages 143–158 in *A new century for natural resources management* (R.L. Knight and S.F. Bates, editors). Island Press, Washington, DC.

Brunson, M.W., and K.J. Richardson. 1997. Perceived fairness and effectiveness of rangeland collaborative partnerships. Paper presented to the 50th annual meeting, Society for Range Management, February 16–21, 1997. Rapid City, SD.

Brunson, M.W., G.A. Rasmussen, and K.J. Richardson. 1996a. Acceptability of range practices and policies among general and ranching publics. Pages 72–73 in *Rangelands in a sustainable biosphere: proceedings of the Fifth International Rangeland Congress* (N.E. West, editor). Society for Range Management, Denver, CO.

Brunson, M.W., D.T. Yarrow, S.D. Roberts, D.C. Guynn, Jr., and M.R. Kuhns. 1996b. Nonindustrial private forest owners and ecosystem management: can they work together? *Journal of Forestry* 94:14–21.

Cancian, F.M. 1975. *What are norms?* Cambridge University Press, New York.

Cannon, J.R. 1996. Whooping crane recovery: a case study in public and private cooperation in the conservation of endangered species. *Conservation Biology* 10:813–821.

Colfer, C.J.P., and A.M. Colfer. 1978. Inside Bushler Bay: lifeways in counterpoint. *Rural Sociology* 43:204–220.

Crowfoot, J., and J. Wondolleck. 1990. *Environmental disputes: community involvement in conflict resolution*. Island Press, Washington, DC.

Deci, E.L. 1975. *Intrinsic motivation*. Plenum Press, New York.

Dyson-Hudson, R., and E. Alden-Smith. 1978. Human territoriality: an ecological reassessment. *American Anthropologist* 80:21–41.

Ellickson, R.C. 1991. *Order without law: how neighbors settle disputes*. Harvard University Press, Cambridge, MA.

Forbes, G.J., and J.B. Theberge. 1996. Cross-boundary management of Algonquin Park wolves. *Conservation Biology* 10:1091–1097.

Fortmann, L. 1990. Locality and custom: non-aboriginal claims to customary usufructuary rights as a source of rural protest. *Journal of Rural Studies* 6:195–208.

Fulgham, R. 1988. *All I really need to know I learned in kindergarten: uncommon thoughts on common things*. Random House, New York.

Hobbes, T. 1651. *Leviathan*. New edition, 1994. J.M. Dent, Rutland, VT.

Holling, C.S., and G.K. Meffe. 1996. Command and control and the pathology of natural resource management. *Conservation Biology* 10:328–337.

Jorgensen, J.G. 1984. Land is cultural, so is a commodity: the locus of differences among Indians, cowboys, sod-busters, and environmentalists. *Journal of Ethnic Studies* 12:3–21.

Kennedy, J.J. 1985. Viewing wildlife managers as a unique professional culture. *Wildlife Society Bulletin* 13:571–579.

Kennedy, J.J. 1988. The symbolic infrastructure of natural resource management: an example of the U.S. Forest Service. *Society and Natural Resources* 1:241–251.

Krannich, R.S., M.S. Carroll, S.E. Daniels, and G.B. Walker. 1994. *Incorporating social assessment and public involvement processes into ecosystem-based management: applications to the East Side Ecosystem Management Project*. Report prepared for the USDA Forest Service, Interior Columbia Basin Ecosystem Management Project, Walla Walla, WA.

Kunioka, T., and L.S. Rothenberg. 1993. The politics of bureaucratic competition: the case of natural resource policy. *Journal of Policy Analysis and Management* 12:700–725.

Lee, R.G. 1972. The social definition of outdoor recreation places. Pages 68–84 in *Social behavior, natural resources, and the environment* (W.R. Burch, N.H. Cheek, and L. Taylors, editors). Ann Arbor Science Publishers, Ann Arbor, MI.

Loomis, C.P. 1960. *Social systems: essays on their persistence and change*. Van Nostrand, Princeton, NJ.

Lorenz, K. 1967. *On aggression*. Bantam Books, New York.

Mandryk, C.A.S. 1993. Hunter-gatherer social costs and the nonviability of submarginal environments. *Journal of Anthropological Research* 49:39–71.

Manfredo, M.J., editor. 1992. *Influencing human behavior: theory and applications in recreation, tourism, and natural resources management*. Sagamore Publishing, Champaign, IL.

McBeth, M.K., and R.H. Foster. 1994. Rural environmental attitudes. *Environmental Management* 18:401–411.

Nelson, G.L. 1952. *The Mormon village*. University of Utah Press, Salt Lake City, UT.

Rokeach, M. 1973. *The nature of human values*. Free Press, New York.

Sack, R. 1983. Human territoriality: a theory. *Annals of the Association of American Geographers* 73:55–74.

Sax, J.L., and R.B. Keiter. 1987. Glacier National Park and its neighbors: a study of federal interagency relations. *Ecology Law Quarterly* 14:207–263.

Schroeder, H.S. 1996. *Voices from Michigan's Black River: obtaining information on "special places" for natural resource planning*. USDA Forest Service, General Technical Report NC-184. North Central Forest Experiment Station, St. Paul, MN.

Sommer, R. 1969. *Personal space*. Prentice-Hall, Englewood Cliffs, NJ.

Stegner, W. 1970. *Mormon country*. Duell, Sloan and Pearce, New York.

Thibaut, J.W. 1975. *Procedural justice: a psychological analysis*. Erlbaum, Hillsdale, NJ.

Tinbergen, N. 1953. *The study of instinct*. Oxford University Press, London.

Tyler, T.R. 1989. The psychology of procedural justice: a test of the group-value model. *Journal of Personality and Social Psychology* 57:830–838.

Ulrich, R.S. 1993. Biophilia, biophobia and natural landscapes. Pages 73–137 in *The biophilia hypothesis* (S. Kellert and E. Wilson, editors). Island Press, Washington, DC.

Williams, D.R., M.E. Patterson, J.W. Roggenbuck, and A.E. Watson. 1992. Beyond the commodity metaphor: examining emotional and symbolic attachment to place. *Leisure Sciences* 14:29–48.

Wilson, E.O. 1978. Introduction: what is sociobiology? Pages 1–12 in *Sociobiology and human nature* (M. Gregory and A. Silvers, editors). Jossey-Bass, San Francisco.

Wrong, D. 1961. The oversocialized conception of man in modern sociology. *American Sociological Review* 26:183–193.

Chapter 4

Laws and Institutions in Cross-Boundary Stewardship

Errol E. Meidinger

Cross-boundary stewardship depends heavily on the legal and institutional context in which it is practiced. This chapter provides an overview of laws and institutions affecting cross-boundary stewardship in the United States. This introductory section states some general propositions about boundaries and stewardship. The next two sections describe the basic types of resource owners in American law and the laws governing how they interact with each other and society. Because the laws both reflect and support larger institutional structures, the fourth section outlines the broad institutional patterns that seem best to describe our current structure and how it may be changing. The fifth section highlights key areas of stress and change in the present system, and the concluding section discusses the implications of the preceding analysis.

What are boundaries? They are not merely human gashes across the natural landscape. Rather, boundaries mark divisions of control over and responsibility for resources among individuals, organizations, and governments. These divisions usually do not take the form of simple disjunctions, voids, or impermeable barriers. Just as ecological boundaries are best understood as zones of transition (Risser 1993), gradients of change (di Castri et al. 1988), and membranes (Norton 1992), social boundaries are areas of both difference and change, and of contact and interaction. Social boundaries typically are governed by rules and conventions that define the terms of engagement between the actors and organizations they simultaneously separate and connect. Moreover, as is vividly demonstrated by other chapters in this book, social boundaries can reshape and sometimes even create ecological ones.

The premise animating this book and much ecological writing is that boundaries, at least social boundaries that do not match ecological ones, are bad. This line of thought highlights several generic problems with boundaries. First, boundaries can make it difficult to coordinate behavior among individuals, organizations, and communities. Where ecological resources are shared, lack of coordination can lead to inefficient, inconsistent, wasteful, or destructive resource management. Second, boundaries can impede and disrupt information flows among organizations, thus making it difficult for any actor to understand the full state of the system involved or its likely future, and hence to act intelligently. Third, boundaries can encourage organizations and communities to externalize the costs of their activities to other social units while seeking to retain the benefits. Thus it is common to see environmental "bads," such as pollution sources and waste sites, placed next to boundaries, so that some of their costs will be borne by outsiders. Similarly, people often cluster along the boundaries of environmental "goods," such as parks and wilderness areas, in attempts to capture special benefits for themselves without fully paying the costs.

Given these problems organizational and jurisdictional boundaries often are seen as irrational human follies that need to be overcome, if not eliminated. However, boundaries perform useful functions as well. Often these are simply the converse of the problems they pose. First, boundaries can slow the movement of disturbances or misguided policies from one entity to another, and thereby provide time for adaptive or corrective responses (Naiman and Decamps 1990, Morehouse 1995). Second, they can facilitate efficient resource and information flows within organizations and communities, by delineating who is permitted and who is required to know about a given matter (Williamson 1985). Third, boundaries can facilitate clear allocation of management control and responsibility, connecting actors to the consequences of their acts (Ellickson 1993). Accordingly, the problem of cross-boundary stewardship is not likely to be as simple—or as unworkable—as eliminating or even redrawing boundaries on a broad scale. Rather, it will require building a much better understanding of the dynamics and effects of boundaries, and then adjusting our laws and institutions to make them as functional as possible for stewardship.

But what is stewardship? Conceptually, the answer seems straightforward. Lynton Caldwell's definition, "socially and ecologically responsible custody of the land" (Caldwell 1986), is fairly typical and probably noncontroversial. So is the proposition that stewardship responsibility extends to both present and future generations. Most people might even agree that stewardship means preserving the integrity and productive capacity of the land. At the point of implementation, however, consensus drops sharply. First, American landowners as a class have neither accepted nor been placed under a general duty to practice stewardship (although many laws constrain them from doing things that would be inconsistent with stewardship). Second, we lack a robust understanding of what stewardship means in concrete terms. Although it is possible to say that some actions clearly are stewardship and others are not, there is a large middle range subject to great uncertainty and contention. We simply do not know the full effects of many of our actions. Even if we did, we would still have to work out what effects are acceptable and who should pay the costs of taking or not taking action. Progress on both fronts is under way, but remains preliminary.

The cross-boundary dimension of stewardship seems to exacerbate the problem, but may actually help to clarify it. Cross-boundary stewardship requires coordinated behavior, and coordination generally requires creating shared understandings and values. Cross-boundary stewardship thus may turn out to be doubly pivotal—first as a major forum for working out the practical meaning of stewardship, and second as a sensitive barometer of progress, as both the greatest achievements and the greatest problems are likely to be evident along boundaries.

Cross-boundary stewardship is a system problem. The model landscape in Figure 4.1 suggests the nature of the system involved. Just as a landscape consists of plant and animal communities, landforms, streams, and

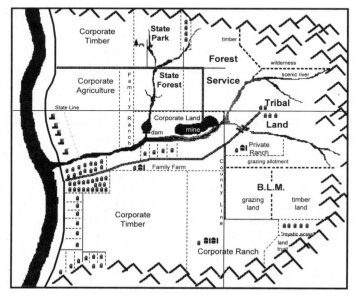

Figure 4.1. Model landscape.

nutrient flows, it also consists of social organizations, communities, institutions, information flows, and exchange systems. These elements are as central to an adequately conceived ecosystem as the plant, animal, and physical interactions that traditionally dominate the attention of ecologists. As in any ecosystem, the concrete nature of the social elements varies enormously from place to place, but many of the categories and types of relationships are general. The next four sections describe the basic types of social actors and the rules and institutions affecting cross-boundary stewardship in the United States.

Landowners

American landowners exercise enormous jurisdiction over natural resources. Although these powers vary among states and are always subject to some uncertainty, they generally include rights to determine the overall use of land, harvest plants, change habitats, mine solid minerals, and capture mobile publicly owned resources such as water, natural gas, petroleum, fish, and wildlife. Landowners' capacity for cross-boundary stewardship is heavily affected by what they can do within their boundaries, which in turn is affected not only by their property rights, but also by the legal form in which they operate and their individual management policies.

Private Landowners

Each type of private landowner in Figure 4.1 operates with a different set of legal and organizational capacities. Corporate landowners generally have the capacity to pool large quantities of investment capital, but operate under a duty to maximize profits to investors. Exactly which strategies will maximize profits in an uncertain and changeable environment is rarely apparent. So corporate managers exercise considerable discretion and their land management practices vary. Whether the profit duty is fundamentally compatible with stewardship is highly contested and cannot be resolved here. But the profit motive clearly does little to promote long-term stewardship, since future generations are not present to bid in current markets and the nature of the interest rate makes a dollar in the future worth less than a dollar today. Accordingly, laws requiring stewardship practices are very important to framing the legal environment in which profit maximization is defined.

Noncorporate private landowners also experience pressures to generate revenues, but generally have no legal duty to maximize profits (with the partial exception of private trusts) and enjoy flexibility to pursue other goals, such as retaining a family land base or maintaining wildlife habitat. Whether they pursue such goals, however, is highly variable, depending on value commitments, financial circumstances, and other factors.

Not-for-profit landowners, such as land trusts and conservancy organizations, generally have authority to manage for stewardship goals such as biological integrity, scenic beauty, or historic preservation. Their need to garner resources, however, sometimes leads to revenue-producing land uses.

Government Landowners

In addition to performing the regulatory functions to be discussed, governments at all levels, local, tribal, state, and federal, own considerable quantities of land. Various agencies manage that land, and their policies vary by law and tradition. The National Park Service usually is mandated to preserve lands in their "natural" condition, but the Federal Bureau of Land Management (BLM) and the USDA Forest Service manage lands for "multiple use," which allows significant changes in the condition of land but not impairment of its productivity. All federal agencies use forms of internal "zoning" to allocate land to specific functions (hence the wilderness/scenic river and timber/grazing boundaries in the Forest Service and BLM lands in Figure 4.1). They also do relatively broad-scale, long-term planning. The National Environmental Policy Act (NEPA) requires federal agencies to consider the direct, indirect, and cumulative effects of their significant actions, including effects beyond their own boundaries (42 U.S.C. §102; 40 CFR §1508.8), and to consult with one another and consider possible conflicts with other federal, state, and local agencies' policies (42 U.S.C. §4332; 40 CFR §§1501-04). Federal management agencies also have authority under other statutes to coordinate with private landowners (Meidinger 1997). In sum, the federal land management agencies are mandated to perform stewardship of their own lands and arguably to perform cross-boundary stewardship. They have sufficient discretion, however, that actual cross-boundary stewardship will depend on their making significant policy changes and learning to collaborate with other landowners. There has been some movement in this direction, but it remains preliminary and partial (Keiter 1994, Interagency Ecosystem Management Task Force 1995).

Indian tribes occupy large areas of land in many ecosystems. Traditionally, the federal government has held that land "in trust" for tribes, managing it in their "best interests" as determined by Congress and the Federal Bureau of Indian Affairs (BIA). Although the best interests criterion would seem to imply a stewardship responsibility, BIA management, driven by a mix of congressional and societal hostility, paternalism, and bureaucratic rigidity, often has been wasteful and short-sighted (Wilkinson 1987). The BIA's response to recent federal legislation reducing its policy control may make management of Indian lands more responsive to tribal needs and values (Allen 1989) and more oriented to stewardship on the whole, although there will still be much disagreement about appropriate land management policies.

States own large quantities of land subject to many mandates. Many state lands, such as parks, are managed for purposes compatible with cross-boundary stewardship. Some, however, are formally held "in trust" to support specified public functions, such as education. Important questions have arisen about the meaning of trust mandates. Some parties argue that state agencies have a narrow duty to maximize revenue streams to beneficiaries of the trust (Thorud 1994), whereas others see more latitude to serve the general public interest and preserve options for future generations (Arum 1990). Of course, even if states have a narrow duty to maximize revenues, there is still a big question of which strategies will achieve that end. Hence, state agencies could follow some corporations in concluding that long-term revenues will be maximized by preserving biodiversity and negotiating proactive habitat conservation plans. In any case, the general legal argument that state trust lands must be managed exclusively to maximize revenue streams is not strong. Unlike most private trusts, government trusts are generally permanent, covering many generations, and government trustees necessarily exercise broader discretion than private ones.

Summary About Landowners

Private and government landowners are important actors whose mandates and practices vary enormously. Only some government and a few private landowners such as land trusts have mandates to practice cross-boundary stewardship, but most others probably have the capacity to do so. Whether they do depends heavily on laws and institutions structuring landowner relationships with one another and society.

Cross-Boundary Laws

Cross-boundary relationships tend to reflect years of ad hoc problem solving and local custom. When informal mechanisms prove inadequate, laws established and enforced by governments come into play.

Common Law

Perhaps the most basic boundary rule is the prohibition on trespass. In essence, trespass law protects owners from unauthorized "touchings" or entries to their property. Trespass law can promote stewardship by ensuring that owners "reap what they sow," at least in the near term and within the bounds of their property. It also can be used to obtain compensation for physical invasions of property such as oil spills. Because trespass law governs only entries by humans or objects they control, and because it is difficult to illustrate human control in many ecological processes, its ability to encourage cross-boundary stewardship is limited. Nonetheless, it creates an important legal baseline from which bargaining, negotiation, and coordination can occur.

"Nuisance" law gives landowners and the public the right to be free from land-use activities that "substantially and unreasonably interfere" with the use and enjoyment of their property or public rights. Possible nuisances include the production of pollution or odors and the depletion of shared resources. Nuisance law is quite general, and what activities are defined as unreasonable changes over time, as knowledge and social values change. This has hindered and helped cross-boundary stewardship at different times. During the early industrial period, for example, a coal mining company whose runoff water pollution ruined the drinking water, killed the fish, and destroyed various other domestic uses of downstream landowners was held not liable for those effects. According to the court, "the necessities of a great public industry, which although in the hands of a private corporation, serves a great public interest" justified such "trifling inconveniences to particular persons" (*Pennsylvania Coal Co. v. Sanderson*, 1886). After about World War II, courts increasingly found such interferences with use and enjoyment of neighboring property to be nuisances. But knowledge limitations combined with the difficulty of bringing individual law suits have limited the role of nuisance law in promoting cross-boundary stewardship.

Another important body of interowner law involves "easements," "real covenants," and "equitable servitudes," often lumped together as "servitudes." Servitudes are rights held by one party either to use or limit the use of land owned by another. Landowners can use servitude law to negotiate and enforce almost any agreement they might wish regarding acceptable uses of each other's property. The agreement can be made binding on subsequent owners who were not involved in its negotiation. Moreover, recently developed "conservation easement" laws allow governments and not-for-profit organizations such as land trusts (regardless of whether they own neighboring land) to negotiate arrangements limiting owners' use of land in specified ways. Although these laws vary among states (see Diehl and Barrett 1988 for a summary), they generally are quite flexible. For example, a conservation easement for one piece of land might permit timber harvesting (perhaps at a set rate) but not mining or subdivision, whereas that for another might permit only recreational uses and limited housing development.

Nuisance and servitude law help illustrate a more general truth about landownership: not *all* the rights in a particular piece of land are ever held by one landowner. In addition to the concurrent rights of neighbors, the public, land trusts, and others outlined earlier, rights to the same parcel of land often are further divided in space and time. Thus rights to the *minerals* (coal, oil, natural gas, precious metals, etc.) may be held by one party, whereas rights to the *surface* (grazing, timber, residence, etc.) are held by another. Similarly, rights to use either type of interest may be held in the *present* by one party (for a set number of years or a specific lifetime) and in the *future* by another. Of course, because these different types of owners often have inconsistent interests and can significantly help or hurt one another, it is necessary to work out rules governing their relationships. Relations between present and future interest holders, for example, are partly governed by the judicially created law of "waste," which essentially prohibits present possessors from using property so as to "unreasonably" interfere with the interests of future possessors. As in nuisance law, what uses are reasonable and unreasonable varies greatly with time and place. Because of its vagueness, and a general preference of the American legal system for encouraging resource use, the law of waste has done very little to promote cross-boundary stewardship.

Environmental Law

The many cross-boundary environmental effects wrought by the industrial revolution led to demands for new types of laws to limit and control those effects. Because environmental problems were soon understood as too complicated and changeable for generalist, nonexpert judges, they were frequently assigned to specialized government agencies. These agencies' responsibilities gradually expanded from simply enforcing laws, to developing and revising them, to sometimes spotting and attacking new problems. Initially, local governments were most active in environmental regulation. In the nineteenth century they passed laws prohibiting maladies such as "dense smoke" and disposal of dead animals in water bodies. In the early twentieth century they adopted comprehensive zoning ordinances relegating different kinds of activities to different "zones." Those strategies proved inadequate, however, because environmental problems are quite complex and readily cross municipal boundaries. After World War II, first the states and then the federal government became increasingly involved in developing uniform environmental standards applicable across large geographic areas.

Today there are major federal statutes regulating air pollution, water pollution, endangered species management, and hazardous chemical production, transportation, and disposal, as well as narrower ones seeking to protect coastal zones, estuaries, wild and scenic rivers, and wetlands. In essence, almost all of them are efforts to control cross-boundary problems through rules. Most involve setting general standards and then using permit programs (often administered by states and localities) to implement them. Many focus on "end of pipe" solutions and do little to prevent problems from arising or to link them to underlying causes such as high energy consumption. More important, in the process of trying to solve typical types of problems in a uniform way across ownership boundaries, these laws have created new jurisdictional boundaries among agencies and programs. Although each program probably made sense when it was created by focusing on a reasonably tractable problem, the aggregate result is a plethora of programs, each of which imposes its own set of rules on regulated parties. There are few good mechanisms for coordinating programs run by different bureaucracies under different statutory frameworks. Although interagency memoranda of understanding are being developed in some areas of federal policy, it seems unlikely that they will overcome the effects of statutory variation and bureaucratic momentum.

Coexistent state and local regulatory programs increase regulatory complexity. Federal agencies exert significant control over many state and local programs, but the overall system remains loosely coordinated. Federal programs typically use two mechanisms to induce state and local conformance to federal policies: (1) making federal funding for state programs contingent on the state program meeting federal guidelines, and (2) threatening to impose a direct federal regulatory program if the state fails to produce a satisfactory one. Federal agencies sometimes have authority to require state programs that interfere with those of other states to make appropriate changes, but have rarely used it (*New York v. EPA*, 1988). In sum, while federal programs have produced increased consistency over time, much variation remains. This situation also has a positive side, however, since it allows for local experimentation and variation.

"Nonenvironmental" Law

The laws shaping cross-boundary stewardship are not limited to the traditional category of "environmental" law. Just as stewardship can be significantly affected by legal definitions of the duties of corporate managers, so it can be affected by laws governing valuation of assets and financing. Liberal debt-financing laws, for example, can encourage rapid resource liquidation and a refusal to develop joint resource management plans with neighbors. In tax law, although income tax deductions can encourage conservation easement donations, high federal estate taxes and local property taxes reflecting development potential can encourage rapid resource liquidation, sale, or subdivision, which can in turn create new cross-boundary stewardship problems (Small 1989). In a still emerging way, intellectual property law may have comparable effects on cross-boundary stewardship, as rules on ownership of genetic codes, trade secrets, and the like shape and reshape incentives and disincentives to cooperate and share information. Antitrust law may also influence cross-boundary stewardship. Lawyers representing forestry companies have argued that the information-sharing and joint decision-making involved could expose their clients to antitrust liability (Pauw et al. 1993). For public agencies, general rules of administrative law governing matters such as collection and dissemination of information and use of advisory committees may be at least as important as their land management mandates.

Summary About Cross-Boundary Laws

The legal and institutional context of natural resource management is multilayered and complex, beginning with several types of legally constructed owners (private, corporate, governmental), all with different mandates and incentives, proceeding to include a variety of interlinking rights and duties among them and other actors, and then including many types of general laws (water, air, land use, wildlife, antitrust, etc.) implemented by a variety of governmental bodies operating at several levels. Although all of these laws can be important to cross-boundary stewardship, they are too numerous, variable, complex, and dynamic to be analyzed simply by cataloguing and adding them up. Rather, both the laws and the prospects for cross-boundary stewardship are best analyzed in terms of the larger institutional patterns they reflect and maintain and how those patterns may need to change to facilitate cross-boundary stewardship.

Fundamental Institutional Patterns

Institutions are basic, widespread patterns of social organization. They often reflect widely shared, taken-for-granted assumptions that serve as social templates (Meidinger 1987, Shannon in press). Three basic institutional models, feudal, liberal, and networked, are helpful for conceptualizing the challenges of cross-boundary stewardship.

Feudal Order

Feudal order takes the form of the nested hierarchy depicted in Figure 4.2. Commands and protection flow downward and information and resources flow upward. Cross-boundary problems are handled through ris-

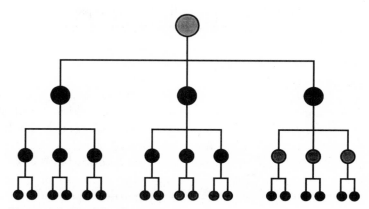

Figure 4.2. Feudal order.

ing layers of officials responsible for coordinating the activities of the lower units, although much decision making remains decentralized. The government and property systems are largely synonymous, with the sovereign serving as both the supreme governmental official and the ultimate owner of all land, while the lower members of the hierarchy both manage discrete parcels of land and perform local governmental functions. Individuals are defined largely by their roles in the system.

Liberal Order

Reflecting direct opposition to the feudal order, the liberal order has four key elements (Figure 4.3). First, property is separate from government. In fact, although largely created by government, property rights are seen as a bulwark against it. Second, law is used as a buffer between government and property. Those in charge of government rule by properly passing and enforcing laws rather than by giving direct orders to individuals—hence the "government of laws and not of men" refrain. Third, society is conceived as a collection of atomistic or semiautonomous individual units that add up to make the whole. Operating in their spheres of control, subject only to general laws applicable to all, property owners are presumed to have what Blackstone so evocatively described as "that sole and despotic dominion which one man claims and exercises over the external things of the world, in total exclusion of the right of any other individual in the universe" (1769). Fourth, hierarchies remain alive and well in distributed form. Most units of society, such as families, firms, and government agencies, remain deeply hierarchical. Thus an adequate graphical depiction would include a hierarchy of some kind at each dot in Figure 4.3. Similarly, most, if not all, of the land parcels of Figure 4.1 would be topped by hierarchical organizations of varying form and extent.

Networked Order

Even if existing institutions are dominated by hierarchical and liberal structures, there is nonetheless good reason to think that the challenges of cross-boundary stewardship imply networked structures of the kind depicted in Figure 4.4. Many of the reasons are described in Breckenridge (1995) and Meidinger (1997a). The key characteristics of networked order are the use of horizontal alliances and partnerships to achieve coordinated action, a heavy reliance on communication and information

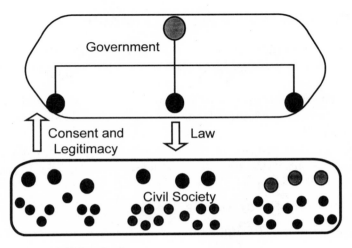

Figure 4.3. Liberal order.

flow, and an emphasis on flexibility and adaptation. Environmental and natural resource organizations with networked structures are appearing at every social level from local watersheds (Wondolleck and Yaffee 1994) to international systems (Meidinger 1997b). Naturally, their emergence creates some strains with traditional institutions, which stress hierarchy, control, fixed jurisdiction, division between private and public functions, and reliance on formal rules. If networked structures aiding cross-boundary stewardship are to flourish, key elements of existing structures will have to change. The next section reviews four broad patterns of change in natural resource institutions that may be crucial to the prospects for cross-boundary stewardship.

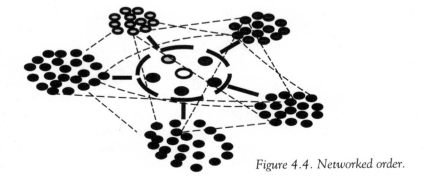

Figure 4.4. Networked order.

Key Changes in Policies and Institutions

A number of current policy developments may be important for success-ful cross-boundary stewardship. Although multidimensional, they are organized in terms of four broad tendencies: privatization of policy mak-ing, movement from rules to discretion, decentralization, and politiciza-tion of information. Although the prior sections indicate that develop-ments such as these are important to the expansion of cross-boundary stewardship, they are not unalloyed goods. They embody a variety of goals and potential negative consequences.

Privatization of Policy Making

As suggested in the "Institutional Patterns" section, boundaries between private and public domains may be the central achievement of the lib-eral order. Those boundaries are enforced in part by judicial interpreta-tions of the Constitutional prohibition of uncompensated "takings" of private property and in part by laws defining acceptable public participa-tion in government policy making. These seem to be going in different directions, but both may actually support growing private control of policy making. Thus, courts and legislatures have recently shown a ten-dency to reduce government's ability to adjust private property rights in response to new knowledge and social values (e.g., *Lucas v. South Car-olina Coastal Council*, 1992). These developments may seriously inhibit society's ability to appropriately value and protect natural resources (Freyfogle 1993, Sax 1993, Meidinger 1993, 1997a). They certainly min-imize the likelihood of legally mandating cross-boundary stewardship, as any landowner required to coordinate management with neighbors could readily claim a taking of previously enjoyed property rights.

Conversely, rules confining public policy making to governments may be opening somewhat. Thus, the Negotiated Rulemaking Act of 1990 explicitly encourages federal agencies to convene stakeholder groups to draft important regulations, and agencies such as the Environmental Pro-tection Agency (EPA) have made extensive use of it (Freeman 1997). Moreover, the Federal Advisory Committee Act (FACA), which sharply constrains federal agency relationships with groups seeking to influence public policy, has been interpreted by the Supreme Court as applying only to groups established or controlled by the federal government (*Pub-lic Citizen v. U.S. Dept. of Justice*, 1989) and was recently amended to remove strictures on federal contracts with state, tribal, and local governments, which in turn will become forums for public–private policy negotiation (Lynch 1996).

Expanded private policy making also is evident in the increasing use of Habitat Conservation Plans (HCPs) to protect endangered species. These are essentially negotiated agreements in which landowners develop and commit to implementing long-term habitat conservation programs in return for federal permits allowing "incidental take" of protected species. Although many HCPs involve individual landowners, several regional efforts involving multiple landowners, agencies, and species have been undertaken (Interagency Ecosystem Management Task Force 1995). Similarly, the EPA has long given companies discretion to "trade" air and water pollution amounts both within and among sources (e.g., Meidinger 1985).

Possibly the most important change in public–private relationships is the growing amount of "public" policy making occurring almost entirely outside of government processes. Best known to American scholars are the plethora of recent watershed and landscape planning processes such as the Applegate Partnership in southwestern Oregon. These generally involve multiple landowners and agencies working to develop consistent cross-boundary stewardship plans (Wondolleck and Yaffee 1994). Equally important are private and quasi-private *global* processes. For example, a global nongovernmental organization (NGO) called the Forest Stewardship Council (FSC) is working to develop consistent field-based standards for sustainable forest management applicable to all the forests of the world (Meidinger 1997a). Similarly, the International Standards Organization (ISO), which has relationships with many governments but operates separately from them, is developing a series of environmental management standards aimed at making businesses' environmental management practices globally consistent (Meidinger 1997b). Although the ISO is more industry-oriented, both the FSC and ISO efforts involve NGO–business partnerships seeking to set legitimate standards in a nongovernmental context.

Industry and trade associations also are taking a much more direct and public role in standard setting and enforcement. Important examples include the chemical industry's Responsible Care Program for controlling hazardous chemical management worldwide (Gunningham 1995); the American Waterworks Association's stakeholder process for developing regulations defining the information to be provided in "consumer confidence reports" required by recent amendments to the Safe Drinking Water Act (Inside EPA 1996a); and the Association of Metropolitan

Sewage Agencies' intensive effort to design and sell a program in which EPA would set total maximum daily water pollution limits on a watershed basis and allow local dischargers to negotiate and enforce arrangements for meeting them (Inside EPA 1996b).

These developments are important because they are creating new local, national, and international environmental programs and because they shift policy making outside governmental processes. Thus, like it or not, governments are placed in the role of being participants in local, national, and global policy networks, rather than near-exclusive makers and enforcers of public policy. This trend is positive insofar as it involves a larger sector of society in defining and implementing cross-boundary policies, but it may pose significant problems by reducing the long-term capacity of government to define and enforce standards.

Rule to Discretion

Although the categories of rule and discretion may not be intuitively obvious to many readers, they are closely connected to the public–private boundaries of liberalism discussed. A basic premise of liberalism is that government should use clear legal rules, rather than ad hoc commands or vague norms, to govern behavior. Rules have been the primary mechanism for promoting cross-boundary stewardship to date. There are two major problems with this approach. The first is that rules generally cannot be written precisely enough to produce appropriate outcomes in every real-world situation. They will generally prohibit some behavior that would be benign or beneficial (the problem of "overinclusiveness") and also will allow behavior that would be destructive ("underinclusiveness"; see Boyer and Meidinger 1985). These problems are recurrent in natural resources policy. For example, it may be clear that driving a heavy vehicle across a stream will often, but not always, damage spawning habitat. If a blanket rule banning driving across streams is enforced to achieve cross-boundary stewardship, a number of harmless crossings will be prevented, imposing potentially significant costs. Yet, it will be virtually impossible to write a rule clearly defining every situation in which it is or is not acceptable to drive across a stream. Conditions are simply too variable and information too limited. Underinclusiveness also is a problem; driving across streams is only one kind of activity that might harm fish, and it will be impossible to write rules controlling all of the others. Thus, it is possible that discretion exercised according to appropriate principles in a network of accountability would be more functional than rules. But rules remain the accustomed way of doing things.

The second problem with rules is that they add up, quickly producing a dense, complicated legal environment (Orts 1995). The agglomerated rules often fit together poorly and work at cross purposes, making compliance difficult. Even a small company may have a dozen major reports and certifications to file with a half-dozen different environmental agencies every year. This situation gives rise not only to complaints about "red tape," but also to noncooperation and occasional political counterattacks. One scholar argues that existing federal laws for biodiversity protection create such a counterproductive tangle that it would be best for the federal government to start completely over by selecting key ecosystems, suspending current laws, setting a serious goal of biodiversity protection, inviting stakeholders to work out how to achieve it, and conferring a federal permit if the plan they come up with is sound (Ruhl 1995).

Although such sweeping proposals seem unlikely to be implemented soon, a number of more modest efforts to bypass dysfunctional rule clusters are under way. Some of these are occurring in the watershed and landscape management efforts already described, as well as the FSC. Others are being sponsored by government agencies. The EPA's Project XL, for example, encourages regulated parties to propose innovative ways of achieving environmentally superior results without necessarily conforming to all existing rules. The Habitat Conservation Planning Processes described take a similar tack. Although it remains to be seen how well they will work in a context of potentially opportunistic regulated parties and rule-habituated bureaucracies and interest groups, each of these initiatives exemplifies an effort to use stakeholder negotiation and site-specific decision making to achieve better results than those produced by juxtaposed rule systems.

Decentralization

For decades environmental policy seemed to be evolving toward a system of centralized policy making and local implementation. Recently, states have played a growing role in policy making (Gade 1996). They have done this by redefining their regulatory functions to include a higher level of information provision and "customer service," changing enforcement policies to seek a higher level of "voluntary" compliance, inviting regulated parties to make proposals for better ways of achieving regulatory objectives, and simply communicating more with each other and not just with the federal government. The EPA is attempting to support state and local innovations through a variety of initiatives such as its Performance Partnership System, which seeks to give states greater flexibility in implementing environmental laws.

Again, where this movement will lead is unclear. In some areas, the federal government seems at risk of losing much control. For example, almost half the states have adopted "audit privilege" laws, which shield results of environmental audits from discovery for litigation and enforcement purposes. The EPA opposes these laws, but has yet to exert effective control over them. Conversely, state initiatives in other areas are almost completely blocked. State efforts to control solid waste disposal have been seriously hampered by a series of court decisions holding that the "commerce clause" of the Constitution (Art. I, §8 [3]) impliedly prevents states and localities from planning primarily for garbage from their own regions (*Fort Gratiot Sanitary Landfill v. Mich. Dept. of Natural Resources*, 1992) or limiting access to landfills to waste generators with good recycling programs (*National Solid Wastes Management Assoc. v. Myers*, 1995).

Politicization of Information

Some of the most far-reaching changes in environmental policy have occurred in the relationship between research and policy making. Although conventionally treated as separate functions, they are becoming increasingly intertwined. Perhaps best known are the "science assessments" recently prepared for large ecoregions such as the western and eastern slopes of the Cascades, the Southeastern Appalachian Ecosystem, the Northern Forest of the northeastern states, and the Sierra Nevada Ecosystem. Although these assessments vary in content, they share the assumption that radically upgraded, shared information bases are necessary for improved cross-boundary coordination. Less explicit, but no less important, is the assumption that better information will *cause changes* in policy and management. This assumption helps explain the intense battles among both scientists and policy makers over methodology, information distribution, and concept definition (Meidinger et al. 1996).

The importance of information can increase the difficulty of compiling it. Private and corporate landholders frequently resist sharing information with government agencies on grounds that freedom of information laws will make it available to the world at large, including people who should not have it. These include trespassers using information to poach valuable or protected plants and animals, real estate developers using it to modify sensitive areas before they can be legally protected, and even competing scientists using it unfairly to claim credit for themselves. The landowners have a point. Unless ecological information involves a trade secret, would invade personal privacy if released, or includes geological or geophysical data about an oil or gas well, federal agencies are unlikely to be able to withhold it under the Freedom of Information Act (FOIA, 5 U.S.C. §552). Of course, resistance to sharing information also may reflect less worthy fears, for example, that it will be used to develop or enforce environmental protection policies. These fears can never be fully overcome, but could be isolated by amending FOIA to allow the nondisclosure of information when it involves the kinds of risks just listed.

Sharing information often is resisted, but laws compelling its provision are a powerful and growing force. The "community right to know" law (42 U.S.C. §§11001 et seq.), which requires businesses to report all releases of toxic chemicals, whether illegal or not, has had a large impact both in prompting industry to reduce use of toxic chemicals and in galvanizing communities to demand safeguards from industry. These safeguards often are formalized in "good neighbor agreements" between companies and communities, thus creating a new cross-boundary stewardship mechanism. The EPA recently proposed regulations requiring disclosure of all toxic chemicals stored and used by businesses, not just releases, and provoked a storm of industry protest. As noted, the Safe Drinking Water Act was recently amended to require water utilities to send "consumer confidence reports" detailing the chemical and biological content of water to all customers, and this is likely to create new pressures for improving water quality. These developments are consistent with those in Europe, where disclosure provisions are becoming a cornerstone of environmental policy (Orts 1995). Finally, as noted in the "privatization" section, NGOs are increasingly relying on certification systems and ecolabeling to achieve policy goals. In every case, information is being deployed as a tool to coordinate and control resource use, a phenomenon that is creating both new mechanisms for cross-boundary stewardship and new resistance to it.

Conclusions

After reading this chapter, one is unlikely to feel a surge of confidence that cross-boundary stewardship will soon be widely and effectively practiced. The question then arises, What should be done? It is a question that cannot entirely be answered. One possibility would be to cut through the whole system and make cross-boundary stewardship legally mandatory. Although appealing, this option seems implausible, not only for political reasons, but also because cross-boundary stewardship probably cannot be defined with sufficient clarity to determine when it is or is not being practiced. The idea of stewardship is as vague and open-ended as it is compelling. It exudes the need for judgment, for learning, for new knowledge, for experimentation and reflection. It also exudes the need for dialog and deliberation. In short, as Aldo Leopold observed about the land ethic in 1949, cross-boundary stewardship is a social ideal, not a legal standard, and probably will remain so for some time (Leopold 1949).

Law's inability unilaterally to produce stewardship does not make law irrelevant. Although the Interagency Ecosystem Management Task Force (1995) recently found little need for legal change, the analysis in this chapter suggests that many legal changes will have to occur over time. Almost every legal area discussed, from nuisance to antitrust, could adapt to facilitate stewardship without undermining its core objectives. Details often will have to be worked out in light of further experience and research, but the general contours of several desirable changes are apparent at this stage.

First, if ongoing, deliberative collaboration is to occur among landowners, communities, and federal agencies, FACA should be amended to allow federal officials to make and keep commitments developed through group deliberations. Although there are several possible ways to do this, perhaps the most straightforward simply is to make FACA inapplicable where (1) a group is working to develop cross-boundary resource management strategies, (2) the group is open to anyone who wishes to participate, and (3) federal officials keep detailed, publicly available records of group deliberations. If limiting participation in the group becomes important, then the agency can charter a FACA committee.

The FOIA also is a clear candidate for amendment. The simplest solution to its current disincentives for sharing information is to exempt from disclosure to nongovernmental parties information that can reasonably be expected to lead to poaching, preemptive development, or loss of commercial value. Although antitrust laws have received little attention, there also are good reasons to think that they will have to be revised to allow stewardship consultations including competing producers. This could conceivably be done by Congress, the courts, federal agencies, or the states (Meidinger 1997). The best near-term option seems to be for the states to shield cross-boundary steward-ship activities by creating state-managed processes in which they can occur.

Numerous other areas of law also would benefit from reassessment and possible revision, including the huge patchwork of federal environmental law. Yet whether and how it should be changed is hard to say, partly because the questions are very complicated, and partly because we have not produced a systematic body of research on environmental law and institutions. At present most commentary consists of pronouncements by lone scholars or partisan interest advocates. Our methodology remains far more based on case law than empirical, and our style of analysis is more dissective than synthetic. Furthermore, we are far more comfort-able studying individual decisions and laws than studying systems. This may be changing, as legal and policy researchers develop working rela-tionships with ecological researchers and managers. But if its goals are to be fulfilled, this book will have to be an early step in building an ongo-ing network of inquiry and dialog among the scientific, policy, and man-agement disciplines, as well as landowners, public interest groups, com-munities, and others. If that happens, then in ten years we will know much more about cross-boundary stewardship. If not, this chapter will remain current.

ACKNOWLEDGMENTS

Research for this chapter was supported in part by funding from the USDA Forest Service, Pacific Northwest Research Station, People and Natural Resources Program, through a cooperative agreement on Legal Issues in Ecosystem Management. The research assistance of Michael Kotin and Carol Messito, the computer assistance of Chris Meidinger, and the substantive comments of Margaret Shannon, Barry Smith, and members of the SUNY–Buffalo Environmental Policy Colloquium are gratefully acknowledged.

REFERENCES

Allen, M. 1989. Native American control of tribal natural resources develop-ments in the context of the federal trust and tribal self-determination. *Boston College Environmental Affairs Law Review* 16:857–79.
Arum, J.B. 1990. Old growth forests on state school lands—dedicated to obliv-

ion? Private trust theory and the public trust. *Washington Law Review* 65:151–169.

Blackstone, W. 1861 (originally 1769). *Commentaries on the laws of England*. J.B. Lippincott, Philadelphia.

Boyer, B.B., and E.E. Meidinger. 1985. Privatizing regulatory enforcement: a preliminary assessment of citizen suits under federal environmental laws. *Buffalo Law Review* 35:864–965.

Breckenridge, L.P. 1995. Reweaving the landscape: the institutional challenges of ecosystem management for lands in private ownership. *Vermont Law Review* 19:363–422.

Caldwell, L.K. 1986. Land and the law: problems in legal philosophy. *University of Illinois Law Review* 1986:319–337.

di Castri F., A.J. Hansen, and M.M. Holland, editors. 1988. A new look at ecotones: emerging international projects on landscape boundaries. *Biology International Special Issue* 17:1–163.

Diehl, J., and T.S. Barrett. 1988. *The conservation easement handbook*. Land Trust Exchange, Alexandria, VA.

Ellickson, R.C. 1993. Property in land. *Yale Law Journal* 102:1315–1400.

Fort Gratiot Sanitary Landfill v. Mich. Dept. of Natural Resources, 504 U.S. 353 (1992).

Freeman, J. 1997. Collaborative governance in the administrative state. UCLA. *Law Review* 45:1–98.

Freyfogle, E.T. 1993. *Justice and the earth: images for our survival*. The Free Press, New York.

Gade, M.G. 1996. The devolution revolution has already occurred. *State Environmental Monitor*, March 4.

Gunningham, N. 1995. Environment, self-regulation, and the chemical industry: assessing responsible care. *Law and Policy* 17:57–109.

Inside EPA. 1996a. Water utilities craft recommendations for new drinking water reporting. *Inside EPA* November 22:17.

Inside EPA. 1996b. Wastewater officials push for a watershed based CWA. *Inside EPA* November 22:19–20.

Interagency Ecosystem Management Task Force. 1995. *The ecosystem approach: healthy ecosystems and sustainable economies*. U.S. Government Printing Office, Washington, DC.

Keiter, R.B. 1994. Beyond the boundary line: constructing a law of ecosystem management. *Colorado Law Review* 65:293–333.

Leopold, A. 1949. *A Sand County almanac* (1970 Reprint). Ballantine, New York.

Lucas v. South Carolina Coastal Council, 505 U.S. 1003 (1992).

Lynch, S. 1996. The Federal Advisory Committee Act: an obstacle to ecosystem management by federal agencies? *University of Washington Law Review* 71:431–459.

Meidinger, E. 1985. On explaining the development of "emissions trading" in U.S. air pollution regulation. *Law and Policy* 7:457–489.

Meidinger, E. 1987. Regulatory culture: a theoretical outline. *Law and Policy* 9:355–386.

Meidinger, E. 1993. The changing legal environment of northern forest policy making. Pages 125–137 in *Sustaining ecosystems, economies, and a way of life in the northern forest.* The Wilderness Society, Washington, DC.

Meidinger, E. 1997a. Legal and organizational challenges for ecosystem management. Pages 361–379 in *Creating a forestry for the twenty-first century: the science of ecosystem management* (K.A. Kohm and J.F. Franklin, editors). Island Press, Washington, DC.

Meidinger, E. 1997b. Look who's making the rules: environmental standard setting by the forest stewardship council and international standards organization. *Human Ecology Review* 4(1):52–54.

Meidinger, E., R.N. Clark, and M.A. Shannon. 1996. *Science and policy in natural resources: conceptual propositions drawn from case studies and the literature.* Pacific Northwest Research Station, USDA Forest Service, Seattle, WA.

Morehouse, B. 1995. A functional approach to boundaries in the context of environmental issues. *Journal of Borderlands Studies* 10:53–74.

Naiman, R. J., and H. Decamps, editors. 1990. *The ecology and management of aquatic–terrestrial ecotones.* UNESCO Press, Paris.

National Solid Wastes Management Assoc. v. Myers, 63 F.3d 652 (1995).

New York v. EPA, 852 F.2d 574 (1988).

Norton, B.G. 1992. A new paradigm for environmental management. Pages 23–41 in *Ecosystem health: new goals for environmental management* (R. Costanza, B.G. Norton, B.D. Haskell, editors). Island Press, Washington, DC.

Orts, E.W. 1995. Reflexive environmental law. *Northwestern University Law Review* 89:1227–1339.

Pauw, J., T.J. Greenan, and D.C. Ross. 1993. *Balancing endangered species regulation and antitrust law concerns.* Working Paper 54. Washington Legal Foundation, Washington, DC.

Pennsylvania Coal Co. v. Sanderson, 113 Pa. 126 (1886).

Public Citizen v. U.S. Dept. of Justice, 491 U.S. 440 (1989).

Risser, P.G. 1993. Ecotones. *Ecological Applications* 3:367–368.

Ruhl, J.B. 1995. Biodiversity conservation and the ever-expanding web of federal laws regulating nonfederal lands: time for something completely different? *University of Colorado Law Review* 66:555–673.

Sax, J.L. 1993. Property rights and the economy of nature: understanding *Lucas v. South Carolina Coastal Council*. *Stanford Law Review* 45:1433–1454.

Shannon, M.A. In press. Understanding social organizations and institutions. In *Ecology and management of streams and rivers in the pacific northwest ecoregion* (R.J. Naiman and R.E. Bilby, editors). Springer Verlag, New York.

Small, S.J. 1989. *Preserving family lands: a landowner's introduction to tax issues and other considerations*. Preserving Family Lands, Boston.

Thorud, D.B. 1994. The role of the board of natural resources and the duties and responsibilities of its members as trustees. Paper submitted to the Washington State Board of Natural Resources, Olympia, WA.

Wilkinson, C. 1987. *American Indians, time, and the law: native societies in a modern constitutional democracy*. Yale University Press, New Haven.

Williamson, O. 1985. *The Economic institutions of capitalism*. Free Press, New York.

Wondolleck, J. M., and S. L. Yaffee. 1994. *Building bridges across agency boundaries: in search of excellence in the United States Forest Service*. School of Natural Resources and Environment, University of Michigan, Ann Arbor.

TYPES OF ADMINISTRATIVE BOUNDARIES

Part II addresses a variety of different boundary types in natural resources management. Accordingly, the four chapters cover wilderness, recreation, private forestry, and private–public land boundaries. Each chapter illuminates key issues relative to a particular boundary type and suggests ways to mitigate harmful effects.

We begin with a chapter titled "Boundary Effects on Wilderness and Other Natural Areas," by Peter Landres and his colleagues. Within the broad rubric of wilderness, Landres et al. include national parks and monuments, research natural areas, areas of critical ecological concern, and natural areas privately held by nongovernmental organizations. The theme of their chapter states that

> Managers of protected areas face the difficult challenge of maintaining boundaries, or certain aspects of boundaries, that protect and sustain these areas, while working to erase or diminish the negative effects of these same boundaries. Facing this challenge will require many different qualities in the people charged with managing and protecting natural areas. One of the more important of these qualities will be the capacity to understand first why wildness is unique and the benefits our society derives from natural areas and then why and how this uniqueness resides within an ecological, social, and managerial context. Such an understanding comes from both an intellectual grasp of these issues and the feeling for an area that develops only by spending much time on the land.

Landres et al. describe ecological impacts originating along administrative borders that affect natural areas. This discussion covers beneficial flows of species and ecological processes into and out of a natural area. For example, wildernesses in the Sierra Nevada of California with fire-dependent conifer ecosystems occur at high elevations. Yet the primary ignition source for many of these higher-elevation areas are fires that begin at lower elevations and burn up into the protected areas. Landres et al. point out that these lower-elevation fires often are actively suppressed on multiple-use areas, resulting in important vegetation changes throughout the higher protected areas.

Landres et al. also explore the recreational component of different boundary types on wilderness areas, including those caused by abrupt changes in recreational use at wilderness edges and those caused by recreation trails and destinations straddling wilderness boundaries. These effects include noise and visual impacts, both of which may alter some of the primary benefits of wilderness and natural area settings. In both cases, the authors stress the importance of landscape-scale planning in the maintenance of wilderness values as the matrix of land surrounding a protected area is just as important as the wilderness itself.

The authors conclude with a discussion of two approaches to wilderness stewardship. One approach, that practiced by the U.S. Forest Service and the Bureau of Land Management, treats wilderness as a resource "separate" from the surrounding land. Such a mind-set, the authors argue, leads to wilderness areas being isolated and trivialized within the agency. The contrasting approach, practiced by the National Park Service and the U.S. Fish and Wildlife Service, views wilderness as "similar" to the surrounding land. A concern with this approach is that wilderness and natural areas then may be viewed as simply a part of other agency resources and the unique and special qualities of wilderness may be lost.

The authors do not suggest that solutions to these dilemmas are simple. Instead they stress a more holistic approach that requires both broader mind-sets within the agencies responsible for protected areas and planning at a larger spatial scale. When traditional land management planning is changed to incorporate the impacts of administrative boundaries that sever beneficial flows and enhance detrimental flows and the incompatible and conflicting uses of adjacent lands the authors believe that wilderness areas will be better protected.

———

Traditionally, public lands were viewed as sources for extracting natural resources, such as logs, grass, minerals, and game. Today, our public lands are being viewed increasingly as places for urban populations to recreate outdoors. Not only are the numbers of recreationists visiting public lands increasing, but also the different types of recreational activities continue to grow. Accordingly, boundaries that separate recreation from other land uses, as well as boundaries that divide different types of recreationists are of critical importance. This is the topic that Clinton Miller and Mark Gershman address in "Outdoor Recreation and Boundaries: Opportunities and Challenges."

Miller and Gershman explain how the nature of administrative boundaries shapes recreational experiences and the land-use or management goals on either side of the line. For example, restrictions placed on one side of a boundary that are incongruent with uses allowed across the line may result in visitor dissatisfaction and a variety of human behaviors that lead to other resource management problems. If managed with a cross-boundary perspective, however, recreationists with different expectations and desires can be accommodated. Increasingly, Miller and Gershman argue, land management agencies are structuring borders so as to separate conflicting recreational uses both spatially and temporally. For example, rock climbers are separated from sensitive cliff-nesting species by seasonal closures.

Miller and Gershman next examine how different types of boundaries encountered by recreationists shape their attitudes and experiences. These types include: (1) boundaries between different public agencies, (2) boundaries within an agency, and (3) boundaries that divide private from public land. Visitors are sometimes surprised to find that land management agencies have different priorities regarding nature protection, recreational opportunities, and resource extraction. In addition, an agency may be expected to accommodate all of these activities simultaneously, though not necessarily on the same parcel of land at the same time. How agencies handle these issues, both within their own organizations and across different agencies, has profound impacts on attitudes developed by recreational visitors. Even more challenging are the difficulties presented when public land abuts private land. Recreationists may be following a trail across a national forest only to find it enters a private parcel. Unless agencies and private landowners cooperate on activities that cross their borders, frustration and legal issues such as trespass and property damage may result.

Challenges associated with recreational conflicts caused by boundary differences are not insurmountable. Miller and Gershman conclude their chapter by presenting a protocol to address these issues. The approach includes: (1) anticipating problems, (2) identifying conflicts when they occur, (3) developing communication with other landowners, land managers, and stakeholders, (4) generating workable solutions, and (5) implementing and evaluating these solutions. They illustrate this approach with an example of pedestrians with and without dogs crossing open-space lands in Boulder, Colorado. The technique required cooperation from both land managers and affected groups and individuals. It required lengthy meetings and deliberations that resulted in a model that is presently being implemented and evaluated. The authors conclude that there seldom are simple solutions to recreational demands and conflicts that arise from the complex patterns of lines we have drawn across the land. Answers occur when land managers and stakeholders agree to work cooperatively.

———

Nowhere, it seems, do boundary effects constrain commodity production more than in the timber industry, on both private and public lands. William Wall addresses this issue in "Boundaries or Barriers: New Horizons for Conservation and Private Forests."

Wall assumes that commodity production is an essential component of our civilization and that food and fiber will continue to be produced on working landscapes. He also believes that the greatest advances in resource conservation will occur by integrating societal and conservation goals. To do this, he writes, ways will have to be found that bridge or diminish the barriers created by organizational and individual differences and information boundaries. Although he considers that these differences will always exist, they diminish cooperation when they are perpetuated by a lack of understanding, short-term vision, or unwillingness of individuals to cross boundaries.

Differences in missions and resulting cultures create boundaries between organizations. This is worsened by the tendency for organizations to resist major changes that affect internal culture. These dynamics lead to different approaches to natural resource management. For example, a federal agency charged with the protection of an endangered species in the face of scientific uncertainty may err on the side of the species with a conservative response. A timber production company may focus on a least-cost alternative to maintain habitat, whereas an environmental organization may be reluctant to accept any solution short of habitat preservation through a "hands-off" alternative. Whereas Wall says that each approach may achieve species persistence, the contention among the organizations comes from the interaction of the three approaches. Agency personnel and environmentalists think that the company only wants to make money, whereas the timber company believes these two groups only want to present roadblocks to harvesting timber. These chasms also exist among individuals. Differences in basic beliefs and values within the professional and scientific communities of resource managers, conservation activists, and private land biologists can create significant barriers. Wall asks, Do scientists advocate or simply inform and illuminate alternatives?

Wall suggests that information boundaries inhibit cooperation in three ways: (1) mistrust of information interpretation, (2) incompatible data, and (3) reluctance to share information. For example, those in the private sector believe that the Freedom of Information Act requires information in federal hands be made available to the public. Private landowners may be reluctant to share information with agencies if they perceive the information may be requested by an outside party and used against the landowner.

So what to do? Is there a way beyond these organizational, individual, and informational complexities that will foster cooperation in commodity production and resource stewardship? Wall believes there is and describes two examples in which the private timber industry worked with agencies and environmental groups to bridge barriers. These examples show that consensus can be reached between resource managers and stakeholders, regardless of the complications of personal beliefs, organization cultures, and differences in levels of information exchanged. The key, Wall asserts, is whether individuals are willing to break out of organizational and cultural roles to take the chances necessary for change.

———

Because America is approximately half private land and because these lands play important roles in sustaining native biological diversity and contributing to vital ecological processes, what occurs on private lands where they join public lands is critical. Richard Knight and Tim Clark in "Boundaries between Public and Private Lands: Defining Obstacles, Finding Solutions" discuss ecological implications that occur on either side of public–private borders and suggest approaches to soften the harmful effects of development.

Although there are a variety of private land-use categories that occur adjacent to public lands, conversion of agricultural and timber lands to housing and commercial development are the fastest growing changes. Three general trends that result from this growth are: (1) increasing human densities adjacent to public lands, (2) increasing economic activities that depend on public land resources (principally tourism and amenity-lifestyle factors), and (3) alteration of biotic communities and ecological processes on both sides of the boundaries.

Commercial and residential development usually result in increases in buildings and roads and an accompanying increase in human densities. These factors, in turn, often contribute to increases in dog and cat populations, automobile traffic, night lights, nonnative species, and human disturbance. Knight and Clark suggest that the consequences of these changes are altered wildlife and plant communities. A hypothetical pattern following development may be more human-adapted species and fewer species that are sensitive to humans and their enterprises. The authors also suggest that there will be interruptions in ecological processes such as fire and water regimes. Not surprisingly, these changes emanating on one side of the private–public boundary will affect the public lands.

Because private-land development adjacent to public lands is not expected to decrease any time in the near future, individuals, organizations, and agencies will want to meet at their boundaries to begin planning for development to minimize harmful effects. Not only is the integrity of public lands at risk when development occurs with little thought and planning, but, Knight and Clark believe, the biodiversity and ecological processes on private lands also are in jeopardy. They present a number of suggestions to facilitate cooperation across these boundaries: (1) developing shared perceptions of issues, (2) identifying shared goals among key participants, (3) increasing cooperation between elected officials, private landowners, and public land management agencies, and (4) increasing appreciation of the consequences of historic trends. These approaches to boundary planning along private and public lands are worked out and understood yet they need to be applied site-by-site to be contextually relevant. Knight and Clark suggest this approach may offer an opportunity to sustain the ecological, economic, and societal needs of diverse communities and organizations that share common borders.

Chapter 5

Boundary Effects on Wilderness and Other Natural Areas

Peter B. Landres, Susan Marsh, Linda Merigliano,
Dan Ritter, and Andy Norman

Boundaries delineate wildernesses and other natural areas from lands managed for other purposes and uses. These adjacent land uses may fragment a natural landscape, causing a host of isolation impacts to the remnant natural areas (see Chapter 2). The land uses that occur on adjacent lands may also directly threaten natural areas by providing sites where exotic plants, animals, and pathogens may gain access to the natural area. These threats to natural areas, both direct and indirect, are the "eternal external threat" noted by Janzen (1986), and they continually and irreversibly ratchet down the quality of these areas, causing unaltered natural ecosystems to become increasingly rare in our human-dominated landscape. At the same time, natural areas are increasingly valued by many people for the ecological services they offer, as well as the social benefits people derive from them (Bengston 1994, McDonald and Brown 1995). The purpose of this chapter is to examine boundary impacts on the ecological, social, and managerial aspects of areas managed for their natural values and benefits to society. We explore whether the same boundaries that define and protect natural areas also compromise their ecological integrity and social values—whether these areas are at risk of becoming "prisons rather than fortresses" (Hales 1989).

This chapter examines the impacts of administrative boundaries on the ecological systems within natural areas, as well as on the social benefits derived from these areas. It also discusses the internal management boundaries that are created within agencies that administer natural areas and the positive and negative effects of these management boundaries.

This chapter draws largely from examples in designated wilderness administered by the USDA Forest Service because most of our personal and professional experiences with natural areas are rooted in national forest wilderness. The concepts we develop apply equally to all areas protected for their natural values, such as national parks and monuments, research natural areas, areas of critical environmental concern, and natural areas that are privately held and protected by groups such as the Audubon Society, The Nature Conservancy, and other private land trust organizations.

Ecological Impacts of Boundaries

Boundary effects on ecological systems were reviewed earlier (Chapter 2). Here we examine those effects that are specific to natural areas. When lands in the United States were first formally protected for their natural values, starting in the latter half of the nineteenth century, ecological reasons for protection were not considered, and it was presumed that these areas would function as self-contained "living museums" or "vignettes of primitive America" (Leopold et al. 1963) in perpetuity.

As early as the 1930s, however, boundary-related and adjacent-land impacts became evident to managers of protected areas (Freemuth 1991), and awareness of these impacts has grown steadily since. In a synthesis of four separate surveys of USDI National Park Service (NPS) and USDA Forest Service wilderness managers conducted from 1980 to 1985, Peine et al. (1988) found that nearly 30 percent of the managers in their sample had boundary-related problems. In a survey of threats to parks worldwide, Machlis and Tichnell (1987) identified development external to the parks as a significant threat to park values. In a series of interviews and surveys conducted in 1990 with NPS personnel to identify problems (Buechner et al. 1992) and potential solutions (Schonewald-Cox et al. 1992), Buechner et al. (1992) found that "all of the park personnel interviewed or surveyed felt that activities adjacent to parks are important influences on the parks' biological diversity." Boundary-related problems were clearly recognized at the highest level within the NPS: "we've all been aware for some time that the most serious threats to the long-term preservation of park resources originate outside park boundaries. . . . Parks are not units unto themselves; they're not *separate*" (Ridenour 1990, quoted in Buechner et al. 1992; emphasis in original). And most recently, Kelson and Lilieholm (1997) surveyed ninety-two wilderness managers from the Forest Service, NPS, USDI Fish and Wildlife Service

(FWS), and USDI Bureau of Land Management (BLM) to assess the perceived impacts from sixty different adjacent land activities: fire management, military overflights, and exotic plant introductions were thought to have the greatest impacts.

Recent scientific concern for boundary impacts was presaged by Wright et al. (1933) and Wright and Thompson (1935), who focused on animal populations and suggested that the boundaries of Yellowstone National Park needed adjustment to account for the movement of migratory and widely dispersing animals, that the park was generally too small, and that "This matter of external influence incessantly acting upon the faunal resources of a national park cannot be overestimated. The success of a sanctuary depends largely upon what is done outside the sanctuary to make it a real and adequate haven for wildlife" (Wright and Thompson 1935). Thompson (1935) also stated that "Wild animals know nothing about the arbitrary boundaries which man draws on maps to indicate areas set aside for his different types of wilderness use. Animals wander back and forth, as seasons and quest for food dictate, across refuge or hunting ground, park or forest, as the case may be. What affects deer or cougars in the environs will also affect them in the game sanctuary itself."

Theoretical interest in boundary effects on natural areas was sparked by the development of island biogeography theory (e.g., Diamond and May 1976, Forman and Godron 1981). Empirical research on boundary impacts lay largely dormant until Newmark (1985) examined the congruence of ecological and administrative boundaries, and the resulting impacts to populations of wide-ranging species. Combining theory with data, Schonewald-Cox and Bayless (1986) developed a "boundary model" to examine the effects of administrative borders on nature reserves and applied this model to Organ Pipe Cactus National Monument and Redwoods National Park, concluding that protection of natural areas may be "more dependent upon what crosses the boundary than upon any internal processes alone." Buechner (1987) developed a simulation model of animal movement across park boundaries, showing that the boundary perimeter-to-park-area ratio was as important as park size for protecting animal populations. Reviewing the spectrum of impacts from adjacent lands that may cross the boundaries of national parks, Shafer (1994) concluded that park context, or the matrix of land surrounding a park, is just as important as park content, emphasizing the importance of large-scale, regional planning in the maintenance of park values and benefits.

A Conceptual Framework for Examining Boundary Effects

The primary ecological effect of differing land uses associated with an administrative boundary is the change in flows or fluxes across the boundary zone, with resulting impacts on ecological processes and species' populations, both near and far from the boundary (see Chapter 2). These impacts were reviewed by Saunders et al. (1991) and Harris and Silva-Lopez (1992) and include fragmentation of habitat with a consequent reduction in the functional size of the natural area and an increase in the perimeter-to-area ratio; disruption of processes such as fire, water movement, and population dispersal that flow across a landscape; creation of population "sinks" that lose individuals from areas that were formerly "sources" of individuals; the increased likelihood of population extirpation caused by genetic problems such as inbreeding depression and genetic drift, or lack of recolonization following catastrophes; effects that ripple or cascade throughout a community because of the loss of prey or predator species; reduced number of species; and increased invasion of exotic plants, animals, and pathogens.

We offer a conceptual framework to help organize and understand this multitude of impacts caused by the administrative borders surrounding protected areas. There are beneficial flows both into and out of the natural area (Figure 5.1; Cole and Landres 1996). Land uses that conflict

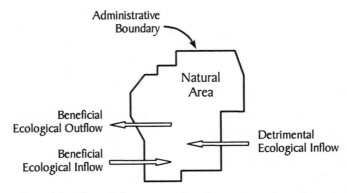

Figure 5.1. Types of ecological flow across the administrative boundary of a natural area. From the perspective of the natural area, flows move into or out from the area. Beneficial flows result from normal or typical ecological functions, such as migratory dispersal, and may be vital to sustaining the ecological integrity of the natural area. Detrimental flow results from adjacent land inflows to the natural area, from invasive exotic plants and animals, predators, and pathogens.

across boundaries cause adverse impacts to natural areas by disrupting beneficial flows either into or out of the area or by increasing detrimental flows into the area (Figure 5.2).

Beneficial flows of species and ecological processes *into* a natural area are disrupted by adjacent land uses. For some species, for example, immigration of new individuals into the population may be more important than birth and death rates of the population itself (Fahrig and Merriam 1994). When adjacent land uses prevent this dispersal and immigration, populations within the protected area may die out even though habitat conditions within the area are adequate in other respects. For example,

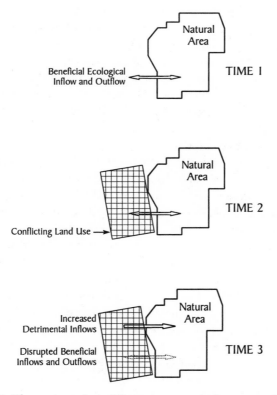

Figure 5.2. Change in ecological flows over time with incompatible land-use adjacent to a natural area. At time 1, normal ecological flows into and out from a natural area are vital to the area. At time 2, adjacent land is developed for uses that may be incompatible with the natural area, resulting at time 3 in disruption of the beneficial or normal ecological flows into and out from the natural area and an increase in detrimental flows into the natural area.

one of the primary reasons for the decline of the northern spotted owl (*Strix occidentalis caurina*) is the increasing distance between suitable habitat patches and the consequent increasing difficulty for juvenile owls in dispersing among these suitable habitat patches (Noon and McKelvey 1996).

Many wildernesses and national parks in the Sierra Nevada in California are at higher elevations in fire-dependent conifer ecosystems. Yet the primary ignition source for many of these higher-elevation areas is fire originating at lower elevations that burns up into the protected areas, and fires at these lower elevations are actively suppressed (McKelvey et al. 1996). Suppression of fire in these adjacent, lower elevations is now causing significant changes in the vegetation throughout the protected Sierran wildernesses and parks. Disruption of hydrologic flow regime outside Everglades and Grand Canyon national parks has likewise caused significant changes to the plants and wildlife within these parks (Kushlan 1987, Johnson and Carothers 1987, respectively).

Beneficial flows *out from* a natural area may also be disrupted by adjacent land goals and uses, adversely affecting populations or processes within the natural area. For example, nearly 70 percent of the mortality of wolves in Algonquin Park, Canada, from 1987 to 1993, occurred when the wolves dispersed out of the Park (Forbes and Theberge 1996). Similarly, the primary cause of mortality for several of Florida's endangered species is being struck by motor vehicles as individuals leave protected areas and attempt to cross roads (Harris and Silva-Lopez 1992).

Crucial ecological processes such as fire also are disrupted within natural areas when these processes flow across a landscape and encounter an administrative boundary. Fires that start within natural areas are suppressed when they approach the boundary and threaten economic or other values that lie outside the protected area (van Wagtendonk 1995). Even the potential risk of fire has been grounds for suppressing naturally ignited fires. For example, in California the combined Lassen Volcanic National Park/Caribou Wilderness Fire Plan describes conditions for prescribed natural fires in these two areas, yet Little and Schonewald-Cox (1990) found that naturally ignited fires within 61 percent of the Park would be suppressed because of the risk of fire spreading into commercial forest surrounding the Park and Wilderness. This problem is especially acute in small protected areas where boundary-related fire suppression can dominate the entire area (Husari 1995).

Detrimental flows into natural areas typically increase when very different goals are established for lands adjacent to natural areas. Air- and waterborne pollutants freely flow into natural areas from extractive industries and agricultural fields, causing many different types of impacts (air pollutant impacts were reviewed by Stottlemyer 1987). The most recent potential threat from an airborne pollutant is xenobiotic chemicals (or chemicals that are foreign to biological systems), primarily herbicides and pesticides wafted in from agricultural fields, that may disrupt endocrine function in amphibians, thus adversely affecting reproduction and development, even though the chemicals are present in extremely small quantities (Stebbins and Cohen 1995). Exotic plants, animals, and pathogens that surround most natural areas today, and in some cases were intentionally introduced to control soil erosion following disturbances such as fire, pose a significant threat to many natural areas. The impacts of exotic plants and animals on nature reserves are reviewed by Usher (1988), MacDonald et al. (1989), Loope (1992), and Cole and Landres (1996), and the impacts of exotic wildlife diseases are reviewed by Alonso et al. (1995). In general, these studies show that exotics flowing into natural areas reduce the number, distribution, and reproduction of native plants and animals and may alter ecological processes such as succession and the fire regime typical for an area.

Boundary Congruence

Concern about the congruence of administrative and ecological boundaries was raised by Newmark (1985) and Wilcove and May (1986), generating considerable discussion among scientists and managers. Even following the sound guidelines offered by Theberge (1989) to minimize their ecological impact, boundaries will always cross and disrupt some natural disturbance paths or dispersal routes, causing adverse impacts to the natural area. If a natural area is managed solely for a particular species, then the size and boundary of the area could be adjusted to fit the population needs for that species, minimizing adverse boundary impacts. However, in areas designated broadly to protect "naturalness," such as wilderness, stochastic disturbance processes such as fire may be vital to the long-term ecological integrity of the area. In this latter case, altering the size and boundary of the area to prevent or mitigate adverse boundary effects will be much more difficult, and less likely to succeed. As discussed in Chapter 2, working to maintain large areas and to ensure compatible land-use goals and actions across administrative boundaries may be the most important actions for the long-term protection of wilderness and other areas managed for their natural values.

Social Impacts of Boundaries

Recreation—the chance to find challenge, beauty, and a connection with a natural world that is largely missing from the lives of many Americans—is one of the primary benefits of wilderness and other natural areas. Nearly seventeen million recreation-visitor-days were recorded in the nation's wildernesses in 1994 (Cole 1996). People recreate in natural areas for many reasons, including the experience of personal challenge, serenity, and spiritual renewal.

Wilderness is defined in large part by its recreation setting, including scenery and primitive character. The Recreation Opportunity Spectrum (ROS), a system in common use among land management agencies (USDA Forest Service 1986), defines primitive recreation in wilderness as one end of a range of settings that runs from highly developed resorts to undeveloped or primitive backcountry areas. Policy objectives for managing wilderness recreation are based on the Wilderness Act and the ROS setting criteria and these direct managers to "provide, consistent with management of the area as wilderness, opportunities for public use, enjoyment, and understanding of the wilderness, through experiences that depend upon a wilderness setting" (USDA Forest Service 1990a).

Primitive areas are distinguished by having little or no evidence of human use. They are large (usually over 5,000 acres), remote, and uncrowded. Wilderness management plans often divide the primitive ROS setting into finer gradations, with the remotest areas having different management standards than high-use portals. However, all areas are to be managed as wilderness and to accommodate compatible types of recreation use. Primitive recreation can be compromised by nearby developments, sources of noise, or scenic intrusions. How we manage land uses on both sides of the wilderness boundary can mitigate or exacerbate the negative effects of incompatible activities. Two general types of wilderness boundary problems are discussed: those caused by abrupt changes in recreation settings and land use at the wilderness boundary, and those caused by recreation trails and destinations straddling the wilderness boundary.

Abrupt Changes in Recreation Settings and Land Use Across a Boundary

Often wilderness boundaries are defined with no consideration for recreation settings, the experience of the wilderness visitor, or compatibility with adjacent land uses. By the time legislation is enacted, other land uses may have already altered much of the surrounding land, making it unsuitable for inclusion in the wilderness, which is then carved out of the remaining roadless area. Two examples of results are given here: the first discusses noise intrusion from an all-terrain vehicle (ATV) route that runs adjacent to a wilderness; the second discusses the visual impacts of clearcuts seen from the wilderness.

Noise Intrusion

The boundary of the Mokelumne Wilderness, California, was drawn around several old roads that have become popular ATV trails. These trails form "cherry stems," long, narrow exclusions reaching up drainages where roads and other developments were already in place at the time of wilderness designation. The wilderness is supposed to offer primitive recreation, yet noise from the ATV trails is clearly heard inside the wilderness. Noise from the ATVs compromises many visitors' expectations for quiet, natural sound, and when the ATV trails receive heavy, continuous use, noise is a continual disruption.

Rerouting ATV trails may be feasible in some cases, although not where the trail corridor is surrounded by wilderness. Newer ATVs are less noisy, so the main problem is when mufflers have been removed or have fallen off and not been replaced. In the short run, regulations to require mufflers, lower speed limits, or a reduction of noise levels below a threshold decibel level could be used. In the long run, preventing or mitigating this type of impact will require recreation settings that are compatible across administrative boundaries, rather than attempting to manage for intrusive or noisy activities directly adjacent to primitive settings.

Visual Intrusion

The Alpine Lakes Wilderness, Washington, includes high peaks and popular hiking trails with views into areas where timber harvest is the primary land use. National Forest is mingled with private lands in a checkerboard pattern; both have been heavily cut. Visitors to the Alpine Lakes Wilderness see large, straight-edged clearcuts and roads on steep terrain, along with resort and summer home developments, drawn-down reservoirs, and city lights. Their expectations for a wilderness experience are often not met. As with noise, the effects are experiential and aesthetic, which are hard to quantify, but are of foremost importance to many wilderness visitors.

What can be done to mitigate these visual impacts that cross administrative boundaries? Prevention of scenic intrusions is more effective than mitigation. At the interface with private lands there is an opportunity for the Forest Service to design timber sales at property boundaries to reduce the straight-line effect of clearcutting to the section line. In cases where clearcutting has turned forested mountainsides into scarred, bald knobs, only planting new trees and time will help. As regrowth occurs, the straight, square edges begin to fade, and the openings look more natural, or at least not as harsh.

The Alpine Lakes Wilderness was designated after much of the logging had already taken place. After the wilderness was established, scenic and recreation values in the surrounding area were emphasized in a special management area. Recent logging on the Wenatchee National Forest near the Alpine Lakes Wilderness has met scenic quality objectives, primarily because clearcutting has been replaced with partial cuts that appear from the wilderness as irregular patches of thinner forest cover. In one timber sale, seen from the Chatter Creek Trail in the Alpine Lakes Wilderness, the sale designer hiked the trail to envision how the cut area would look from viewpoints within the wilderness.

A special management area is not necessary; applying the Forest Service's scenic management system, by designing timber cuts to appear more compatible with the surrounding landscape, can be done anywhere. The problem is that protecting scenic quality often is considered optional, of less importance than an economically efficient timber sale.

Recreation Trails and Destinations That Straddle a Boundary

If wilderness boundaries are drawn without regard for recreation settings, they may ignore trails and water routes that cross into the wilderness. Cherry stems eliminate roads from the wilderness, although not all of their effects. But what of the trails that may be open to motor vehicles and bicycles until they cross the wilderness boundary? What about wilderness boundaries that are drawn to exclude part or all of lakes where motors are allowed? Examples of these situations follow.

Trails That Cross a Boundary

Goodwin Lake, in the Gros Ventre Wilderness, Wyoming, lies within easy access of Jackson Hole. The lake is less than four miles from the trailhead, and the wilderness boundary cuts the trail about ¾ mile from the lake. Although there are several scenic viewpoints along the way, the primary destination is Goodwin Lake.

Illegal trespass into the wilderness by mountain bikes and occasional motor vehicles has created conflict. It is a source of visitor complaints, as well as frustration for the bikers who can legally ride to within a mile of the lake. There is no alternative attraction outside the wilderness that mountain bikers can be directed to that is accessible from this trail. Adding to the problem is a history of ignorance on the part of those promoting recreation in the area, who have in the past included Goodwin Lake in various mountain biking guides. Several years ago, a Jackson newspaper printed an article about the Goodwin Lake trail, recommending it as a "good workout" for mountain bikers. When contacted by the Forest Service, the reporter said she did not know that bikes were not allowed in wilderness, nor that the trail even entered wilderness.

To mitigate the problem, the Forest Service increased its efforts to educate the media and bike users. Posters were placed at the trailhead information board and at the wilderness boundary. The Forest Service cooperated with Bikecentennial, Inc., to publish a guide to mountain biking in the Jackson Hole area, giving bikers options for rides outside the wilderness. Outreach to local bike shops and publishers of trail information helped spread word about the problem as well as offer ideas on other places to ride. As a result, incidents of illegal bicycle use have fallen. In this case, education was the principal solution to this cross-boundary conflict.

Other solutions are possible in different situations. On another popular trail that leads to the Gros Ventre Wilderness, a backcountry bike rack was installed at the wilderness boundary to allow people to ride the six miles of trail open to bikes without encouraging illegal use inside the wilderness. In this situation, the bike rack worked well because there is no lake or other obvious destination within a mile of the wilderness boundary, and the trail becomes quite steep just beyond the boundary, thus discouraging bike use.

Closing a trail to bikes at the trailhead is another potential solution. This would eliminate the conflicting uses on the wilderness trail, but precludes an otherwise suitable use outside the wilderness. In other situations, it may be possible to take advantage of alternatives. Is there another attraction outside the wilderness that a new trail could give access to? Is there a way to create a loop outside the wilderness, so bikers can have an alternative to illegally entering the wilderness?

Another possibility comes into play just after a wilderness is designated. There is a year or so during which the final legal boundaries are described, with an opportunity to make boundary adjustments. This was done after the Lee Metcalf Wilderness in Montana was designated. A ridge defines the eastern boundary of the Taylor-Hilgard Unit of the wilderness. Before wilderness designation, trails open to motor vehicles gained the ridge at two places. The ridge trail dropped in and out of the wilderness, defined by the hydrologic divide. As the legal description was finalized, a compromise placed all of the northern section of the trail inside the wilderness, thereby closing it to vehicles, and the southern part was left outside. Thus the management headache of a trail that for several miles goes in and out of the wilderness was avoided.

Navigable Waters That Cross a Boundary

At Green River Lakes in the Bridger Wilderness, Wyoming, the upper lake is in the wilderness but the lower lake is not. The wilderness boundary wraps the shore of the lower lake, drawn to accommodate historical use by motorboats. In the past there has not been much conflict between traditional small motor craft (used mostly for fishing) on the lake and the adjacent wilderness, even though the first two miles of the Highline Trail are within sight and sound of motorboats on the lake. Although the lake is open to motorboats, most people use canoes, kayaks, and rowboats.

Recent increase in the use of "personal watercraft," or jet skis, has begun to create conflict among lake users. These craft are loud and usually travel fast, disturbing both wilderness users and anglers. The section of the Green River between the two lakes is inside the wilderness, and, along with the upper lake, it is closed to motorboat use. However, it is easily navigable and trespass into the wilderness is becoming a problem and a source of visitor complaints. Most people who canoe to the upper lake do so to distance themselves from the sight and sound of motors. Although the wilderness boundary is marked, it is difficult to patrol and prevent trespass.

What is being done to reduce the problem? Because the state regulates watercraft, the Forest Service has been working with state agencies to impose regulations on motorized use of the lake. The state of Wyoming has banned jet skis from lower Green River Lake, which helps reduce the conflict considerably. Signs at the boat launch and wilderness boundary inform visitors about where the wilderness begins and that motorboats are not allowed within it. Information about the other lakes at the foot of the Wind River Range is available; at other lakes that are more accessible, boat launches that accommodate larger craft are provided to give motorboaters and jet skiers alternatives to Green River Lakes.

Management Boundaries

Wilderness and other protected areas are embedded within a larger land base of national forests, parks, and wildlife refuges administered by several different public agencies. Attitudes and internal policies toward natural areas create boundaries within agencies among people with different views of management (also see Chapter 3) that generally follow one of two approaches: treating natural areas similarly to the surrounding land base, or treating them as separate entities that are set aside from other lands. Both approaches offer certain benefits and problems in managing protected areas, particularly in terms of planning, budgeting, work force organization, information collection, and reporting. In the remainder of this chapter we examine the benefits and problems of these two approaches in the management of natural areas, based on our experiences with Forest Service administration of designated wilderness.

Two Approaches to Wilderness Stewardship

The Wilderness Act of 1964 directs managers to administer wilderness "for the use and enjoyment of the American people in such manner as will leave them unimpaired for future use and enjoyment as wilderness, and so as to provide for the protection of these areas, the preservation of their wilderness character." Wilderness management seeks to retain naturalness and wildness with minimal or no manipulation, in contrast to traditional land management, which seeks to manipulate vegetation, wildlife, and water for the needs of people (Merigliano and Kovalicky 1993). These differences in management goals and the fact that wilderness is a congressionally designated area rather than a commodity raise the significant question of where wilderness should fit within the agency's system of management. This dilemma is captured by Hales (1989), who observed: "By over-emphasizing the special, we sacrifice too much of the necessary. If we over-emphasize the necessary, we will lose the special." In other words, if treated as a separate resource apart from other agency resources, wilderness may be isolated and trivialized within the broader agency, but if treated similarly to other agency resources, the unique and special quality of wilderness may be lost.

In general, the NPS and the FWS have taken the approach of treating their designated wildernesses like other agency-held lands (called "wilderness similar" hereafter). The NPS, with its preservation roots, saw little difference between wilderness and other park lands and has only recently begun to focus attention on wilderness as a distinct resource (Kennedy 1996, Henry 1996). The FWS, with its specific mandate to protect wildlife species and habitat, views wilderness legislation as "within and supplemental" to the primary purposes of wildlife refuges (Jerome 1996). For both of these agencies, wilderness management duties are typically dispersed among many people in different divisions rather than contained within a single program.

In contrast to the NPS and the FWS, the Forest Service and BLM have adopted the approach of treating designated wildernesses differently from their other agency-held lands (called "wilderness separate" hereafter). The roots of this approach in the Forest Service run deep. Despite the Forest Service's leadership role in developing the wilderness concept, the agency's roots are anchored in a utilitarian conservation philosophy (Allin 1990). Such a philosophy creates a mind-set that in areas where land is not to be treated or manipulated (e.g., wilderness), there is no need for management. Despite provisions in the Multiple Use–Sustained Yield Act of 1960 (one of the guiding pieces of legislation for National Forest management), which states that "the establishment and maintenance of areas of wilderness are consistent with the purposes and provisions of this Act," the "wilderness separate" mind-set was sufficiently strong to deter active management by the agency (Hendee et al. 1990). In addition, Roth (1995) suggests that the resistance to fully embrace wilderness as part of the National Forest System was a reaction by the agencies against special congressional designation. This special status challenged agency authority for the first time and signaled the beginning of citizen-based initiatives to gain statutory protection for wildlands. Furthermore, there was little public pressure for agency involvement in wilderness management because many citizens believed that the job of protecting and preserving wilderness was accomplished once the wilderness boundary was drawn around the area. Many people felt that ongoing agency involvement in wilderness was neither needed, desired, nor philosophically appropriate.

Throughout the 1970s, increasing recreation use of wilderness, increasing development adjacent to wilderness, and improving knowledge about threats to ecological systems allowed greater public awareness of the threats and impacts to wilderness and other natural areas nationwide. With this increasing knowledge and awareness, wilderness management could no longer be ignored but was still given low priority in terms of overall agency attention and budget. Congressional pressure in the late 1980s brought focused attention on the need for wilderness management, but the approach was still "wilderness separate," only now with more stature and legitimacy.

Implications of the "Wilderness Similar" Approach

The effects and implications of these two approaches are summarized in Table 5.1. The "wilderness similar" approach of the FWS and NPS is problematic in terms of legal compliance, visibility, accountability, and ability to compete for funds. When wilderness is assumed to be no different from surrounding lands, managers typically do not have opportunities to learn about the Wilderness Act and the concept of wildness. Thus, they are not as likely to develop plan direction or alter their management practices to meet the intent of the act. When the wilderness program is buried within the agency structure and not identifiable, it is difficult to track accomplishments, management needs, funds, and conditions and trends within wilderness. Furthermore, wilderness projects must compete for funds against projects where visitor use is higher or management targets are more readily measurable.

Implications of the "Wilderness Separate" Approach

The "wilderness separate" approach of the FS and BLM is problematic in terms of planning, work force integration, and information availability. When wilderness is treated as an island within surrounding lands, planning is viewed as somehow different, thus direction for stewardship of the resource is not integrated within broader agency plans. When wilderness is assumed to be a separate discipline with its own work force, the skills necessary to adequately care for a multidiscipline resource are not in place. This limited range of skills and expertise results in the collection of only some types of information. Thus, managers making decisions about a broad range of issues affecting wilderness often do not have the quantity and quality of information necessary to make informed choices.

Planning: An Example of the "Wilderness Separate" Approach

Increasing concern about the stewardship of wilderness prompted congressional scrutiny of the Forest Service wilderness program in the late 1980s and early 1990s. In response to this scrutiny, attention to wilderness increased within the agency. The visibility of a separate program allowed funding to be targeted to wilderness, so budgets increased substantially. The presence of a separate program also enabled managers quickly to establish an accounting and reporting system to track funds, accomplishments, conditions, and needs. To respond to questions regard-

Table 5.1. Contrasting approaches to wilderness management within agencies

Attributes of Management System[a]	AGENCY APPROACHES[b]	
	Wilderness Separate	Wilderness Similar
Legal compliance. Management plans and practices comply with Wilderness Act	More likely	Less likely
Planning. Efficiency of process and integration within agency	Less likely	More likely
Budgeting. Ability to compete for funds within agency	More likely	Less likely
Reporting and accountability. Ability to track funding and trends in conditions	More likely	Less likely
Work force. Interdisciplinary skills needed to manage wilderness	Less likely	More likely
Information. Quantity and quality available for decision making	Less likely	More likely
Visibility. Ability of public and Congress to target the wilderness program	More likely	Less likely

[a]Identify tasks and how an agency accomplishes its mission.
[b]The designations "More likely" and "Less likely" are our judgments about whether the particular agency approach ("Similar" or "Separate") is more or less likely to meet the goals of the management system attribute compared with the alternate approach.

ing the scope and cost of wilderness stewardship, planning efforts began. However, wilderness managers, rather than planners within the agency leading the effort, were assigned this task. Wilderness managers typically were trained in recreation and lacked formal knowledge about planning and National Environmental Policy Act (NEPA) procedures. Unfamiliarity with broader forest planning frameworks caused wilderness managers to use the Limits of Acceptable Change (LAC) planning framework that had recently been pilot-tested in a wilderness and was known throughout wilderness networks. Supervisors did not attempt to steer wilderness managers toward forest planning frameworks, perhaps believing that because managing wilderness was different, the planning frameworks also must be different.

By viewing LAC as a separate framework rather than integrating LAC concepts into the broader forest planning framework, additional barriers were created within the agency resulting in lost time and duplicated work efforts. As products from the wilderness planning process were still subject to NEPA analysis, they had to be cut apart into separate documents to fit the two decision levels (programmatic and project) of traditional forest planning. Communication barriers developed between wilderness managers and forest planners because of different terminology used in their respective efforts.

A lack of information also hampered planning efforts. Developing integrated plan direction depended on information from basic resource inventories, but wilderness managers often found that this information did not exist because forest inventories typically stopped at the wilderness boundary. The management of recreation impacts or fire are just two areas where this lack of information made it difficult to make informed decisions. Two reasons may explain why resource information stopped at the wilderness boundary. First, there were no commodity values derived from timber harvest and other active manipulation of the land within designated wilderness, so there was little perceived need for resource information. And second, the general perception among the public and managers was that, once wilderness boundaries were drawn, the primary work of protection was accomplished and resource information was simply not needed.

On the positive side, approaching planning from a different perspective led to insights that will continue to improve broader forest planning frameworks. In addition, because people knowledgeable about wilderness as a distinct resource were leading the planning effort, there was a sincere effort to translate the spirit and letter of the Wilderness Act into direction for a particular area. The challenge managers face today is in creating the mental and administrative distinctiveness needed to comply with the spirit and letter of the Wilderness Act while at the same time integrating the wilderness program into broader agency systems. Facing this practical challenge and opportunity will require consciously maximizing the positive aspects of the boundaries created by both the "wilderness similar" and "wilderness separate" approaches while minimizing the negative effects of these boundaries.

Conclusions: Toward a Landscape View of Natural Areas

Boundaries, whether congressional, administrative, or managerial, have significant positive and negative effects on the ecological and social values of protected areas. Managers of protected areas face the difficult challenge of maintaining boundaries, or certain aspects of boundaries, that protect and sustain these areas, while working to erase or diminish the negative effects of these same boundaries. Facing this challenge will require many different qualities in the people charged with managing and protecting natural areas. One of the more important of these qualities will be the capacity to understand why wildness is unique and the benefits our society derives from natural areas and then why and how this uniqueness resides within an ecological, social, and managerial context. Such an understanding comes from both an intellectual grasp of these issues and the feeling for an area that develops only by spending much time on the land.

Many of the impacts from administrative boundaries discussed in this chapter are attributable to the inadequacies of traditional land management planning that allow incompatible and conflicting uses of adjacent lands that in turn sever beneficial flows and enhance detrimental flows into natural areas. One reason for these incompatible uses is that agencies with adjacent lands have differing policies toward their natural areas, for example regarding fire or recreation. Another reason is that management plans within an agency typically divide the land into a patchwork of discrete areas, each reflecting a land use or commodity product to be emphasized, such as developed recreation or timber harvest. In this traditional view, wilderness, for example, is just another land allocation and not the "enduring resource" envisioned by the Wilderness Act, nor is it the core of relatively unaltered land and wildness within a landscape dominated by people. Although the traditional approach describes the goals and activities for each piece of ground, it ignores how one land use relates to adjacent ones and how flows across administrative boundaries may be necessary to sustain an area and the values associated with it. Traditional planning approaches often fail to consider each piece of ground within a larger land mosaic and the contributions, both negative and positive, that each piece of land brings to every other piece.

One potential solution to these boundary-related problems would be to adjust the spatial and temporal scale of planning and analysis to fit the particular issue. Recreation settings, for example, may require a spatial scale of one to five square kilometers and a temporal scale of a few years. Fire or highly mobile wildlife, on the other hand, may require a spatial scale of ten to hundreds of square kilometers and a temporal scale of a hundred or more years.

Protected natural areas, such as wilderness, should influence how adjacent lands are managed, just as adjacent land uses influence the kind of management possible in any protected area. The Forest Service policy manual for wilderness management, for example, states that "Because wilderness does not exist in a vacuum, consider activities on both sides of wilderness boundaries during planning and articulate management goals and the blending of diverse resources in forest plans" (USDA Forest Service 1990b). This direction clearly directs Forest Service managers to consider wilderness as an area that affects and is affected by adjacent lands.

Stewardship across boundaries must include consideration for how wilderness and other natural areas are not only a place apart from our usual lives in a highly altered world, but also a part of a continuum from wild to human-dominated landscapes, providing unique social and ecological benefits. Wilderness and all areas protected for their natural values are a special and integral part of the landscape.

ACKNOWLEDGMENTS

We are indebted to the many dedicated people within agencies and other organizations who work everyday to protect our natural and wild landscapes. Review comments on a draft of this chapter from Greg Aplet, Tim Hogan, and Madeline Mazurski are greatly appreciated.

REFERENCES

Allin, C.W. 1990. Agency values and wilderness management. Pages 189–205 in Outdoor recreation policy: pleasure and preservation (J.D. Hutcheson, Jr., F.P. Noe, and R.E. Snow, editors). Greenwood Press, New York.

Alonso, A., E.E. Starkey, and D.E. Hansen. 1995. Wildlife diseases in national park ecosystems. *Wildlife Society Bulletin* 23:415–419.

Bengston, D.N. 1994. Changing forest values and ecosystem management. *Society and Natural Resources* 7:515–533.

Buechner, M. 1987. Conservation in insular parks: simulation models of factors affecting the movement of animals across park boundaries. *Biological Conservation* 41:57–76.

Buechner, M., C. Schonewald-Cox, R. Sauvajot, and B.A. Wilcox. 1992. Cross-boundary issues for national parks: what works "on the ground." *Environmental Management* 16:799–809.

Cole, D.N. 1996. *Wilderness recreation use trends, 1965 through 1994.* USDA Forest Service Research Paper INT-RP-488, Intermountain Research Station, Ogden, UT.

Cole D.N., and P.B. Landres. 1996. Threats to wilderness ecosystems: impacts and research needs. *Ecological Applications* 6:168–184.

Diamond, J.M., and R.M. May. 1976. Island biogeography and the design of natural reserves. Pages 163–186 in *Theoretical ecology: principles and applications* (R.M. May, editor). W.B. Saunders, Philadelphia.

Fahrig, L., and G. Merriam. 1994. Conservation of fragmented populations. *Conservation Biology* 8:50–59.

Forbes, G.J., and J.B. Theberge. 1996. Cross-boundary management of Algonquin Park wolves. *Conservation Biology* 10:1091–1097.

Forman, R.T.T., and M. Godron. 1981. Patches and structural components for a landscape ecology. *BioScience* 31:733–740.

Freemuth, J.C. 1991. *Islands under siege: national parks and the politics of external threats.* University of Kansas Press, Lawrence.

Hales, D. 1989. Changing concepts of national parks. Pages 139–144 in *Conservation for the twenty-first century* (D. Western and M. Pearl, editors). Oxford University Press, New York.

Harris, L.D., and G. Silva-Lopez. 1992. Forest fragmentation and the conservation of biological diversity. Pages 197–237 in *Conservation biology: the theory and practice of nature conservation, preservation, and management* (P.L. Fiedler and S.K. Jain, editors). Chapman and Hall, New York.

Hendee, J.C., G.H. Stankey, and R.C. Lucas. 1990. *Wilderness management,* 2nd edition. North American Press, Golden, CO.

Henry, W. 1996. Status and prospects for wilderness in the US National Park Service. *International Journal of Wilderness* 2:19.

Husari, S.J. 1995. Fire management in small wilderness areas and parks. Pages 117–120 in *Proceedings: symposium on fire in wilderness and park management* (J.K. Brown, R.W. Mutch, C.W. Spoon, and R.H. Wakimoto, technical coordinators). USDA Forest Service General Technical Report INT-GTR-320, Intermountain Research Station, Ogden, UT.

Janzen, D.H. 1986. The eternal external threat. Pages 286–303 in *Conservation biology: the science of scarcity and diversity* (M.E. Soulé, editor). Sinauer, Sunderland, MA.

Jerome, P. 1996. Status and prospects for wilderness in the US National Wildlife Refuge System. *International Journal of Wilderness* 2:22.

Johnson, R.R., and S.W. Carothers. 1987. External threats: the dilemma of resource management on the Colorado River in Grand Canyon National Park, USA. *Environmental Management* 11:99–107.

Kelson, A.R., and R.J. Lilieholm. 1997. The influence of adjacent land activities on wilderness resources. *International Journal of Wilderness* 3:25–28.

Kennedy, R. 1996. Managing wilderness in perpetuity and in democracy. *International Journal of Wilderness* 2:6–9.

Kushlan, J.A. 1987. External threats and internal management: the hydrologic regulation of the Everglades, Florida, USA. *Environmental Management* 11:109–119.

Leopold, A.S., S.A. Cain, C.M. Cottam, J.N. Gabrielson, and T.L. Kimball. 1963. Wildlife management in the national parks. *American Forests* 69:32–35, 61–63.

Little, R.L., and C. Schonewald-Cox. 1990. Fire management policy and boundary effects on parks: Lassen Volcanic National Park: case study. Pages 249–256 in *Examples of resource inventory and monitoring in National Parks of California, proceedings of the third biennial conference on research in California's national parks* (C. van Ripper, T.J. Stohlgren, S.D. Veirs, and S.C. Hillyer, editors). USDI National Park Service, Washington, DC.

Loope, L.L. 1992. An overview of problems with introduced plant species in national parks and biosphere reserves of the United States. Pages 3–28 in *Alien plant invasions in native ecosystems of Hawaii: management and research* (C.P. Stone, C.W. Smith, and J.T. Tunison, editors). University of Hawaii Cooperative National Park Resources Study Unit, Honolulu.

MacDonald, I.A.W., L.L. Loope, M.B. Usher, and O. Hamann. 1989. Wildlife conservation and the invasion of nature reserves by introduced species: a global perspective. Pages 215–256 in *Biological invasions: a global perspective, Scope 37* (J.A. Drake, H.A. Mooney, F. di Castri, R.H. Groves, F.J. Kruger, M. Rejmanek, and M. Williamson, editors). John Wiley and Sons, Chichester, England.

Machlis, G.E., and D.L. Tichnell. 1987. Economic development and threats to national parks: a preliminary analysis. *Environmental Conservation* 14:151–156.

McDonald, B.L., and M.B. Brown. 1995. The redefinition of natural resources and changing social values. Pages 256–260 in *Proceedings of the fourth international outdoor recreation and tourism symposium and the 1995 national recreation resource planning conference* (J.L. Thompson, D.W. Lime, B. Gartner, and W.M. Sames, compilers). University of Minnesota Press, St. Paul.

McKelvey, K.S., C.N. Skinner, C. Chang, D.C. Erman, S.J. Husari, D.J. Parson, J.W. van Wagtendonk, and C.P. Weatherspoon. 1996. An overview of fire in the Sierra Nevada. Pages 1033–1040 in *Sierra Nevada Ecosystem Project: final report to Congress*, Vol. II, *Assessments and scientific basis for management options*. Centers for Water and Wildland Resources, University of California, Davis.

Merigliano, L., and T. Kovalicky. 1993. Toward an enduring wilderness resource: a stewardship primer. *Journal of Forestry* 91:16–17.

Newmark, W.D. 1985. Legal and biotic boundaries of western North American national parks: a problem of congruence. *Biological Conservation* 33:197–208.

Noon, B.R., and K.S. McKelvey. 1996. Management of the spotted owl: a case history in conservation biology. *Annual Review of Ecology and Systematics* 27:135–162.

Peine, J., J. Burde, and W. Hammitt. 1988. Threats to the National Wilderness Preservation System. Pages 21–29 in *Wilderness benchmark 1988: Proceedings of the national wilderness colloquium* (H.R. Freilich, compiler). USDA Forest Service General Technical Report SE-51, Southeastern Forest Experiment Station, Asheville, NC.

Ridenour, J.M. 1990. The directors report: working with our neighbors. *Courier* 35:1.

Roth, D.M. 1995. *The wilderness movement and the national forests*. Intaglio Press, College Station, TX.

Saunders, D.A., R.J. Hobbs, and C.R. Margules. 1991. Biological consequences of ecosystem fragmentation: a review. *Conservation Biology* 5:18–32.

Schonewald-Cox, C.M., and J.W. Bayless. 1986. The boundary model: a geographical analysis of design and conservation of nature reserves. *Biological Conservation* 38:305–322.

Schonewald-Cox, C.M., M. Buechner, R. Sauvajot, and B.A. Wilcox. 1992. Cross-boundary management between national parks and surrounding lands: a review and discussion. *Environmental Management* 16:273–282.

Shafer, C. 1994. Beyond park boundaries. Pages 201–223 in *Landscape Planning and ecological networks* (E.A. Cook and H.N. Vanlier, editors). Elsevier Science Publishers, England.

Stebbins, R.C., and N.W. Cohen. 1995. *A natural history of amphibians*. Princeton University Press, Princeton.

Stottlemyer, R. 1987. Evaluation of anthropogenic atmospheric inputs on U.S. national park ecosystems. *Environmental Management* 11:91–97.

Theberge, J.B. 1989. Guidelines to drawing ecologically sound boundaries for national parks and nature reserves. *Environmental Management* 13:695–702.

Thompson, B.H. 1935. National parks and wilderness use. Pages 47–35 in *Fauna of the National Parks in the United States: wildlife management in the National Parks* (G.M. Wright and B.H. Thompson, editors). USDI National Park Service, Fauna Series No. 2. U.S. Government Printing Office, Washington, DC.

USDA Forest Service. 1986. *The 1986 recreation opportunity spectrum book.* USDA Forest Service, Washington, DC.

USDA Forest Service. 1990a. *Forest Service Manual 2300—Recreation, wilderness, and related resource management,* Washington Office Amendment 2300-90-2, Chapter 2320—Wilderness Management, Section 2323.11. USDA Forest Service, Washington, DC.

USDA Forest Service. 1990b. *Forest Service Manual 2300—Recreation, wilderness, and related resource management,* Washington Office Amendment 2300-90-2, Chapter 2320—Wilderness Management, Section 2320.3. USDA Forest Service, Washington, DC.

Usher, M.B. 1988. Biological invasions of nature reserves: a search for generalizations. *Biological Conservation* 44:119–135.

van Wagtendonk, J.W. 1995. Large fires in wilderness areas. Pages 113–116 in *Proceedings: symposium on fire in wilderness and park management* (J.K. Brown, R.W. Mutch, C.W. Spoon, and R.H. Wakimoto, technical coordinators). USDA Forest Service General Technical Report INT-GTR-320, Intermountain Research Station, Ogden, UT.

Wilcove, D.S., and R.M. May. 1986. National park boundaries and ecological realities. *Nature* 324:206–207.

Wright, G.M., and B.H. Thompson. 1935. *Fauna of the National Parks of the United States: wildlife management in the National Parks.* USDI National Park Service, Fauna Series No. 2. U.S. Government Printing Office, Washington, DC.

Wright, G.M., J.S. Dixon, and B.H. Thompson. 1933. *Fauna of the National Parks of the United States: a preliminary survey of faunal relations in National Parks.* USDI National Park Service, Fauna Series No. 1. U.S. Government Printing Office, Washington, DC.

C h a p t e r   6

Outdoor Recreation and Boundaries: Opportunities and Challenges

Clinton K. Miller and Mark D. Gershman

The popularity of outdoor recreation has increased dramatically since the 1950s (Flather and Cordell 1995). Because outdoor recreation can alter natural and cultural resources (Knight and Gutzwiller 1995), land management agencies, which have traditionally concentrated on the management of fish, wildlife, timber, soil, and water, have begun to emphasize managing for the coexistence of outdoor recreation with healthy ecosystems (Clark and Stankey 1979, Freimund et al. 1996, Johnson and Vande Kamp 1996, Manning et al. 1996b). This shift in focus has had both positive and negative effects on recreationists' experiences. Increased outdoor recreation has resulted in more attention by land and resource managers to the impacts of recreation and to providing a positive recreational experience (Wagar 1964, Chavez 1995, Manning et al. 1996a). The effectiveness of management initiatives focusing on these issues often is affected both positively and negatively by administrative boundaries.

In this chapter we provide examples of how boundaries are used to benefit natural resources, such as when they are used to protect cliff nesting raptors (Richardson and Miller 1997). We provide examples of how boundaries may be used for separating different types of recreationists seeking different outdoor experiences, such as off-road vehicle (ORV) users and individuals seeking wilderness solitude. We also explore how administrative boundaries affect the recreational experience and describe situations where boundaries are ineffective and become a barrier to recreation. Finally, we provide recommendations on how to overcome the cross-boundary issues that negatively affect the recreational experience.

Effects of Administrative Boundaries on Outdoor Recreation

Administrative boundary and recreation interactions are determined to a large degree by two factors: (1) the nature of the boundary (that is, internal, multiagency, or between public and private lands), and (2) the management goals on each side of the boundary. Failure to consider the effects of land management practices across boundaries, whether it be a property line or the limits of an agency's jurisdiction, can result in impacts to resources and can degrade a visitor's experience. Boundaries also can significantly affect the experience of outdoor recreationists. For example, if recreationists have negative experiences because of differing management on either side of a boundary, they may be unwilling to continue spending time and money recreating in that area.

The impacts of recreation on natural resources have been well documented (for summary see Knight and Gutzwiller 1995). The effects range from hunters overharvesting sensitive wildlife populations to exotic plant species that become established along trails that bisect native plant communities. Impacts of this sort can be exacerbated by problems associated with administrative boundaries. For example, public trails that dead-end at private property usually result in development of a trail system on adjacent property. These new trails are typically unwanted, unmaintained, and the source of conflict between neighbors.

Where resource managers fail to address visitors' expectations, they run the risk of creating resource problems elsewhere, often on neighboring property. Consider a public fishing area that is heavily used, but not well maintained. Discouraged by the condition of the public facility, some users may seek out other areas, potentially damaging sensitive wetlands or nearby shorelines. If the area of public ownership is small, users may trespass onto adjacent private land in an attempt to find room. This not only creates the potential for resource damage, but also threatens the agency's relationships with its neighbors.

Restrictions placed on recreationists on one side of a boundary may have effects on other agencies, neighboring landowners, or the local economy. For example, a rock climber who has traveled a long distance to a specific destination may be frustrated by a seasonal closure designed to protect cliff-nesting raptors. Inadequate educational signs or a lack of directions to other climbing sites may exacerbate the climber's dissatisfaction. Climbers may ignore such boundaries, may shift their use to private lands, or may visit another publicly owned property without such restrictions or where the chances of being found (and fined) are less. Dissatisfaction with an overly regulatory approach to resource management may result in less support for other, unrelated management objectives of a particular agency or for the agency itself.

An increasing trend among recreational users of public lands is backcountry travel (Flather and Cordell 1995). Many visitors to public lands place a value on being able to find a remote location where they will not be disturbed by other users. Some agencies that manage wilderness or backcountry areas near large urban centers limit the number of hikers or campers allowed in an area through a permit system or other means. The regulations protect the solitude of the visitor and may mitigate environmental impacts. Backpackers who disregard the permit system or designated boundaries by accessing remote areas through adjacent and unregulated lands threaten the very solitude they and others seek.

As the visitor experience or natural resource degrades, visitors may lose motivation to return. If a sensitive population of game animals is overharvested, it may cause increased access (legal or illegal) on adjacent property where healthy populations still exist. Finally, if the resource is ultimately degraded beyond the point where visitors are no longer attracted to the area, there may be financial impacts on the local economy. This also could influence the political support and revenues of the agency responsible for management of the recreational resource (e.g., hunting and fishing revenues).

Boundaries As a Tool for Recreation and Resource Protection

As illustrated in other chapters in this book, boundaries can take numerous forms. They can be internal boundaries (such as designated wilderness areas or sensitive resource closures), multiagency boundaries (such as those between different public agencies) or between public and private land. The role different boundaries play in recreation management is as important for improving a recreationist's experience as it is for protecting the natural and cultural resources.

Separation of Recreational Activities

Boundaries can provide an effective means to accommodate different recreational uses and satisfy demand for a variety of outdoor recreational experiences. Land management agencies typically try to accommodate a variety of recreational uses by separating recreational activities both spatially and temporally. Because some recreational uses are viewed as incompatible (such as snowmobilers and cross-country skiers), separating perceived conflicting uses can alleviate potential user conflicts. For example, mountain bikes and hikers are sometimes incompatible on certain trails (Chavez 1996). These two activities can be spatially separated by designating sections of a park or forest as hiking only and another area or trail type as hiking and biking compatible. Because multiple-use trails can be controversial (Zaslowsky 1995), identification of designated areas or zones for various recreational activities can help reduce visitor conflicts and enhance recreationists' experiences.

Protection of Natural and Cultural Resources

Boundaries can be as effective at separating recreation from natural or cultural resources as at separating different recreational uses. Temporary or permanent closures (with designated spatial boundaries) can be useful in protecting sensitive natural or cultural resources from vandalism or disturbance. For example, for more than seven years the city of Boulder, Colorado, has used seasonal closures to protect cliff-nesting raptors (Richardson and Miller 1997).

Wilderness or natural area designation has helped protect areas from negative impacts of recreation and resource extraction. At the same time, the more restrictive regulations characteristic of these areas may positively or negatively affect a recreationist's experience (Johnson and Vande Kamp 1996). Friedland et al. (1973) found that restrictions are more likely to be followed if compliance is seen as benefiting the visitor rather than the agency alone.

Boundaries also may separate land used to buffer and protect core areas of high natural or cultural resource value. For example, land that allows unrestricted recreational activities could be buffered by increasingly restrictive zones to protect a core area with limited recreational activities.

Improving Recreation Management

Boundaries can be used to improve visitor management by providing users areas where the predictability of their recreational experience remains somewhat certain. Recreationists have certain expectations of services depending on where they are on public land. In the "front country," for example, a visitor would expect a more routine presence of uniformed law enforcement and interpretive personnel than in designated backcountry or wilderness areas (Johnson and Vande Kamp 1996). Establishing and communicating the boundaries of such zones increases predictability for users and improves their level of satisfaction. Such boundaries also can provide the public with a variety of visitor experiences (e.g., campgrounds, backcountry wilderness backpacking).

When Are Boundaries Ineffective

Boundaries become ineffective when they interfere with the ability of landowners or managers on either side to meet their land management goals. Poor cooperation between adjacent landowners and managers can cause unsatisfactory visitor experiences and adverse impacts of recreationists on natural resources. This section characterizes the major factors facing those who manage outdoor recreation across administrative boundaries. We provide examples from a variety of different types of boundaries, resource management goals, and recreational uses.

Recreationists' Attitudes

Pleasure and enjoyment are fundamental to a person's experience in the outdoors and can be affected by boundaries (Ellis and Rademacher 1989). The amount of pleasure derived from a visit shapes users' desire to return, their commitment to protect natural resources, and their attitudes about a land management agency (Manfredo et al. 1995). Expectations are pivotal in determining how pleasurable a recreational experience will be. A negative experience may lead to detrimental impacts on natural resources or have negative impacts on local economies. For example, snowmobilers restricted or banned from Yellowstone National Park may abandon the Yellowstone area or may shift their use to adjacent areas (Keiter and Boyce 1991). If they quit using the region, an essential component of the tourism-based economy would disappear. If use is shifted to adjacent lands, the land managers who receive this increase or new use may find themselves facing a management nightmare. Such a situation would cause negative relations between neighbors if the agency receiving the increase was not involved in the decision to cease or modify recreational use on adjacent land.

Access to Recreation

Access to recreational opportunities is especially important because it may be difficult or expensive to find desirable areas for recreation. Convenience and affordability enhance a user's experience as they do with any other commodity. When access to a destination is complicated by restrictions or high costs, a recreationist is less likely to have a positive experience (Bialeschki and Henderson 1988). For example, mountain bikers may wish to access trails in the southern portion of the City of Boulder Open Space near Boulder, Colorado. The most direct access is via unpaved trails that connect with paved bike paths within the city. However, the central portion of the Open Space area specifically prohibits bikes to avoid conflicts with hikers on popular, high-use trails. Cyclists' only available alternative to reach the trails open to bikes is via on-street bike paths or a busy highway. Mountain bikers may not want to risk on-street alternatives to reach their destination or may choose to drive to the trailhead. In this case, an administrative boundary compromises the convenience of the biker for the quality of other trail users' experiences. The result is a less-than-satisfactory outdoor experience and diminished enjoyment or illegal (trail) use by bicyclists.

Surrounding Land Use

Surrounding land use can affect qualities of remoteness and "appropriateness" sought by outdoor recreationists (Freimund et al. 1996). For example, controversy surrounded the recent proposal to establish a gold mine near Yellowstone National Park (Barker 1996). Some of the debate centered around the ecological implications of the proposed mine, but there was significant concern about the visual impact of the mine. Even if it were to be located far from the areas typically traveled by visitors, imagine the visual impact of the open pit or processing facilities of a city-sized mine! Boundaries of management units often are treated differently to screen human-caused disturbances from view. For example, land management agencies typically maintain vegetative buffer strips between extractive uses and travel corridors or high-use areas. In some places, the Federal Aviation Administration, the National Park Service, and USDA Forest Service have worked together to ensure that flight paths for commercial air traffic avoid passing over national parks and wilderness areas. These "boundaries in the sky" were established in response to the public's expectation that outdoor recreation experiences should not be disturbed by the noise or sight of aircraft.

Resource management agencies can coordinate activities along their boundaries through the use of spatial or temporal boundaries separating incompatible uses to enhance a recreationist's experience. For example, backcountry anglers may appreciate the opportunity to fish where only artificial flies and lures are allowed. An angler looking for a challenging "natural" fishing experience would not be satisfied with an area where hatchery fish could be caught with bait. Therefore, separate sections of river could be managed differently and the management changes communicated to anglers with signs. Such administrative boundaries could help accommodate the needs of different users.

Rules and Regulations

The consistency of rules and regulations across boundaries also affects a user's experience. The amount of enforcement may differ across boundaries and can be difficult for the visitor to ascertain. A visitor may wonder, for example, whether there is active enforcement of rules and regulations. This knowledge is important for people who seek the comfort of a routinely patrolled campground or trail. The more complicated and inconsistent regulations are across boundaries, the less compliance a recreationist is likely to demonstrate. Regulations that appear arbitrary or those that are not clearly communicated are more likely to be ignored and generally reduce the satisfaction of the visitor. Unless warned to the contrary, visitors expect consistent aesthetics, access, allowable uses, regulations, law enforcement, and emergency response on public lands even as they cross administrative boundaries. For example, along the eastern Front Range of Colorado, numerous raptors take advantage of the plentiful cliffs and rock faces for nesting. To protect these nesting areas land managers seasonally close areas to rock climbing. Climbers can expect consistent treatment for all climbing sites each year. Therefore, land managers have an increased likelihood of climbers respecting and adhering to the boundaries (both spatial and temporal) of such closures. Inconsistent enforcement and application of variable closures across agencies or from year to year would confuse visitors and lead to disruption of the birds' nesting.

Recreationist Satisfaction in a Variety of Boundaries

How do predictability, access, safety, remoteness, appropriateness, and consistency affect recreationists' satisfaction? The answer varies according to the type of boundary. We explore two categories of boundaries commonly encountered by outdoor recreationists: (1) boundaries between two types of public land, including those within a system managed by a single public land management agency (e.g., wilderness areas within a national forest), and boundaries between public lands managed by different agencies (e.g., national parks and national forests); and (2) boundaries between public and private land.

Public Land Boundaries

As most visitors to public lands in the United States do not distinguish among the various parts (i.e., wilderness versus multiple use) of each park or forest, there is a similar monolithic view of public land agencies. Parks, forests, and other types of management areas often are divided into zones defined by specific management goals. These zones may be established to protect sensitive or interesting resources (e.g., wilderness areas, research natural areas), be used for commodity production (e.g., silviculture, agriculture, mining), or provide developed facilities for recreational use (e.g., campgrounds, marinas). A visitor to public lands in the United States, for example, would face a wide variety of land management goals among agencies that manage the majority of America's public lands. Different agencies (National Park Service, Fish and Wildlife Service, Forest Service, Bureau of Land Management) emphasize resource protection, commodity production, and recreational use to varying degrees. This multitude of different boundary types may confuse recreationists and contribute to a dissatisfactory outdoor experience.

Sensitive Resource Protection

Special designations for the protection of sensitive resources often are unanticipated by recreationists. Most visitors to public lands are generally unaware that the forest that looks so uniformly green in the road atlas is really a mosaic managed to meet a variety of goals, only one of which may be recreation.

Areas set aside for sensitive resource protection are usually more heavily regulated than adjacent areas. Some public land management agencies have established areas where access is prohibited or restricted, such as sensitive archaeological sites. Recreationists may feel that their experiences are degraded by such special restrictions (Johnson and Vande

Kamp 1996). For example, in arid climes, closing off a riparian area to hikers may take away the most interesting areas for nature observation. Big-game hunters may be disappointed if they are not able to retrieve downed game using an off-road vehicle in a wilderness area. However, hikers desiring solitude may seek out a designated wilderness in a national forest, never anticipating that their experience could be legally interrupted by the gunshots of hunters.

Commodity Production

Outdoor recreationists are sometimes surprised to learn that commodity production is a legitimate use of public lands. Aesthetic contrasts between areas managed for commodity production and areas managed for their natural beauty often are dramatic. Examples of visually obtrusive land uses that take place on public lands include open pit mines in the deserts of the southwestern United States, overstocked pastures in native grasslands, and clearcuts in forested landscapes.

It is difficult to ensure public safety around agriculture, mining, and forestry activities. Heavy equipment and dangerous situations are commonplace. Increasing attention to legal exposure has prompted many land management agencies to restrict public access in areas of commodity extraction.

Areas Developed for Recreation

The boundaries around developed recreation areas, such as campgrounds, beaches, and boat landings, usually focus on human activity. Like sensitive resource zones, recreation areas also have special rules and regulations to minimize social conflicts and public safety hazards (e.g., quiet times in campgrounds or no-wake areas in marinas). Although enforcement of the rules can be a problem, most visitors understand the need to maintain order and safety. Visitors often anticipate certain rules to be in place to provide them with the predictability, consistency, and safety they expect on public land managed for recreation.

Boundaries Between Public and Private Land

Public lands, although they may dominate the landscape in some areas, exist within a context of private property. Undeveloped and well-

managed private land contributes significantly to the aesthetic and biological values of adjacent public lands and therefore to the satisfaction of
outdoor recreationists. Scenic vistas in parks and forests often include
nearby private property—much of which looks just like the public land.
However, developed private land adjacent to public lands may not be
compatible with a recreationist's expectations. For example, a hiker in a
national park may be disappointed to find housing developments visible
from the trail.

Recreationists frequently encounter restricted access or no access to
adjacent private land (Brown et al. 1984). Although access may be
restricted in a number of ways, the most common is for landowners to
prohibit access to their property or require an access fee. These charges
often are high and reduce the likelihood that people will use these areas
(Kaiser and Wright 1985). Hunters may be disappointed at being
required to obtain permission or pay a fee to retrieve downed game on
private land. Hiking trails that begin on public property and then dead-
end at a private land boundary are a source of frustration for hikers and
private landowners alike.

A Framework for Solving Boundary Problems in Recreation

The challenges associated with solving recreation and boundary conflicts
are not insurmountable. Schonewald-Cox et al. (1992) and Buechner et
al. (1992) provide useful suggestions and tools for resolving general cross-
boundary problems. Here we provide a simple problem-solving process
for recreation and boundary conflicts that includes: (1) anticipating
problems; (2) identifying conflicts when they do occur; (3) establishing
and maintaining communication with other land owners, land managers,
and stakeholders; (4) developing workable solutions; and (5) implementing and evaluating changes. The following framework provides
guidance for anticipating, identifying, and resolving cross-border conflicts for outdoor recreation.

Anticipate Conflicts

This chapter summarizes the characteristics of recreationist-boundary
issues. In most cases land and resource managers will be aware of existing
problems. However, managers can be vigilant about conflicts that may
arise when property is acquired or when there are proposed changes to

land uses adjacent to a management area. Managers can work to establish and maintain open lines of communication with neighboring landowners or management agencies to increase coordination on recreation projects related to the shared boundary.

Identify the Problem

The initial step toward resolving the cross-boundary recreational issues is to identify the conflict. Problems may be the result of the negative impacts of recreation on natural resources or recreationists' satisfaction level. In either case, the issues need to be clearly stated. This may require site-specific monitoring and research to determine causal relationships (if any) and explain the role boundaries play. Visitor-use surveys (Zeller et al. 1993) or research on recreationists' attitudes and behavior are valuable tools for delineating problem areas. Vase et al. (1995) provides an excellent review of methodology for identifying potential problems, particularly for recreationists' reactions to boundaries. A thorough summary of the problems and potential conflicts assists with the next step, identifying stakeholders.

Identify the Stakeholders

It is important to identify all parties involved in a cross-boundary conflict. This includes not only the property owners and land managers, but also the users who may have an interest in the specific problem. Each stakeholder needs to be informed of the relevant issues. This step is especially important because stakeholders may not be aware of the conflict or may not recognize the cross-boundary issue as a problem. It is critical that each stakeholder understand his or her role in resolving the conflict. Because of local attachment and investment by neighbors and constituents, community-based partnerships can be a powerful way to ensure success (Buechner et al. 1992, Selin 1995).

Identify Management Goals

The group of stakeholders, which may include agencies, landowners, private citizens, or special-interest groups, needs to identify the management goals for the particular cross-boundary recreation issue. For example, a management goal for a recreational planner or trail user might be to provide a positive recreational experience. Other members of the group would set standards for natural resource protection, commodity production, and other issues relevant to the specific topic. The role of the administrative boundary in helping or hindering these goals should be clearly identified. Can aesthetic conditions be improved? Can access easements be negotiated? Can rules and regulations be made more consistent across boundaries? Prior to implementation of solutions, a mechanism for monitoring the success or failure of changes needs to be agreed upon by the stakeholders. Management goals should be measurable and include recommendations to determine whether the goal has been met.

Develop a Matrix of Potential Solutions

After the management goals and implementation techniques have been developed, a matrix can be used to select the package of techniques that offers the greatest likelihood of success. The matrix should include the management goals along one axis and the implementation techniques along the other. The implementation of any recommended strategy needs to be evaluated in the context of the appropriate constraints (e.g., legal, biological, financial). Written agreements, such as memorandums of understanding, are good tools for documenting cooperative management strategies (Tilghman and Murray 1995).

Implementation and Evaluation

Monitoring can be accomplished by site-specific natural resource studies or review of recreationists' attitudes after a specified period. A designated review period and individuals responsible for evaluation should accompany any implementation strategy to appraise the strategy's success (Tilghman and Murray 1995).

Cross-Boundary Conflict Resolution: A Case Study

During the development of the City of Boulder Open Space Department's Long Range Management Policies (LRMP), a section addressing the management of dogs was removed because of public opposition to increasing restrictions for dogs on Open Space lands. Other concerns were expressed by the Boulder Mountain Parks (MP) staff who manage adjacent city-owned land. The LRMP proposed that regulations be changed from voice and sight control of dogs to require that all dogs be leashed. The desire for a leash regulation on the Open Space property was born out of a concern for quality visitor experience, potential environmental impacts of large accumulations of dog waste along trail margins, and the disruption of wildlife by dogs. The MP staff did not view the off-leash policy as inconsistent with the management goals of the Mountain Parks that emphasized recreational use. However, they feared that changes in regulations on Open Space would result in drastically increased use of the adjacent MP by dog owners, who preferred not to leash their dogs, which could diminish enjoyment of visitors on already crowded trails.

Soon after language relating to dog control was removed from the polices, the LRMP were approved by the city council and a committee was established to develop dog management recommendations. The Dog Roundtable was composed of several citizen interest groups (dog advocates and environmentalists), as well as representatives from the land management agencies (Open Space and MP).

The first task was the identification of problems with the proposed policies, existing regulations, and the potential impacts of the new regulations. Issues included vague language and inconsistent standards for the existing regulations, degraded visitor experience and user conflicts from too many dogs, dog waste along trails, and potential harmful impacts to wildlife and the environment. The cross-boundary issues identified included indistinguishable borders, different management goals and positions regarding dog management and their potential impacts to visitors and the environment, and lack of coordinated visitor and natural resource management goals between Open Space and MP.

The management goals for each agency and the citizen interest groups were identified and summarized as follows: (1) provide a rewarding visitor experience to those with and without dogs, and (2) provide adequate environmental protection of the ecological resources. Extensive meetings and input from all the stakeholders led to the development of a matrix of potential solutions (Table 6.1). This matrix also included legal and practical constraints such as enforceability of regulations by ranger staff. Through an extended public process, the solutions and constraints were presented to the public and the Dog Roundtable developed compromise solutions. No party got all of what they wanted. For example, the Open Space land system has four separate dog regulations depending on what part of the system a user visits (on leash, voice and sight, voice and sight on trail, and no dogs). Educational information was developed and public seminars were used to help reduce visitor conflict and enhance environmental protection. In addition, a two-year monitoring and evaluation period with specific measurable goals was agreed on.

Table 6.1. Problem-solving matrix developed for the dog management case study, highlighting proposed solutions and their relationship to visitor and environmental protection goals

Proposed Solutions	MANAGEMENT GOALS		
	Visitor Experience	Environmental Protection	Conditions and Constraints
Dogs under voice and sight control (current OS and MP regulations with several minor exceptions)	Uncontrollable conflicts with others' dogs Unsatisfactory recreational experience for non–dog owners	Allows off-trail travel by dogs with increased impacts to wildlife and increased dispersal of weeds and feces	Difficult to enforce with consistency Inconsistent enforcement by property owners
Dogs on leash	Decreased pleasure for dog owners and dogs Increased pleasure for non–dog owners	Restricts dogs to immediate vicinity of trail Minimizes disturbance to wildlife Allows owners to find and remove feces more easily	Enforcement is difficult because of the high ratio of visitors to enforcement staff Consistent with other regional Open Space programs
Combination of policies: Leash Voice and sight (on and off trail) No dogs allowed	Provides opportunities for those who want to have dogs unrestricted to do so Gives opportunities for those not wanting contact with dogs to avoid dog areas	Recognition of potential impact a large number of dog visits can have on wildlife Opportunity to restrict dog activity and change specific designations depending on sensitivity of natural resource and management goals	Requires development of criteria for site designation depending on environmental sensitivity and visitor use Requires cooperation and communication between OS and MP regarding signs between property boundaries and dog management zones Requires education and enforcement with cross-training among agencies

Conclusions

In this chapter we reviewed how boundaries affect outdoor recreation. We showed how boundaries can be positively used to protect natural and cultural resources and how to use boundaries to enhance recreationists' outdoor experiences. We also explored situations when boundaries become ineffective and how different types of boundaries (public–public and public–private) affect recreation. In addition, we provided a framework for solving recreation and boundary conflicts. In the case study example we demonstrated that cross-boundary conflicts are not insurmountable, even though they can be controversial and complicated.

There still is much to be learned about the use of boundaries in protecting natural and cultural resources from the negative impacts of recreation and how to use boundaries effectively to enhance recreationists' outdoor experiences. It is imperative that research into the impacts of recreation on the environment continue, particularly on recreational trails and roads (Hackman 1990, Miller et al. in press). Knight and Gutzwiller (1995) provide excellent suggestions for additional research topics on impacts of recreation on the environment.

Another valuable contribution to overcoming cross-boundary recreation problems would be to build on research regarding recreationists' attitudes toward restrictions (Watson and Niccolucci 1995, Johnson and Vande Kamp 1996) and perceived constraints to outdoor recreation participation (Bialeschki and Henderson 1988, Jackson 1994). This kind of information could be useful to resource and recreation managers for identifying particular ways to reduce cross-boundary conflicts and enhance visitor enjoyment while protecting natural and cultural resources. Reviewing future recreational trends (Flather and Cordell 1995) could assist in predicting what potential recreation and boundary conflicts resource managers may encounter (Cordell et al. 1990).

Finally, resource and recreation managers need to continue to explore better ways of communicating with recreationists about resource and visitor management goals and the role boundaries play in protecting recreationist interests and sensitive natural and cultural resources. It will be critical to share this information with other resource managers and the public through publication, symposia, or other public means (see Manning et al. 1996a for additional suggestions). Schonewald-Cox et al. (1992) and Buechner et al. (1992) provide examples of tools for resolving cross-boundary conflicts such as personal contacts, developing a supportive local constituency, and sharing information. Bringing together a collection of case studies on boundary and recreation issues and synthesizing them to develop principals for use in solving cross-boundary management problems also would be useful for resource and recreation managers to avoid duplicating efforts.

ACKNOWLEDGMENTS

The authors would like to acknowledge the following individuals for their support during the development of this chapter: J. Gershman, N. Gershman, A. Guthrie, B. Miller, J. Miller, P. Miller, and B. Winter.

REFERENCES

Barker, R. 1996. Grassroots grit beat "the mine from Hell." *High Country News*, September 2, 1996.

Bialeschki, M.D., and K.A. Henderson. 1988. Constraints to trail use. *Journal of Park and Recreation Administration* 6:20–28.

Brown, T.L., D.J. Decker, and J.W. Kelley. 1984. Access to private lands for hunting in New York: 1963–1980. *Wildlife Society Bulletin* 12:344–349.

Buechner, M., C. Schonewald-Cox, R. Sauvajot, and B.A. Wilcox. 1992. Cross-boundary issues for national parks: what works "on the ground." *Environmental Management* 16:799–809.

Chavez, D.J., technical coordinator. 1995. *Proceedings of the second symposium on social aspects and recreation research.* USDA Forest Service, General Technical Report PAW-156. Pacific Southwest Research Station, Albany, CA.

Chavez, D.J. 1996. *Mountain biking: issues and actions for USDA Forest Service managers.* USDA Forest Service, Research Paper PSW-RP-226. Pacific Southwest Research Station, Albany, CA.

Clark, R.N., and G.H. Stankey. 1979. *The recreation opportunity spectrum: a framework for planning, management and research.* USDA Forest Service, General Technical Report PNW-98. Pacific Northwest Forest Experiment Station, Portland, OR.

Cordell, H.K., J.C. Bergstrom, L.A. Hartmann, and D.B.K. English. 1990. *An analysis of the outdoor recreation and wilderness situation in the United States: 1989–2040.* USDA Forest Service, General Technical Report RM-189. Rocky Mountain Forest and Range Experiment Station, Fort Collins, CO.

Ellis, G.D., and C. Rademacher. 1989. Making barriers manageable: a call for the use of paradigms in barriers research. Pages 455–466 in *Outdoor Recreation Benchmark 1988* (A.H. Watson, editor). USDA Forest Service, General Technical Report SE-GTR-52. Southeastern Forest Experiment Station, Asheville, NC.

Flather, C.H., and H.K. Cordell. 1995. Outdoor recreation: historical and anticipated trends. Pages 3–16 in *Wildlife and recreationists: coexistence through management and research* (R.L. Knight and K.J. Gutzwiller, editors). Island Press, Washington, DC.

Freimund, W.A., D.H. Anderson, and D.G. Pitt. 1996. Developing a recreation and aesthetic inventory framework for forest planning and management. *Natural Areas Journal* 16:108–117.

Friedland, N., J. Thibaut, and L. Walker. 1973. Some determinants of the violation of rules. *Journal of Applied Social Psychology* 3:103–118.

Hackman, S. 1990. Evidence of edge species attraction to nature trails within a deciduous forest. *Natural Areas Journal* 10:3–5.

Jackson, E.L. 1994. Constraints on participation in resource-based outdoor recreation. *Journal of Applied Recreation Research* 19:215–245.

Johnson, D.R., and M.E. Vande Kamp. 1996. Extent and control of resource damage due to noncompliant visitor behavior: a case study from the U.S. national parks. *Natural Areas Journal* 16:134–141.

Kaiser, R.A., and B.A. Wright. 1985. Recreational access to private land: beyond the liability hurdle. *Journal of Soil Water Conservation* 40:478–481.

Keiter, R.B., and M.S. Boyce. 1991. *The Greater Yellowstone Ecosystem: redefining America's wilderness heritage*. Yale University Press, New Haven.

Knight, R.L., and K.J. Gutzwiller, editors. 1995. *Wildlife and recreationists: coexistence through management and research*. Island Press, Washington, DC.

Manfredo, M.J., J.J. Vase, and D.J. Decker. 1995. Human dimensions of wildlife management: basic concepts. Pages 17–31 in *Wildlife and recreationists: coexistence through management and research* (R.L. Knight and K.J. Gutzwiller, editors). Island Press, Washington, DC.

Manning, R.E., N.L. Ballinger, J. Marion, and J. Roggenbuck. 1996a. Recreation management in natural areas: problems and practices, status and trends. *Natural Areas Journal* 16:142–146.

Manning, R.E., D.W. Lime, and M. Hof. 1996b. Social carrying capacity of natural areas: theory and application in the U.S. national parks. *Natural Areas Journal* 16:118–127.

Miller, S.G., R.L. Knight, and C.K. Miller. In press. Recreational trails and bird communities. *Ecological Applications*.

Richardson, C.T., and C.K. Miller. 1997. Recommendations for protecting raptors from human disturbance: a review. *Wildlife Society Bulletin* 25:634–638.

Schonewald-Cox, C., M. Buechner, R. Sauvajot, and B.A. Wilcox. 1992. Cross-boundary management between national parks and surrounding lands: a review and discussion. *Environmental Management* 16:273–282.

Selin, S. 1995. A content analysis of USDA Forest Service recreation partnerships. Pages 89–92 in *Proceedings of the second symposium on social aspects and recreation research*. USDA Forest Service, General Technical Report PAW-156. Pacific Southwest Research Station, Albany, CA.

Tilghman, B.N., and R. Murray. 1995. Seeking common ground: establishing interpark partnerships. Pages 93–97 in *Proceedings of the second symposium on social aspects and recreation research*. USDA Forest Service. General Technical Report PAW-156. Pacific Southwest Research Station, Albany, CA.

Vase, J.J., D.J. Decker, and J.J. Manfredo. 1995. Human dimensions of wildlife management: an integrated framework for coexistence. Pages 32–49 in *Wildlife and recreationists: coexistence through management and research* (R.L. Knight and K.J. Gutzwiller, editors). Island Press, Washington, DC.

Wagar, J.A. 1964. *The carrying capacity of wild lands for recreation*. USDA Forest Service Monograph 7, Society of American Foresters, Washington, DC.

Watson, A.E., and M.J. Niccolucci. 1995. Conflicting goals of wilderness management: natural conditions vs. natural experiences. Pages 11–15 in *Proceedings of the second symposium on social aspects and recreation research*. USDA Forest Service, General Technical Report PAW-156. Pacific Southwest Research Station, Albany, CA.

Zaslowsky, D. 1995. The battle of Boulder. *Wilderness* (Summer):25–33.

Zeller, M., H.C. Zinn, and M.J. Manfredo. 1993. *Boulder Open Space visitation study*. Report prepared for City of Boulder Open Space Real Estate Department, Boulder, CO.

Boundaries or Barriers: New Horizons for Conservation and Private Forests

William A. Wall

I have just returned from an opportunity to warm myself next to an oak campfire in front of a particular old wooden shed in Wisconsin. The building had its humble beginnings as a chicken coop, but later gained a footnote in history as Aldo Leopold's "Shack." This was my third visit to Leopold's Shack for the annual Conservation Network meeting. Our purpose at this meeting was to discuss crossing boundaries and removing barriers to conservation. I had the privilege of being presented Nina Leopold Bradley's personal copy of *A Sand County Almanac* (Leopold 1949). Many quotations had been marked in that copy, but the following quotation was typed on a separate sheet of paper:

> One of the anomalies of modern ecology is the creation of two groups, each of which seems barely aware of the existence of the other. The one studies the human community, almost as if it were a separate entity, and calls its findings sociology, economics and history. The other studies the plant and animal community and comfortably relegates the hodge-podge of politics to the liberal arts. The inevitable fusion of these two lines of thought will, perhaps, constitute the outstanding advance of the present century.

These were several lines from an unpublished note of Leopold's found on a piece of stationary from a hotel in Berlin, Germany. Leopold had a profound understanding of the enigmas associated with conservation in our modern society. In four sentences, he captured the heart of this chapter: that our greatest advances in resource conservation will occur by integrating societal and conservation goals.

The purposes of this chapter are to explore the organizational, individual, and information boundaries that have potential to create barriers and to describe two case studies that successfully bridged these barriers. The opinions and examples expressed in this chapter are based on my ten years of experience working as a wildlife biologist for private forest-product companies. My observations are not made from the perspective of a trained student in sociology, psychology, or history, but as a biologist who has recognized the dilemmas of integrating conservation and societal demands. I share the view expressed by Leopold when he stated that his primary interests were the relationship of humans to other humans and the relationship of humans to the land (Leopold 1949).

Organizational boundaries within society will always exist. Barriers, however, are built and perpetuated by a lack of understanding, short-term vision, or unwillingness of individuals to cross boundaries. A key to success is to treat recognizable boundaries as opportunities to solve issues, rather than as lines of demarcation. Even more significant is the need for practical application of processes that bridge these boundaries.

This chapter is developed in three parts. First, I present a brief historical perspective on the major stages affecting natural resource use and conservation in this century. It is important to keep a perspective of how we arrived at the numerous resource management debates today. This is not an explicit historical review, but a reminder of how the values, attitudes, and administrative cultures that create boundaries in natural resource management developed. Second, I describe and categorize organizational cultures, individual beliefs and values, and administrative boundaries that occur today in corporate, environmental, and regulatory organizations. And third, I describe two case studies of efforts designed to bridge boundaries. These efforts are expanding the horizons of forest commodity producers, environmentalists, and regulators and illustrate ways to remove barriers.

Historic Perspective

During the twentieth century natural resource management in the United States moved through three important stages and is, it is hoped, entering a fourth one (Meine 1995). No clear boundaries exist between these stages, but movement from one stage to another is revealed by changes in philosophies for resource use that result in major shifts in management methodologies and policy. Although public policy attitudes have evolved throughout the twentieth century, actual management planning and implementation practices transformed more slowly. Shifts in commodity production have primarily been in response to financial market incentives. Public attitudes expressed in the form of policy and regulatory pressures have only recently significantly influenced forest commodity production (Wall 1995a).

The first stage, commodity extraction, can be characterized as an exploitative or pioneer approach to resource use and reached its pinnacle at the turn of the twentieth century. Dramatic ecosystem alterations occurred through improved technologies in agricultural conversion, flood control, logging without replanting, grazing, fire exclusion, market hunting, introduction of exotic species, and other resource extractions. Momentum from this approach continued into the middle of the twentieth century. A good example of policy-based ecosystem change was the conversion of the Mississippi River Basin bottomland hardwood ecosystem to soybeans. This was accomplished primarily through federal incentives to landowners to convert massive forested wetland areas to soybean production (David Pashley, American Bird Conservancy, personal communication). Many landowners are now being paid, through federal programs, to convert the marginal agricultural lands back to forest. Such examples demonstrate how ecosystems are directly affected by human economics and policies.

The second stage began with the recognition that unmitigated resource use could not be sustained. This recognition served as the impetus for early conservation efforts by the leaders of the conservation movement, such as John Muir and Aldo Leopold. These efforts were highly successful in laying the foundation for more effective scientific resource management, restoration of many forested areas, and development of federal forest reserves, refuges, parks, and wildlife management areas. However, a country hungry for economic expansion and a growing population caused this original effort to be only partially successful at slowing significant alteration of ecosystems.

Stage three grew from the earlier conservation efforts and the economic expansion created in the late 1940s and 1950s. Out of the conservation community came the recognition that commodity extraction had to become commodity production with care taken to provide for environmental amenities. However, out of the push for economic expansion came the drive to produce forest commodities quickly and cheaply, leading to a primary focus on fiber and not on the other environmental amenities of the forest. Thus stage three became a period of strong environmental laws and high-yield intensive forestry.

Through strong regulations, the dynamic interactions between intensive commodity production and the environmental community produced several significant results: (1) it increased awareness of environmental issues for management of natural resource commodities and the simultaneous maintenance of biodiversity; (2) it led to public and regulatory pressure for real change in the approaches used by resource management agencies and private, industrial landowners; (3) it increased efforts to improve the science of managing within the dynamics of ecosystems and viability of species; (4) it increased intensity of the policy and legal debate surrounding the production of commodities from forested ecosystems; (5) it moved much of responsibility for management decisions out of the hands of local and regional resource managers and stakeholders into the courts because of regulatory conflicts; and (6) it resulted in inefficient and costly bureaucratic planning processes within land management agencies.

The frustration on all sides with achieving appropriate goals led to the fourth phase, now in its infancy. This phase involves new efforts of cooperation and collaboration, especially at local and regional levels (Ruckelshaus 1995). Polarization is substituted by a healthy respect for divergent viewpoints and a willingness to try new approaches and to learn by doing. These trends are being accomplished in the face of historic distrust and cumbersome regulatory processes. However, ecological sustainability at large scales must be achieved in social frameworks that integrate ideas, information, and institutional and individual capabilities (Chapter 14). New paradigms for the three primary combative cultures— economically driven commodity-producing organizations, resource regulatory agencies, and environmental activist organizations—must emerge if we are going to move to the next phase in resource conservation. This historic perspective documents the emergence of three types of boundaries: organizational, individual, and informational.

Types of Boundaries

Many different types of boundaries affect private forestry. Three are discussed here: boundaries between organizations, boundaries between individuals with different beliefs and values, and boundaries created by access to information.

Organization Cultures

Organizations (agencies, corporations, and nongovernmental organizations) develop internal cultures based on their missions, administrative policies, history of mission implementation, and attitudes of personnel. Over time, organizations develop cultural inertia and institutionalized methodologies that can in turn create boundaries between organizations. If individuals fail to communicate or understand differences in the missions and cultures among their organizations, these boundaries become barriers.

Organizational culture forms a feedback loop to individual philosophies within an organization. Thus, differences among various organizations' approaches to the implementation of their missions are expressions of attitudes, beliefs, and even values of personnel interacting with the organizations' policies and rules. Cultural inertia can reinforce organizational boundaries and personal bias and thus create barriers.

Organizational culture may be expressed differently in autonomous regions because of differences in regional cultures. For example, cultures differ significantly between the southeastern and northwestern United States. Thus organizations can express regional differences in their approaches to fulfilling missions. For example, forest management issues are more polarized in the Northwest than the Southeast, and, therefore, collaboration on landowner and agency agreements are more complicated and expensive in the Northwest.

Organizations tend to resist major changes that affect internal culture. The magnitude of resistance is based on internal cultural inertia. Cultural inertia is a construct of organizational mission, political relevancy, regional public attitudes, financial drivers, and employee attitudes, values, and beliefs. Resistance to change within organizations is manifested by influencing individuals to incorporate the organization's cultural values into their personal beliefs. Obviously, this is a generalization and many individuals within organizations do act as agents of change. However, personal experience has shown me that organizational culture can affect individual attitudes.

Internal organizational dynamics leads to vitally different approaches to natural resource management. For example, the basic approach of a federal agency charged with protecting endangered species in the face of scientific uncertainty is to err on the side of the species with a conservative response. A basic premise from a commodity production perspective is to focus on an active management solution. The commodity producer would prefer the least-cost alternative to maintain habitat through flexible management. A third perspective is that of environmental activists who may be driven by aesthetic values and a reluctance to accept any solution short of habitat preservation through a "no management" alternative.

Each approach may sustain habitat, but the conflict comes from the interaction of the three approaches. Thus activists and agency personnel believe that the corporation thinks only about money, and corporation personnel think the agency just wants to place road blocks to resource use and impose their values on private land management. Differences of perspective often result in mistrust and tremendous difficulty in communication. These are significant, yet subtle, barriers that make cooperation between some organizations difficult. Opportunities for win–win solutions are lost simply because of the inability of individuals to communicate across organizational boundaries. Individuals willing to break out of organizational cultural roles and take chances are necessary to create change.

Individual Beliefs and Values

The divergent values and beliefs that are expressed by lay supporters of commodity production within forests versus those expressed by lay opponents to forest management are obvious and expected. Less obvious are the differences in basic beliefs and values within the professional and scientific communities of resource managers and conservation biologists. Seemingly minor influences on approaches to conservation, these differences can create significant barriers. For example, there is debate as to whether scientists should be advocates, using their expertise to influence policy (Sweeney and Stangel 1995). Some argue that scientists have an obligation to advocate. Others say that the role of a scientist is to inform and illuminate alternatives, but not advocate. Either way, science is involved in resource management policy debates and in the specific implementation of organizations' missions. Policymakers suggest using the "best available science" as if it were an absolute. But, who interprets the data? And what are their personal interests, beliefs, and values? Are spotted owls an old-growth obligate, or are there specific habitat components within mature, forested stands and across managed landscapes that meet their requirements for nesting, foraging, and dispersal? These questions can apply to many species in forested ecosystems. Thus, the structure of the questions that are asked and the interpretation of data are influenced by personal values regarding land use and management.

Botkin (1990) stated that the greatest impediments to developing solutions to many of our environmental issues are our basic assumptions about nature. These assumptions often are deeply rooted in historic beliefs perpetuated through history and the evolution of ecological theory. Botkin states that in striving to be objective in the scientific development and interpretation of information, we are all influenced by our basic individual beliefs of the way ecosystems respond to human disturbance.

Professional beliefs strongly interact with organizational cultures, oftentimes strengthening boundaries to the point of creating barriers. An example of organizational and professional interaction is the difference between agency and private-land biologists in their approaches to conservation strategies for sensitive or candidate species. Although many strategies for habitat conservation have been described, two primary approaches exist (Everett and Lehmkuhl 1996, Haufler et al. 1996). Some strategies are based on a system of planned reserves across a landscape, and others are based on large-scale, shifting mosaics of vegetation. Even though both approaches may be effective, the first appeals to conservation biologists and environmentalists, whereas the second is more palatable to commodity producers.

Information Boundaries

In the context of this section, information refers to all forms of data, maps, and knowledge to support management, including species survey data, analysis methods, ecosystem planning and landscape classification methods, GIS map layers, peer-reviewed and nonreviewed literature, as well as policies that enhance or hinder the sharing of information. Information boundaries can be significant barriers to cooperation in three ways: mistrust of information interpretation, incompatible data, and reluctance to share information. Mistrust of information between organizations starts with the interpretation of "best available information" and continues to "good science" that must be defined by people with inherent values, beliefs, and organizational missions. Uncertainty abounds in "good science," as does mistrust between people in different organizations. It is this uncertainty that becomes the barrier when information is interpreted by people with opposing beliefs or organizational missions.

As natural resource management moves to landscape and ecosystem approaches, greater amounts and different forms of multiple-scale information are needed to support new methods. To be useful, information must be credible to all parties. In addition, it must be compatible with the various analytical and planning methodologies developed by agencies and landowners.

Many in the private sector believe that the Freedom of Information Act (FOIA) requires that information in federal hands be open to the public, except under certain circumstances. A concern is that information generated by a private landowner and shared in a cooperative spirit could be requested by an outside party and used against the landowner. Thus private landowners may be reluctant to share information with federal or state agencies. The Federal Advisory Committee Act (FACA) produces a similar effect in that sharing information and participation in collaborative approaches to some federal processes are prohibited. Without full participation from people with a wide variety of perspectives, management approaches are limited in scope and may create more problems and barriers than solutions. At the same time, private landowners are wary of public processes, such as the National Environmental Protection Act (NEPA), affecting their lands.

The Antitrust Act does not allow private entities to share certain types of information, such as inventory levels, production rates and timing, and any information that could be construed to limit production and fix prices within the free marketplace. This means that two forest products companies operating within the same watershed cannot collaborate on production levels and timing within that watershed. The Act does not disallow a cooperative watershed analysis or working together to solve any problems in the drainage, but it does dictate types of information that can be shared. Companies can share information on stream condition, road building, or landslide hazards, as well as biological information on species distributions.

Thus ownership and organizational boundaries can become informational barriers for several reasons, including proprietary ownership, compatibility of collection techniques, scale and precision of information, credibility of the information, as well as FOIA, EPA, and FACA policies.

Summary of Types of Boundaries

The boundaries that must be crossed to develop collaborative ecosystem approaches to resource management are impressive. They range from personal to institutional, historic to current, real to perceived. Despite

these obstacles, when a diverse group decides that it is going to find reasonable solutions, all barriers can be bridged in some way.

Innovative Approaches to Crossing Boundaries

The following two case studies illustrate the interactions of organizations
involved in ongoing issues. Many participants were able to cross many
historical boundaries, some were not. A key point is that boundaries are
crossed by efforts of individuals made on behalf of organizations.

The maturation of the following collaborative process required understanding the initial positions of organizations and their responses and
changes. My intent is to demonstrate how these types of collaborative
processes require breaching barriers built on traditional organizational
responses. It also demonstrates internal organizational paradigm shifts
and resistance to new approaches.

The Black Bear Conservation Committee

In June 1990 the U.S. Fish and Wildlife Service (USFWS) proposed listing the Louisiana black bear (*Ursus americanus luteolus*) as a threatened
species under the Endangered Species Act (ESA). The proposal listed
habitat conversion and illegal kill as the major threats to the bear. This
proposed listing occurred at the height of the controversy over spotted
owls in the Northwest and red-cockaded woodpeckers in the Southeast.
On December 30, 1991, the USFWS announced its decision to list the
Louisiana black bear as threatened. Included in the decision was an innovative attempt to exempt normal forest management in bear habitat,
with certain limitations, from any habitat modification rulings. This was
the first use of the "4d rule," a rule-making process within ESA, in that
way, and it exemplified the flexibility of the ESA to remove disincentives
for private landowners. This was significant because more than 90 percent of the historic range of the Louisiana black bear is in private ownership today (Bullock and Wall 1995).

The proposal to list the bear in light of the national ESA controversies was very contentious. The scientific community was divided on the
validity of subspecies designation for the bear. Some groups believed that
listing would save the bear and its habitats. Others viewed the listing as
detrimental to the animal's well-being by increasing the regulatory burden on private landowners, creating a strong deterrent to increase bears
or bear habitat on private land.

The Solution Process

On July 19, 1990, the Louisiana Forestry Association (LFA) hosted a meeting to discuss black bear biology, management, and the implications of the proposed listing. After the discussion the LFA's Wildlife and Recreation committee invited key local environmentalists to a meeting and formed the Black Bear Conservation Committee (BBCC). The BBCC evolved from an initial gathering of eighteen individuals into a broad coalition of more than sixty members, including landowners, state and federal agencies, private conservation groups, forest industry, agricultural interests, and the academic community, all working to address management and restoration of the Louisiana black bear (Bullock and Wall 1995). The coalition agreed that, although some organizations supported listing and many did not, the common goal was bear restoration. Each organization could respond to the listing process outside the context of the BBCC as it wished. However, the only requirement of membership was to work toward stabilizing current populations and to support efforts to restore populations to suitable habitat in Louisiana, Mississippi, and East Texas. At meetings, all individuals representing an organization were required to set their organizational biases aside and focus on bear restoration. Trust was built at evening socials where many discussions and debates about organizational concerns occurred.

The committee organized itself into four subcommittees: habitat and management, information and education, research, and funding. Since its inception, the BBCC has generated more than $700,000 for research, education, the production of a restoration plan, and a landowner guide for effective bear habitat management. The education and information committee produced newsletters and press releases. Forest-products companies used their hunting club newsletters to educate and gain support from thousands of hunting club members. Some clubs offered rewards and significant peer pressure to stop illegal take during hunting seasons. The logo of the BBCC became "Working Together for the Resource." The official motto is "Restore the Bear," and the rallying cry, which became a bumper sticker, was "Feed Bears—Not Lawyers."

Behind the scenes, a group of several forest-industry biologists and their counterparts in local environmental groups evolved into an unofficial core coalition within the BBCC framework. With differing opinions on listing and management of bear habitat, the members of the group were linked by the determination to demonstrate a successful regional cooperative model to solve an ESA issue. These individuals then had to make a strong stance within their respective environmental and commodity production communities.

The Dynamics of Crossing Boundaries

The scale from which organizations respond to an issue such as the ESA listing process of the Louisiana black bear may create very different responses. National groups do not have vested interests in reaching solutions at local levels, but local and regional organizations do. Crossing organizational, individual, and informational boundaries requires four key attitudes on the part of participants: a desire to solve the problem, trust, flexibility in approaches, and allowing organizations to maintain and meet their internal goals. The dynamics of the BBCC illustrate this perspicacity.

A branch of a national association of forest products companies expressed its intent to sue the USFWS to stop the listing of the Louisiana black bear. Their contention was that the Louisiana subspecies was neither a unique subspecies nor a unique population. This contention was based on the fact that Louisiana bear populations had been enhanced through stocking of Minnesota bears by the Louisiana Wildlife and Fishery Department and that the current "best available information" on subspecies status was ambiguous. The association's concern was that listing was a strategy by environmental groups to restrict forest management within hardwood ecosystems. Another concern was that listing the bear as a subspecies or a unique population would set a precedent for further listings of other subspecies or populations. The industry association intended to expend significant resources in fighting the listing. Regional forest-industry biologists convinced the association that, although some of their concerns might be real, the best way to deal with the issue was through a new approach: a regional coalition to restore the bear. Not only did these biologists need to convince the trade association, but they also had to make the case to the land managers of their own organizations. After a brief debate, the association became a charter member of the BBCC and eventually paid for publication of the "Landowner Habitat Management Handbook."

On the national environmental front, two groups had interest in the listing process for various reasons. A national wildlife organization had recently launched a promotional program focusing on large predators, specifically bears and wolves. The program entailed advocacy and fund raising. Members of the wildlife organizations were invited to all of the meetings of the BBCC and attended most. However, they were initially skeptical of the process, would not join, declared the BBCC a tool of the forest industry, and later initiated a suit to force the USFWS to list the bear. The environmentalists on the BBCC tried to dissuade the lawsuit but were not successful. After the listing, the national wildlife group publicly declared the 4d rule "a loophole big enough to drive a logging truck through." The wildlife group believed that, once the bear was listed, the BBCC would dissolve. The challenge made the coalition more determined to be successful at their original and overriding goals of restoring the bear and demonstrating a model of collaboration. Several years after the bear was listed and the BBCC continued to develop and implement a restoration plan, the wildlife group joined the committee and offered a reward for anyone yielding evidence leading to prosecution for illegal killing of a bear.

This example illustrates the several barriers that the national wildlife group had to overcome to join the process: (1) Did membership in the BBCC meet their national objectives for fund raising and activism for bears? (2) Could they trust the participants at the table, and the forest industry specifically, to actually work for the bear? (3) Could they trust the interpretation of forest management effects on bear habitat? (4) If organizations such as timber management companies were allowed to meet their goals of forest management, would this allow the wildlife group to meet its national agenda? (5) Was their agenda the restoration of bear populations or influencing forest management on private lands? Because the committee focused on bear restoration, the wildlife group was able to get through their institutional barriers, as did all of the member organizations, and become a productive member of the BBCC.

Another group, a litigation branch of a major national environmental organization, saw the delay in the listing process by USFWS as an opportunity to sue for listing of the bear. This group had successfully litigated on behalf of other species, and from their perspective this was the appropriate approach to save the bear and its habitat. The president of the state chapter of this organization, one of the primary instigators of the BBCC, and several other environmentalists met with the national representatives and tried to explain the advantages of the regional coalition. If private landowners view the black bear as a threat, no amount of regulation would ever help bear populations recover. After discussion, the local chapter was unable to convince national representatives that suing was inappropriate. The local chapter then resorted to a strong stance: either the national organization cease litigation or the local chapter would release a story to the press that the national agenda was attempting to undermine a positive regional coalition supporting bear restoration. The national organization reluctantly withdrew its litigation, but it was clear that no barriers were breached or new horizons embraced by this national group. However, trust within the regional coalition was magnified by the willingness of both industry and environmental partners to make a stand within their own organizational cultures for a regional solution-oriented process that benefited the bear. The scale from which potentially polarizing issues are addressed through collaboration is very important. National perspectives infuse a different set of barriers in a process as demonstrated by the national versus regional agendas in the BBCC.

The third significant event in the success of the BBCC process was the development of the special 4d rule. Both the local office and the national office of USFWS were involved in removing the greatest concern from the private sector: the ability to continue to manage private forests. The 4d rule was possible because of the preponderance of evidence based on "good science" that bear habitat management was compatible with quality forest management. The USFWS was able to capitalize on the opportunity through the support of the BBCC.

Barriers Crossed and Accomplishments

There are several key elements to the success of the BBCC. Each has to do with crossing boundaries that had historically been barriers. No organization that participated in the BBCC had ever dealt with an issue of this magnitude in a collaborative process before. One member stated, "We were too naive to know that it wouldn't work." Each organization's management had to trust their representatives who promoted the BBCC approach and be willing to allow the development of trust, communication, and understanding of each group's needs and limitations. The environmental and industry core group, with the help of a few key academicians and agency personnel, created the critical mass to lead the way. Once BBCC organizational momentum was begun by individuals, the organizations followed.

The BBCC accomplished more for the bear in a short time than any one organization or regulatory framework could alone. The committee structure allowed for specific focus on key areas of need. The BBCC has made significant progress toward its goal of restoring the bear through the following accomplishments: (1) increasing public awareness about the black bear's historic prominence, population status, and habitat management needs; (2) promoting the bear as an asset rather than a regulatory liability; (3) staffing and funding a full-time BBCC coordinator to serve in administrative and extension capacities; (4) coordinating a regional research effort and helping secure sufficient funding; (5) publishing two editions of the "Black Bear Habitat Management Handbook" to assist landowners; (6) developing a protocol for handling nuisance bears and mediating disputes that arise over bear problems; and (7) completing a comprehensive restoration plan for the tristate region of Louisiana, Mississippi, and East Texas that sets objectives for restoration, establishes bear management units, and designates those responsible for implementation. The plan was developed cooperatively by all public and private stakeholders and served as the template for the USFWS Draft Recovery Plan for the Louisiana Black Bear (Bullock and Wall 1995).

The BBCC is currently implementing the regional restoration plan. The group meets at least twice a year to review progress. Popular support has been engendered within local communities and especially with hunting clubs. The BBCC won the conservation group of the year award from the Wildlife Society in 1995, and both state and federal agencies lauded the BBCC for efforts to make bear conservation work within local communities. The BBCC model has recently been used to develop a similar group to deal with bear conservation in Florida.

The Conservation Network

The Conservation Network is a direct spinoff of the BBCC. The intent in developing this ad hoc group was to propagate the model of cooperation developed within the BBCC at a national scale. The goal was to bring participants from the national environmental community, the USFWS, and industry together in an atmosphere where greater understanding could be reached. Several people from each group were assembled in September of 1994 under the auspices of the Shack Foundation at Aldo Leopold's Shack located near Baraboo, Wisconsin. Original participants included the BBCC coordinator, two Washington staff from USFWS, professionals from six national environmental groups, biologists from five national forest-products corporations, representatives for small private landowners, and the Sand County Foundation. The difference between this meeting and other meetings of this sort was the participants. Other meetings have brought high-level managers to a table to discuss common ground. Their ability to breach organization cultures and get beyond political organizational rhetoric was limited by their ability truly to communicate on a personal level. The Conservation Network was intentionally targeted at mid-level staff who focus on natural resource environmental issues and who shape and implement their organizations' responses to issues. These participants do not have full responsibility directly to change organizational policy, but they all share an understanding of the need to change culture within organizations. The success of this effort depended on the appropriate mix of participants.

The agenda was simple: use the model of the BBCC to build a network of compatible people that were willing to move across the historic boundaries, attack the barriers, and develop solution-based projects. The idea was to establish a core group that could cultivate a high level of trust and recognize the boundaries and needs created by each organization's missions. With that understanding, the core group was to pioneer ways of bridging the historic barriers formed by differences in organizations needs, regulations, and historic distrust. Armed with greater understanding and a willingness to work together, the group could then initiate and support local and regional efforts similar to those of the BBCC.

The first meeting was successful in building the understanding and trust needed to continue. A second meeting was held the following spring. The first project of this ad hoc group was to develop a White Paper on Candidate Species Conservation Agreements with incentives for private landowners (Wall 1995b). This "White Paper" outlines the incentives for Conservation Agreements from the perspective of the private landowner, the requirements for species conservation from the USFWS perspective, and the need for participation and input from the environmental community. This effort helped support a draft proposal by the USFWS for Conservation Agreements as a mechanism for solving problems with species prior to a listing, where more restrictive regulation mechanisms are imposed.

Conclusions

The common ground that resource managers and stakeholders must reach is complicated by the interactions of personal beliefs, organization cultures, societal or management policies, and economic and aesthetic motivators. We must pursue collaborative models that integrate the concepts of Leopold's land ethic with a scientific approach to ecosystem management. As we attempt to integrate these concepts, we must work through the strengths and weaknesses of individuals and organizations.

Individuals within organizations instigate and make collaborative processes successful. There are no institutional, political, economic, cultural, or informational boundaries that cannot be crossed or barriers that cannot be breached if a diverse core group of individuals desires solutions.

REFERENCES

Botkin, D.B. 1990. *Discordant harmonies: a new ecology for the 21st century.* Oxford University Press, New York.

Bullock, J.F., Jr., and W.A. Wall. 1995. Proactive endangered species management: a partnership paradigm. *Transactions of the North American Wildlife and Natural Resources Conference* 61:436–446.

Everett, R.L., and J.F. Lehmkuhl. 1996. An emphasis-use approach to conserving biodiversity. *Wildlife Society Bulletin* 24:192–199.

Haufler, J.B., C.A. Mehl, and G.J. Roloff. 1996. Using a coarse-filter approach with species assessment for ecosystem management. *Wildlife Society Bulletin* 24:200–208.

Leopold, A. 1949. *A Sand County almanac: with essays on conservation from Round River.* Oxford University Press, New York.

Meine, C. 1995. The oldest task in human history. Pages 7–35 in *A new century for natural resources management* (R.L. Knight and S.F. Bates, editors). Island Press, Washington, DC.

Ruckelshaus, W.D. 1995. Stopping the pendulum. Paper presented before the Environmental Law Institute, October 18, 1995, Washington, DC.

Sweeney, J.M., and P.W. Stangel. 1995. Walking the line: science versus advocacy. *Transactions of the North American Wildlife and Natural Resources Conference* 60:1–5.

Wall, W.A. 1995a. The need for partnerships in ecosystem management: opening remarks. *Transactions of the North American Wildlife and Natural Resources Conference* 61:413–414.

Wall, W.A. 1995b. Conservation agreements: innovative solutions or missed opportunities—a corporate lands perspective. *Transactions of the North American Wildlife and Natural Resources Conference* 61:496–500.

Chapter 8

Boundaries Between Public and Private Lands: Defining Obstacles, Finding Solutions

Richard L. Knight and Tim W. Clark

Nearly 70 percent of the United States, outside of Alaska, is privately owned (Natural Resources Conservation Service 1996). Accordingly, boundaries that separate private from public lands are both prevalent and important. Stewardship of ecological resources across boundaries between public and private lands is one of several defining goals of contemporary ecosystem management. Ideally, viable wildlife communities and ecological processes can be maintained or reestablished in ways that also are societally and economically sustainable (Doob 1995, Goodland 1995, Interagency Ecosystem Management Task Force 1995, Reid 1996, Callicott and Mumford 1997).

Three private land-use categories that relate to boundaries between public and private lands include: (1) urban centers and commercial development, (2) rural development, and (3) amenity and commodity uses (recreation, agriculture and timber management). Our chapter focuses on the first two categories as they have been the fastest growing land-use changes that relate to boundaries with public lands (Ambrose and Bratton 1990, Riebsame et al. 1996). In addition, boundary issues related to management of amenities and commodities are covered elsewhere in the book (see Chapter 6 on recreation, Chapter 10 on ranching, and Chapter 7 on timber management).

Human development along the interface between public and private lands results in declines of plant and animal populations, degradation of riparian and other plant communities, and the alteration of ecological processes (Janzen 1983, Knight et al. 1995, Buechner and Sauvajot 1996, Theobald et al. 1996, Dobson et al. 1997). In a survey of threats to world parks, it was reported that 24 percent of these threats arose exclusively from outside the park boundaries (Machlis and Tichnell 1987). As more urban and rural development occurs adjacent to public lands, these pernicious wildlife and ecological trends are expected to grow (Knight and Mitchell 1997). As a result, concern for ecological resources across boundaries between public and private lands has emerged as a principal interest of land management agencies and conservation organizations (Yaffee et al. 1996). The key to improving this situation is enhanced cooperation among landowners, elected officials, private organizations, and public land managers (Long and Arnold 1994, Chapters 3 and 14). Our chapter examines aspects of the public–private land border issue, offers suggestions to enhance communication across these borders, and discusses information needs on this topic.

What Are the Current Trends?

Three general trends pertain to the interface between public and private lands: (1) increasing human densities, (2) increasing economic activities that depend on public land resources, and (3) alteration of biotic communities and ecological processes.

Growth Along the Borders

There is widespread and rapid growth in the density of people living adjacent to public lands, a trend typified by a recent realty ad in the Fort Collins newspaper, *The Coloradan* (June 6, 1996): "Your own piece of heaven! Private entrance from your ranchette adjacent to thousands of acres of national forest. Elk, deer, trout and vistas that don't end." Between 1982 and 1992, for example, 6.4 million hectares of pasture and rangeland were taken out of use and 5.6 million hectares of agricultural lands were developed, primarily for homes and commercial projects (Natural Resources Conservation Service 1996). Private lands adjacent to public lands of any type (county, state, or federal) are particularly coveted for development because of their amenity values (Power 1996).

This rural growth has particular consequences for the American West because of the preponderance of public lands in that region. Counties that contain federal wilderness lands in Colorado, Wyoming, Montana, Idaho, Utah, Nevada, Arizona, and New Mexico have grown in population considerably faster than all other counties (Rudzitis and Johansen 1989, Riebsame et al. 1996). In addition, rural areas of these states grew more than rural areas nationwide (Cromartie 1994, Fuguitt 1994). Here, agricultural land adjacent to public land is being purchased and subdivided at an increasing rate (e.g., Maxwell 1993, Gersh 1996, Romme 1997). Over 500,000 hectares of private lands in the Yellowstone ecosystem have already been subdivided (see Chapter 11).

The East River Valley, near Crested Butte, Colorado, represents a typical pattern of private land development adjacent to public land. This valley of approximately 35,327 hectares forms a peninsula of private land surrounded by USDA Forest Service, USDI Bureau of Land Management, and state-owned lands. Within the valley, roughly 20 percent of the private land has been subdivided into parcels smaller than 18 hectares (Theobald et al. 1996). Since the mid-1960s, 2,489 hectares have been subdivided into ranchettes providing 171 housing units, and 546 hectares have been developed into high-density subdivisions providing 1,371 housing units. The total length of roads in the valley increased by 62 percent, of which 82 percent led to individual homes. Parcels that abut public lands were especially targeted because of the amenity of public land access.

Another example is found in northern Larimer County, Colorado, where ranches adjacent to the Roosevelt National Forest are being subdivided (Figure 8.1). Here, homes are first built on lots adjacent to the forest boundary and spread outward over time. Portions of the forest now

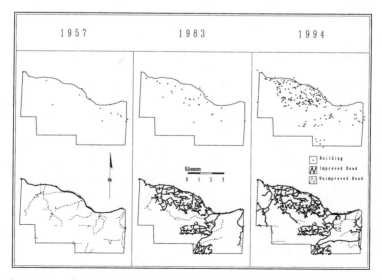

Figure 8.1. A ranch in Larimer County, Colorado, adjacent to Roosevelt National Forest, that was subdivided into ranchette homes showing the increase in homes and roads between 1957 and 1994. (From Knight and Mitchell 1997.)

have more than a dozen layers of homes emanating outward from the boundary.

Commercial Development Along the Borders

A second trend seen along public–private borders has been an increase in commercial development, usually of a type that depends on commodities or amenities found within the public lands (e.g., Machlis et al. 1990, Wilkinson 1995). Decisions made by natural resource managers regarding types and levels of land use are intensely scrutinized by the chambers of commerce of towns whose economies depend on public lands (e.g., Gale 1991, Jackson et al. 1995, Power 1995). Differences in agency management goals and expectations of local businesses frequently create land management dilemmas that end in litigation or bitter recriminations (e.g., Bama 1996). Examples abound: businessmen in Jackson Hole, Wyoming, want the airport in Grand Teton National Park expanded to accommodate more commercial airplane flights, but the park and allied interests oppose the expansion because it is contrary to the land protection goals of national parks (Hayden 1993). Developers at Snowmass, Colorado, want access to more Forest Service land so they can enlarge their ski facilities, but many local people are concerned about the ecological, societal, and economic costs that accompany further growth (Larmer 1993).

Changes in Biological Diversity and Ecological Processes

A third trend along the interface between public and private lands is the alteration of flows and fluxes of biotic and abiotic factors (see Chapter 2). Two of the most conspicuous changes following increases in residential and commercial development along public land boundaries are an increase in buildings and roads and an accompanying increase in human densities (Figure 8.1). Additional factors that may change following these developments include: increases in (1) dog and cat populations, (2) automobile traffic, (3) night lights; (4) nonnative species; and (5) human disturbance (Knight et al. 1995). Each of these changes has the potential to alter native biological diversity on both sides of the public–private land border.

First, increasing rural dog and cat populations may result in greater predation on wildlife, ranging from small mammals and songbirds up to medium and large mammals (see references in Jurek 1994). For example, almost 80 percent of rural homeowners in Wisconsin had cats, and each household had on average eight cats (Coleman and Temple 1994). Collectively, these subsidized predators (Soulé et al. 1988) may reduce both native wildlife populations and potential prey populations for native predators such as hawks and medium-size carnivores (Soulé et al. 1988).

Second, the roads that serve developments usually are dirt or gravel, may be constructed across steep slopes with inadequate grading, and usually are traveled daily. The marked increase in total kilometers of roads following subdivision results in increased soil erosion, habitat fragmentation, and wildlife mortalities (see references in Schonewald-Cox and Buechner 1992). Roads also serve as barriers to wildlife dispersal and as conduits for the dispersal of weeds and harmful plants. Some wildlife species appear particularly susceptible to road effects, including those that do not do well in edge habitat, are sensitive to humans, are unwilling to cross roads, and seek roads for heat or food (and therefore run the risk of being run over).

Third, housing and commercial developments result in more outdoor lights. Although the topic has not adequately been studied, it appears that lights at night may alter the movement of certain wildlife species. Headlights from automobiles and yard lights may collectively cause developed areas to be less suitable for dispersing wildlife. Beier (1995), for example, noted that mountain lions (Felis concolor) avoided artificial lights when moving through the Santa Ana Mountains of California.

Fourth, people in housing and commercial developments often landscape their homes and businesses with nonnative plants, disturb substrates near buildings, and disperse weeds with their vehicles, all of which may alter native plant communities (e.g., Shafer 1990, Tyser and Worley 1992, Drayton and Primack 1996).

Fifth, because human activities are one of the principal ways that wildlife are disturbed, increases in human density and activity may alter the composition of wildlife communities (references in Knight and Gutzwiller 1995 and Buechner and Sauvajort 1996). Not all wildlife species demonstrate equal sensitivity to human presence. Some species tend to avoid humans whereas others are attracted to them (Friesen et al. 1995, Blair 1996, Bowers and Breland 1996, Harrison 1997). For example, Engels and Sexton (1994) recorded decreases of golden-cheeked warblers (Dendroica chrysoparia), a rare species, and increases of blue jays (Cyanocitta cristata), a common predator of songbird nests, with increasing housing development.

Collectively, these trends and consequences suggest that the composition of native wildlife and plant communities will be altered in the vicinity of housing and commercial development and that these changes also may affect adjacent public lands (Knight et al. 1995, Buechner and Sauvajot 1996, Dobson et al. 1997). A hypothetical pattern following increased development suggests more human-adapted species (native and alien) and fewer species that are sensitive to humans and their associated enterprises (Knight 1997). A study by Bock et al. (in press) on public lands in Boulder County, Colorado, illustrates this point. Bird surveys on public grasslands adjacent to housing developments showed more suburban species (e.g., European starling [*Sturnus vulgaris*], common grackle [*Quiscalus quiscula*], house sparrow [*Passer domesticus*]) than species found on grasslands away from development (e.g., savannah sparrow [*Passerculus sandwichensis*], bobolink [*Dolichonyx oryzivorus*], and grasshopper sparrow [*Ammodramus savannarum*]).

Public lands also serve as sources of biotic and abiotic factors that create social conflicts between private landowners and public land agencies. For example, wildlife, such as bears, ungulates, and mountain lions may cross from public lands onto private lands, creating a nuisance (e.g., Meagher 1989, Torres et al. 1996). Forbes and Theberge (1996) document how Algonquin Park in Canada serves as a population source for gray wolves (*Canis lupus*), yet these animals frequently leave the park to hunt on surrounding private lands. Private landowners feel that wolves encroach on their rights and threaten their safety. One result was that, during a six-year study, most wolf deaths were attributed to human-caused mortality across the park's borders. In another example, public lands in California serve as sources for mountain lions. With increasing housing development adjacent to public lands, there has been a sharp increase in lion depredation on dogs and cats, an increase in lion attacks on people, and a marked increase in permits issued to kill offending lions (Torres et al. 1996).

Similarly, increased human densities and economic activities along public land borders have altered the ability of agencies to implement management activities that may cross over onto private lands (Clark and Minta 1994). For example, fire is being restored to public lands to recreate historic patterns of landscape heterogeneity. Fire, however, may threaten homes that border public lands (Cortner et al. 1990, Stanton 1995). Prescribed burning in areas of intermixed houses and public lands calls for cooperation. Zoning, building codes, and state legislation will all be components of cooperative fire programs that must incorporate local fire-fighting organizations with the federal agencies (e.g., Pyne et al. 1996).

Because the trend of increased housing and commercial development adjacent to public land borders is expected to continue, agencies, organizations, and individuals must begin now to plan for development while minimizing harmful ecological effects. When development occurs with little thought and planning the integrity of public lands are at risk and the biological diversity and ecological processes on private lands are in jeopardy (Bean and Wilcove 1997). Most species have 80 percent or more of their known habitat on nonfederal lands, and over a third have all of their known habitat there (General Accounting Office 1994). Here we offer suggestions that can increase cooperation across boundaries between public and private lands, reducing the barriers and maintaining the positive aspects of borders.

Suggestions for Cooperation Across Boundaries

Increasingly the very fabric of our society and our relationship with one another and with the natural world have been under intense reappraisal (Brunner 1994). As part of this, federal and state land management agencies in the United States are now addressing the challenge of managing ecosystems (Interagency Ecosystem Management Task Force 1995). This has necessitated a shift from focusing on specific, small-scale units to an emphasis on the health of more broadly defined ecosystems. Under ecosystem management, it is inappropriate for agencies to operate as if their administrative boundaries form an impregnable wall, within which they have control and outside of which they are powerless. Because land management agencies commonly share borders with private land, ecosystem management must acknowledge these neighbors and find ways to cooperate. This can be effective only by creating an interactive network of participants, information, and practices. This network should represent the diverse legitimate interests and capabilities of a pluralistic society. It also must address the problems arising from the highly fragmented distribution of information, resources, and power across geographic boundaries, social groups, organizations, agencies, and disciplines (Lasswell 1970, Wondolleck and Yaffee 1994). This is largely a matter of using democratic mechanisms that clarify and secure our common interests.

Citizens, businesses, and public officials must learn to work collaboratively with land management agencies to develop effective decision processes. Because private actions may directly or indirectly affect the ecological integrity of the public lands (e.g., rural subdivisions adjacent to public lands and commercial businesses dependent on some public land resources), it is critical that agencies form inclusive, problem-oriented decision processes on cross-border issues.

To minimize these difficulties, participants can seek to: (1) develop shared perceptions of issues, (2) identify shared goals among key participants, (3) increase cooperation between elected officials, private landowners, and public land managers, and (4) increase appreciation of the consequences of historic trends, both harmful and helpful.

Improving Perspectives and Problem Definition

Developing shared perspectives on the issues comes from analyzing and opening up communication on participants' identities, expectations, and demands. What belief systems, organizations, and communities do people identify with? What do they expect will happen? What claims are they making on each other and society? Once people see which elements of their various perspectives and values are shared and which are exclusive, they can begin to come together to define the problems at hand. Setting up and managing effective decision processes via genuine problem-solving exercises, policy exercises, or other vehicles offer the best means for coming to a common problem definition, and thence to a course of action that will more likely solve the problems and enjoy community support.

Improving Consensus on Goals

Managing ecological resources in a consistent, rational, and adaptive manner across ownership boundaries is a goal of ecosystem management, but it is not always a shared goal among key participants in the public–private land boundary issue (Yaffee et al. 1996). Clarifying goals and developing effective decision processes can help. It may require that agencies jointly develop land management goals that cross their own administrative lines. Although institutional barriers make this difficult, agencies are increasingly finding ways to realign administrative units with more ecologically meaningful land borders (e.g., Larmer 1996).

In addition, implementing shared goals is essential. Good implementation requires sharing information across agencies and with the diverse publics. Information should not be viewed as an end in itself but rather as a means to foster interagency cooperation and public empowerment in joint problem solving. Adaptive management, which includes organizational and policy learning as well as technical learning, is one way to proceed (Clark 1996). This kind of learning, however, must be planned, actively managed, and rewarded, or it will not happen.

Improving Cooperation Among Participants

The key to improving cooperation is to build a decision process by which participants can clarify and secure their common interests (see Chapter 14). Mechanisms must be developed to facilitate exchange of information, open discussion, and evaluation of management policies (Clark and Brunner 1996).

Communication on complex policy issues can be addressed through workshops and exercises, policy dialogs, mediation, alternative dispute resolution procedures, and negotiation (Dryzek 1990). Problems should be framed so that people can grapple with them cognitively and practically. Thus, cross-boundary management efforts should be focused on specific sites where existing or potential problems exist and prospects for their resolution are greatest. These prototypes can then become models for improving efforts in other arenas.

For example, in Madison County, Montana, a memorandum of understanding on coordinated land-use planning has been drawn up among public agencies, local public officials, and diverse private organizations (see Chapter 11). About 56 percent of the county is in state or federal ownership and both public and private participants acknowledged that they have direct and significant effects on each other. They agreed that it was in their common interest to join to develop and implement countywide plans. In addition, local and regional conservation groups are working with state and county officials to provide information to the public on ways builders and homeowners can protect wildlife, minimize soil erosion, and soften their impact on landscapes (e.g., Jackson Hole Wildlife Foundation and Jackson Hole Alliance for Responsible Planning 1995).

Consequences of the Trends

Besides the harmful trends, such as loss of wildlife and habitat, there also are helpful trends such as the growing movement toward ecosystem management (Yaffee et al. 1996). Understanding these trends, projecting their probable courses into the future, and applying this information in decision-making processes are important components of rational problem solving.

Cooperation will require agencies to give up a "command and control mentality" when dealing with diverse publics on border issues and to establish open decision processes focused on genuine democratic problem solving (Knight and Meffee 1997). Agencies will develop a new role as true partners, cooperators, or catalysts in decision processes (e.g., Jones 1996). In a time when agencies are being asked to "do more with less," it is appropriate that this approach stresses partnerships (Clark and Brunner 1996). Agencies no longer have the resources necessary to address the increasingly complex issues along their public–private borders. Partnerships reduce duplication, encourage efficiency and cooperation, and make collective resources available to solve common problems.

Information Needs

Improving the management of boundaries between public and private lands will require various kinds of information. First, our understanding of ecological issues relating to cross-boundary topics is rudimentary. We need to know more about spatial and temporal changes in landscape mosaics along these borders, differences and similarities in wildlife and plant communities on both sides of borders, and alterations in ecological processes, both biotic and abiotic, across the interface between public and private lands.

Because land-use practices on opposite sides of public–private borders are driven by different sets of economic and societal pressures, it is expected that landscape mosaics across borders might be quite different (Ambrose and Bratton 1990, Turner et al. 1996, Wear et al. 1996). Although it is widely believed that there are substantial land-use conversions of private land adjacent to public lands (e.g., ranchland to rural subdivisions), there are few case studies from which to create reliable patterns (Theobald et al. 1996).

We need empirical studies that define plant and animal communities along an ecological gradient of human densities and land uses along borders (sensu Blair 1996). Although scientists suspect that increasing development adjacent to public lands simplifies biodiversity, causing reductions in naturally rare and specialist species and increases in human-adapted species, the degree to which these activities cross borders onto public lands and the degree to which native species are affected on both sides are not known. There are a variety of biotic and abiotic fluxes that cross boundaries between public and private lands. Further study of several issues would be helpful—from the increasing level of wildlife–human interactions to the role of fire on landscapes where this process has been long suppressed (Pyne et al. 1996).

Second, there are a variety of societal issues concerning public–private borders about which we need more information. Most important, because much of the development occurring adjacent to public lands represents a conversion of lands previously in agriculture, this cultural-economic change requires study. When the prevailing economies of an area go through a relatively sudden and drastic shift (e.g., agriculture to housing development), there are long-lingering impacts on the residents and businesses who had been there before (Larmer and Stuebner 1994, Rasker and Glick 1994, White 1996, Knight 1997). In addition, because much of this new growth is fueled by quality-of-life amenities, there are additional impacts on other sectors of society. These more affluent people often depend on service personnel, from landscape gardening to security, yet these jobs may not provide service workers with an income sufficient to live in the communities where they work (e.g., Ring 1995). What are the long-term implications of widening class and income distinctions?

Information about public knowledge and attitudes over private land development is needed. In the face of increasing conflict on the issue of growth adjacent to our public lands detailed surveys are essential to discuss these issues. For example, a study among visitors to Steamboat Springs, Colorado, indicated that ranchlands contributed overwhelmingly to the enjoyment of their stay (Walsh et al. 1993). In addition, 46 percent said they would not return to Steamboat Springs if ranchlands were converted to golf courses and resort housing. Surveys may add important information to the dialog between elected officials, nongovernmental organizations, and management agencies when preparing a blueprint for future land use.

Third, information on the economics of growth adjacent to public lands is necessary. Evidence suggests that property taxes from this type of growth do not cover the costs of county services to these often far-flung developments. For example, in Gallatin County, Montana, population growth increased by almost 15 percent between 1990 and 1994 with increasing demands on local government to provide services. Haggerty (1996) found that for every dollar generated by residential land during 1994, the county government and school districts had to spend $1.45 to provide county and education services to residential landowners. Alternatively, it was found that only $0.25 had to be spent to provide these same services to agricultural landowners for every dollar raised in revenues from their lands. Education was the single most costly service provided.

Information also is needed about economic costs to public land agencies of private development and business growth adjacent to public lands.

For example, what are the increased costs to agencies of fighting fires that cross borders and threaten residential and commercial development on private land? In addition, are there additional costs to agencies to manage resources on public lands that are increasingly threatened by phenomena originating on private lands?

Conclusions

Boundaries between public and private lands require thoughtful discussion because human activities on one side of the boundary can significantly affect values on the other side. In recent decades, urban and rural development near public lands has caused wildlife and habitat losses and disruption of ecological processes. It is important to address ecological, economic, and societal issues in a consistent, rational, and adaptive manner. By focusing on shared perspectives and tracing past and likely future trends, there is an increased likelihood of cooperation and collaboration.

General solutions to the boundary problem between public and private lands are known and need to be applied site by site to be contextually relevant. Practical solutions require reliable information, planning, open discourse, clear management recommendations, constructive dispute resolution, and ongoing policy appraisal. This approach may offer an opportunity to sustain the ecological, economic, and societal needs of diverse communities and organizations that share borders.

ACKNOWLEDGMENTS

Richard L. Knight is indebted to George Wallace, Curt Meine, Alvin Johnson, Peter Landres, and Heather Knight for discussion and insights on this issue. TWC thanks the many wonderful people at Yale University, the Northern Rockies Conservation Cooperative in Jackson, and elsewhere across the Greater Yellowstone Ecosystem. Denise Casey provided invaluable editorial assistance.

REFERENCES

Ambrose, J.P., and S.P. Bratton. 1990. Trends in landscape heterogeneity along the borders of Great Smokey Mountains National Park. *Conservation Biology* 4:135–143.
Bama, L. 1996. Yellowstone: a park boss goes to bat for the land. *High Country News* 28(8):1, 8–12.

Bean, M.J., and D.S. Wilcove. 1997. The private-public problem. *Conservation Biology* 11:1–2.

Beier, P. 1995. Dispersal of juvenile cougars in fragmented habitat. *Journal of Wildlife Management* 59:228–237.

Blair, R.B. 1996. Land use and avian species diversity along an urban gradient. *Ecological Applications* 6:506–519.

Bock, C.E., J.H. Bock, and B.C. Bennett. In press. Songbird abundance in grasslands at a suburban interface on the Colorado High Plains. In *Ecology and conservation of grassland birds in the Western Hemisphere* (P. Vickery and J. Herkert, editors), Studies in Avian Biology.

Bowers, M.A., and B. Breland. 1996. Foraging of gray squirrels on an urban–rural gradient: use of the GUD to assess anthropogenic impact. *Ecological Applications* 6:1135–1142.

Brunner, R.D. 1994. Myth and American politics. *Policy Sciences* 27:1–18.

Buechner, M., and R. Sauvajot. 1996. Conservation and zones of human activity: the spread of human disturbance across a protected landscape. Pages 605–629 in *Biodiversity in managed landscapes* (R.C. Szaro and D.W. Johnston, editors). Oxford University Press, New York.

Callicott, J.B., and K. Mumford. 1997. Ecological sustainability as a conservation concept. *Conservation Biology* 11:32–40.

Clark, T.W. 1996. Learning as a strategy for improving endangered species conservation. *Endangered Species UPDATE* 13(1&2):5–6, 22–24.

Clark, T.W., and R.D. Brunner. 1996. Making partnerships work: an introduction to the decision process. *Endangered Species UPDATE* 13:1–5.

Clark, T.W., and S.C. Minta. 1994. *Greater Yellowstone's future: prospects for ecosystem science, management, and policy.* Homestead Press, Moose, WY.

Coleman, J.S., and S.A. Temple. 1994. Rural residents' free-ranging domestic cats: a survey. *Wildlife Society Bulletin* 21:381–390.

Cortner, H.J., P.D. Gardner, and J.G. Taylor. 1990. Fire hazards at the urban–wildland interface: what the public expects. *Environmental Management* 14:57–62.

Cromartie, J. 1994. *Recent demographic and economic changes in the West.* Economic Research Service, U.S. Department of Agriculture, Washington, DC.

Dobson, A.P., J.P. Rodriguez, W.M. Roberts, and D.S. Wilcove. 1997. Geographic distribution of endangered species in the United States. *Science* 275:550–553.

Doob, L.W. 1995. *Sustainers and sustainability: attitudes, attributes, and actions for survival.* Praeger, Westport, CT.

Drayton, B., and R.B. Primack. 1996. Plant species lost in an isolated conservation area in metropolitan Boston from 1894 to 1993. *Conservation Biology* 10:30–39.

Dryzek, J.S. 1990. *Discursive democracy*. Cambridge University Press, New York.

Engels, T.M., and C.W. Sexton. 1994. Negative correlation of blue jays and golden-cheeked warblers near an urbanizing area. *Conservation Biology* 8:286–290.

Forbes, G.J., and J.B. Theberge. 1996. Cross-boundary management of Algonquin Park wolves. *Conservation Biology* 10:1091–1097.

Friesen, L.E., P.F. Eagles, and R.J. MacKay. 1995. Effects of residential development on forest-dwelling neotropical migrant songbirds. *Conservation Biology* 9:1408–1414.

Fuguitt, G.V. 1994. Population change in nonmetropolitan America. Paper prepared for the National Rural Studies Committee, Department of Rural Sociology, University of Wisconsin–Madison.

Gale, R.P. 1991. Forest resource-dependent communities and the new forestry: how wide the welcome mat in the Pacific Northwest. *The Northwest Environment Journal* 7:7–33.

General Accounting Office. 1994. *Endangered Species Act: information on species protection on nonfederal lands*. GAO/RCED-95-16. U.S. General Accounting Office, Washington, DC.

Gersh, J. 1996. Subdivide and conquer. *Amicus Journal* 18(3):14–20.

Goodand, R. 1995. The concept of environmental sustainability. *Annual Review Ecology and Systematics* 26:1–24.

Haggerty, M. 1996. *Fiscal impact of different land uses on county government and school districts in Gallatin County, Montana*. Local Government Center, Montana State University, Bozeman, MT.

Harrison, R.L. 1997. A comparison of gray fox ecology between residential and undeveloped rural landscapes. *Journal of Wildlife Management* 61:112–122.

Hayden, R. 1993. Critics say big jets and national parks don't mix. *High Country News* 25(18):3.

Interagency Ecosystem Management Task Force. 1995. *The ecosystem approach: healthy ecosystems and sustainable economies*, vol. 1. U.S. Department of Commerce, Springfield, MA.

Jackson, D.H., D. Doyle, E. Schuster, and B.J. Stelzenmuller. 1995. *Sources of community well-being in Montana resource-dependent communities*. Discussion Paper 3, Bolle Center for People and Forests, School of Forestry, University of Montana, Missoula, MT.

Jackson Hole Wildlife Foundation and Jackson Hole Alliance for Responsible Planning. 1995. *Welcome to the neighborhood: ways builders and homeowners can protect wildlife in the Jackson Hole area*. Jackson, WY.

Janzen, D.H. 1983. No park is an island: increase in interference from outside as park size decreases. *Oikos* 41:402–410.

Jones, L. 1996. Howdy neighbor: as a last resort Westerners start talking to each other. *High Country News* 28(9):1, 6, 8.

Jurek, R.M. 1994. *A bibliography of feral, stray, and free-roaming domestic cats in relation to wildlife conservation*. Nongame Bird and Mammal Program Report No. 94-5. California Department of Fish and Game, Sacramento, CA.

Knight, R.L. 1997. Field report from the new American West. Pages 181–200 in *Wallace Stegner and the continental vision* (C. Meine, editor). Island Press, Washington, DC.

Knight, R.L., and K.G. Gutzwiller, editors. 1995. *Wildlife and recreation: coexistence through research and management*. Island Press, Washington, DC.

Knight, R.L., and G.K. Meffee. 1997. Ecosystem management: agency liberation from command and control. *Wildlife Society Bulletin* 25:676–678.

Knight, R.L., and J. Mitchell. 1997. Subdividing the West. Pages 270–272 in *Principles of conservation biology*, 2nd edition (G.K. Meffe and C.R. Carroll, editors). Sinauer Associates, Inc., Sunderland, MA.

Knight, R.L., G.N. Wallace, and W.E. Riebsame. 1995. Ranching the view: subdivisions versus agriculture. *Conservation Biology* 9:459–461.

Larmer, P. 1993. Does Aspen need thousands more skiers? *High Country News* 25(18):4–5.

Larmer, P. 1996. A Colorado county tries a novel approach: work the system. *High Country News* 28(9):11–13.

Larmer, P., and S. Stuebner. 1994. "Wise use" plans abhor change. *High Country News* 26(16):16–17.

Lasswell, H.D. 1970. The emerging conception of the policy sciences. *Policy Sciences* 1:3–14.

Long, F.J., and M. Arnold. 1994. *The power of environmental partnerships*. Dryden Press, New York.

Machlis, G.E., and D.L. Tichnell. 1987. Economic development and threats to National Parks: a preliminary analysis. *Environmental Conservation* 14:151–156.

Machlis, G.E., J.E. Force, and R.G. Balice. 1990. Timber, minerals and social change: an exploratory test of two resource dependent communities. *Rural Sociology* 55:411–424.

Maxwell, J. 1993. A realtor runs through it. *Audubon* 44–48.

Meagher, M. 1989. Evaluation of boundary control for bison of Yellowstone National Park. *Wildlife Society Bulletin* 17:15–19.

Natural Resources Conservation Service. 1996. *America's private land: a geography of hope*. USDA Natural Resources Conservation Service, Washington, DC.

Power, T.M. 1995. Thinking about natural resource dependent economies:

moving beyond the folk economics of the rear-view mirror. Pages 235–253 in *A new century for natural resources management* (R.L. Knight and S.F. Bates, editors). Island Press, Washington, DC.

Power, T.M. 1996. *Lost landscapes and failed economies.* Island Press, Washington, DC.

Pyne, S.J., P.L. Andrews, and R.D. Laven. 1996. *Introduction to wildland fire.* Wiley, New York.

Rasker, R., and D. Glick. 1994. Footloose entrepreneurs: pioneers of the New West? *Illahee* 10:34–43.

Reid, W.V. 1996. Beyond protected areas: changing perceptions of ecological management objectives. Pages 442–453 in *Biodiversity in managed landscapes* (R.C. Szaro and D.W. Johnston, editors). Oxford University Press, New York.

Riebsame, W., H. Gosnell, and D. Theobald. 1996. Land use and landscape changes in the Colorado Mountains I: theory, scale and patterns. *Mountain Research and Development* 16:395–405.

Ring, R. 1995. The New West's servant economy. *High County News* 27(7):1, 8–12.

Romme, W.H. 1997. Creating pseudo-rural landscapes in the Mountain West. Pages 139–161 in *Placing nature: culture and landscape ecology* (J. Nassauer, editor). Island Press, Washington, DC.

Rudzitis, G., and H.E. Johansen. 1989. Migration into western wilderness counties: causes and consequences. *Western Wildlands* (Spring):19–23.

Schonewald-Cox, C., and M. Buechner. 1992. Park protection and public roads. Pages 373–395 in *Conservation Biology* (P.L. Fiedler and S.K. Jain, editors). Chapman and Hall, New York.

Shafer, C.L. 1990. *Nature reserves: island theory and conservation practice.* Smithsonian Institution Press, Washington, DC.

Soulé, M.E., D.T. Bolger, A.C. Alberts, J. Wright, M. Sorice, and S. Hill. 1988. Reconstructed dynamics of rapid extinctions of chaparral-requiring birds in urban habitat islands. *Conservation Biology* 2:75–92.

Stanton, R. 1995. Managing liability exposures associated with prescribed fires. *Natural Areas Journal* 15:347–352.

Theobald, D.M., H. Gosnell, and W.E. Riebsame. 1996. Land use and landscape change in the Colorado Mountains II: a case study of the East River Valley. *Mountain Research and Development* 16:407–418.

Torres, S.G., T.M. Mansfield, J.E. Foley, T. Lupo, and A. Brinkhaus. 1996. Mountain lion activity in California: testing speculations. *Wildlife Society Bulletin* 24:451–460.

Turner, M.G., D.N. Wear, and R.O. Flamm. 1996. Land ownership and land-cover change in the Southern Appalachian Highlands and the Olympia Peninsula. *Ecological Applications* 6:1150–1172.

Tyser, R.W., and C.A. Worley. 1992. Alien flora in grasslands adjacent to road and trail corridors in Glacier National Park, Montana (U.S.A.). *Conservation Biology* 6:253–262.

Walsh, R.G., J.R. McKean, and C.J. Mucklow. 1993. *Recreation value of ranch open space*. Department of Agricultural and Resource Economics, Colorado State University, Fort Collins, CO.

Wear, D.N., M.G. Turner, and R.O. Flamm. 1996. Ecosystem management with multiple owners: landscape dynamics in a southern Appalachian watershed. *Ecological Applications* 6:1173–1188.

Wilkinson, T. 1995. Snowed under. *National Parks* 69(1–2):32–37.

White, R. 1996. Are you an environmentalist or do you work for a living?: work and nature. Pages 171–185 in *Uncommon ground: towards reinventing nature* (W. Cronin, editor). Norton, New York.

Wondolleck, J.M., and S.L. Yaffee. 1994. *Building bridges across agency boundaries: in search of excellence in the United States Forest Service*. Pacific Northwest Research Station Report, Seattle, WA.

Yaffee, S.L., A.F. Phillips, I.C. Frentz, P.W. Hardy, S.M. Maleki, and B.E. Thorpe. 1996. *Ecosystem management in the United States: an assessment of current experience*. Island Press, Washington, DC.

PART III

CASE STUDIES

Part III contains five examples of individuals, organizations, and agencies that have found ways to cross their administrative boundaries and promote stewardship of natural resources. Florida, Colorado, Idaho, Montana, Wyoming, Arizona, and New York are the settings and each example is remarkably different from the other ones. Collectively, however, they demonstrate that cross-border collaboration can occur and that it is individuals with open minds that seem to be the only common prerequisite.

Our first example occurs in Florida where Fred Fagergren describes the creation and development of a new national preserve in "Big Cypress National Preserve: The Great Compromise." This case study describes a coalition (often called the The Great Compromise or The Unholy Alliance) among those who would use and those who would preserve wetlands south and west of Lake Okeechobee. Historically, these lands had served a remarkable variety of different functions, from hunting and off-road vehicle use, development of oil and gas, land-promotion schemes, and uses by Native Americans. In the 1960s Dade County targeted the area for an airport. This posed a sufficiently large threat to the other users that they came together and worked with the National Park Service and a variety of other state and federal agencies to form the Big Cypress National Preserve. A national preserve, however, is far from being a national park. Accordingly, a variety of uses were allowed in the Big Cypress that one would seldom see in a national park, such as oil and gas development, hunting, and off-highway vehicle use.

The real challenges for cross-boundary stewardship, however, lay in dealing with the borders created by an array of private inholdings and within-agency cultures. Over 200 private landholdings still remained within the preserve's borders and over 500 hunting camps also were built. In addition, individuals within the National Park Service viewed a national preserve as a very nontraditional idea and found the concept

193

unsettling. Fagergren describes how he and his staff maneuvered through these murky waters and eventually developed a plan that allows Big Cypress to be managed effectively.

The approach they took in developing the plan was unusual: because they recognized that the lands they managed represented only parts of natural systems, they initially disregarded their own administrative borders and instead focused on critical and sensitive resources of the Big Cypress. Only later did they overlay their own artificial boundaries established by law and identify their responsibilities. By first concentrating on the land and its resources, regardless of ownership, they were able to prepare a management plan that did the right thing for the land, rather than simply doing things right.

To describe the benefits of this approach, Fagergren presents a summary of conditions before and after the plan. For example, prior to the planning effort, hunting occurred 321 days of the year and off-highway vehicle use was unrestricted except for one area. No programs existed for protected plant species, exotic plants were largely ignored, and prescribed fire was not used. Afterward, hunting did not exceed 171 days annually, hunting dogs, other than bird dogs and retrievers, were prohibited on the preserve, off-highway vehicle use was regulated, protected plants were managed and exotic plants controlled, and a prescribed fire program was implemented. Fagergren concludes with the belief that coordination and cooperation across artificial boundaries, whether they be federal, state, county, or private, can occur when individuals are willing to meet and discuss desired outcomes.

The next case study is by John Mitchell and George Wallace and is titled "Managing Grazing and Recreation across Boundaries in the Big Cimarron Watershed." This case study explores the twin issues of grazing and outdoor recreation within a landscape of public and private lands where resolution of conflicts required a study of different land-use boundaries.

To understand grazing and recreational issues on the mixture of public and private lands that blanket western landscapes one must understand that ranchers who graze public lands also own private property to support their livestock most of the year. A typical ranching operation will keep livestock on this privately owned, lower-elevation property during fall, winter, and spring, where they are fed hay produced on those same lands during the summer. In early summer, the animals are moved on to public lands to graze sites that may include designated wilderness areas.

Recreation on wilderness areas is popular and increasing. Each of the three landscape components (private, public, and wilderness) utilized by the public–private grazing systems exhibits different recreationist–livestock interactions. It is these interactions that have the greatest implications for cross-boundary management. This topic is of interest because boundaries of livestock allotments rarely coincide with wilderness boundaries, yet recreational activities and expectations are sharply defined by boundaries between multiple-use and wilderness areas.

Land-management agencies are interested in curtailing the scope and severity of impacts caused to wilderness visitors. Likewise, they have focused on biophysical indicators of rangeland health to manage livestock grazing. Mitchell and Wallace suggest that managers may soon begin to incorporate social indicators and standards for wilderness conditions with the goal of mitigating some impacts of livestock grazing on wilderness visitors.

The third case study is "Overcoming Boundaries: The Greater Yellowstone Ecosystem" and occurs in portions of Idaho, Montana, and Wyoming. Dennis Glick and Tim Clark describe the complexities of working across administrative lines that include twenty-five federal, state, and local agencies, in addition to the boundaries of thousands of private landowners. It is not surprising, Glick and Clark argue, that such complex boundaries have led to habitat fragmentation, disruption of ecological processes, and human–wildlife confrontations. Because these issues transcend administrative and land-ownership boundaries, they underscore the need to take a broader, more integrated view of land management activities in the Greater Yellowstone.

Recognizing the need for better coordination between federal land managers, state and county governments, and private individuals, a variety of groups and organizations have begun to work cooperatively to bridge their own boundaries and ensure the ecological and economic vitality of this region. Collectively these examples demonstrate practical progress toward resolving cross-boundary issues. While each project had its own unique qualities, they all share common elements including (1) the collection and dissemination of good data before undertaking action;

(2) the creation of forums for dialog where information can be discussed; (3) the decision to give stakeholders a voice and role in management decisions; (4) identification of a shared set of goals; and (5) continual evaluation and modification to reflect changing conditions.

Glick and Clark conclude that the traditional top-down, short-term, and narrowly focused approaches to land management do not address the more complex challenges that face managers today. The Greater Yellowstone Ecosystem has always been fragmented by diverse ownerships and jurisdictions, but its problems are exacerbated by the phenomenal population growth the region is experiencing. Collaborative approaches that seek common goals across administrative lines, they argue, are the best hope to minimize harmful ecological effects that in time will jeopardize the sustainability of human enterprises in this region.

─────

The next case study explores the advantages of forging partnerships that span the boundaries of private landowners with those of public lands. Arizona is one of America's most rapidly growing states. What happens when that growth reaches the boundary of a national park? In their chapter titled "Partnerships across Park Boundaries: The Rincon Institute and Saguaro National Park," Luther Propst, William Paleck, and Liz Rosan describe the efforts of individuals and organizations that met along the abrupt line between Tucson and Saguaro National Park and then crossed over.

Saguaro National Park protects almost 37,000 hectares of Sonoran Desert and the "sky islands" of the Rincon Mountains. When the park was established in 1933, it stood as an isolated wilderness 19 kilometers from the edge of Tucson. Since then, growth has swept up alongside the park's borders and redefined it as a suburban wilderness. Many of the ecological values that defined the park's very character were being eroded by the pressure of high human densities alongside its boundary. Not surprisingly, this residential and commercial development was threatening the park's integrity, yet it was proximity to the park's amenities that drew people to live and work there in the first place.

The proposal of a 2,428-hectare development along 8 kilometers of the park's borders served as a catalyst to bring people together. The developer, national park service officials, local and national conservationists, and the county formed a unique partnership to ensure that any new development would be highly sensitive with respect to the park's natural and cultural resources.

What resulted was called the Rincon Institute, an independent, non-profit conservation organization whose mission was to help protect Saguaro National Park and adjoining lands. As the authors describe, the results from this consensus-based approach have been remarkable. The developer agreed to sell 95 percent of the area's most important wildlife habitat to the National Park Service and to restore damaged riparian habitat that issued from the park and ran through the proposed development. The developer also reduced the total number of homes from 21,000 to less than 7,000 and set aside one half of the area as open space. In addition, the developer agreed to fund the Rincon Institute to ensure long-term monitoring, compliance, and implementation of these commitments.

Since that time the Rincon Institute has successfully lobbied Congress to increase the size of the park and has developed a variety of conservation research, land management, and environmental educational programs. The authors believe that this emerging trend of forging collaborative solutions integrating conservation with development will continue, particularly as more and more Americans are choosing to live in rural areas adjacent to public lands.

The final case study is by Thomas Pasquarello and is titled "Wilderness and Working Landscapes: The Adirondack Park As a Model Bioregion." Adirondack Park in New York State encompasses two and one-half million hectares and is larger than Yellowstone, Yosemite, Olympic, and Everglades national parks combined. Unlike traditional parks, however, this state park is a mixture of private (60 percent) and public (40 percent) ownership. The park also is home to approximately 150,000 permanent and 125,000 seasonal residents and is visited by an estimated 15 million tourists annually. The park is divided into 105 units of town and village government across 12 counties, and each of the 5 state agencies that provide services to park residents and visitors have divided it into a different geographic pattern of administrative units. Protecting the park's natural resources requires cross-boundary cooperation, perhaps more so than for most landscapes.

Pasquarello explores the historical, legal, and ecological dimensions of wilderness and working landscapes, an alliterative description of the patchwork of public and private lands that makes the Adirondack one of the oldest and largest bioregions of the world. Understandably, the difficulties of uniting such complex boundaries over such a large area would be a daunting task for any single organization or entity. Pasquarello explores four approaches that appear to be the most responsible for the successes the park has experienced. First, is the idea of regional land use planning. The linchpin of this process is the Adirondack Park Land Use Map created in the 1970s, that designates the Park into different land-use categories influencing what is developed and what is protected.

Second, the New York State Department of Environmental Conservation, in consultation with others, prepares unit management plans for areas of the park to remain in wilderness or other designations of minimal use. This effectively controls growth or unrestricted outdoor recreation and ensures the park remains "forever wild."

The third approach is within the category of compatible economic development. The Adirondack Park Agency has created regional zoning regulations that classify private land within six designations from industrial to agricultural. Within the park, farms and forest lands are the most prevalent working landscapes, but both are under intense pressure from development. The Adirondack Park Agency and other organizations have intervened using a variety of market incentives and tools to keep these lands from being further developed. As the same time, small towns have the least restrictions as they are designated as the growth and service centers of the park.

The final category of tools that Pasquarello describes falls under the heading of stewardship. Stewardship, to Pasquarello, is a sense of responsibility that helps protect biodiversity by providing both the means and the motives to sustain a landscape in the face of economic, political, and social pressures. For stewardship to work, Pasquarello believes, the park's residents and visitors need access to information, opportunities to be heard by officials, a decision-making process that is open to all relevant interests, an explicit legal base for decision-making authority, public accountability, written reasons for important decisions, and an independent appeal process.

Pasquarello concludes with the belief that Adirondack Park is a grand experiment in bioregionalism. Building on successes and learning from failures, the park offers lessons that form a practical toolkit that may be used to reduce the difficulties of managing bioregions across human boundaries.

Big Cypress National Preserve: The Great Compromise

Fred J. Fagergren

For some south Floridians there is no confusion if one speaks of "The Great Compromise" and "The Unholy Alliance." Those who use and those who would preserve natural resources came together in the early 1970s to protect a portion of the south Florida ecosystem called the Big Cypress Swamp. Individuals with beliefs from opposite ends of the natural resource spectrum made an unusual compromise and alliance to establish a new kind of unit for the National Park Service: a national preserve.

Where subtle elevation changes and varying soil depths create a diverse landscape of swirling, intertwined vegetation, the U.S. Congress chose section and township lines to enclose and establish the Big Cypress National Preserve, making a compromise between opposing interests and solving their problem. Congress then charged the National Park Service (NPS) with managing the area within these human-conceived boundaries as though it were a national park, yet insisted many preexisting consumptive uses be allowed to continue. Although Congress had ended their debate, it left it to the NPS to translate a unique congressional mandate into management plans and policies that accommodate legal boundaries, social issues, and a natural ecosystem. The experience of the NPS at Big Cypress provides an example of how to work within the dimensions of artificial boundaries to manage and preserve a remnant of an ecosystem, while still influencing the entire ecosystem.

Area Description

The Florida lands south of Lake Okeechobee were once called the Everglades, or the "Glades": the last home of the Seminoles and Miccosukees. Shallow fresh waters flowing south from Lake Okeechobee, bounded by ocean waters around the peninsula, create a complex ecosystem where freshwater outflow and saltwater intrusion find a fragile balance. The characteristics that made it such an ideal refuge for these American Indians—difficult to enter and cross—continue to shape options for this complex ecosystem.

The western portion of this system became known as the Big Cypress Swamp—607,000 hectares east of Naples, Florida (Figure 9.1). In many ways this is a confusing name. The cypress are seldom big: the area was named for the quantity of cypress trees, not for their size. "Swamp" fails to describe the area's complexity: the area inundated varies each year from as much as 90 percent to as little as 10 percent. Within the Big Cypress Swamp, the waters flow south and westward toward the Ten

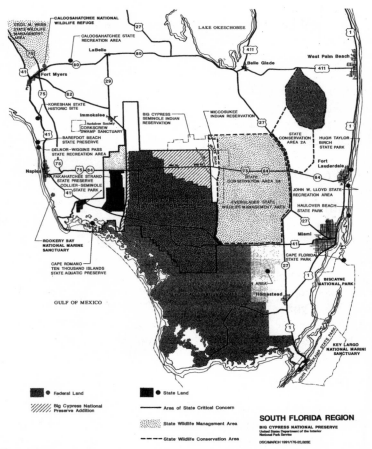

Figure 9.1. The regional context of Big Cypress National Preserve in southern Florida.

Thousand Islands and the Gulf of Mexico and are distinct from the waters in Everglades National Park. Water depths and salinity, soil depth and composition, and elevation all combine in an infinite array to create old-growth pinelands, grass prairies or marshes, cypress strands, hardwood swamps and sloughs, hardwood hammocks, and mangrove forests. A change of merely a centimeter of elevation or soil depth, whether more or less, changes the vegetation. The rich diversity of the landscape was historically inhabited by a diverse fauna, including the Florida panther (*Felis concolor coryi*), endemic tree snails (*Liguus fasciatus*), alligators (*Alligator mississippiensis*), white-tailed deer (*Odocoileus virginianus seminolus*), and hundreds of bird species (Duever et al. 1986).

Unused and unentered by European settlers, this area was only traversed east to west by the Tamiami Trail (U.S. 41) and Alligator Alley (I-75) in the relatively recent past (Figure 9.1). Historic and environmental conditions resulted in coastal settlements with large absentee ownership of the interior lands. Hot and humid Florida initially attracted only hardy souls who explored the Glades with flat-bottom dugouts, following the Miccosukee and Seminole example. Eventually, mechanical ingenuity and home design brought about "swamp buggies" and "airboats," unique off-road craft that could traverse the shallow waters. For generations these folks and the American Indians were minor intruders in this vast area.

Automobiles and air conditioning brought south Florida an increasing human population and demands for improved access. The development of the Tamiami Trail and Alligator Alley in 1928 and 1967, respectively, inspired interest and exploration in the region, which in turn brought about subdivision of landownership, additional roads, and increased land speculation and development. These changes, plus loss of the wild lands, decreasing bird populations, and increasing tourism, led to the establishment of Everglades National Park in 1947.

Although an effort was made by some to include the Big Cypress Swamp within Everglades National Park, this did not occur for several reasons: the perceived threat to Big Cypress was less; recreationists did not want to lose hunting and off-road vehicle opportunities; major landowners did not want to lose opportunities for oil and gas development or land subdivision; and Congress did not want to purchase the oil and gas mineral rights.

In the late 1960s conditions again changed. Public concerns were raised by the drainage of wetlands for land speculation, development in the western portion of the Big Cypress Swamp, and the 1968 construction of the Dade Jetport at the eastern edge of the Swamp. Envisioned as a major airport 80 kilometers west of Miami, Dade Jetport was seen as the answer to the transportation needs of the booming east coast of Florida. The immediate impacts of the taxi and runways (massive dredge and fill of hundreds of hectares), plus concerns over development that normally accompany an airport's completion, prompted various special interests to seek congressional action to protect their vision for the Big Cypress (Gore 1976).

The environmental community wanted the Big Cypress added to Everglades National Park or established as a separate national park. Hunters and off-road enthusiasts wanted an area where their uses would take priority. Private landowners wanted the protected area to be as small as possible, with the assurance of compensation for land acquisitions and the ability to continue oil and gas development. The Miccosukee and Seminoles wanted to continue to use Big Cypress resources and continue their religious practices. The attention drawn to the Dade Jetport brought national interest, and the special concerns and visions of south Floridians were soon mixed with other national agendas. Differing opinions tend to slow congressional action, so protection of these lands languished for several years. Finally, dialog began between those who use the Big Cypress Swamp and those who would preserve it. Believing their individual efforts might fail, they made what will always be called "The Great Compromise." The written legislation seems to say the NPS will satisfy all the demands of all interests, or perhaps it says the NPS will not satisfy any of the demands completely. This unique enabling Act, Public Law 93-440, established Big Cypress National Preserve on October 11, 1974 (correspondence from Assistant Secretary N.P. Reed of the Department of the Interior to John Jones and Calvin Stone, March 2, 1972, and U.S. Senate 1973, U.S. House of Representatives 1974). The Act states: "That in order to assure the preservation, conservation, and protection of the natural, scenic, hydrologic, floral and faunal, and recreational values of the Big Cypress Watershed . . . and to provide for the enhancement and public enjoyment thereof, the Big Cypress National Preserve is hereby established."

That seemingly direct and simple statement is followed by many specifics that: (1) direct acquisition of all lands, waters, or interests, except certain improved properties already in place and oil and gas interests; (2) require the lands be administered as a unit of the National Park System in a manner that assures their natural and ecological integrity in perpetuity; (3) allow hunting and fishing, off-road vehicle use, and grazing to the extent these activities are shown to be compatible with protection of the preserve's resources; and (4) ensure the Miccosukee and

Seminole tribes their usual and customary use and occupancy, including traditional tribal ceremonials and hunting, fishing, and trapping on a subsistence basis.

However, public law does not stand alone. Congressional testimony and House and Senate reports on a public law are recognized as legislative history and provide clarification and direction. Public Law 93-440 is accompanied by House Report 93-502 and Senate Report 93-1128, and these provide some additional direction (U.S. Senate 1973, U.S. House of Representatives 1974). Unfortunately, in the case of Big Cypress National Preserve, the bills and public hearings with their extensive testimony give limited clarification, although they clearly articulate the many conflicts that would challenge the management skills of the NPS. Key comments from House Report 93-502 (U.S. House of Representatives 1974 include (emphasis added):

> anything that interferes with the natural flow of fresh water will radically alter this sensitive subtropical environment . . . (any construction activities which divert the water . . . will ultimately affect all forms of life . . . since the water level is the most significant factor. . . .

> Since the area . . . is largely undeveloped . . . and because it will *be managed in a manner which will assure its return to the true wilderness character which once prevailed,* it will offer . . . recreation opportunities. . . . While the use of all terrain vehicles must be carefully regulated. . . . to protect the natural, wildlife and wilderness values . . . , the bill does not prohibit their use along designated roads and trails.

> The committee chose to call the area a preserve rather than a reserve . . . feeling such distinction may be important. Reserve refers to stock—a commodity held for future use. Preserve refers . . . to the keeping or safeguarding of something basically protected and perpetuated. . . .

> *The principal thrust of these areas should be the preservation of the natural values which they contain.* They might differ . . . from national parks . . . insofar as administrative policies are concerned. Hunting . . . subject to reasonable regulation . . . *could be permitted to the extent compatible with the purposes for which the area is established. . . . All management activities . . . should be directed toward*

maintaining the natural and scientific values. . . . National preserves
may accommodate significant . . . uses . . . but such . . . would be
*limited to activities where, or periods when, such human visitation
would not interfere with or disrupt the values which the area is created
to preserve.*

These statements seem clear, with limited room left for interpretation.
Along with similar statements from Senate Report 93-1128, they clarify
the public law and provide an extraordinary standard not given in other
national park enabling legislation. True, the preserve would be subject to
more extensive recreational use than a national park, but other national
park and environmental laws direct managers to ensure that resources are
protected. This prompts managers to focus on measuring the extent to
which activities are detrimental, and, as a result, they feel unable to act
until damage to the resource is shown. For example, the Redwoods Act
(Public Law 95-250) directs park managers to ensure resources are not
degraded, and the Endangered Species Act requires action when harm to
a species is documented (Mantell 1990, Dilsaver 1994). The Big Cypress
legislation clearly set a stronger standard: human activities could occur
to the extent they are shown to be compatible with the protection of the
resources. This clarified two points that bring advantages to management: (1) we do not need to allow an activity until or unless we prove it
is detrimental, and (2) the NPS does not have to shoulder the burden of
proof that it is detrimental. If the NPS does not have the time or
resources to show compatibility between an activity and resource protection, the NPS can take a very conservative approach until a level of compatibility is shown. If outside forces believe the activity is compatible,
they may wish to collect and present data to the NPS themselves.

Arrival of the National Park Service

At the time Big Cypress and Big Thicket in Texas were the first national
preserves established by Congress, and the NPS was directed to proceed
with acquisition and management. On top of this legislative challenge
was the reality of the preserve: 231,000 hectares in the original legislation, carved out of private lands. By number of tracts, this was the largest
land acquisition ever attempted by the U.S. government: 47,000 separate
tracts, the result of subdivision and land speculation. In laying out the
preserve's administrative boundary, the designers attempted to follow the
natural water systems, but human boundaries and interests constrained
possibilities and shaped the final reality. The southern preserve bound-

ary, which is formed by the northern boundary of Everglades National Park, was stair-stepped along section and township lines instead of the natural boundary formed by the mangroves that followed the coastline. The Preserve's northern boundary was meant to separate the water systems of the Big Cypress from waters that flow to the east and eventually into Shark Slough of Everglades National Park, but this boundary also follows the stair-stepped lines of townships and sections. The western boundary parallels State Highway 29 approximately 1.6 kilometers to the east and excludes the Barron River canal that parallels the highway. The waters of the Big Cypress, generally flowing south and west, enter this canal at various points, speeding their loss into the Gulf. Nevertheless, the value of road frontage to private landowners was perceived as a priority over the integrity of the ecosystem. The eastern boundary more closely follows the natural separation between the Big Cypress and Shark Slough drainages.

Adding to the challenges presented by these human boundaries were the internal land circumstances. Lands held in private ownership before November 23, 1971, were not to be acquired unless use of the land came in conflict with the purposes of the preserve. Over two hundred inholdings were thus to remain intact until there was a willing seller. Also unresolved were the restoration and transfer of the 9,650 hectares held by Dade County for the jetport. Lands "suitable for a jetport" were to be found, developed, and then exchanged for the jetport area within the preserve. Potential lands for this exchange are yet to be located, and so the jetport and its runways, which originally prompted the establishment of the preserve, remain in nonfederal ownership and open to different land use and management.

In addition to the lands in private ownership, there were 500 "trespass camps" within the preserve. Over many years, individuals had constructed hunting camps on property they did not own. These camps, some quite elaborate, were focal points for hunting and off-road vehicle use and other resource impacts. Miccosukees and Seminoles also occupy villages and use several religious sites within the preserve and are assured subsistence use throughout the preserve.

How to Make a Preserve Work

Big Cypress was and is different and challenging. The preserve's enabling legislation created something difficult to define, but it also gave a fundamental charge that shapes all decisions regarding the preserve's resources and systems. Preserve managers must protect the resources while allowing human activities to the extent compatible with that protection. This requires them to know more about the preserve and its adjacent natural systems than other national parks. In some circumstances, other national park units have the option to exclude human activities from critical resources or areas. Within the Big Cypress National Preserve, human activities are legislatively included, which requires extensive scientific knowledge of their interaction with preserve resources.

What of federal management and direction? In the case of Big Cypress this task was given to the Southeast Region of the NPS. The preserve was acknowledged, even in its unique legislation, as being a very nontraditional concept for the NPS. How would it be viewed? An opportunity to expand our horizons and experiences? or a threat to tradition and a change we could not comprehend?

In 1981, I was selected as the first superintendent, a position that had evolved from a project supervisor temporarily transferred from a district ranger position in Everglades National Park, to a site manager whose focus was land acquisition. Confusion and indecision were apparent when, en route to the preserve for the first time, I met with the southeast regional director. He shared his understanding that as a new "park manager" I was no doubt excited to get to my area, to learn about the preserve and begin my job. He then explained this was not going to happen! The preserve was established solely to allow water to flow through to Everglades National Park. There would be no active management, there would be no development to meet public needs, there would be no increase in staff. The NPS would not actively plan for or manage this unit! During the balance of my visit, one deputy regional director introduced me as the new superintendent of Big Cypress, and the second deputy introduced me as the new site manager of the preserve.

Although concerned, I hoped time would cure some of these confusing perceptions about the future of the preserve, but my initial months at the preserve did not indicate time was helping. Management of Big Cypress was seen by some as a part of Everglades National Park. If I initiated a telephone call to an associate regional director and left my name and number, the superintendent of Everglades would receive a call and an inquiry about why I might be calling. When I initiated a memorandum requesting regional help with various planning needs and signed it as the superintendent of Big Cypress National Preserve, the rift expanded between those within the NPS who realized the need to fulfill our legislative mandates for the preserve and those who wished to ignore its existence. The need for long-term planning became increasingly evident. Management decisions were being made issue by issue with no regard for the resources or the public.

Finally during one week in 1984 everything changed. I had again sought support from the regional office to develop a management plan for the preserve and had again been informed no management planning would occur. On Friday of the same week I received a call from the head of regional planning who informed me a General Management Plan for Big Cypress was now the number-one priority for regional planning efforts. When I asked how we could have gone from no chance for planning to planning as the top priority, he shared the observation that a certain individual in the region had been transferred.

Shortly thereafter the management of Big Cypress was separated from Everglades National Park and the new regional director, Robert Baker, made the commitment to manage the preserve in a manner consistent with its specific enabling legislation. Of course, this did not resolve all issues at the preserve. It did, however, allow us to embark toward a General Management Plan: the process that would allow long-term management of the Big Cypress ecosystem within and across its administrative boundaries. This would be a difficult and expensive process, full of internal agency and public conflict. I suspect many individuals today still believe it was a mistake, that it would have been better to have pursued the other path—no active management of the preserve. Fortunately, throughout this process we had the continuing commitment and leadership of Regional Director Baker. He quickly developed a vision of the Big Cypress National Preserve and held fast with his support for not simply doing things right, but also doing the right thing.

In reality there was no other option that could resolve the many challenges found within and beyond Big Cypress National Preserve. We tried to use short-term planning efforts such as the Preserve's Statement for Management, an NPS process that provides year-to-year management direction, but too much remained unresolved. Various governmental actions had split ecosystems between private, state, county, National Park, preserve, reservation, and U.S. Fish and Wildlife refuge lands. In Big Cypress, the large, absentee landownership pattern allowed unregulated hunting and trapping of wildlife, and trespass camps facilitated and concentrated those activities. Authorized uses of private inholdings, hunting and off-road vehicles, oil and gas exploration and extraction, and the subsistence rights held by Miccosukees and Seminoles inherently conflicted with overall preservation of natural resources.

Planning Across Administrative Boundaries

It was clear that management success depended on consistent interpretation of the preserve's enabling legislation and knowing as much as possible about the ecosystem. The preserve's management staff acknowledged this challenge: we were to manage and protect these resources forever, yet allow human activities to the extent they were compatible with resource protection. This meant we needed to allow the activities either where the least impact would occur or where mitigation was possible or easiest. Where were these resources? Which resources were most vulnerable? Which resources were most sensitive to which uses? Which were most important? We knew we would never know enough, and yet we could not wait to make decisions until enough was known. We recognized the absolute need for long-range planning, a General Management Plan that would address all these issues. It would have been nice to have had every piece of resource data before we began the General Management Plan, but protection of the resources demanded we make decisions based on what we did know.

Fortunately, active oil and gas exploration and extraction within the preserve prompted some data collection. Requests for federal and state permits for exploration were occurring routinely. Although the responsible agencies recognized the need to avoid sensitive areas when oil roads and pads were placed, the permit process did not consider cumulative impacts. In 1983 the NPS developed a "Proposed Sensitive Resource Areas" report and map that would alert the oil and gas industry to those resources they should avoid, improve protection of preserve resources, and assist preserve staff in processing of oil and gas permits (National Park Service 1983).

This experience, combined with the need to address cumulative impacts, allowed us to base management on important or critical resources. We recognized that the lands we managed represented only parts of the natural systems. We decided to use a stepped approach: the identification of important resources would lead to the development of management zones, and both of these steps would ignore human-made boundaries. Only at the next stage would we return to the artificial boundaries established by law and identify the Planning Units and objectives that applied to those units. This Land Use Planning Process is best conveyed by Figure 9.2 (National Park Service 1991).

We began by returning to the legislative history of the preserve. We reviewed the many federal and state laws, regulations, and policies that

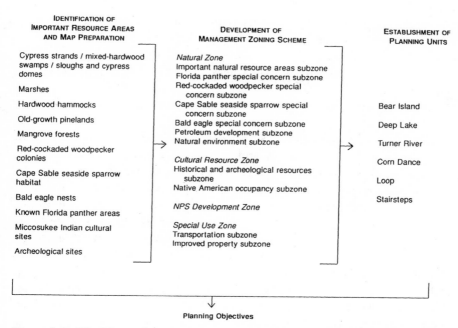

Figure 9.2. *The National Park Service Land Use Planning Process applied at Big Cypress National Preserve.*

also applied to the preserve. These documents helped us identify the important resource values.

We prepared a base map for the preserve from U.S. Geological Survey maps and infrared aerial photographs and developed overlays for each of the important resource categories (e.g., a detailed map identified the vegetation communities). These individual overlays were then used in a composite form to produce the "Important Resource Areas Map" that was released to the public in August 1986 (National Park Service 1986). The following criteria were used in identifying important resource values:

- Areas that contain outstanding examples of the natural, scenic, hydrologic, floral, faunal, and recreational values for which the preserve was established

- Areas essential to protecting the ecological integrity of Everglades National Park by maintaining water flow and quality throughout the preserve

- Areas that provide necessary habitat for the continued survival of threatened or endangered species of flora or fauna

- Areas that contain Native American cultural sites

- Areas with important historic or archeological resources

We defined three categories for important resource values based on these criteria: (1) vegetation and landform resources, (2) wildlife resources, and (3) cultural resources. Within each of these broad categories, specific resource areas were identified and, where possible, mapped.

We then identified management zones based on the important resource areas. Given the emphasis throughout this process on protecting of preserve resources, most of the preserve was placed in the "natural" zone. This included the "subzone" for petroleum develop-ment because those areas would eventually be restored to their natural conditions. Other zones incorporated the important cultural resources and Native American occupancy, NPS development, and special uses such as public roads and the improved property or inholdings.

We then turned to the artificial boundaries, roads and trails, to identify appropriate planning units. The human-made roads, trails, and boundaries allowed us to develop management units with specific objectives (Figure 9.3). These objectives covered the following areas:

- *Visitor use*: To include visitor services, hunting, and off-road vehicle management

- *Natural resource management*: To include hydrologic, mineral, vegetation, fire, and wildlife management

- *Cultural resource management*: To include cultural resources management, cooperation with Native Americans to continue their usual and customary use and occupancy, protection of Native American ceremonial sites, and provision for maximum Native American participation in new revenue-producing visitor services

- *General development*: To include providing visitor services and operations with minimal development while minimizing impacts on flood plains and wetlands, rare and protected species, important resource areas, habitat diversity, and other natural resource values.

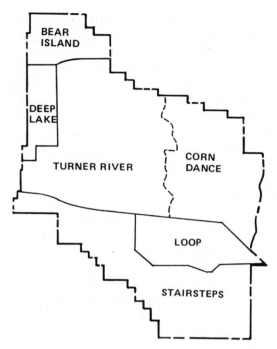

Figure 9.3. Geographic location of each of the planning/management units within Big Cypress National Preserve. (From National Park Service, 1991, General Management Plan.)

We developed planning objectives in each of these areas (generally in response to the need to protect the important resource areas) and identified alternatives for managing toward these objectives. Managing at the status quo was considered unacceptable because the important resource areas would not be adequately protected, and managing the preserve as a national park was unacceptable because this was beyond the legislative authority. The management alternatives that were identified as feasible were shaped by the resource areas, their distribution within each planning unit, the present level of human activity and its impacts on the important resources, and the professional judgment of NPS staff that current levels of human activities were not compatible with protection of the resources. For example, within the Bear Island Unit, current oil and gas activity was believed to be at or beyond an acceptable level. Thus the management action we proposed allowed further oil and gas activity only if the area of direct impact does not exceed the current area of unreclaimed roads, pads, pipelines, and geophysical survey lines in the unit. We also considered important resource areas when we selected a management alternative that permits surface occupancy for exploratory drilling and production only outside important vegetation and cultural resource areas.

For off-road vehicle use, we closed the Deep Lake unit to ORVs because of the important resource areas and documented panther habitat. In the Bear Island unit, we restricted all ORV use to designated trails because it has one of the highest concentrations of important resource areas.

Benefits from Planning

To describe the benefits of this planning approach it is best to provide a summary of before and after conditions. Prior to this effort, hunting occurred 321 days of the year, including 187 nights of raccoon (*Procyon lotor marinus*) hunting with dogs. Concerns for the Florida panther had limited impacts on hunting regulations. Except for the Loop Unit, ORV use was unrestricted. Oil and Gas exploration and production were evaluated as we received each proposal, and important resource areas were protected only where and when possible. No programs were undertaken for protected plant species. The control program for exotic plants was extremely limited, and no prescribed fire program existed for the Cape Sable seaside sparrow (*Ammospiza maritima mirabilis*) or red-cockaded woodpecker (*Picoides borealis*). Efforts were made to protect the hydrology of the preserve, but the effects of existing canals, roads, and other influences on water resources were not mitigated (e.g., Turner River and Birdon Canals and the Loop Road were accepted and no further restoration actions were taken).

Through this comprehensive planning effort, the total time open to hunting will not exceed 171 days annually. Raccoon hunting was eliminated, and check-in, check-out stations operate during hunting seasons. Hunting dogs other than bird dogs and retrievers are prohibited in the preserve, and no dogs of any kind are allowed in the Loop and Deep Lake units. These units are reserved for walk-in hunting and are closed to ORVs. Deep Lake unit is reserved for archery hunting only. Loaded weapons are prohibited on ORVs and during general gun season each management unit has a limited number of daily permits (i.e., they will operate under a quota hunt system).

Now ORVs are regulated and controlled through (1) a vehicle permit system with no more than 2,500 permits issued each year, (2) general regulations governing vehicle operation, and (3) a system of designated access points, areas, or trails for each unit with ORV use. Two units are closed to ORVs: Loop and Deep Lake. In the Bear Island unit ORVs are restricted to designated trails.

We established an acceptable level of exploration and development for oil and gas based on the area of influence. At any given time, only 10 percent of the preserve can be subject to the influence of oil and gas exploration and development. Important vegetation and cultural resource areas will be protected by prohibiting surface occupancy for exploratory drilling and production, and all oil and gas activity is subject to the stipulations of a Minerals Management Plan.

An aggressive program exists for protected species and for eliminating exotic plants. We established a prescribed fire program for Cape Sable seaside sparrow and red-cockaded woodpecker. Also in place is a program of water monitoring, regulatory actions and restoration, and rehabilitation projects for the preserve's hydrology. Turner River and Deep Lake Strand will be restored; Loop Road and Bear Island Road will be rehabilitated to remove current water impoundment; and over 150 acquired tracts with abandoned structures or fill pads and access roads will be restored to allow natural water flow.

Application Beyond the Preserve

How might this land use planning process be used elsewhere? How might future preserve managers and adjacent land managers use this approach? How will future science and refined knowledge fit within the existing plan?

This process, with today's computer technology, has continuing application within the Big Cypress National Preserve and at any location where resources exist and need to be protected. In the future, science and refined knowledge will only benefit the management of human activities and protection of resources. Our experience at Big Cypress began before the NPS had fully developed Geographical Information Systems (GIS) capability. We began by using noncomputerized maps and data, but during the process much of the data were eventually computerized, allowing better comparison and integration of data, GIS development will continue to strengthen at Big Cypress, and baseline scientific knowledge and monitoring of resources and human activities must continue. Expansion of these capabilities will allow refinement of the important resource areas data collected during the general management plan development. On-the-ground application of the planning objectives and management decisions will be more accurate, and greater protection of resources will be possible. Assumptions made during the General Management Plan development can be verified or modified using these continuing systems, and management decisions can be reviewed and revised in light of new data.

Coordination and cooperation across the artificial boundaries between preserve and park, reservation, refuge, state, or county can be increased. The GIS data follow natural boundaries and comprehensive data bases should be shared between agencies and entities. Even if legislation, policy, and management objectives differ among land managers, the identification of resources and the understanding of their importance will allow parties to work more cooperatively.

Application of this process elsewhere requires only the commitment to gain the necessary knowledge of the resources one is charged to protect and an understanding of the level and type of protection with which one is charged. Any location can be described, defined, and mapped by its resources. Those resources can be placed in some hierarchical order of importance, depending on legal mandates, sensitivity, or other criteria. Important resource areas can be identified through layering (whether manually or with GIS capabilities) and organized into management zones. Land managers can then, as appropriate, step back to the artificial boundaries of planning or management units and determine the range of alternatives that will allow human activities consistent with protection of their important resource areas.

Any entities or individuals charged with ownership, stewardship, or management of land should pursue their responsibilities with the fundamental concept that activities on that land should occur only in ways compatible with the long-range objectives of that landownership. Knowledge and data sharing with adjacent landowners will only increase all the parties' ability to fulfill their objectives. No piece of land stands isolated from another—each impacts and influences its neighbor. This is true whether the land is managed by the NPS and must be preserved in perpetuity or whether private landowners wish their property to increase in value through time. Understanding what resources an area contains, how those resources interact and influence one another, the relative importance of those identified resources, their presence within one's specific tract of land, and how one should best manage those resources toward their objectives is a process applicable to any location.

REFERENCES

Dilsaver, L.M. 1994. *America's National Park System: the critical documents*. Rowman & Littlefield Publishers, London.

Duever, M.J., J.E. Carlson, J.F. Meeder, L.C. Duever, L.H. Gunderson, L.A. Riopelle, T.R. Alexander, R.F. Myers, and D.P. Spangler. 1986. *The Big Cypress National Preserve*. National Audubon Society, New York.

Gore, R. 1976. *Twilight hope for Big Cypress*. National Geographic Society, Washington, DC.

Mantell, M.A. 1990. *Managing National Park System resources: a handbook on legal duties, opportunities, and tools*. The Conservation Foundation, Washington, DC.

National Park Service. 1983. *Proposed sensitive resources areas*. National Park Service Mining and Minerals Division, Denver, CO.

National Park Service. 1986. Newsletter, General Management Plan, Environmental Impact Statement, Important Resource Areas. National Park Service Denver Service Center, Denver, CO.

National Park Service. 1991. *General Management Plan*. National Park Service Denver Service Center, Denver, CO.

U.S. House of Representatives. 1973. *Report No. 93-502, Establishing the Big Cypress National Preserve in the state of Florida, and for other purposes*. 93rd Congress, Washington, DC.

U.S. Senate. 1974. *Report No. 93-1128. Establishing the Big Cypress National Preserve, Florida*. 93rd Congress, Washington, D.C.

Chapter 10

Managing Grazing and Recreation Across Boundaries in the Big Cimarron Watershed

John E. Mitchell and George Wallace

Edges, by their very character, have been a challenge to people whose professions or avocations deal with nature. Ecologists have focused on community edges, called ecotones, for the past one hundred years. Contemporary natural resource managers function as applied ecologists who wish to sustain natural landscape structure and ecosystem processes. In doing so, however, they are more often hindered by human-defined boundaries and attendant political and social considerations than by ecological edges (Christensen et al. 1996).

In the western United States, livestock grazing provides a particularly interesting study of cross-boundary management problems and opportunities because it frequently extends across both ecological and political borders. The basis for authorizing and controlling grazing on National Forest System (NFS) lands was contained in the Organic Administration Act of 1897. One control measure that is still effective requires permittees to own sufficient "base property" to support the number of livestock allowed by the permit when the livestock are not on public land (Public Land Law Review Commission 1970). As a result, public lands grazing privileges have become linked to individual ranching operations, and the livestock involved are moved cyclically across boundaries between private and public land.

A typical ranching operation keeps livestock on its privately owned, lower-elevation feeding grounds during late fall and winter where the stock are fed hay and other forage produced on those same lands in summer. Calving and lambing take place in late winter or early spring. In middle to late spring, the animals are moved onto public lands to graze, which in turn allows hay production to begin again on the ranch's irrigated meadows. Often, this means using spring forage on middle-elevation lands administered by the USDI Bureau of Land Management (BLM) first, and then moving onto upper-elevation National Forest System (NFS) lands for the summer and early fall. In some areas summer and fall grazing will also occur on lands that have been designated as wilderness by the Wilderness Act of 1964 and succeeding statutes.

On landscapes where public lands grazing may be found, other uses usually are present, including recreation. Recreationists bring with them a wide range of motives, such as being with friends, experiencing nature, improving outdoor skills, and rest and relaxation. On private lands, recreation commonly centers on ranches or rural resorts. Other recreationists experience the outdoors simply by passing through private rangelands on public roads. Recreation on public lands includes developed and dispersed camping, hiking, fishing, hunting, horseback riding, or using all-terrain vehicles. In wilderness areas, visitors seek the same sorts of activities, but in a nonmotorized setting with higher levels of ecosystem protection and less evidence of human activity (P. Brown and Haas 1980). Ultimately, each of the three landscape components (private, public multiple-use, and wilderness) used by these grazing systems may be expected to exhibit somewhat different interactions between visitors and livestock. It is these interactions that have the greatest implications for cross-boundary management.

Using a case study of a montane watershed on the northern slopes of the San Juan Mountains in Colorado, this chapter examines how institutional policy and visitor attitudes can differ within the three landscape components that cattle and sheep occupy during the year. It also shows how administrators might use such information to reduce constraints presented by these differences, thereby making cross-boundary management more effective.

The Big Cimarron Watershed

The Big Cimarron watershed is mostly contained in the Ouray Ranger District, Uncompahgre National Forest. The district shares common traits with numerous other NFS and BLM lands in the Rocky Mountains, however. It borders privately owned valley lands along its lower edge and extends above timberline to peaks and ridges that frequently rise 4,000 meters above sea level. The highest elevations of the district have been designated as wilderness, in this case the Uncompahgre Wilderness (Figure 10.1).

Lower-elevation lands in the Gunnison River valley, including areas adjoining the Uncompahgre National Forest, are undergoing a fundamental change in land use. Since 1990 urban dwellers have been moving into the rural landscape in Delta, Montrose, and Gunnison counties,

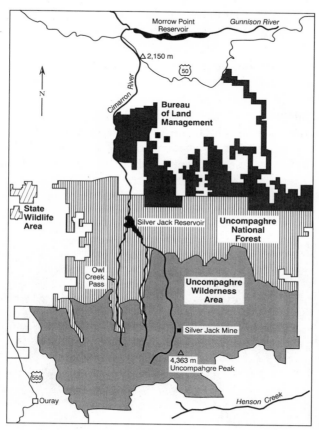

Figure 10.1. Land use and ownership patterns in the Cimarron River watershed of southwestern Colorado: light shading, wilderness; vertical lines, other USDA Forest Service areas; dark shading, USDI Bureau of Land Management; white, private land. The land adjoining the western boundary of the Uncompahgre Wilderness on the left of this figure is a hodgepodge pattern of private and National forest lands, resulting primarily from the patenting of mining claims since the mid-1800s. (Map developed by the authors.)

inhabiting small (less than 15-hectare) ranchettes in a pattern that increasingly fragments both social and ecological landscapes (Theobald et al. 1996). As these new immigrants become settled in the rural environment, they often bring vestiges of their former lifestyles with them. Construction of new fences and roads, free-running dogs, increased vehicular traffic, and the loss of rental pastures combine with other factors to create an "impermanence syndrome" that makes it more difficult for ranchers to maintain their pastoral way of life (Lapping et al. 1983). As land values and liabilities increase, it becomes more tempting for owners to sell ranch land. Once initiated, these changes produce a positive feedback condition that leads a system away from previously established uses provided by agriculture and ranching. The land-use changes, in turn, affect the cross-boundary management of the adjoining public lands, as will be later explained.

On middle-elevation BLM and NFS lands, mining, grazing, and logging were the most prominent historical uses (Figure 10.2). For example, the Ouray Ranger District listed nearly 500 active and inactive mines within their borders, nearly all of which are no longer producing ore. Silver Jack Reservoir, formed in 1971 on the Big Cimarron River just inside the NFS boundary, was named for a locally well-known silver mine.

Figure 10.2. Cattle grazing near the Uncompahgre National forest boundary. Throughout much of the interior western United States, livestock grazing systems cross land use and ownership boundaries during the year.

Since World War II, however, amenity resources such as hiking, fishing, and wildlife viewing have become more central to the public, including those who visit federal lands (Brunson and Steel 1994, Wells 1995). The USDA Forest Service has made a considerable investment in improving and augmenting recreation facilities and infrastructures around Silver Jack Reservoir in response to the expanding number of visitors.

At upper elevations, grazing has occurred for many years on lands that are now a part of the Uncompahgre Wilderness—a condition that is repeated on many other western grazing allotments. Grazing in wilderness is one of several "nonconforming uses" authorized by Section 4 of the Wilderness Act. A nonconforming use is one that, though legal, may not correspond to the spirit of the Act; that is, having a primeval character affected primarily the forces of nature. Nonconforming uses, such as grazing, water impoundments, landing strips, and patented mining claims, are generally allowed to continue in areas where they existed prior to wilderness designation.

Ostensibly, grazing in wilderness would seem to fall under the purview of guidelines included in the Act directing agencies to manage for wilderness values and minimize the impact of nonconforming uses on wilderness character. It seems logical to assume, as many wilderness users do, that wilderness designation creates a boundary condition where grazing management also should change to protect wilderness values and character. We will see that these expectations in the minds of wilderness visitors are seldom reflected in actual practices, which often change inconspicuously where a boundary is traversed between wilderness and nonwilderness.

A large part of the Ouray Ranger District, as demarcated by the Big Cimarron River watershed, incorporates two important administrative boundaries that influence livestock grazing specifically, and recreation and resource management in general: (1) The boundary between NFS land and private lands, some of which remain as rangeland or farmland and some of which have been subdivided into ranchettes or for other nonagricultural uses; and (2) the boundary between designated wilderness and NFS lands managed according to precepts of the Multiple-Use Sustained-Yield Act of 1960. We address both of these boundaries in turn.

The Boundary Between Public and Private Lands

The boundary between federally managed lands and adjoining private property in our case study is spatially complex. In some places, where there are numerous small parcels under different ownerships, the boundary is fragmented and takes an irregular shape. Nonetheless, the boundary clearly separates two legal jurisdictions that are distinct in their ability to control land uses. Activities on public lands are administered and restricted by a suite of federal laws—including the National Environmental Policy Act, Forest and Rangeland Renewable Resources Planning Act of 1974, Federal Land Policy and Management Act of 1976, National Forest Management Act of 1976, and forest stewardship provisions of the National 1990 Farm Bill—all presumably aimed at managing for the public trust.

Land uses on privately owned lands are influenced by market forces and regulated by local governments via the Montrose, Hinsdale, and Gunnison County Commissioners and their planning boards, as well as by subdivision regulations directed by Colorado state statutes. Decisions about other landscape components on private land, such as water and wildlife, are guided by Colorado statutes and also are subject to market forces. Typically, there has been limited interaction between the two jurisdictional or administrative systems on public and private lands.

In places within the Big Cimarron watershed, land administered by the BLM is situated between the Uncompahgre National Forest and private lands to the north. There are other locations where the national forest abuts private land, particularly along the Big Cimarron River itself. If we accept the tenet that both the BLM and the Forest Service have similar management objectives concerning livestock grazing (i.e., keeping or attaining rangelands in overall satisfactory condition) and recreation (i.e., managing for a spectrum of recreation opportunities while recognizing resource constraints), and recognizing that the physiography of agency lands is relatively similar at their respective administrative boundaries with private land, then the subject can be treated as a public versus private distinction.

Cross-boundary differences between public and private lands are commonly described in terms used in landscape ecology: what land uses are most prevalent, how fragmented the landscape is, and what corridors and obstacles to movement exist. Studies have shown that a direct correlation exists between ecosystem fragmentation and the degree of human development (Saunders et al. 1991). Consequently, depending principally on activities and land-use practices on the private side of the line, the transition can range from gradual and undetectable to abrupt and conspicuous. Examples of landscape elements associated with private land include roads, fences, plowed ground, buildings, and yard lights.

The manner in which the landscapes change across the boundary between public and private lands can be divided into two dissimilar categories: agricultural lands, and lands that have been subdivided for more intensive human uses. We examine each of the two boundary types in turn.

Public–Private Boundary with Agricultural Lands

Visitors to NFS lands in the Big Cimarron can enter the valley from two directions. They can follow the river upstream along a county road that leaves U.S. Highway 50 approximately 30 kilometers east of Montrose. Or they can take another county road from U.S. Highway 550 north of Ouray and travel east over Owl Creek Pass (Figure 10.1). In either case, the land between the paved highway and the national forest boundary is largely taken up by ranches and forms more of a vegetation transition than one measured in terms of changes in land use.

Along the Cimarron and Uncompahgre River basins floodplains are customarily irrigated to produce hay, whereas upland pastures are fenced for livestock grazing. Upland vegetation is a mosaic of grasslands and foothills shrubs, dominated by Gambel oak (*Quercus gambelii*) and mountain mahogany (*Cercocarpus montanus*). The shrub communities form a transition zone between more xeric ecosystems at lower elevations and the aspen–mixed conifer forest above (*Populus tremuloides/Pseudotsuga menziesii, Abies lasiocarpa, Picea engelmannii*; Mitchell 1993). The ecological boundary between montane forests and the grassland–shrubland landscape does not coincide with the administrative boundaries of NFS and BLM lands. It extends to lower elevations on north-facing slopes and in draws where colder temperatures prevail and adequate soil water is available.

At a landscape scale, the boundary between private agricultural land and federal lands is what Forman (1995) calls a patch boundary. A patch boundary is a form of soft boundary, which hypothetically differs from a hard boundary in several ways. For example, vertebrates will cross a soft boundary more readily than a hard boundary, perhaps because they do not distinguish a soft boundary as a barrier (Stamps et al. 1987).

The relative softness of an edge can be based on physical or psychological factors. Examples of physical barriers include interstate highways

with fences designed to keep out large ungulates (hard) versus an infrequently traveled country road with a three-strand barbed-wire fence
along one side (soft). A psychological barrier can be portrayed by com-
paring two small mammals: white-footed mice (*Peromyscus leucopus*) will
not leave their habitat in agricultural shelterbelts and range into surrounding fields; however, short-tailed shrews (*Blarina brevicauda*), commonly do so (Yahner 1983). A soft boundary also can be more abstract
from a human point of view. A visitor taking a photograph of a rural
landscape, a firefighter defending a fire line, or a rancher maintaining a
diversion ditch would all find land-use transitions less of a hindrance to
their projects on a landscape with soft boundaries.

Road structure also can change across boundaries in response to land-
use patterns or management objectives (Theobald et al. 1996). However,
road densities on privately owned ranches are similar to the public lands
neighboring them in the Big Cimarron valley. Both improved and unim-
proved (ranch) roads tend to follow drainages and most extend onto public lands. Thus, outwardly the administrative boundary appears relatively
imperceptible in terms of land form, vegetation, wildlife, and road patterns.

One human dimensions factor that differs across the boundary
between public and private range lands concerns accessibility. Most rural
landowners in the Big Cimarron, as throughout the western United
States, lock their gates and post their land (Guynn and Schmidt 1984).
The prevalence of posted rural areas is relatively recent in the West. We
both recall being able to drive for long distances along two-track roads
through privately owned ranch lands in Montana and Colorado until the
1970s. This shift in landowner policy seems to be tied to three phenomena: a disregard by some visitors for the norms and values found in rural
areas, the increasing litigious nature of society in the United States, and
the need to supplement agricultural income by leasing recreation rights
to specific groups of users. The first is illustrated by such activities as leaving gates open, shooting stock tanks, and harassing livestock from off-
road vehicles.

By constraining entry onto private land, access to adjacent public
lands is likewise restricted for the general populace. Interestingly enough,
in spite of increasing restrictions, the public has shown widespread support for actions designed to perpetuate Colorado ranches and farms
(Wallace and DeRuiter 1996). A majority of Coloradans have indicated
that ranches are an important part of their quality of life by providing a
"backdrop" amenity value, the loss of which would be enough to dis-

courage future visits to rural areas (Rosenberger et al. 1996). Some communities in Colorado are now attempting to use open space funds for conservation easements or the purchase of development rights to help maintain farms and ranches, even though public access will remain limited.

Public–Private Boundary with Subdivided Lands

Suppose that you decided to drive into the Big Cimarron basin along the river from U.S. Highway 50 (Figure 10.1). As you approached the National Forest just north of Silver Jack Reservoir and looked to the right in the direction of Fish Creek Reservoirs, it is possible to see a rural subdivision in the woods. The edge between this subdivision and NFS lands, when compared to nearby boundaries involving open rangeland, possesses several unique characteristics associated with hard boundaries.

First, subdividing ranches into tracts for ranchettes or summer cabins alters the physical landscape. The barrier effect caused by improved roads decreases patch sizes and increases edge densities, even if the native vegetation is not altered by horse pastures and other human impacts (Riebsame et al. 1996). Increased edge effects and barriers bring about changes in plant and animal communities (Chapter 8, this volume). Roads have been shown to serve as a conduit for nonindigenous weed species (Hobbs 1989). In a study of the East River valley, located in the upper Gunnison River drainage, Theobald et al. (1996) found that total road length increased at a rate of 17 percent each year during the period 1990–1994, almost solely because of subdivisions for ranchettes.

Inhabited buildings modify the natural landscape in a number of ways. Yard lights, cats and dogs, and noise all affect wildlife populations and other fauna (Knight et al. 1995). Theobald et al. (1996) ascertained that the number of dwelling units in the East River valley increased by 163 during 1990–1994, an annual growth rate of 8 percent due almost exclusively to subdivision.

The rural subdivision just outside the national forest boundary on the Big Cimarron started as sites for summer cabins owned by local residents. The cabins provide a place to relax, fish, and hunt for a few weeks during the year. More recently, as people have started moving into the area from other locations, the composition of the subdivision has begun to change. New construction is usually for larger homes designed for longer, or year-round, occupation.

One consequence of these changing residence patterns has been a cross-boundary demand for water. Water diversions from NFS lands to subdivided rural homesites can constitute a major impact on management plans for wildlife and livestock grazing on adjacent public lands (Personal communication with James Free, District Ranger, Ouray Ranger District). A private landowner or group of landowners will identify an unclaimed spring or seep on the National Forest suitable for piping to their property and request a permit to do so. If a pipeline is approved and constructed, it must then be maintained. Such activities can open the boundary between private and public lands to detrimental human impacts at a locale where none existed before, especially the loss of water intended for wildlife and/or livestock use. Permission to pipe water across boundaries between public and private lands can be denied if the expected impact is too great.

Returning to our human-dimensions example, boundaries harden not only for plant and animal communities but also for the visitor wishing to take pictures of a rural landscape, the firefighter who may now face a much greater effort and expense saving rural residences, and the rancher whose diversion ditch must pass through several fences, the maintenance of which is increased by litter, erosion, and liability.

Not much is known about how homeowners in subdivided rural landscapes feel about livestock grazing. We would expect that their values would reflect whether they are local residents who merely want land for a summer cabin or hunting base camp or whether they emigrated from urban centers. According to data gathered from driver registration records, a distinct movement of people from California to Colorado has taken place since the early 1990s (Larmer and Ring 1994). Other states also have shown a net shift in population to Colorado during this period. It would be informative to be able to assess whether the distribution of values held by inhabitants of subdivided ranches mirror those of other local residents, visitors to public lands, or wilderness visitors.

We have limited knowledge about cross-boundary dynamics between subdivided areas and public lands or private ranches on the Big Cimarron. In the greater Gunnison River valley and similar locations in the Rocky Mountains, privately owned ranches and farms adjoining public lands continue to be subdivided (Theobald et al. 1996). This trend increases appraised land values of neighboring ranches and tends to disrupt or destabilize the agrarian way of life, thus leading more ranchers to sell and retire or move away (Frazier 1993). So an understanding of the attributes of boundaries encircling subdivided rural lands will become increasingly important.

The Boundary Between Multiple-Use and Wilderness Lands

At the boundary of the Uncompahgre Wilderness, interactions between livestock grazing and recreational pursuits create an interesting challenge for managers. Traditionally, the wilderness boundary has had little spatial prominence for those managing grazing allotments. There are two reasons for this. First, boundaries of livestock allotments rarely coincide with wilderness boundaries, and second, the Wilderness Act and subsequent wilderness legislation provide for rangeland improvements and certain motorized activities within wilderness as part of the allotment management plan.

Eight of ten Forest Service allotments that are active on the Uncompahgre Wilderness straddle the wilderness boundary. The one permit administered by the BLM also extends on both sides of the wilderness boundary. All of these allotments have management plans that involve some kind of rotation grazing system incorporating pastures whose edges seldom conform with the wilderness boundary. Thus livestock often move into and out of wilderness with few restrictions.

There are few procedural differences between how federal agencies and livestock permittees manage the portion of an allotment inside the wilderness compared to that outside the wilderness. The Uncompahgre Wilderness was designated by the 1980 Wilderness Act. Like other wilderness legislation, the 1980 Bill included provisions for nonconforming activities that helped secure its enactment into law. It did so with reference to livestock grazing in Section 108 by requiring grazing management to be administered in accordance with guidelines contained in House Committee Report 96-617. In the House Committee Report, fences, water developments, and other livestock management improvements that were present prior to wilderness designation are specifically allowed to be kept and maintained.

Congressional grazing guidelines for National Forest Service wildernesses allow the occasional use of motorized equipment for maintenance and other activities identified in the applicable allotment management plan. For example, permittees are allowed to use chain saws to maintain driveways that enable livestock movement within their allotment. Vehicles have been used to carry fencing materials, caches of other supplies needed to sustain cowboys, sheepherders and their riding stock (like canned goods, oats, and salt), and equipment to set up base camps inside the wilderness. A backhoe could feasibly be employed to maintain a water development, although this has not occurred on the Uncompahgre Wilderness. Wilderness visitors seldom understand these exceptions to the ideal concept of wilderness, however, and bring a different set of expectations with them.

Allotment management plans covering wilderness areas usually restrict the use of motorized vehicles and other equipment to times when recreationists are mostly absent. Such a strategy, in essence, serves to maintain an artificial temporal boundary between wilderness and non-wilderness in lieu of a spatial boundary, except for the brief times when these activities are authorized.

Adverse interactions between livestock grazing and recreation in wilderness can be mitigated by management practices that spatially separate the two uses. Compared to cattle, properly controlled sheep grazing creates fewer conflicts with visitors and causes smaller environmental impacts in higher-elevation watersheds like the Big Cimarron. Sheep can be herded so their distribution does not rely on fences, and they can be moved to and from natural water with relative ease. Moreover, plant communities used for livestock grazing in the high-elevation rangelands are rich in forbs and browse, the kind of vegetation for which sheep are well adapted. Sheep prefer to graze on upland sites away from riparian zones where a greater-than-average likelihood of encountering wilderness visitors has been noted (Johnson et al. 1997). Sheep also can be herded away from trails, campsites, and areas that are not in acceptable range condition.

Although livestock allotments in NFS wilderness generally are better suited for use by sheep than by cattle, since the mid-1950s there has been a gradual transition from sheep allotments to cattle allotments on NFS wilderness areas. On the Uncompahgre Wilderness, all four of the vacant allotments are for sheep permits, a situation found in other national forests in the region; for example, all five vacant allotments on the West Elk Wilderness to the north also are for sheep. The reason for decreased sheep grazing on NFS lands, both wilderness and nonwilderness, are many, but fundamentally involve consumer habits, predation losses, labor procurement, and tariffs.

In the eyes of wilderness visitors, a firm boundary exists between designated wilderness and NFS lands managed for multiple uses. A recent study revealed that two-thirds of all visitors to the Uncompahgre Wilderness thought that cattle and sheep detracted from their recreational experience, and only one in ten considered livestock encounters to add to their visit (Johnson et al. 1997). These proportions were notably different from those found in an earlier study in the larger Big Cimarron watershed that evaluated visitors to NFS lands managed under the precept of multiple use. In the prior study, only about one-third of the visitors felt that livestock detracted from their stay, and an equal number stated that encountering cattle and sheep actually added to their recreational experience (Mitchell et al. 1996, Wallace et al. 1996). The expectation of wilderness visitors that they will encounter a pristine setting with little evidence of human activity clearly creates a boundary distinction that current grazing management only partially recognizes.

Our studies also showed that wilderness and nonwilderness visitors differ in opinion about specific types of livestock encounters. Across the board, wilderness visitors are more dissatisfied with conditions associated with livestock grazing than their fellow visitors to public lands managed for multiple uses. The biggest differences are seen in the dissimilar proportion of visitors who perceive that livestock encounters add to their experience (Table 10.1).

We found that local residents from Montrose, Hinsdale, Ouray, and Gunnison counties composed roughly half of the visitors to nonwilderness NFS lands in the Big Cimarron. These residents were much less likely to identify the presence of cattle and sheep as a source of interference to their visit than visitors from other regions, particularly Texas and the West Coast states (Mitchell et al. 1996). Such a correlation between where a person lives and his or her values concerning agriculture and livestock should not be unexpected. In general, visitors to the Uncompahgre Wilderness who came from rural areas and towns of less than 50,000 people were significantly more likely to support public lands grazing than those from cities with populations exceeding 50,000 people, while those from the largest cities were less apt to understand the concept of public lands grazing (Mitchell et al. 1996 and Table 10.2).

This does not mean that visitors to multiple-use portions of the Forest all agree that encounters with livestock are beneficial. Our study found that visitors to both wilderness and nonwilderness NFS lands in the Big Cimarron were annoyed by cowpies and cattle along the trail to a greater extent than any other type of livestock-related encounter, except cowpies and cattle in campsites (Table 10.1). Wilderness visitors can witness such impacts between the trailhead and the wilderness boundary, which may aggravate their attitudes about grazing once they are inside the wilderness area.

On the Ouray Ranger District, sheep gain access to summer allotments via the East Fork and Middle Fork of the Cimarron River, the Rigestock Driveway, and from trailheads along Henson Creek on the south. At least 50 percent of the sheep follow the Rigestock

Table 10.1. Evaluations of types of livestock-related encounters by wilderness and nonwilderness visitors on the National Forest System lands in the Big Cimarron River drainage

	Detracts (%)	Neutral (%)	Adds (%)
A. Nonwilderness visitors (n = 986)[a]			
Cowpies in camp site	67	28	5
Cattle in camp site	57	29	14
Cowpies along trail	53	42	5
Cattle along trail	42	35	23
Fences	26	60	14
Cowboys herding stock	19	39	42
Cattle in distance	19	37	44
B. Wilderness visitors (n = 537)[b]			
Manure in camp site	88	12	<1
Livestock in camp site	87	9	4
Livestock on or near trails	78	16	6
Manure on or near trails	77	21	2
Fences	74	24	2
Livestock in distance	54	31	15
Cowboys	47	37	16

Sources: From Wallace et al. (1996) and Wells (1995).
[a]Data include a few wilderness visitors. Data collected during 1992 and 1993.
[b]Data collected during 1994.

Driveway. Loading corrals are normally located adjacent to improved roads and close to the start of driveways leading to the combined nonwilderness–wilderness allotments. The steep terrain associated with lower boundaries of high-elevation wilderness areas confines livestock movement to the same valley-bottom areas used by visitors. Even in other locations, sheep and cattle driveways tend to overlap with trails designed for human use both within and outside the wilderness.

Stock driveways became common in the early twentieth century when barbed wire fences started restricting livestock movement between winter and summer rangelands (Hochmuth et al. 1942). The driveways received heavy grazing and trampling pressure over several weeks at least

Table 10.2. Relationship between visitor acceptance of public lands grazing and the size of their home community for those visiting the National Forest lands in the Big Cimarron watershed, 1992–1993[a]

Community Size	Approval	Conditional Approval	Disapproval	Confused by Question	Total
Rural	65 (46.9)	64 (70.4)	23 (25.7)	25 (34.0)	177 (20.1%)
<10,000	53 (45.3)	71 (68.0)	24 (24.9)	23 (32.8)	171 (19.4%)
10,000–49,999	64 (51.6)	69 (77.6)	19 (28.4)	43 (37.4)	195 (22.2%)
50,000–99,999	20 (29.4)	43 (44.1)	23 (16.1)	25 (21.3)	111 (12.6%)
100,000–299,999	12 (14.0)	24 (21.1)	10 (07.7)	7 (10.2)	53 (06.0%)
≥300,000	19 (45.8)	79 (68.8)	29 (25.2)	46 (33.2)	173 (19.7%)
Total	233 (26.5%)	350 (39.8%)	128 (14.5%)	169 (19.2%)	880 (100%)

[a]In each cell the first number is the observed frequency and the number in parentheses is the expected frequency if no causal relationships exist. Pearson chi-square = 54.1 (P < .001).

twice each year, leading to loss of cover by perennial plants and excessive erosion. At that time, the acceptance of "sacrifice areas" was legitimate in range management (Stoddard and Smith 1943). Today, national forest plans cannot accept management alternatives that maintain degraded vegetation and soils on stock driveways. The primary alternative for promoting recovery in highly disturbed areas is to reduce their use.

On the Uncompahgre Wilderness, use of the Rigestock Driveway has been cut in half by requiring some permittees to truck their sheep to corrals near Capitol City, an abandoned mining town on upper Henson Creek. Trucking can significantly increase a permittee's costs, however, so other options, such as opening vacant allotments to decrease livestock densities, must sometimes be examined.

Improving Cross-Boundary Management

Considering visitors' attitudes and preferences about livestock grazing, the boundary separating wilderness from other public lands may be more significant than previously recognized by those administering grazing allotment management plans. Most wilderness users perceive such boundaries to be essential to the integrity of the U.S. wilderness system.

This conclusion is corroborated by key differences between the attitudes of visitors to the Big Cimarron watershed about grazing on wilderness and nonwilderness public lands. At the same time, we have seen how restrictions imposed by time, terrain, and by elements of the Wilderness Act of 1964 and succeeding legislation have effectively diminished the significance of the boundary between the Uncompahgre Wilderness and adjacent public lands managed for multiple resources.

Land management agencies have begun an extensive effort to curtail the scope and severity of impacts caused by wilderness visitors. A nation-wide, interagency "Leave No Trace" educational program has produced a profusion of visitor materials, interpretive displays, activities, and law enforcement techniques (Hammitt and Cole 1987). To many wilderness users, it seems appropriate for those with grazing permits in wilderness to recognize its special nature by working to reduce livestock impacts when-ever possible. Both types of programs are integral to good wilderness management.

Grazing management strategies currently focus on biophysical indica-tors of rangeland health. However, monitoring, assessment, and planning activities can begin to incorporate social indicators and standards for wilderness conditions with the goal of mitigating some impacts of live-stock grazing on wilderness visitation. One management alternative is to place greater emphasis on the timing and location of allotment manage-ment activities. For example, trailing cattle and sheep from roadhead unloading areas to wilderness allotments can be planned for days and times that will minimize visitor interactions. It is unwise, for example, to unload cattle at a trailhead on or around the 4th of July, even if it falls in the middle of the week.

Operating mechanized equipment to achieve the objectives in wilder-ness allotment management plans can, in the same manner, be tempo-rally separated from conflicting visitor use by restricting their employ-ment until after the summer vacation season. Because vehicular activity in spring can cause accelerated erosion and unsightly ruts when soils are wet, the best season for making range improvements usually is during the fall. When it is sensible to do so, pack animals and hand tools should be substituted for motorized machinery.

Increased attention can be given to management practices that mini-mize the amount of time livestock spend near sites visitors use. In wilder-ness areas that have multiple water sources, livestock can be kept away from riparian areas that attract visitors, especially in the main travel cor-ridors. Our studies have shown that livestock seen in the distance affect visitor experience considerably less negatively than do livestock encounters close to visitor-use areas (Johnson et al. 1997).

The boundary between public lands and private holdings also requires innovative management. Actions that increase the management efficiency and longevity of healthy cross-boundary landscapes need the joint participation of federal managers and livestock producers in local land-use planning initiatives where they take place. Although BLM and Forest Service employees have not traditionally been involved in local land-use planning, a number of county and state open-space acquisition programs are now in effect that let ranchers keep part of their equity and still stay in production. Moreover, funding protocols have shown a preference for programs where agencies are involved with private landowners. It is felt that this type of partnership increases the effectiveness of land preserved for open space, thereby softening the transition between public and deeded lands (Covert 1996). With the initiation of ecosystem management as a land management policy, some agencies are hiring or training staff specialists to interact with local entities involved in making land-use decisions.

The presence of livestock on western landscapes invokes strong convictions about how public landscapes are to be managed (Fleischner 1994, J. Brown and McDonald 1995). Present policy, as authorized in federal and state laws and confirmed by numerous ensuing appropriations acts, has consistently mandated the continued use of our public rangelands for livestock grazing (USDA Forest Service 1989). The topic of a possible buffering effect of ranch base properties on public land management has been joined to the debate (Knight et al. 1995).

As our case study suggests, western range livestock operations must routinely cross boundaries between public and private lands and often boundaries between multiple-use lands and wilderness in order to exist. We have seen how those who manage grazing and other public lands resources are faced with cross-boundary complications. Uses of neighboring private lands are unquestionably influenced by public land management and vice versa. Public expectations differ for what happens on each of the three land categories grazed by livestock. Because grazing systems do span these borders, public policies profoundly effect the use of private lands surrounding the public lands of the United States (Public Land Law Review Commission 1970). In the long run, therefore, integration of prudent social and ecological management standards and guidelines on entire ecosystems, regardless of ownership, will provide the goods and services so essential to our nation's vitality.

REFERENCES

Brown, J.H., and W. McDonald. 1995. Livestock grazing and conservation on southwestern rangelands. *Conservation Biology* 9:1644–1647.

Brown, P.J., and G.E. Haas. 1980. Wilderness recreation experiences: the Rawah case. *Journal of Leisure Research* 12:229–241.

Brunson, M.W., and B.S. Steel. 1994. National public attitudes toward federal rangeland management. *Rangelands* 16:77–81.

Christensen, N.L., A.M. Bartuska, J.H. Brown, S. Carpenter, C. D'Antonio, R. Francis, J.F. Franklin, J.A. MacMahon, R.F. Noss, D.J. Parsons, C.H. Peterson, M.G. Turner, and R.G. Woodmaster. 1996. The report of the Ecological Society of America Committee on the Scientific Basis for Ecosystem Management. *Ecological Applications* 6:665–691.

Covert, J. 1996. Overview of the Colorado Coalition of Land Trusts. Presentation to Colorado extension agents. Workshop on land use planning and land trusts, Cooperative Extension Service, Colorado State University, March 12–13, 1996, Fort Collins, CO.

Fleischner, T.L. 1994. Ecological costs of livestock grazing in western North America. *Conservation Biology* 8:629–644.

Forman, R.T.T. 1995. *Land mosaics: the ecology of landscapes and regions.* Cambridge University Press, Cambridge, England.

Frazier, D. 1993. Change on the range. *Rocky Mountain News*, November 7, pages 8A, 18A–20A. Denver, CO.

Guynn, D.E., and J.L. Schmidt. 1984. Managing deer hunters on private lands in Colorado. *Wildlife Society Bulletin* 12:12–19.

Hammitt, W.E., and D.N. Cole. 1987. *Wildland recreation: ecology and management.* Wiley, New York.

Hobbs, R.J. 1989. The nature and effects of disturbance relative to invasions. Pages 389–406 in *Biological invasions: a global perspective* (J.A. Drake, H.A. Mooney, F. di Castri, R.H. Groves, F.J. Kruger, M. Rejmanek, and M. Williamson, editors). Wiley, Chichester, England.

Hochmuth, H.R., E.R. Franklin, and M. Clawson. 1942. *Sheep migration in the Intermountain region.* U.S. Department of Agriculture, Circular 621. Washington, DC.

Johnson, L.C., G.N. Wallace, and J.E. Mitchell. 1997. Visitor perceptions of livestock grazing in wilderness: a preliminary assessment. *International Journal of Wilderness* 3(2):14–20.

Knight, R.L., G.N. Wallace, and W.E. Riebsame. 1995. Ranching the view: subdivisions versus agriculture. *Conservation Biology* 9:459–461.

Lapping, M.B., G.E. Penfold, and S. MacPherson. 1983. Right to farm laws: do they resolve land use conflicts? *Journal of Soil and Water Conservation* 38:465–467.

Larmer, P., and R. Ring. 1994. Can planning rein in a stampede? *High Country News* 26(16)6–8.

Mitchell, J.E. 1993. The rangelands of Colorado. *Rangelands* 15:213–219.

Mitchell, J.E., G.N. Wallace, and M.D. Wells. 1996. Visitor perceptions about cattle grazing on national forest land. *Journal of Range Management* 49:81–86.

Public Land Law Review Commission. 1970. *One third of the nation's land: a report to the president and to the Congress by the Public Land Law Review Commission*. U.S. Government Printing Office, Washington, DC.

Riebsame, W.E., H. Gosnell, and D.M. Theobald. 1996. Land use and landscape change in the Colorado mountains I: theory, scale, and pattern. *Mountain Research and Development* 16:395–405.

Rosenberger, R.S., R.G. Walsh, J.R. McKean, and C.J. Mucklow. 1996. *Benefits of ranch open space to local residents*. Report to County Board of Commissioners, Steamboat Springs, Colorado Department of Agricultural and Resource Economics, Colorado State University, Fort Collins, CO.

Saunders, D.A., R.J. Hobbs, and C.R. Margules. 1991. Biological consequences of ecosystem fragmentation: a review. *Conservation Biology* 5:18–32.

Stamps, J.A., M. Buechner, and V.V. Krishman. 1987. The effects of edge permeability and habitat geometry on emigration from patches of habitat. *American Naturalist* 129:533–552.

Stoddard, L.A., and A.D. Smith. 1943. *Range management*. McGraw-Hill, New York.

Theobald, D.M., H. Gosnell, and W.E. Riebsame. 1996. Land use and landscape change in the Colorado mountains II: a case study of the East River valley. *Mountain Research and Development* 16:407–418.

USDA Forest Service. 1989. *A description of Forest Service programs and responsibilities*. USDA Forest Service, General Technical Report RM-176. Rocky Mountain Forest and Range Experiment Station, Fort Collins, CO.

Wallace, G.N., and D.S. DeRuiter. 1996. *Public attitudes about agriculture in Colorado*. Report submitted to Colorado State Department of Agriculture and Colorado State University, College of Natural Resources, Fort Collins, CO.

Wallace, G.N., J.E. Mitchell, and M.D. Wells. 1996. *Visitor perceptions about grazing on a Forest Service cattle allotment*. USDA Forest Service, Research Paper RM-RP-321. Rocky Mountain Research Station, Fort Collins, CO.

Wells, M.D. 1995. The application of a goal interference recreation model to the public land grazing controversy. Ph.D. dissertation, Colorado State University, Fort Collins, CO.

Yahner, R.H. 1983. Population dynamics of small mammals in farmstead shelterbelts. *Journal of Mammalogy* 64:380–386.

Chapter 11

Overcoming Boundaries: The Greater Yellowstone Ecosystem

Dennis A. Glick and Tim W. Clark

The 8.5-million-hectare Greater Yellowstone Ecosystem (GYE) encompasses portions of Idaho, Montana, and Wyoming and includes national parks, national forests, wildlife refuges, Indian reservations, Bureau of Land Management (BLM) lands, and state and private lands. It is a landscape crisscrossed with almost 4,000 kilometers of administrative boundaries among more than twenty-five federal, state, and local agencies, not to mention the boundaries among thousands of private landholders. Current GYE management is largely piecemeal and problematic. The lack of shared conservation goals among these many stakeholders has led to habitat fragmentation, disruption of ecological processes, and human–wildlife confrontations (Berger 1991, Glick et al. 1991, Clark and Minta 1994). Many of these environmental problems transcend administrative and landownership boundaries. These problems underscore the need to take a broader, more integrated view of land management activities in Greater Yellowstone.

Our chapter describes the GYE and the boundary dilemma, analyzes consequences of this dilemma, and offers recommendations to move us closer to the goal of ecosystem sustainability. Examples of ongoing management efforts that reflect these recommendations are offered.

A Landscape of Boundaries

The GYE is one of the last, essentially intact, temperate zone ecosystems on the planet (Barbee and Varley 1984). This section describes key trends in natural resources and cross-boundary issues, the context within which land management takes place, and projections about the future.

237

A Profile of Greater Yellowstone

Yellowstone, the world's first national park, and Grand Teton National Park lie at the center of the GYE, surrounded by seven national forests, three national wildlife refuges, two Indian reservations, and BLM, state, and private lands (Figure 11.1 and Harting and Glick 1994). This mostly mountainous region harbors nearly every wildlife species encountered by the Lewis and Clark expedition in the early 1800s, although a number of species are now considered threatened (Clark et al. 1989). Yellowstone National Park contains the planet's most diverse and intact collection of geothermal features and is annually visited by close to three million people. Ecological processes such as fire, predation, and ungulate migrations operate in large tracts of roadless lands with relatively little human interference. Greater Yellowstone represents a unique opportunity to manage a large landscape as a "boundary-less" ecosystem to sustain its full complement of biological diversity and its unique natural features and human communities.

The term *Greater Yellowstone Ecosystem* was coined by grizzly bear biologists Frank and John Craighead (Craighead 1979, Clark and Zaunbrecher 1987). During the 1960s and 1970s, their research revealed that the range of Yellowstone grizzlies (*Ursus arctus*) covered at least 2.2 million hectares, of which only 1 million hectares were within the administrative boundary of Yellowstone National Park. Additional research on the park's elk (*Cervus elaphus*), mule deer (*Odocoileus heminous*), mountain lion (*Felis concolor*), bald eagles (*Haliaetus leucocephalus*), trumpeter swans (*Cygnus buccinator*), and other species showed that they, too, utilized habitats outside the park (Greater Yellowstone Coordinating Committee 1987, Clark et al. 1996). Even the integrity of Yellowstone National Park's geothermal features depends on subterranean "plumbing" and ground water recharge areas well beyond the park's boundaries (Greater Yellowstone Coordinating Committee 1987).

People and the Economy of Greater Yellowstone

Over 210,000 people live within or adjacent to the GYE. This twenty-county region is one of the fastest growing rural areas in the United States (33 percent faster than the three states as a whole, Power 1991). Residents take part in diverse outdoor recreation activities in numbers far above the national average (Wyoming Recreation Commission 1985). Indeed, quality of life is the primary magnet for attracting and holding this growing population (Rasker et al. 1992). The region's economy, once based on resource extraction, now depends on resource pro-

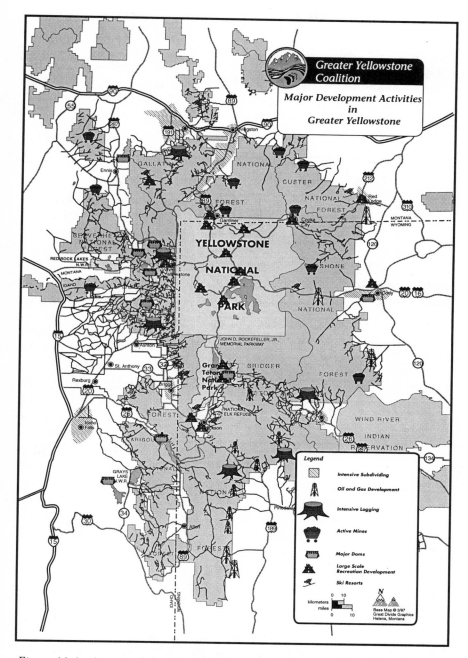

Figure 11.1. A map of the Greater Yellowstone Ecosystem, including Yellowstone National Park, and the three states of Idaho, Montana, and Wyoming showing the diversity of development impacts. (From Greater Yellowstone Coalition, Bozeman, Montana, 1997.)

tection (Power 1995). A growing service sector, transfer payments, and nonlabor-related income now form the backbone of this economy. By contrast, agriculture, mining, timber harvest, wood products, and oil and gas development combined account for less than 8 percent of regional income (Rasker and Glick 1994).

The Boundary Dilemma

Whereas the GYE is defined by its geology, physiography, and plant and animal communities, the jurisdictional boundaries of the various land management agencies have more to do with history than ecology (Keiter 1989). The environmental implications of this situation are becoming ever more obvious. For example, a grizzly bear wandering out of Yellowstone Park in search of food or habitat must deal with clearcuts and forest roading, predator control by livestock grazers, recreationists, subdivisions, backwoods cabins, and other human activities that exponentially increase its chances of being killed or removed from the ecosystem (there were thirty-seven known human-caused grizzly bear mortalities between 1994 and 1996 according to the Interagency Grizzly Bear Study Team). A Yellowstone cutthroat trout faces a similar set of challenges as it moves downstream out of the national park and into stretches of river and streams that may be dewatered for irrigation, polluted by runoff from fields and subdivisions, and overfished by increasing numbers of anglers. Even backcountry recreationists must deal with conflicting human uses such as off-road vehicles, logging, mining, and grazing as they move farther and farther from Greater Yellowstone's wild core.

Added to the mix of diverse land uses is the staggering mix of management agencies. These diverse federal, state, and local government entities manage pieces of GYE, often as though each piece were unconnected to the whole (Appendix 11.1, Schmidt 1991). The public lands of Greater Yellowstone combined with the two Indian reservations (Wind River and Fort Hall) make up about 80 percent of the GYE. The rest, about 1.6 million hectares, is privately owned. Twenty county administrations are superimposed (Glick et al. 1991).

These public and private entities create a dense, highly fragmented, and complex policy arena (Clark and Harvey 1990, Clark et al. 1991). Land managers acknowledge problems associated with boundaries, but little cooperative management exists among public agencies and private landowners (Congressional Research Service 1987). One reason for management conflicts is differing agency missions. For example, the National Park Service Organic Act of 1916 states that the purpose of the parks is to "conserve the scenery and the natural and historic objects and the wildlife therein and to provide for the enjoyment of the same in such manner and by such means as will leave them unimpaired for the enjoyment of future generations." The USDA Forest Service operates under multiple-use policies set forth in the 1897 Organic Act, the 1960 Multiple Use–Sustained Yield Act, the 1964 Wilderness Act, the 1974 Forest and Rangeland Renewable Resources Act, and the 1976 National Forest Management Act. The U.S. Fish and Wildlife Service takes its authority from the 1956 Fish and Wildlife Act and the 1973 Endangered Species Act. The Bureau of Land Management is guided by the 1976 Federal Land Policy and Management Act. The Montana Department of Fish, Wildlife and Parks, Idaho Department of Fish and Game, and the Wyoming Department of Game and Fish have all historically managed wildlife to maximize harvest of game animals (Harting and Glick 1994). Adding to this diversity is a fundamental and profound difference of opinion on federal versus states rights in local and regional management.

Recognizing the need for better coordination between federal land managers, the Park Service and the Forest Service created the Greater Yellowstone Coordinating Committee (GYCC) to improve communication and cooperation between the national parks and forests (Greater Yellowstone Coordinating Committee 1987). The GYCC includes superintendents of the two national parks, the regional director of the Park Service, the forest supervisors of six national forests, and the three regional foresters. Members of this group have met several times a year since the mid-1980s. An effort in the early 1990s to develop and implement a set of shared management goals and guiding principles resulted in the "GYCC Vision document," which met strong opposition by the extractive industries (Litchman and Clark 1994). The first draft promoted ecosystem management much more than the final "Vision," which downplayed ecosystem conservation and promoted multiple use (Harting and Glick 1994).

Additional problems aggravate the boundary problem. Currently, several resource agencies (especially the Forest Service) are in the throes of organizational and cultural transition. Significant budget cuts have resulted in reduced staffs and scaled-back on-the-ground management. There also are disruptions from outside these agencies by people who have legally and in some cases even physically threatened land managers and government property. These pressures and heavy workloads have created a difficult agency environment.

On private land, few of the twenty GYE counties have effective and enforced land-use plans, and only one county has developed a "build out" analysis of the future based on current development trends. This lack of understanding of the consequences of unmanaged growth, combined

with strong ideological views of private property rights, has stymied most
land-use planning (Smith 1994). Subdivisions and scattered homes now
abut national parks and forests in many parts of the GYE with "spillover"
ecological consequences (see Chapter 8).

Cross-Boundary Issues

Management decisions on one side of an administrative boundary will
almost always affect natural resources and people on the opposite side.
Among differing land uses that take place on either side of boundaries are
road building, livestock grazing, recreation development, mining, dam
and irrigation projects, subdivisions, and species management.

Cross-Border Problems and Their Environmental and Economic Impacts

A review of resource use in the GYE shows trends in increased habitat
fragmentation across both public and private lands. This is affecting the
ecological integrity of natural systems and the economic viability of
human enterprises across jurisdictional boundaries.

For example, over 12,000 kilometers of roads have been built on the
national forests and national parks (Greater Yellowstone Coordinating
Committee 1987). On private lands, with 500,000 hectares already in
subdivisions (Glick et al. 1991), road construction is occurring at an
even greater rate. This spaghetti tangle of roads on both public and private lands increases the cross-boundary spread of noxious weeds that
harm both domestic livestock and wildlife. Roads often cause siltation
that affects aquatic life and reduces water quality for human use, in some
cases kilometers from the source of these sediments.

Timber harvest further reduces habitat for many species and can lead
to soil erosion that affects resources throughout a watershed regardless of
owner or manager (Harvey 1994). Over four billion board feet of timber
have been cut on GYE national forests since the 1960s. Reduced timber
harvest on public lands is resulting in increased timber harvest across
forest boundaries on private lands. Environmentalists celebrate their
success at having brought national forest harvest rates down to more
sustainable levels, but with increased cutting on private lands, the overall cumulative affect of timber harvest is still substantive. With fewer
environmental safeguards on private lands, it is possible that there may
be greater ecological damage than from timber harvests on national
forests.

This point is illustrated in the Crazy Mountains at the northern end of the GYE. There, large-scale and poorly managed timber cutting on private land has caused extensive siltation of the Shields River. This has not only devastated trout populations on public land, but also contributes to flooding downstream on private land (Story, personal communication).

Livestock grazing on national forests has degraded important habitats, especially biologically rich riparian areas (Wuerthner 1990). Conversely, the development of private rangeland into rural subdivision affects species associated with public lands. Nearly 50 percent of the public lands in the GYE are open to livestock with an estimated 200,000 head of cattle, sheep, and horses currently grazing on national forest land (Greater Yellowstone Coordinating Committee 1987). Many of these public land permittees also own tracts of deeded land that are currently undeveloped.

Confrontations between wildlife and public land grazers are frequent and well documented, with wildlife generally losing out in subsequent management actions. Over 1,000 Yellowstone bison were destroyed during the winter of 1996–97. This culling occurred because of the fear that brucellosis would spread from bison to domestic cattle when bison, in search of winter range, wandered beyond the border of Yellowstone National Park onto private ranches. Some environmentalists cite this and other livestock-related problems as a reason to end public land grazing. Yet the conversion of farms and ranches to subdivisions and ranchettes could prove more threatening to wildlife that depend on these habitats (Greater Yellowstone Coalition et al. in press; see Chapter 8, this volume).

Recreation-related development further fragments ecosystems and often raises cross-boundary concerns (see Chapter 6). Ski resorts, for example, create spillover problems associated with recreational development. In Greater Yellowstone, most downhill ski areas are located on national forests and are regulated by the Forest Service. However, in many cases, these public land resorts serve as a catalyst for adjacent private land development, which is generally not well regulated by county governments. Grand Targhee Resort, on the border of Idaho and Wyoming near Driggs, Idaho, is currently expanding and seeks a land exchange that would increase its size. Even if this trade is not completed, many residents of adjacent Teton Valley believe that widespread development of that county directly results from expansion of Grand Targhee and other nearby ski hills. Important wildlife habitat has been degraded by this sprawl, and socioeconomic impacts have been dramatic. Once a valley known for its farms and ranches, the area is now being swallowed up by trophy homes and tract developments (Glick 1997).

There are hundreds of hard rock mining claims and several active or proposed mines in Greater Yellowstone. Some of these sites, such as the historic New World Mining District at the northeastern edge of Yellowstone Park, leach toxic wastes into tributaries of important trout streams. A century of mining in that area has left stretches of Soda Butte Creek nearly sterile. Soda Butte Creek flows out of the mining district, through a portion of the Gallatin National Forest, and then into Yellowstone National Park. It eventually flows into the Yellowstone River, which passes through private ranchland and a number of communities.

Though concentrated on private land, rural sprawl is a growing cross-boundary issue. Although not all of the subdivided lands in Greater Yellowstone have been built out, river valleys such as the Gallatin, Paradise, Teton, Star, and Clarks Fork have been heavily affected by sprawl. These developments are often placed in critical wildlife habitat, such as winter range and riparian corridors. Most rural subdivisions use septic systems, which can lead to water quality problems. They also provide fertile ground for the establishment of noxious weeds that can move onto public lands. In addition, private landowners often demand the suppression of natural processes such as wildfire on adjoining national forests and parks (Harvey 1994, Smith 1994; see Chapter 8, this volume).

Besides the obvious destruction of wildlife habitat such as winter range, there are other spillover effects from rural sprawl. Domestic dogs and cats prey on wildlife wandering down from the parks and forests. Sometimes this situation is reversed with calls for increased control of predators that prey on domestic pets. In Montana the allowable take of mountain lions was greatly increased in 1996 over previous years at least in part because of increased confrontations between people and lions in the suburban–wildland interface (Pac, personal communication). Perhaps the most significant cross-boundary impact of rural sprawl has been the changing attitudes of the public toward once-admired wildlife species such as elk, deer, bear, and moose. In rural areas of Greater Yellowstone, subdivision residents are beginning to view wildlife as pests rather than amenities (Pac, personal communication). This change in attitude presents a new set of challenges for wildlife agencies and will certainly affect how they manage species on public lands.

Each of these development activities has affected plant and animal species as well as the ecological processes that sustain them. Seven percent of the vascular plants of GYE are now considered rare. Nineteen animal species are listed under the Endangered Species Act. Six are endangered, one is threatened, and twelve are candidate species (Harting and Glick 1994). Other species that are currently on the rebound or even at higher numbers than they have been in decades (e.g., moose) could experience declines if habitat alteration continues at its current pace.

Although the relationship between landscape alteration and the health of natural communities is generally understood, there is less awareness of the correlation between environmental health and the economic well-being of the GYE's human residents. Surveys have documented the important role of the natural environment and recreational amenities in attracting and holding businesses in the area (Johnson and Rasker 1993).

Natural amenities represent the GYE's competitive advantage in the business world (Power 1995). Environmental damage on both public and private lands has not yet degraded these amenities to the point where businesses and residents have begun leaving in great numbers, but there are indications that this is beginning to occur. Towns such as Bozeman, Montana, and Jackson, Wyoming, once known for their scenic beauty, are today known for their congestion and cluttered rural landscapes (Kenworthy 1997).

The Management Morass

The dozens of agencies, entities, and committees charged with administering the GYE share neither the same management policies nor cooperative motivations. Even if they did, it is doubtful whether, under their current administrative structure, economic development policies, and information management and monitoring programs, they could carry out the activities needed to sustain the GYE.

No magic bullet will quickly and effectively facilitate ecosystem conservation across borders. Laws, for example, are an important aspect of ecosystem protection. Many existing laws, such as the Endangered Species Act, are helpful if effectively applied. But in the GYE, a lack of monitoring, incentives, and enforcement renders some of them inadequate. Along with ecosystem-friendly laws that simply need to be enforced are many others that are outmoded or have done more harm than good (Wilkinson 1990). Some, such as the 1872 Mining Law or many of the water-related laws, were written in the 1800s when the West was newly settled. They make little sense on the eve of the twenty-first century when society now values ecosystem protection as well as the resources these lands offer.

Some of the GYE's environmental problems also can be traced to economic policies and tax codes that work against conservation goals. Some basic changes would help protect public wildlands and support economic sustainability in local communities. Much of the logging on national forests has actually cost more than it generates in revenue (Wilderness Society 1987). The 1996 Draft Management Plan for the Targhee National Forest, a forest that already has had two billion board feet of timber cut since the 1960s, called for additional logging primarily to maintain the local economy (USDA Forest Service 1996). In reality, logging is now a fraction of this economy, about 7 percent of total income in Fremont County, Idaho, where much of this took place (Greater Yellowstone Coalition and the Wilderness Society 1993).

Managing the GYE as an ecosystem will require land managers to give up more than just outmoded ideas and practices. It requires giving up some control and administrative power (Holling and Meffe 1996). Resource administration in GYE is very much a top-down process. Decisions affecting on-the-ground management often are made far from the affected sites.

Some agency personnel are quite comfortable in their current, semi-isolated management roles. Ecosystem management would require that they leave the security of their agencies and closely interact with the public and private sectors. There are examples of land managers who are building constructive relationships with other land managers and with the general public, but these are the exception, not the rule. To quote a former Yellowstone Park Superintendent, "Adventurism for bureaucrats is not rewarded" (Barbee, personal communication).

However, not all the blame should be placed on state and federal agencies. Local elected officials, private landowners, and environmentalists have contributed to the air of distrust and miscommunication. Many regional residents still hold a "rearview mirror" perception of the regional economy, that the backbone of economic development is resource extraction from public lands and unrestricted development of private lands. New public land initiatives such as "ecosystem management, rangeland reform, and watershed protection," are perceived as threats to traditional culture, economy, and political power. Much of their interaction with land managers revolves around resurrecting diminishing extractive industries, not working collaboratively on cross-border issues.

The regional environmental community has for the most part placed itself somewhere between these two views. On one hand, environmentalists have been consistent and vocal critics of the actions of public land managers and strong proponents of a whole-ecosystem approach to resource management. However, they often have demonstrated "cold feet" when it comes to the thought of relinquishing land management decisions to communities and private landowners. Although this concern is sometimes well justified, it ultimately undermines the trust needed to effectively involve stakeholders in cross-border issues.

In a very real sense, a leap of faith is required by those affected by cross-boundary problems to work through solutions. Such a leap is not expected any time soon, but cautious first steps are being taken.

Blurring the Boundaries

Minimizing cross-boundary issues in the GYE requires changes in resource law, administration and policy, economic policies and tax incentives, resource management, science, and education. A series of case studies illustrates how these reforms are being addressed on the ground in the GYE. Efforts to implement these in a comprehensive, ecosystemwide fashion have generally not been well received by regional residents. What appears to be more palatable is the incremental application of these changes on a site-by-site basis.

Progress toward cross-boundary ecosystem management depends on the evaluation, diffusion, and adaptation of innovative models (Clark 1996). The following section describes site-specific cooperation in Greater Yellowstone. Four GYE prototypes show particular promise. Each is noteworthy in that it deals with cross-boundary issues, actively involves different stakeholders, employs good science and data collection, and facilitates civil discourse. Although these illustrations are viewed as potential success stories, they need to be thoroughly evaluated and prototypical elements adapted to other situations.

Beaverhead County Partnership

The first example is an ecosystem planning effort in Beaverhead County, Montana, in the northwestern corner of the GYE. The Beaverhead National Forest initiated a landscape analysis on public lands in the county. At the same time, the county was beginning to develop a comprehensive land-use plan. The county did not have a planner or planning budget, let alone computing equipment and geographic information system (GIS) skills. Human, financial, and equipment needs served as a catalyst for local government interest in cooperating with federal agency officials on countywide "ecosystem" planning.

A Memorandum of Understanding (MOU) was signed among the

Beaverhead County Commissioners, the Forest Service, the U.S. Fish and Wildlife Service, the National Park Service, the Bureau of Land Management, the Montana Department of Fish, Wildlife, and Parks, and the Montana Department of State Lands. These agencies provided the county with funding, equipment, technical assistance, and data to help planning efforts. The Forest Service is now including private lands in its landscape analysis work, which will provide the technical underpinnings of management. As Forest Service District Ranger Mark Patroni (personal communication) stated, "we have erased administrative boundaries. We can now look at the whole area."

Periodic meetings are held among all these entities to discuss issues of shared concern (e.g., noxious weed control). A countywide "consensus council" has been created to bring the public into this partnership and decision process (Clark and Brunner 1996). Through this council, a dialog has been initiated between the environmental and ranching communities on public land policies and growth management on private lands. These two groups are currently exploring the possibility of jointly sponsoring a workshop or project aimed at keeping ranchers on the land and protecting privately owned wildlife habitat.

Using this MOU as a model, the Beaverhead National Forest has now signed a similar agreement with Madison County, and the Gallatin National Forest has signed an agreement with Gallatin County (Patroni, personal communication). Such MOUs among federal, state, and local officials and the general public could be a useful vehicle for dealing more effectively with cross-border issues. The growing concern over changing public land-use policies, such as grazing fees, coupled with the inability of counties and towns to deal with land-use planning, may be the catalyst needed to spur collaboration on landscapewide issues.

Madison Range Landscape Assessment and Adaptive Management Project

The second example is the Madison Range Landscape Assessment and Adaptive Management Project. The Hebgen Lake District of the Gallatin National Forest in Montana is completing a landscape assessment of its district with the help of GIS. They are making major strides in bringing other land management agencies, elected officials, and diverse publics into the process. Through this effort, a baseline by which to measure the impacts of resource management prescriptions across administrative boundaries is being created.

As background, Forest Service staff spent years collecting data on an array of natural features ranging from vegetation to wildlife, visitor use, and natural processes such as fire. This information has been entered into a multilayered database that illustrates ecosystem elements affected by proposed land uses. Throughout this data analysis, important landscape elements for management were identified. Project supervisor Alan Vandiver (personal communication) notes that not only did this turn out to be a socially acceptable approach to data collection and interpretation, but it also was very cost-effective: "it expanded my staff from 12 to 50 by involving other private and government organizations."

A number of on-the-ground projects that cross borders have emerged from this initiative, including assistance to owners of in-holdings in the forest for the crafting of conservation plans, a cooperative project with Yellowstone National Park to control noxious weeds, a forest transportation plan that reduces impacts on wildlife, a prescribed fire plan as part of an overall vegetation management plan, and the initiation of fish habitat restoration projects (Vandiver, personal communication).

Data collection and analysis have proven to be useful tools for resolving site-specific resource issues that involve several players. In one drainage, the Forest Service had proposed a number of timber sales to generate funds needed to purchase private in-holdings. Because of important habitat values, the environmental community was concerned about the cutting of any timber, yet supportive of the idea of purchasing the private property. Through the Landscape Assessment Project and GIS database, landowners, biologists, environmentalists, and Forest Service staff were able to explore options for timber sales and identify potential impacts of each scenario. The idea of timber sales is still a difficult pill for environmental groups to swallow, but their comfort level has increased because of hands-on involvement in the sale design. The involvement of private citizens has significantly modified the Forest Service's initial proposal.

The Henry's Fork Watershed Council

The third example is the Henry's Fork Watershed Council. Frustrated by the public agencies' inability to manage the Henry's Fork watershed, farmers and environmentalists in eastern Idaho are building a foundation for ecosystem management. The Henry's Fork watershed is a microcosm of the GYE. Twenty-five state and federal agencies work in the watershed, and there are numerous and diverse resource users, many areas in need of conservation, and no centralized data base.

The Henry's Fork Foundation (a nongovernmental conservation group) and the 1,700-member Fremont–Madison Irrigation District now work together on water rights and water management. A watershed center has been created with an ambitious research and data-gathering component (including the establishment of a watershed GIS). This center is supplying the Watershed Council with the scientific information needed to make good decisions on water management and a host of other resource issues.

The Council (which may number up to 100 people) meets on a regular basis. It includes representatives from many different organizations, as well as interested citizens. Public officials participate as equals in this process, but are not "in charge." Decisions are made by consensus, and the group employs the WIRE (Watershed Integrity Review and Evaluation) criteria for project evaluation. The group is gaining support and respect within the region and data produced by the GIS team are utilized by agencies for their watershed plans (Brown, personal communication).

The Greater Yellowstone Coalition Stewardship Program

The last case study involves the Greater Yellowstone Coalition (GYC) Stewardship Program, which features the collection and application of information related to land use on private lands. The project has brought together a variety of agencies and individuals to work on the complex issues of growth management in a twenty-county area. Because of the link between public land management (particularly grazing policies) and private land use (ranching and the maintenance of open lands), this program has addressed a broad spectrum of ecological, economic, cultural, and administrative issues.

Several research projects are under way that have for the first time in the Greater Yellowstone quantified the extent and impact of rural sprawl. In collaboration with county officials, university faculty, land-use planners, and ranchers, "studies of cost of community services" have been developed to identify the fiscal and economic costs of various land uses (Haggerty 1996). In addition, GIS maps are being completed to pinpoint the extent of subdivided land over a several-county area. With this information, alternative development scenarios are being created to demonstrate that communities can meet their housing needs in a more environmentally benign manner and at a lower cost to taxpayers.

Another component involves outreach to landowners themselves and direct assistance in identifying options for the conservation of their landholdings. Because most large landowners are farmers or ranchers, activities have focused on reducing the economic problems faced by the agricultural community. Workshops have explored options for improving the economic viability of ranches, use of conservation easements for maintaining open lands, market- and incentive-based approaches to species conservation, and citizen-generated land-use plans.

This project has the ultimate goal of creating a Greater Yellowstone land ethic among both the public and private sectors. To be shared among all stakeholders, it must be created by these stakeholders. To be fully embraced, it must be built not only on an understanding of the science and economics surrounding these issues, but also on their sociocultural characteristics.

Lessons Learned

These four prototypes have demonstrated practical progress toward resolving cross-boundary issues. In each case, participants build on current practices. As goals are clarified and scientific data become available, they are incorporated.

Each case study has its own characteristics, but they all share some common elements: (1) the collection and dissemination of good data before undertaking major management actions, (2) the creation of forums or mechanisms for civic dialog where information can be discussed and used in a constructive manner, (3) the decision to give stakeholders a voice on resource management issues and an opportunity to play a greater role in management decisions, (4) identification of a set of shared management goals, and (5) continual evaluation and modification to reflect changing conditions.

These prototypes may or may not serve as prototypes for other cross-boundary resource problems, but they suggest what is working and what is not. It appears as if environmental protection efforts in Greater Yellowstone are at a crossroad. Traditional top-down, short-term, and narrowly focused approaches have not been a total failure, but they have caused problems that are becoming more serious as development pressures mount. Even though they have undeniably protected wildlands, additional conservation gains using solely this approach will be difficult to achieve.

Though most stakeholders admit that a new management paradigm is needed, this model is far from fully developed. The five elements shared by the projects appear to be keys to success, but there are various interpretations on how they should be applied. For instance, what constitutes "good data" may be debatable. When data are collected and analyzed by one agency or organization, they may not be considered credible by others. The most successful data collection and analyses have been done in a collaborative fashion (e.g., Forest Service staff working with the Montana Department of Fish, Wildlife, and Parks, the county planning office, and private landowners to map elk [*Cervus elaphus*] migration routes). Economic data collected by a community generally is more trusted by the community than data presented to them by an outside organization (Rasker, personal communication).

The creation of forums for civil dialog also has its pitfalls. There are a number of examples in Greater Yellowstone where these forums or processes have fallen apart because stakeholders are unable to engage in honest communication (Clayton, personal communication). Development of the trust needed for effective communication is a slow, painstaking process that can be frustrating for participants. There is the danger that consensus or compromise on an issue will not meet the biological needs of wildlife affected by a resource issue. There is a legitimate concern that in the rush to find common ground and resolve cross-boundary problems, more emphasis is placed on achieving consensus rather than really solving a problem. Practice has shown that if these groups begin with the most straightforward, easily resolved issues, they stand a better chance of building the foundation needed to get beyond merely "handholding."

Giving stakeholders a voice in management decisions is perhaps the most controversial paradigm shift of all. Resource users such as ranchers and loggers convincingly argue that, because of their hands-on knowledge of the land, they possess the skills needed to fine tune management practices. Professional resource managers claim that because of their academic training, they are most capable of applying good science to cross-boundary problems. Environmentalists often argue that neither resource managers nor resource users represent the general interests of the public. There is a certain amount of truth to each of these claims. But while all stakeholders need to be at the table, each needs to share a common understanding of the issue. Consensus decisions based on a misinterpretation of ecological and socioeconomic realities will invariably result in bad decisions.

The development of shared management goals among stakeholders generally is not so difficult when goals remain general. Community and agency visioning and planning processes have usually resulted in surprisingly similar outcomes. Far more difficult is the crafting of specific management actions that all affected parties can accept. As one land-use planner noted, "plans without implementation strategies are like a New Year's resolution, they more than likely will not be adhered to" (Propst, personal communication).

Finally, using an adaptive management approach that continually evaluates and modifies management actions is a major change for many organizations and individuals. Agencies, resource users, and environmentalists often are slow to modify their perceptions and actions, even when it is clear that they are no longer relevant. Change is uncomfortable, and flexibility is generally not in the vocabulary of public land managers. Although many organizations pay lip service to the need to evaluate, few are effectively and continually evaluating their progress.

Conclusions

Effective cross-boundary resource management in the GYE still is in its infancy. Progress is evident, but the challenges facing ecosystem conservation remain varied and dynamic. Historic trends show rapid growth in population and development, and this is having harmful effects on ecological integrity and the sustainability of human enterprises. Current management by government agencies and local officials and landowners is disjointed and unable to address many immediate problems, much less longer-term sustainability issues. Practice-based approaches appear to be producing the most progress. Ecosystem conservation that resolves and prevents future cross-boundary issues will require a set of actions that are currently being created, monitored, refined, and adapted to new situations by a few pioneering individuals. Citizens and managers have a means to bring about ecosystem sustainability. It remains to be seen whether they will use it to advantage.

APPENDIX

Following is a list of agencies, committees, and organizations involved with resource management in the Greater Yellowstone Ecosystem (after Schmidt 1991).

U.S. Department of Interior

National Park Service
  Yellowstone and Grand Teton National Parks and J.D. Rockefeller Parkway
U.S. Fish and Wildlife Service
  Gray's Lake, Elk Refuge, and Red Rocks Lake National Wildlife Refuges and fisheries in Yellowstone National Park

Bureau of Land Management
Bureau of Indian Affairs
Bureau of Reclamation
Bureau of Mines
Office of Surface Mining

U.S. Department of Agriculture

Forest Service: seven national forests in three different regions

Other Federal Agencies
Environmental Protection Agency
Department of Energy
  Bonneville Power Administration and
    Federal Energy Regulatory Commission
Army Corps of Engineers

State Agencies and Regulatory Bodies
Idaho Department of Fish and Game
Montana Department of Fish, Wildlife,
  and Parks
Wyoming Department of Game and
  Fish
Departments of State Lands or equiv-
  alent in each state
Department of Environmental Quality
  or equivalent in each state

**Interagency Committees and
  Working Groups**
Greater Yellowstone Coordinating
  Committee
Interagency Grizzly Bear Committee
Greater Yellowstone Ecosystem Bald
  Eagle Working Group
Montana Bald Eagle Working Group

Western Idaho Bald Eagle Working
  Group
Jackson Hole Cooperative Elk Studies
  Group
Pacific Flyways Council's Committee
  on the Rocky Mountain Trumpeter
  Swan Population
Montana Peregrine Falcon Recovery
  Team
Western States Peregrine Falcon
  Recovery Team
Northern Rocky Mountain Wolf
  Recovery Team
Wolf Management Committee
Cooperative Rocky Mountain Canada
  Goose Project
Greater Yellowstone Ecosystem
  Committee on Outfitters and Guides

County Planning Offices
Most of the twenty Greater Yellowstone Ecosystem counties have
  planning offices and planning
  commissions that review proposed
  private land developments.

ACKNOWLEDGMENTS

Hunter Coleman of Desktop Assistance calculated boundaries from GYE maps produced by Great Divide Graphics, Helena, Montana. Pete Feigley provided detailed comments on early drafts.

REFERENCES

Barbee, R.D., and J. Varley. 1984. The paradox of repeating error: Yellowstone National Park from 1872 to Biosphere Reserve and beyond. Presentation at the Conference for Biosphere Reserves, Great Smokey Mountains National Park, Gatlinburg, TN.

Berger, J. 1991. Greater Yellowstone's native ungulates: myths and realities. *Conservation Biology* 5:353–363.

Clark, T.W. 1996. Learning as a strategy for improving endangered species con- servation. *Endangered Species UPDATE* 13:5–6, 22–24.

Clark, T.W., and R.D. Brunner. 1996. Partnerships in endangered species conservation: attending to the decision process. *Endangered Species UPDATE* 13:1–4.

Clark, T.W., and A.H. Harvey. 1990. The Greater Yellowstone Ecosystem policy debate. *Society and Natural Resources* 3:281–284.

Clark, T.W., and S. Minta. 1994. Greater Yellowstone's future: prospects for ecosystem science. *Management and Policy*. Homestead Press, Moose, WY.

Clark, T.W., and D. Zaunbrecher. 1987. The Greater Yellowstone Ecosystem: the ecosystem concept in natural resource policy and management. *Renewable Resources Journal* 5:8–16.

Clark, T.W., E.D. Amato, D.G. Whittemore, and A.H. Harvey. 1989. *Rare, sensitive, and threatened species of the Greater Yellowstone Ecosystem*. Northern Rockies Conservation Cooperative, Montana Natural Heritage Program, The Nature Conservancy, Mountain West Environmental Services, Jackson, WY.

Clark, T.W., E.D. Amato, D.G. Whittemore, and A.H. Harvey. 1991. Policy and programs for ecosystem management in the Greater Yellowstone Ecosystem: an analysis. *Conservation Biology* 5:412–422.

Clark, T.W., D. Glick, and J. Varley. 1996. Balancing scientific, social, and regulatory concerns in biodiversity management. Pages 630–646 in *Biodiversity in managed landscapes: theory and practice* (R.C. Szaro and D. Johnston, editors). Oxford University Press, New York.

Congressional Research Service. 1987. *Greater Yellowstone Ecosystem, an analysis of data submitted by federal and state agencies*. U.S. Government Printing Office, Washington, DC.

Craighead, F. 1979. *Track of the grizzly*. Sierra Club, San Francisco.

Glick, D. 1997. Going downhill fast? *Greater Yellowstone Coalition Greater Yellowstone Report* 13:1–7.

Glick, D., M. Carr, and B. Harting. 1991. *An environmental profile of the Greater Yellowstone Ecosystem*. Greater Yellowstone Coalition, Bozeman, MT.

Greater Yellowstone Coalition, Environmental Defense Fund, and World Wildlife Fund. In press. *Tools for protecting wildlife habitat on private land*. Greater Yellowstone Coalition, Bozeman, MT.

Greater Yellowstone Coalition and the Wilderness Society. 1993. *Economic profiles of the twenty Greater Yellowstone counties*. Greater Yellowstone Coalition, Bozeman, MT.

Greater Yellowstone Coordinating Committee. 1987. *The Greater Yellowstone area, an aggregation of national park and national forest management plans*. U.S. Government Printing Office, Washington, DC.

Haggerty, M. 1996. *Fiscal impact of different land uses on county government and school districts in Gallatin county, Montana*. Montana State University, Bozeman, MT.

Harting, B., and D. Glick. 1994. *Sustaining Greater Yellowstone, a blueprint for the future*. Greater Yellowstone Coalition, Bozeman, MT.

Harvey, A.H. 1994. The aliens among us: introduced species in the Greater Yellowstone Ecosystem. *Northern Rockies Conservation Cooperative, NRCC News:* 74:5, 7.

Holling, C., and G. Meffe. 1996. Command and control and the pathology of natural resource management. *Conservation Biology* 10:328–337.

Johnson, J., and R. Rasker. 1993. Local business climate and the quality of life. *Montana Policy Review* 3:11–19.

Keiter, R. 1989. Taking account of the ecosystem on the public domain: law and ecology in the Greater Yellowstone region. *University of Colorado Law Review, Natural Resource Issue* 60:924–1007.

Kenworthy, T. 1997. Homes, homes on the range. *The Washington Post*, February 12, A1.

Litchman, P., and T.W. Clark. 1994. Rethinking the "vision" exercise in the Greater Yellowstone Ecosystem. *Society and Natural Resources* 7:459–478.

Power, T. 1991. Ecosystem preservation and the economy in the Greater Yellowstone area. *Conservation Biology* 5:395–404.

Power, T. 1995. *Lost landscapes and lost economies*. Island Press, Washington, DC.

Rasker, R., and D. Glick. 1994. Footloose entrepreneurs: pioneers of the new west? *Illahee Journal for the Northwest Environment* 10:34–43.

Rasker, R., N. Tirrell, and D. Kloepfer. 1992. *The wealth of nature*. The Wilderness Society, Bozeman, MT.

Schmidt, K. 1991. *Conserving Greater Yellowstone, a teacher's guide*. Northern Rockies Conservation Cooperative, Jackson, WY.

Smith, L. 1994. The land rush is on. *Greater Yellowstone Report* 10:1–5.

USDA Forest Service. 1992. *Our approach to sustaining ecological systems*. U.S. Forest Service Northern Region, Missoula, MT.

USDA Forest Service. 1996. *Targhee National Forest Draft Forest Plan*. Targhee National Forest. U.S. Government Printing Office, Washington, DC.

Wilderness Society. 1987. *Management directions for the national forests in the Greater Yellowstone Ecosystem*. The Wilderness Society, Washington DC.

Wilkinson, C. 1990. Crossing the next meridian: sustaining the lands, water, and human spirit in the West. *Environment* 32:10.

Wuerthner, G. 1990. Grazing the western range: what costs, what benefits. *Western Wildlands* 16:27–29.

Wyoming Recreation Commission. 1985. *State comprehensive outdoor recreation plan*. State of Wyoming, Cheyenne, WY.

Partnerships Across Park Boundaries: The Rincon Institute and Saguaro National Park

Luther Propst, William F. Paleck, and Liz Rosan

Perhaps the most pervasive and intractable threat to the long-term integrity of national park units and other protected areas is incompatible development of adjacent lands. This chapter concerns the conflicts between conservation and development that arise along the boundaries of public and private lands, and offers a collaborative approach to reconciling these conflicts.

Boundary pressures are greatest in settings such as Shenandoah National Park, Virginia, where private lands border 90 percent of the park's 566-kilometer boundary. In 1982, approximately 10 percent of the boundary was occupied by residential development; by 1992, this figure had risen to nearly 40 percent, transforming the park into an isolated habitat island (J. Davis, The Conservation Fund, personal communication). As Shenandoah tries to deal with immediate threats to wildlife habitat and viewsheds from housing construction ringing its boundaries, opposition to potential expansion of the park has grown among neighboring landowners. This antagonism stems from historical fears that the Park Service may condemn private land and from a more realistic concern regarding the fiscal impact of removing donated or acquired land from the local tax rolls (Fordney 1996).

Public land and resource managers increasingly point to declining ecological conditions within their jurisdictional boundaries: isolation of wildlife habitat and populations, invasion by exotic plants and animals, degradation of historic and cultural sites, and declining air and water quality. To understand the cause and scope of these resource-related

257

problems, the U.S. General Accounting Office conducted a survey of National Park Service superintendents, who reported that 85 percent of parks experience threats from sources outside their boundaries (U.S. General Accounting Office 1994a). These threats are likely to grow given the increased interest and mobility among Americans to flee congested suburbs and live next to protected lands.

Urbanization along the borders of protected areas that is not carefully planned affects natural processes in ways both striking and subtle. Residential subdivisions around natural areas, for example, isolate wildlife habitat and sever migratory and travel corridors, creating fragmented habitat "islands" that are too small to guarantee the long-term maintenance of species diversity. A study examining fourteen North American national parks reveals the extent of this trend: post-establishment extirpations occurred in all but the Banff-Jasper-Yoho Park complex in Canada (Newmark 1987). This study confirms what the Leopold Committee, an advisory board that influenced basic park management philosophy, concluded as early as 1962: "Few of the world's parks are large enough to be self-regulatory ecological units" (Leopold et al. 1963).

Native flora and fauna also are threatened by invasion of exotic plants and animals introduced by nearby development. Competition from introduced plant species, particularly those closely associated with disturbance, often plays a major role in the extinction of native species (Bowers and Turner 1985, Rondeau et al. 1992). The relationship between development and exotic bird species such as the European starling (*Sturnus vulgaris*) and the house sparrow (*Passer domesticus*) is well established: as the number of houses and large turf areas (grass lawns, golf courses, etc.) increases, so does the presence of exotic birds (Mills et al. 1989, Bibles and Mannan 1992). These species may then outcompete and displace native avifauna. Competition with European starlings for nest sites has contributed to the decline of native species throughout the United States (Yoakum et al. 1980).

The traditional response to protecting nationally significant resources from imminent adjacent development has relied heavily on federal acquisition. In 1988, Manassas National Military Park in Virginia, for example, acquired a 219-hectare parcel to prevent the development of Stuart's Hill, the site of Robert E. Lee's battlefield headquarters during the second Battle of Manassas. This protection, however, came at great cost. The park acquired the parcel only after the public became outraged by county approval of a 1.2 million square-foot regional mall and 560 residential units, thus costing the public $118 million for land that was purchased for $11 million two years earlier. This price tag was more than twice the amount the National Park Service spent on all other land acquisitions that year (Stone 1989).

In search of new approaches to prevent and resolve cross-boundary controversies, The Conservation Foundation (1985) published a seminal study entitled *National Parks for a New Generation: Visions, Realities, Prospects*. The most promising approach to such challenges, it concluded, is to devise protective measures tailor-made for the unique local circumstances surrounding each park, rather than following a uniform, nationwide methodology. The report called for creating "diverse cooperative mechanisms involving landowners and local governments in ways that reflect the needs and aspirations of adjacent communities." Last, the report recommended that such mechanisms are likely to be more effective if they involve strong local constituencies that recognize the contribution that national parks make to local quality of life.

Public land management agencies are increasingly adopting this important cross-boundary approach to park protection, encouraging their stewards to manage along ecological rather than political or administrative boundaries. This broader approach, often referred to as a component of "ecosystem management," acknowledges the limitations of managing solely within current borders and instead advocates promoting stewardship across boundaries, thereby "ensur[ing] the sustainable long-term use of natural resources . . . and prevent[ing] future ecological and economic conflicts from becoming intractable" (U.S. General Accounting Office 1994b). Ecosystem management demands what experts in community-based conservation describe as "a new matrix of expectations and relationships—to include both rights and responsibilities, accountability as well as trust, long-term patience, equitable partnership, flexibility, a more enlightened apportioning of costs and benefits, a vision of nature from which humans are inextricable, and a seamless linkage between conservation efforts and community development" (Liz Claiborne and Art Ortenberg Foundation 1993). To make such lofty goals real, the National Park Service is striving to include the human component in resource protection. The current NPS policy document (USDI National Park Service 1988) stresses that the key to fulfilling park stewardship obligations depends on working collaboratively with adjacent communities to promote improved communication, planning, and education.

A number of promising partnerships involving public land managers and adjacent communities have formed across the country. In many cases, what initially appears to be an irreconcilable conflict turns into a productive alliance where the participants strive to achieve common goals. A 1995 University of Michigan study of 105 ecosystem management efforts around the United States noted that collaboration among public land managers and neighboring communities was the most commonly reported factor facilitating successful initiatives (Yaffee et al. 1995). Our chapter features an example of this collaborative approach to reconciling conservation and community development situated at Saguaro National Park on the outskirts of Tucson, Arizona.

Controversy over Threats to Saguaro National Park

The two units of Saguaro National Park sit on the east and west sides of the Tucson Basin like mountainous bookends struggling to contain the city's 48 square kilometers of urban sprawl (Figure 12.1). Named after the majestic saguaro cactus (*Carnegiea gigantea*), the symbol of the American Southwest, this park protects 36,960 hectares of lush Sonoran Desert vegetation and the "sky islands" of the Rincon Mountains, including 28,895 hectares of legislatively designated wilderness.

Although it is considered the most lush and diverse of North American deserts, the Sonoran Desert receives fewer than 31 centimeters of rainfall a year. Annual rainfall in Saguaro National Park increases substantially as the Rincon Mountains rise from 665 meters to 2,641 meters, averaging 102 centimeters at elevations above 2,438 meters. These ele-

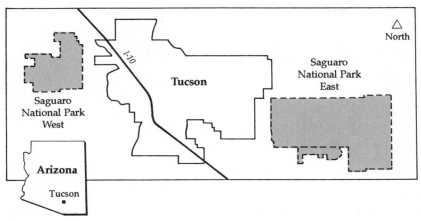

Figure 12.1. Location of Saguaro National Park, East and West Units.

vation changes in the park provide for six distinct biotic communities: desertscrub, desert grassland, oak woodland, pine–oak woodland, pine forest, and mixed conifer forest. This diverse landscape is home to common desert dwellers, including javelina (*Tayassu tajacu*), gila monsters (*Heloderma suspectum*), western diamondback rattlesnakes (*Crotalus atrox*), coyotes (*Canis latrans*), bobcats (*Felis rufus*), black bears (*Ursus americanus*), mountain lions (*Felis concolor*), gila woodpeckers (*Melanerpes uropyqialis*), red-tailed hawks (*Buteo jamaicenis*), and mule deer (*Odocoileus hemionus*). Petroglyphs remind visitors that the Hohokam people, part of the Chichimeca culture, once occupied this region. Archaeologists remain uncertain about the meanings of these petroglyphs, but consider these indigenous people innovators of prehistoric desert farming based on extensive networks of irrigation canals. With a growing national population interested in natural and cultural history and outdoor recreational activities, Saguaro National Park, like other protected natural areas, has experienced a surge in visitation since the early 1990s, skyrocketing from two to three million visitors annually.

When the Rincon Mountain District of Saguaro National Park was established in 1933, it stood as an isolated wilderness situated 19 kilometers from Tucson's eastern urban boundary. Since then, particularly since the mid-1950s, Tucson has experienced rapid growth averaging 2.8 percent annually, almost twice the national average. The population in Pima County has doubled since 1970, reaching over 700,000 today, and is expected to double again in the next twenty-four years (Pima Association of Governments 1994). Embracing classic patterns of sunbelt sprawl, this growth pushed development to the park's very boundaries and redefined it as a suburban wilderness. Unplanned sprawl also is eroding the natural and ecological integrity of the other protected sky island mountains adjacent to the city, including Coronado National Forest, Tucson Mountain Park, and Tortolita Mountain Park.

Since 1985 local officials have approved the construction of six major high-end resort and residential communities in the scenic foothills adjoining the city's pristine mountain backdrop. Ironically, the growing demand for resort, residential, and commercial development in these natural settings is threatening the very reason people are attracted to them in the first place. In many cases, the development of property adjacent to park and forest trailheads has eliminated or severely restricted access to popular recreational trails. At the same time, the residents of new subdivisions near large natural areas have created their own paths into the desert and foothills. This not only increases disturbance and impacts, but also can lead to a confusing and destructive mish-mash of intertwined, overlapping, and parallel "rogue" trails.

Development pressure in sensitive natural areas is likely to continue given Tucson's projected rise in population over the next few decades. Property adjacent to protected lands is particularly attractive to the growing number of people seeking to escape the urban environment. As a leading Tucson developer points out, "From a market perspective, land adjoining Saguaro National Park is the closest thing in southern Arizona to ocean-front property."

As in so many other western cities grappling with rapid growth, Tucson's expansion has stirred great controversy. In the mid-1980s, Tucsonans were particularly troubled by the "cookie cutter" tract developments stamped over large expanses of previously undisturbed desert uplands and the rapid conversion of tree-lined arroyos to concrete-lined flood control channels. With limited funds for public acquisition of significant buffer lands and local elected officials largely supportive of growth, concerned citizens worked with Saguaro National Park Superintendent Rob Arnberger to develop a regulatory approach that would mitigate the impacts of development adjacent to protected lands.

The State of Arizona imposed a moratorium on any rezoning within 1.6 kilometers of Saguaro National Park while legislators studied the issue. During this time, a citizen-generated referendum to make this temporary moratorium permanent readily secured sufficient signatures to appear in the next election, but was ruled unconstitutional by the state supreme court. The state eventually passed legislation that eliminated the ability of local jurisdictions instantaneously to approve rezonings by invoking governmental "emergency" powers, a practice that had become routine in Tucson. The arena for continuing this debate then shifted from the state level to the local level.

Sobered by the near-loss of local zoning control through referendum and examination by state legislators, Pima County appointed a diverse group of local developers, environmental activists, biologists, realtors, and agency officials to prepare a zoning ordinance to encourage more ecologically sensitive development near the protected areas of the Tucson Basin. After nearly two years of investigation, debate, and compromise, their efforts resulted in a proposal that came to be known by its unfortunate acronym, BOZO: the Buffer Overlay Zone Ordinance. BOZO addressed a wide variety of concerns, including prohibited and recommended landscape plant species, night lighting and sunlight reflective standards, minimum percentage of open space, riparian habitat pro-

tection, and minimum setbacks from the boundaries of the protected natural areas. Throughout the community, BOZO was hotly debated. Some
argued that it went too far, whereas others maintained that it failed to
secure long-term protection of the ecological integrity and character of
the Tucson Basin and its quality of life. Eventually, in June 1988 a paper-
tiger version of the ordinance was approved.

Rather than providing any meaningful protection for park ecosystems
and any certainty for landowners, the compromise on BOZO only
heightened the conflict and polarization over development adjacent to
sensitive desert lands. Following this effort, a vocal and frustrated anti-
growth constituency emerged to challenge new development proposals
in the Tucson Basin.

The Rincon Institute: A New Approach to Conservation

Nowhere in the Tucson Basin did the polarized debate over development
play out more contentiously than in the review of the Rocking K Ranch,
a proposed large-scale resort development sharing an eight-kilometer
boundary with the Rincon Mountain District of Saguaro National Park
east of Tucson (Figure 12.2). What resulted, however, was not the usual

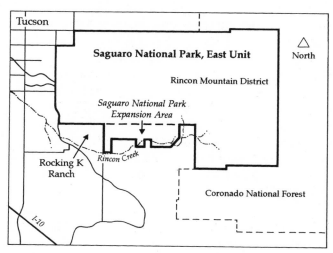

Figure 12.2. Location of the Rocking K Ranch in relation to Saguaro National Park East.

bitter compromise. Instead, the landowner, National Park Service officials, local and national conservationists, and the county formed a
unique partnership to ensure that the new development would be highly
sensitive to adjacent natural and cultural resources.

In a climate of failed expectations following the BOZO ordinance,
prominent Tucson investors and land developers presented the 2,428-
hectare Rocking K Ranch for rezoning to the Pima County Board of
Supervisors. With picketers standing outside closed hearing doors and
rumors of a bomb threat, the Rocking K Ranch became the most controversial development proposal in Pima County's history. The proposed
plan included a resort and residential development, complete with
21,000 residential units, four resorts, 243 hectares of commercial space,
and three golf courses, that would support a new community of over
50,000 in the Rincon Valley. This proposal raised serious concerns,
threatening to transform this rural valley into a new suburb of Tucson,
and directly compromising the park's ecological and scenic integrity. Surprised by the intensity of the debate sparked by the proposal, the Rocking K Development Company withdrew its initial plan from consideration.

As a native of Tucson, Bill Paleck, new Superintendent of Saguaro
National Park, had watched the Old Pueblo rapidly become a sprawling
urban metropolis with few measures to protect outlying public lands.
What he most feared was the prospect of settling for another county-
approved development without any long-term environmental safeguards
to preserve the park's resources. Among the many resources Superintendent Paleck saw threatened were:

- *Riparian habitat.* Large areas of impervious surfaces (created primarily by roads and parking areas) increase water runoff and invariably
  lead to the channelization of stream beds. The resultant loss of
  riparian habitat has a negative impact on the majority of the Sonoran Desert's wildlife species, which frequently visit or live in riparian areas during at least part of their life cycles. In addition, a variety of threatened and endangered wildlife species already depend
  on this critical habitat for their survival (Ohmart and Zisner 1993).

- *Desert tortoise.* Construction of sprawling residential development
  and its attendant infrastructure often destroys the habitat of the
  protected desert tortoise (*Gopherus latrans*). Subsequent disturbance and handling of the survivors by curious residents can stress

these reclusive animals, thereby reducing their resistance to disease and illness. People also illegally remove tortoises from the wild to keep as pets.

- *Mule deer.* Interruption of, or barriers to, movement along the threads of riparian habitat that issue from the mountain reaches and intertwine on the valley floor can have devastating effects on mule deer (*Odocoileus hemionus*). Deer travel up and down these corridors to access water, forage, and bedding areas during the critical dry period before the arrival of the summer monsoon rains. When they give birth, does use riparian corridors to move to higher elevations away from predators on the valley floor. During periods of great natural stress, blockage of these corridors by fences and harassment from domestic dogs running at large invariably result in lowered fawn survival rates and increased adult mortality.

- *Scenic and "night sky" views.* Architecture that clashes with surrounding landforms and traditional building materials and designs, highly reflective surfaces that glisten and shine distractingly, and exterior lighting that reduces the luster of the natural "night sky" can individually and cumulatively diminish the scenic quality of the Sonoran Desert landscape, which is highly valued by many residents, recreationists, and visitors.

Superintendent Paleck was determined to continue the efforts of his predecessor and committed himself to making development in the Rincon Valley support a more ecologically benign community. To better understand the potential impacts of the proposed Rocking K Ranch development and the feasibility of alternative land uses, he approached two national conservation organizations with extensive experience in reconciling development and land protection: World Wildlife Fund and The Conservation Foundation (WWF; The Conservation Foundation was absorbed by WWF in 1990), and the National Parks and Conservation Association (NPCA). These organizations evaluated several factors for Paleck to consider in response to the Rocking K Ranch development proposal: (1) Rocking K's water rights, (2) the property's ownership and financing, (3) metropolitan growth trends and projections for eastern Pima County, (4) the history of development review in Pima County, and (5) the history of judicial review of local land-use decisions. What they concluded was that county approval and successful development of the site were almost inevitable.

First and foremost, the probability of the Rocking K Ranch's owners (Rocking K) abandoning the project or declaring bankruptcy, a common occurrence in the late 1980s, was remote. In the mid-1970s, experienced investors and land developers had purchased the ranch with the intention of developing an exclusive, high-end resort. Land records revealed that there was no mortgage-backed debt on the property; consequently, Rocking K would not be financially crippled by delays in the development review process, allowing them to view this as a long-term project.

Second, the value of the property had appreciated considerably since acquisition. Rocking K was thus even more inclined to weather delays in developing the ranch since selling it would result in a substantial capital gains tax.

Third, adequate water for the project already had been secured. According to the Arizona Department of Water Resources, the Rocking K Ranch had an adequate supply of on-site groundwater, an annual supply of approximately 5 million cubic meters, for the next 100 years. In addition, Rocking K had obtained water rights to 4 million cubic meters annually from the Colorado River through the Central Arizona Project (CAP), providing the development with twice the amount of water needed to supply the projected population.

Fourth, given population trends, sharp reductions in congressional funding for park acquisition, and pro-growth county land-use ordinances and court rulings, development over the next 25 years in the Rincon Valley appeared imminent. Moreover, no major development proposals in the past two decades in Pima County had been defeated.

Fifth, the option to protect the park's resources through the traditional land acquisition approach appeared infeasible: a large portion of the Rocking K Ranch did not merit national park status and protection; Congress had never appropriated funds to acquire park additions in Arizona; funds appropriated by Congress from the Land and Water Conservation Fund had dropped off precipitously; and the Arizona delegation would not support acquisition without the developer's approval.

Based on this comprehensive land-use analysis, Superintendent Paleck concluded that the Rocking K Ranch proposal in some form would almost certainly gain local approval. He also reasoned that a successful national campaign to oppose Rocking K would at best result in the type of unplanned development that already characterized lands adjoining the Tucson Mountain District of Saguaro National Park, development that was both ecologically incompatible with park values and fiscally draining for local taxpayers.

Given these circumstances, WWF and NPCA recommended that the park most likely stood to gain from a cooperative partnership with Rocking K. To ensure the protection of the park's desert ecosystems and the quality of the visitor's experience, Paleck concluded that a proposed master-planned development with significant environmental measures would be less intrusive and damaging than the incremental, piecemeal subdivision occurring elsewhere in the Tucson Basin. Over the next ten months, the National Park Service worked with Rocking K and a variety of local leaders to craft a mutually acceptable plan that included provisions for the park's protection as an integral element of the development proposal for the Rocking K Ranch.

At the top of Superintendent Paleck's list was to ensure that the site design and planning would not fragment migratory routes and create isolated wildlife habitat islands too small to support biological diversity. He particularly wanted to consider the positive attributes of limiting development to carefully designed clusters. This planning approach reduces the extent of disturbance, not only of the building footprints themselves, but also of the network of road, water, power, and sewer infrastructure required. It reduces the area of impervious surfaces and can provide opportunities to deal with water runoff in ways that do not lead to stream channelization and riparian habitat degradation. In addition, visual intrusions can be more easily mitigated and the extent and nature of exotic decorative plantings can be substantially reduced.

To evaluate the regional impacts of the proposed development, Superintendent Paleck recruited the chair of the University of Arizona's Department of Wildlife Biology to map critical habitat and wildlife corridors in the park and on the Rocking K Ranch. Extensive wildlife, vegetation, and hydrology studies were conducted and a prime resource area was identified that included about 809 hectares on the ranch. These studies revealed that limiting the overall density of the development alone would not provide adequate wildlife habitat protection (Shaw et al. 1992). The development also needed an environmentally sensitive plan that integrated wildlife corridors. Fortunately, the scale of the Rocking K Ranch development could accommodate this type of carefully planned site design.

National Parks and Conservation Association argued that these wildlife protection measures should be coupled with public acquisition of the critical habitat identified on the Rocking K Ranch. Rocking K Development Company agreed to sell the National Park Service 95 percent of the area that had been identified as prime wildlife habitat. They would not, however, sell the resort site at the edge of this critical area, as its dramatic location was essential for a successful resort project.

While these site planning provisions were crucial, Superintendent Paleck knew that alone they were insufficient to adequately protect Saguaro's long-term ecological integrity from regional growth pressures. The challenge was how to ensure stewardship of environmental values, not just in the short term, but through a succession of homeowners over the next several decades. This was a particularly relevant concern considering that the transient urban population of Tucson "rolled over" every 7.5 years. Paleck feared merely token commitments from the developer to educate residents about wildlife and ecosystem stewardship.

In one recent Tucson development, for example, initial buyers of lots adjoining critical wildlife habitat received a notebook about wildlife protection and a figurine of a bighorn sheep family for their mantelpiece. These measures were designed to verse the new residents in habitat protection needs. Subsequent homeowners, however, never received further information. With such a cursory and short-term commitment invested in its residents, it was clear that this community's conservation ethic would not be sustained. To prevent this kind of superficial environmental stewardship, Paléck wanted long-term, built-in guarantees from the developer to enhance the development's conservation commitments and to protect park resources.

With these considerations in mind, the National Park Service, Rocking K Development Company, and conservation leaders proposed to create the Rincon Institute: a new, independent, nonprofit conservation organization whose mission would be to help protect the natural resources of Saguaro National Park and adjoining lands. A diverse board of directors was recruited to ensure that the Rincon Institute incorporated sound policy and science into its activities. To guarantee representation from key actors in this partnership, the Superintendent of Saguaro National Park, the Director of Pima County Parks and Recreation Department, and the President of Rocking K Development Company would serve as board members in a nonvoting and ex officio capacity.

The Rincon Institute would enter into a long-term funding agreement with Rocking K to provide four major conservation priorities:

- Manage approximately 182 hectares of natural open space within the Rocking K Ranch for educational, scientific, conservation, and outdoor recreational purposes.

- Provide environmental education in partnership with the National Park Service for students, residents, guests, employees, builders, realtors, and the greater Rincon Valley.

- Conduct long-term ecological research on wildlife habitat, plant salvage, and riparian restoration.

- Provide professional guidance and oversight on environmentally sensitive development, management, and restoration strategies for the Rocking K Ranch and landowners in the Rincon Valley.

What distinguished the Rincon Institute from other conservation approaches was its pioneering partnership with the Rocking K Ranch: the development process would generate long-term funds for the Institute's conservation activities. As a condition of local approval, the Rocking K Development Company agreed to impose deed restrictions binding all future homeowners and businesses to financially support the Rincon Institute's conservation programs. The restrictions include nightly surcharges on hotel rooms, occupancy fees on commercial and retail outlets on the site, monthly fees assessed to homeowners, and real estate transfer fees that apply to both initial conveyances and resales. Under this agreement, the nightly surcharge from a proposed 400-room hotel, for example, would generate approximately $50,000 per year (50 cents per guest per night). When fully built, the development anticipated generating between $200,000 to $300,000 a year for resource conservation adjacent to Saguaro National Park.

After months of negotiations, the National Park Service and Rocking K Development Company finally agreed to the following four key provisions to protect the park's fragile ecosystems. Rocking K Development Company would:

- Sell 95 percent of the ranch's most significant wildlife habitat, about 809 hectares in all, to the National Park Service when the boundary of the park was legislatively expanded. (In addition, the National Park Service eventually agreed to purchase another 648 hectares of neighboring ranch lands.)

- Restore critical riparian habitat along a four-kilometer stretch of Rincon Creek, a major drainage in the Tucson Basin that issues from the park and has been severely degraded by decades of ground-

water mining, cattle grazing, and farming. Given that desert riparian environments provide as much as ten times more productive
wildlife habitat than do desert uplands, this restoration, with an
estimated cost of six to eight million dollars, is critical to the Rincon Valley's wildlife.

- Reduce the total number of homes from 21,000 to 10,000 units and
  cluster the development sites. This revised plan would support
  24,000 new residents and preserve one-half of the site as open space
  in a system of integrated wildlife corridors and 24 kilometers of public hiking and equestrian trails into the park. (In July 1996 Rocking
  K Development Company entered a joint venture partnership with
  Lowe Development Resorts of Santa Barbara, California, and
  agreed further to reduce the total number of units to 6,500 and
  eliminate one major resort.)

- Create and fund the Rincon Institute to ensure long-term monitoring, compliance, and implementation of environmental commitments. County development approval mandated the Institute's
  funding, thereby ensuring the organization's financial autonomy.
  Furthermore, the Rincon Institute is structured as a 509(a) support
  organization for the Sonoran Institute, a 501(c)(3) organization
  that was founded at the same time in 1991. This arrangement
  ensures tax-exempt status and deductible donations even though a
  substantial portion of the Rincon Institute's budget comes from a
  single source. The Sonoran Institute was created to promote community-based strategies that preserve the ecological integrity of
  protected lands, and at the same time meet the economic aspirations of adjoining landowners and communities. Underlying the
  Sonoran Institute's mission is the conviction that community-
  driven and inclusive approaches to conservation produce the most
  effective results. (In summer 1996, the Rincon Institute and Rocking K Development Company renegotiated to increase long-term
  funding and simplify financial administration.)

In December 1990, Rocking K Development Company presented its
revised proposal to Pima County Supervisors. With supervisors aware of
the importance of including these environmental mitigation measures,
Pima County approved the new specific plan for the Rocking K Ranch.
The reality of the situation was characterized by a supervisor in a public
statement: "In the world of real choices, this plan represents a dramatic

departure from past practices of unplanned sprawl and spot zoning. Our challenge now is to assure that all future development conforms to these high standards."

Despite these unprecedented elements in a county-approved development plan, public skepticism remained strong. During the year-long approval process, the Rincon Valley Coalition, a citizens' group opposed to the Rocking K plan, had staunchly contested any development of the ranch other than 0.4-hectare and 1.2-hectare lots and refused to discuss alternatives with Rocking K or Saguaro National Park. Accordingly, the Coalition viewed Paleck as a turncoat and the Rincon Institute as nothing more than a clever ploy to gain development approval without an authentic environmental commitment to the valley.

Following county approval, the Rincon Valley Coalition organized a petition drive to force a referendum, hoping to overturn the County's decision by popular vote. As WWF and NPCA had pointed out earlier, Arizona courts tightly enforce technical rules governing the referendum process when used to overturn site-specific zoning decisions. True to tradition, the courts disallowed the petition drive for failing to submit an adequate number of valid signatures. Consequently, the issue never appeared on the ballot as a referendum question.

Fostering Stewardship at Saguaro National Park and the Rincon Valley

In 1991, its first year, the Rincon Institute initiated a range of conservation activities designed to protect wildlife habitat and to assess the potential impacts of developments on natural resources in Saguaro National Park, the Rocking K, and throughout the Rincon Valley. Most notably, the Institute spearheaded a coalition of organizations that convinced Congress to add nearly 1,619 hectares to the Rincon Mountain District of Saguaro National Park. With continued support from these local organizations, the Institute helped add another 1,416 hectares to the Tucson Mountain District and redesignate Saguaro National Monument as a National Park in 1994.

By attracting a diverse and professional board of directors from the Tucson community, the Rincon Institute has built a strong constituency among private landowners in the Rincon Valley, federal and state agencies, and a variety of other public and private organizations. Over the past five years, the Rincon Institute has specialized in conservation research, land protection, landowner outreach efforts, and environmen-

tal education at Saguaro National Park, the Rincon Valley, and the Tucson Basin.

Conservation Research and Land Management Program

In partnership with Saguaro National Park, the University of Arizona,
U.S. Geological Survey, and Harris Environmental, Inc., the Rincon
Institute completed a two-year inventory of wildlife populations and
riparian habitat on the Rocking K Ranch, Saguaro National Park, and
the Rincon Valley. Amphibians, small mammals, reptiles, and birds were
inventoried as part of a long-term wildlife monitoring effort to assess
potential pressures on these populations. The riparian habitat inventories documented data on biotic components (streamside vegetation communities) and abiotic components (groundwater, streamflow, and channel morphology) of riparian ecosystems at four permanent study sites
along a 13-kilometer stretch of the Rincon Creek. These inventories will
serve as the basis for long-term monitoring of the area's natural resources
and increase empirical understanding of how development and urbanization affect protected natural areas as well as how these impacts can be
minimized (Briggs et al. 1996).

The Rincon Institute also is responsible for developing a comprehensive restoration plan for the 4-kilometer reach of Rincon Creek that
winds through the ranch. To help guide these restoration efforts, the
Institute evaluated the results of many conservation and rehabilitation
efforts throughout Arizona. An early result of this effort was the publication of *Riparian Ecosystem Recovery in Arid Lands: Strategies and References*
(Briggs 1996). This guidebook targets resource managers, biologists,
hydrologists, government planners, and concerned citizens interested in
developing site-specific recovery plans for damaged riparian areas in the
southwestern United States and northwestern Mexico.

As part of the Rocking K Ranch's comprehensive land management
plan, the Rincon Institute will manage approximately 182 hectares of
natural open space and trails within the ranch and coordinate conservation activities and needs with the park. To protect cross-boundary
wildlife corridors, Saguaro National Park, in partnership with the developer and Pima County, will develop the design and construction criteria
for the 24-kilometer public trails system within Rocking K. When the
development breaks ground in 1998, the Institute will initiate a plant salvage operation to reduce the impacts of development on biodiversity in
the valley and encourage volunteer participation in habitat restoration
and maintenance projects.

Natural Area Protection and Outreach Program

To mitigate the impacts of adjacent development on Saguaro National Park, the Rincon Institute is promoting conservation approaches that include public land acquisition measures as well as expanded conservation options for private landowners.

In 1992, Saguaro National Park and the Institute sponsored a conference at which more than 100 Tucsonans—from builders and developers to environmentalists and government officials—identified collaborative ways to reconcile conservation and development. As a direct result of this conference, the Institute spearheaded the formation of a citizens' committee for open space and parks to identify and prioritize critical natural areas in Pima County that should be saved from development. With increasing pressure to develop near protected natural areas, this committee is working with the Citizens Bond Advisory Committee and the Pima County Parks and Recreation Department to coordinate a $31 million bond referendum to acquire the most sensitive and scenic natural areas in the Tucson Basin. Working closely with the County, the Institute also intends to create a mechanism that will offer developers incentives to cluster housing and preserve open space in all new development.

With decreasing funding for public land acquisition, the Institute also is working with private landowners in the Rincon Valley and along the adjoining upper Tanque Verde Creek to develop and implement landowner-based strategies to protect this area's desert riparian ecosystems. The Partnership for Riparian Conservation in Northeastern Pima County (PROPIMA) addresses the need to preserve privately owned riparian habitats in a manner that protects private property rights and promotes citizen stewardship. Thus far, the Institute has helped secure one conservation easement on private property along Tanque Verde Creek in support of this effort.

Environmental Education Programs

The Institute's environmental education programs emphasize increased understanding of desert ecosystems while instilling a high level of environmental awareness among participants. Fundamental to these programs is conveying the message that stewardship of the area does not begin or end at park boundaries. Rather, the long-term integrity of the park will depend in large part on the stewardship role of Rincon Valley residents.

Targeting elementary school students, the Institute and teachers in the Vail School District developed a program called "Parks As Classrooms" to take students out of the classroom and into Saguaro National Park to learn about the habitat needs of wildlife and the importance of conservation in a fragile desert environment. To involve the community in this project, the school district initiated a docent training program for "Parks As Classrooms" in cooperation with Saguaro National Park and the Institute.

Long-term environmental education plans include building an environmental education center adjacent to Saguaro National Park that will incorporate classrooms, research and exhibit space, and outdoor interpretive trails. This center will provide comprehensive environmental education and natural and cultural history programs geared for residents, guests, employees, and students. In addition, the Institute will develop an education program to help homeowners build environmentally sensitive and energy-efficient designs in the new community. Homeowners also will learn about their rights and responsibilities related to natural resource protection of the development and adjacent park as established in the deed restrictions.

Sources of Support

This innovative blend of conservation and development has attracted support from a range of foundations, individuals, and state and federal conservation agencies. The Institute has secured major project funding from the Arizona Game and Fish Department, Arizona Water Protection Fund, ARCO Foundation, National Fish and Wildlife Foundation, National Park Foundation, and World Wildlife Fund. In 1995 the National Park Foundation and the U.S. Department of the Interior awarded Saguaro National Park and the Rincon Institute the prestigious National Park Partnership Leadership Award in recognition of their collaborative programs.

Reflections on Cross-Boundary Solutions

Win–win solutions are now being crafted across the country to enhance long-term protection of park resources and enrich local quality of life and economic vitality. Independent of formal theories, standard practices, or traditional conventions, developers have established similar nonprofit organizations as integral and permanent conservation elements of new communities bordering protected areas. These organizations are playing an important role in addressing local land development and conservation issues while reducing polarization and providing new methods for financing conservation efforts in an era of public funding cutbacks. Their unconventional approach to financing conservation has emerged in several diverse markets, including Arizona, California, Florida, South Carolina, and Washington.

This emerging trend of forging collaborative solutions that integrate conservation with development will continue to gather momentum as more Americans choose to live adjacent to national parks or other areas with significant natural amenities. As part of this trend, an increasing number of homebuyers are willing to pay a premium for development projects that demonstrate an authentic long-term commitment to environmental quality. To capture this growing market niche, developers are creatively responding with approaches such as the Rincon Institute that make this lasting promise to conservation. Moreover, from a market standpoint, protecting these natural assets clearly adds value to their real estate investments, helps earn broad local support, and reduces the need for governmental mandates.

Organizations such as the Rincon Institute invest new communities with a conservation ethic that takes hold before the first spadeful of soil is turned for construction and lasts long after the developers leave. This model demonstrates some clear advantages over earlier organizational models that own and manage common open space, including local government authorities (such as county or municipal parks or schools), or homeowners' associations. These latter approaches to land protection often meet with initial success. However, as time passes and competing priorities evolve, the commitment to natural open space tends to lose precedence and attention. Schools and parks often must choose between protecting riparian habitat and buying a new roof for the gymnasium. Homeowners' associations must choose between spending funds to protect and maintain open space or replacing the community swimming pool pump. The Rincon Institute model, on the other hand, can avoid this difficult reality of choices by vesting responsibility in an independent, nonprofit third party with a secure source of income and a conservation focus.

As private lands neighboring our wild areas become increasingly urbanized, public land managers are recognizing the importance of solutions that address issues beyond their formal boundaries. In the past, Americans successfully preserved cherished landscapes by setting aside more parks, forests, refuges, and wilderness areas. Natural resource managers can no longer rely on isolation and federal laws to protect the integrity of these areas. International and now domestic experience teach us that this jurisdictional boundary approach to ecosystem management and protection is inadequate to deal with the magnitude and complexity of air, habitat, and water systems, as well as neighboring urban issues of traffic, crime, increased infrastructure costs, water rights, and development controversies. In response to these challenges, federal land managers are working directly with local residents, developers, and county officials to develop conservation strategies that reflect and integrate the diverse needs of protected areas with those of adjacent landowners and communities. Without big-picture, landscape-level solutions, protected areas will become veritable islands in a rising sea of development.

Inevitably, we will need to search for new pragmatic and workable paradigms that manage growth in a sustainable manner while protecting local natural resources. The model described in this chapter cannot reconcile all natural resource boundary conflicts. Rather, it represents one strategy among many for minimizing the impacts of development in cases where development bordering a protected area appears inevitable. Most notably, this approach demands a fresh way of thinking about the role of human communities in relation to the natural environment—by placing resource stewardship in the hands of each new community.

ACKNOWLEDGMENTS

We appreciate the editorial assistance of Mary Schmid in improving this chapter.

REFERENCES

Bibles, B., and R.W. Mannan. 1992. Impacts of exotic cavity-nesting birds on native cavity-nesting birds in Saguaro National Monument. Pages 195–199 in *Proceedings of the symposium on research in Saguaro National Monument* (C.P. Stone and E.S. Bellantoni, editors). National Park Service, Rincon Institute and Southwest Parks and Monuments Association, Tucson, AZ.

Bowers, J., and R. Turner. 1985. A revised vascular flora of Tumamoc Hill, Tucson, Arizona. *Madroño* 32:225–252.

Briggs, M. 1996. *Riparian ecosystem recovery in arid lands: strategies and references*. University of Arizona Press, Tucson, AZ.

Briggs, M., L. Harris, J. Howe, and W. Halvorson. 1996. Using long-term monitoring to understand how adjacent land development affects natural areas: an example from Saguaro National Park, Arizona (USA). *Natural Areas Journal* 16:354–361.

The Conservation Foundation. 1985. *National parks for a new generation: visions, realities, prospects*. The Conservation Foundation, Washington, D.C.

Fordney, Chris. 1996. Boundary wars. *National Parks* 70:24–29.

Leopold, A.S., S.A. Cain, C.M. Cottam, I.N. Gabrielson, and T.L. Kimball. 1963. Study of wildlife problems in national parks. *Transactions of the North American Wildlife and Natural Resources Conference* 28:28–45.

Liz Claiborne and Art Ortenberg Foundation. 1993. *The view from Airlie: community based conservation in perspective*. Liz Claiborne and Art Ortenberg Foundation, New York.

Mills, G.S., J.B. Dunning, Jr., and J.M. Bates. 1989. Effects of urbanization on breeding bird community structure in southwestern desert habitats. *Condor* 91:416–428.

Newmark, W.D. 1987. A land-bridge island perspective on mammalian extinctions in western North American parks. *Nature* 325:430–432.

Ohmart, R.D., and C.D. Zisner. 1993. *Functions and values of riparian habitat to wildlife in Arizona: a literature review*. Submitted to Arizona Game and Fish Department, Phoenix, AZ.

Pima Association of Governments. 1994. *Community information database*, third edition. Tucson, AZ.

Rondeau, R., T. Van Devender, P. Jenkins, C.D. Bertelsen, and R. Van Devender. 1992. Extirpated plant species of the Tucson Mountains. Pages 141–143 in *Proceedings of the Symposium on Research in Saguaro National Monument* (C.P. Stone, and E.S. Bellantoni, editors). National Park Service, Rincon Institute, and Southwest Parks and Monuments Association, Tucson, AZ.

Shaw, W.W., A. Goldsmith, and J. Schelhas. 1992. Studies of urbanization and the wildlife resources of Saguaro National Monument. Pages 173–180 in *Proceedings of the symposium on research in Saguaro National Monument* (C.P. Stone and E.S. Bellantoni, editors). National Park Service, Rincon Institute, and Southwest Parks and Monuments Association, Tucson, AZ.

Stone, Roger. 1989. National parks and adjacent lands. *Conservation Foundation Letter*, no. 3, Washington, DC.

USDI National Park Service. 1988. *Management policies*. U.S. Government Printing Office, Washington, DC.

U.S. General Accounting Office. 1994a. *Activities outside park borders have caused damage to resources and will likely cause more*. U.S. General Accounting Office, GAO/RCED-94-59. Washington, DC.

U.S. General Accounting Office. 1994b. *Ecosystem management: additional actions needed to adequately test a promising approach*. U.S. General Accounting Office, GAO/RCED-94-111. Washington, DC.

Yaffee, S., A. Phillips, I. Frentz, P. Hardy, S. Maleki, and B. Thorpe. 1995. *Ecosystem management in the U.S.: an assessment of current experience*. Island Press, Washington, DC.

Yoakum, J., W.P. Dasmann, H.R. Sanderson, C.M. Nixon, and H.S. Crawford. 1980. *Habitat improvement techniques*. Pages 329–403 in *Wildlife management techniques manual* (S.D. Schemnitz, editor). The Wildlife Society, Washington, DC.

Chapter 13

Wilderness and Working Landscapes: The Adirondack Park As a Model Bioregion

Thomas Pasquarello

The loss of biological diversity is one of the most pressing environmental problems facing the world today, and Wilson (1992) has demonstrated that only the protection of natural ecosystems will reverse this trend. Bioregions are geographic constructs that unite natural ecosystems across human boundaries and may thus help to protect them from the adverse effects of human development, fragmentation, and boundary effects documented in recent studies by Newmark (1985), Tilman et al. (1994), Knight et al. (1995), and Cole and Landres (1996). As used here, the term *bioregion* refers specifically to units of government that protect natural ecosystems, and not the small-scale economic communities advocated by Kirkpatrick Sale (1985) and other "deep ecologists." There is inherent tension between the *ecological concept* of a bioregion and the essentially *political exercise* of defining and managing them that stems from the fact that ecologists and geographers can only define the boundaries of bioregions in a "rough and ready way" (Brennan 1988), while the rights and prerogatives assigned to even the most arbitrary of human boundaries are generally strictly defined and upheld by courts, legislatures, and executive agencies (see the Supreme Court's decision on the issue of "takings" in *Dolan v. Tigard* 1994, for example). "Wilderness and working landscapes" is an alliterative description of the patchwork of public and private lands that make New York's Adirondack Park one of the oldest and largest bioregions in the world. This case study utilizes the Adirondack Park as a grand experiment in bioregionalism, building on its successes and learning from its failures to create a practical "toolkit" that may be used to reduce the inherent difficulties of defining, managing, and governing bioregions across human boundaries.

279

The Adirondack Park encompasses 2.5 million hectares and is larger than Yellowstone, Yosemite, Olympic, and Everglades National parks *combined*. Unlike these more heralded national parks, this state park joins public (40 percent) and private (60 percent) land in a manner similar to the national parks of Europe, although on a much larger scale. Within its boundaries are over 1 million hectares of wilderness, 46 peaks over 1,220 meters in altitude, more than 1,800 lakes and ponds, 48,000 kilometers of brooks and streams, nearly 4,827 kilometers of wild and scenic rivers, and most of the plant and animal species indigenous to the northeastern United States.

The Adirondack Park also is home to approximately 150,000 permanent and 125,000 seasonal residents, and is visited by an estimated 15 million tourists each year. In few other places on earth are human beings and natural ecosystems integrated to such a degree. The Park is divided into 105 units of town and village government across 12 counties, and each of the 5 state agencies that provide services to Park residents and visitors have divided it into a different geographic pattern of administrative units. These factors make the Adirondack Park an important experiment in light of the threat posed to natural ecosystems by human development and administrative boundaries. Because the boundaries and administrative structures that define the Adirondack Park are the result more of complex historical interactions than of ecological principles, it is useful to place this experiment in historical context.

A Brief History of the Adirondack Park

Until the mid-1800s the Adirondack region of New York State, with its thin soil, rugged terrain, and short growing season was bypassed as settlers pushed west to more-productive farmlands. However, the industrial revolution that transformed the U.S. economy in the latter half of the nineteenth century was dependent on wood for fuel and raw materials, and the Adirondack forests soon echoed with the sound of axe and saw. By the 1870s much of the Adirondack forest had been clear-cut or burned when the sparks from steam locomotives set fire to logging debris. Anglers and hunters upset with the loss of fish and game, and business interests concerned that the eroded Adirondack landscape would result in floods and droughts that would harm the economically important Erie Canal, joined forces to call for legislation to protect the region. In 1884 the state legislature authorized funds to purchase scattered parcels of land in the Adirondacks for New York's State Forest Preserve. Eight years later the legislature drew a line around the scattered parcels of land it had purchased and created the Adirondack Park, declaring its intention to purchase all the lands within the boundary. Because this line was drawn in blue ink on the legislator's maps, the boundary of the Park became known as the "blue line," a moniker that persists to this day.

Despite the creation of the Forest Preserve and the Adirondack Park, widespread logging continued on state lands in the Adirondacks. In 1894 the New York Constitution was amended to provide stronger protection for the Forest Preserve. The "Forever Wild" clause, as this amendment has come to be known, states that "The lands of the State, now owned or hereafter acquired, constituting the Forest Preserve as now fixed by law, shall be forever kept as wild forest lands. They shall not be leased, sold, or exchanged, or be taken by any corporation public or private, nor shall the timber thereon be sold, removed, or destroyed" (Graham 1978).

This landmark action, and the declining importance of wood and wood products in the U.S. economy, put a halt to the destruction of the Adirondack forest. As the forest regenerated, New York eventually abandoned its plan to purchase all of the land within the park, and created the patchwork of public and private land that has persisted through subsequent expansions of the park boundary.

By the late 1960s approximately 60 million people lived within a day's drive of the Adirondack Park, and many were developing an appetite for recreation in a natural setting. More leisure time and greater disposable income allowed an increasing number of visitors and seasonal residents to satisfy this appetite in the park. A proposal to create a national park in the Adirondacks was defeated by a coalition of residents who realized that large private inholdings were not consistent with the national parks model used in the United States, and conservationists who believed that the "Forever Wild" clause offered better protection to the Adirondack wilderness than national park status. However, faced with growing tourism and second-home development, and the fact that only about 10 percent of the land in the park was under local land use regulation, the state legislature yielded to the efforts of Governor Rockefeller and his Temporary Study Commission on the Future of the Adirondacks and created the Adirondack Park Agency (APA) in 1972.

The APA was granted authority to develop and administer a land-use plan for *both* public and private land within the park, and residents protested against the increased regulation through a variety of means: "The town of Clare voted to secede from the park. Aggrieved parties hurled eggs at and dumped manure on APA property. An agency lawyer, returning to its headquarters in Ray Brook late one night to pick up some documents found a man inside trying to set the place on fire" (Graham 1978).

Over the next few years an uneasy peace seemed to develop between park residents and the APA, but another "development crisis" brought unresolved issues back to the surface.

A four-lane highway from Albany to Montreal (the Northway) that ran through the park was completed in 1968, but development in the park was held in check by gasoline shortages and a series of economic recessions through the early 1980s. In the mid-1980s, economic expansion, falling interest rates, and tax policy that allowed deductions for second-home mortgages fueled fears of a new development boom in the Adirondack Park. These fears accelerated when corporate raiders conducted leveraged buyouts of forest products companies with Adirondack land holdings based on the development potential of those lands. Environmental groups such as the Adirondack Council began to raise concerns, and articles warning of an impending Adirondack "development crisis" began to appear in newspapers and magazines.

Responding to this pressure, the Governor's Commission on the Adirondack Park in the 21st Century was established in 1989. From the start, the commission met with stiff resistance from park residents, who opposed the lack of "real" (by their definition) Adirondackers among its members, the preponderance of former members of environmental agencies and/or interest groups on its staff, and the paucity and timing of its open hearings (only two open hearings were held in the Park, and those took place after most of the final report was already written). When residents learned that the commission was calling for a one-year moratorium on new development in the park, stricter density zoning regulations, and the acquisition of 600,000 additional acres for the forest preserve, some resorted to protests, civil disobedience, and scattered acts of vandalism and violence to make their resentment known. Two "rolling blockades" tied up traffic on the Northway, the headquarters of the Adirondack Council was splattered with paint, and the Commission's executive director was threatened with bodily harm on a number of occasions. Various attempts were made to translate the report into legislation, but none made it to the floor of the state Senate.

In 1994 the newly elected governor altered the makeup of the APA by appointing a new executive director and several new commissioners, who serve as a policymaking "board of directors" for the APA. These appointees were widely perceived by environmental groups as more "pro-development" than their predecessors. In 1995 the governor's decision not to allow extensive salvage cutting of timber downed during a massive storm in July won praise from environmentalists, but his 1996 proposal to cut ten positions from the APA staff in his executive budget brought the polarization between environmental groups and residents back to the surface, as a recent exchange on the editorial pages of the *Syracuse Post Standard* illustrates. On July 1, 1996, a former APA staff member and spokesperson for the Adirondack Council and the Audubon Society, wrote an op-ed piece arguing that the recent appointments and cuts were "undermining the Adirondack Park Agency and throwing New York's greatest natural treasure to the wolves." Two days later, the director of communications for the New York Farm Bureau responded that the "APA has done everything in its power to trample the rights of the farmers and other landowners who live within the park. The environmental activists wishing to protect the APA [from] cuts, or worse yet, expand the APA, fail to realize that humans who live in the park are also part of the environment."

Over the past 100 years the Adirondack Park has transformed an area of severe environmental degradation into a preserve that contains the largest wilderness in the contiguous United States, but the controversy that surrounds Park politics today illustrates how difficult it can be to unite natural ecosystems across human boundaries. Just as aeronautical engineers learn from airplane designs that both pass and fail the rigors of wind tunnel tests, the successes and failures of the Adirondack Park can be used to define a series of tools that may reduce the negative consequences of boundary effects on wilderness and biodiversity.

Land-Use Planning for Bioregions

The first category of tools that are used to define and manage the Adirondack bioregion falls under the heading of regional land-use planning. Since the amount of biological diversity that an ecosystem will support is directly proportional to its size, Wilson (1992) proposes that "parcels of land will have to be set aside as inviolate preserves. Others will be identified as the best sites for extractive reserves, for buffer zones used in part-time agriculture and restricted hunting, and for land convertible totally to human use." This describes the regional land-use planning process used in the Adirondack Park since 1972.

The linchpin of this process is the Adirondack Park Land Use Map, the end product of the Adirondack Park State Land Master Plan. The

map was created in the early 1970s using biological inventories and pre-
cursors to geographic information systems (GIS) techniques. Extensive
field surveys were made to determine existing human uses and growth
patterns; physical limitations relating to soils, slopes, and elevations;
locations of unique features such as gorges and waterfalls; locations of
rare or endangered species and fragile ecosystems (swamps, bogs, and
marshes); locations of historic sites and viewsheds; and the proximity of
private holdings to public lands. These surveys were translated into manual cartographic data using paper and plastic overlays. Different shadings
produced by the overlays were used to designate different land-use categories in essentially the same manner that data layers are used in digital
GIS mapping. More than 500 changes were made during an appeal
period to produce the map that remains—subject to periodic review and
revision—the primary land-use planning tool for the Adirondack Park
today.

The Adirondack Park Land Use Map illustrates the enormous potential that biological inventories and GIS techniques hold for defining
bioregions. But the task of managing and governing the Adirondack
bioregion across those boundaries is even more complex than the process
of defining them. Additional categories of tools are needed to protect
the park's wilderness, to sustain its working landscapes, and to promote
a sense of stewardship for the Adirondack Park among residents and
visitors.

Wilderness and Bioregions: Protecting the Core

The second category of tools that emerges from a study of the Adirondack Park falls under the heading of wilderness protection. Nash (1982)
describes wilderness as essentially a *cultural* construct. Under the right
circumstances and with sufficient forethought it is a construct that may
be transformed into a useful policy instrument, as Howard Zahniser did
in the Wilderness Act of 1964 by defining wilderness as lands "untrammeled by man," a phrase that cleverly conveys the cultural essence of
wilderness, without making it off-limits to appropriate human activity.
The Adirondack Park State Land Master Plan also defines wilderness in
terms that transform a cultural construct into a useful policy instrument.
More than 400,000 hectares of Adirondack Forest Preserve are classified
as "wilderness" lands, where camping, hiking, canoeing, fishing, hunting,
trapping, snowshoeing, and ski touring are allowed, but motorized equipment and permanent structures are prohibited. "Wild forest" lands in the

Adirondack Park are managed in a similar fashion to "wilderness," but motorized vehicles may be operated in designated areas of "wild forest." A small portion of the Adirondack Forest Preserve is designated as "intensive use areas" for downhill ski centers, public campsites, developed beaches, and boat launch sites.

Working within the framework of the AP State Land Master Plan, the New York State Department of Environmental Conservation (DEC), in consultation with the APA, prepares unit management plans for each discrete unit of the Adirondack Forest Preserve. The unit management plans use detailed information about specific natural features and resources to translate the broad policy directives of the AP State Land Master Plan into specific management actions that maximize conservation and appropriate recreational access while reducing conflicts between different types of recreational users. Classifying and managing state lands as different types of wilderness strengthens the broad coalition of preservationists and recreational users that has helped sustain the Adirondack Park for more than 100 years.

Classification alone will not protect wilderness from development pressures. The legal protection embodied in the "Forever Wild" clause puts teeth in the Adirondack Park's wilderness designation. The "Forever Wild" clause employs two important mechanisms to protect the Adirondack wilderness from economic pressure: a delaying mechanism and provisions for a popular referendum. Because it is part of the New York State Constitution, changes to the "Forever Wild" clause must be approved in two consecutive sessions of the state legislature, then passed by popular referendum in the next general election. Since New York's legislature is only in session January to June, any change to the "Forever Wild" clause is subject to almost two full years of public scrutiny. In practice, this allows conservation groups to research thoroughly proposed changes and rally public support against proposals that threaten the environmental integrity of the park. For example, in the 1940s and 1950s, preservationists defeated thirty-eight different proposals to build reservoirs that would have flooded parts of the Adirondack Forest Preserve. The last of these was defeated in a popular referendum in November 1955 by over a two-to-one margin.

Given the nature of wilderness, it is difficult to develop strategies for its management that provide adequate protection without severely restricting access. Certain parts of the Adirondack wilderness, especially the "High Peaks" region, are experiencing environmental degradation due to dramatic increases in the number of visitors. Trail erosion and destruction of fragile arctic tundra habitats have been two of the most salient problems. Both have been mitigated to some degree by volunteer programs. Members of the Adirondack Mountain Club voluntarily perform trail maintenance using primitive equipment and materials that conform to wilderness conditions, and volunteer "Summit Stewards" station themselves amidst the High Peaks' alpine tundra, educating visitors about this rare habitat and encouraging them to stay on the trails and thereby protect what they've just learned to appreciate.

The recently completed High Peaks Wilderness Master Plan suggests that in the future wilderness management in the most popular parts of the Adirondack Park will involve increased restrictions on access and activities. But these restrictions will not protect biodiversity and wilderness experiences in the park if the working landscapes that provide buffer zones are not also protected.

Compatible Economic Development

Compatible economic development is the third category of tools that compose the Adirondack Park model bioregion. Wilson demonstrates that "to save species is to study them closely, and to learn them well is to exploit their characteristics in novel ways" (1992) and goes on to describe the wealth of knowledge and useful products that have already emerged from the study of biological diversity, as well as the huge potential benefits that have yet to be realized. Wilson terms this perception of the practical value of wild species the "New Environmentalism," and concludes that "only new ways of drawing income from land already cleared, or from intact wildlands themselves, will save biodiversity from the mill of human poverty. The race is on to develop methods, to draw more income from the wildlands without killing them, and so give the invisible hand of free-market economics a green thumb" (Wilson 1992).

In other contexts "free-market" solutions to environmental problems have been based on an unfounded trust in laissez-faire economics, but the Adirondack Park model specifically rejects this notion. Instead, it calls for government intervention to restructure markets in a manner that will help preserve biological diversity within the Adirondack bioregion. For example, working landscapes are "areas used for economic activities that do not irretrievably alter the natural ecological conditions and that enhance historic traditions, environmental objectives, and scenic objectives" (New York State 1991). Working landscapes are analogous to the "buffer zones" in Wilson's regional zoning scheme. In practice, however, they often are not easy to sustain without market interventions. In the Adirondack Park, farms and forest products lands are the most prevalent working landscapes. Both are under development pressure in certain areas of the park, and both have benefited from a variety of market interventions.

The regional zoning regulations created by the APA as part of the Adirondack Park State Land Master Plan are the most salient form of market intervention practiced in the Park today. Private land is zoned using six classifications ordered from least to most restrictive: Industrial Use Areas, Hamlets, Moderate Intensity Use Areas, Low Intensity Use Areas, Rural Use Areas, and Resource Management Areas. For each classification "overall intensity guidelines" prescribe the approximate number of principal buildings that are allowed in a square mile of the particular land-use area, and a "character description" and statement of "purposes, policies, and objectives" describe it. "Development considerations" point to possible adverse impacts of projects. Lists of "compatible uses" for each land use area serve to guide development. In addition, all projects that require review and approval by the agency are listed. These "regional projects" vary with each area. In the case of subdivisions, for example, the Agency's jurisdiction generally ranges from a 100-lot project in hamlets to a two-lot subdivision in resource management areas (New York State 1991).

Under the current classification scheme, areas zoned as "hamlets" have the fewest restrictions of all residential areas and are designated as the growth and service centers of the Park. All uses are permitted in hamlet areas, and no limits are set on development intensity. In contrast, areas zoned for "resource management" have the most restrictions. Special care is given to protecting the natural open-space character of private property designated as resource management lands. Compatible uses include agriculture and forestry, game preserves, and recreation. Residential development is compatible only at a very low density of fifteen principal buildings per square mile (17.3 hectare average lot size) (New York State 1991).

On balance these categories have been reasonably successful in directing and clustering development to minimize its impact on the park's natural resources and open spaces, but they also have created a great deal of friction between the APA and park residents. Once again, it has proven far easier to establish land-use boundaries within the Adirondack bioregion than it has to manage and govern the bioregion across those boundaries. Residents frequently complain about the long period of time (over a year in some instances) that it takes the APA to process permits, and it seems reasonable to assume that recent staff reductions at APA must either lengthen or weaken its review process.

Conservation easements have been used to protect both wilderness and working landscapes in the Adirondack Park when the state, or an environmental organization such as The Nature Conservancy, purchases the rights to a specific *use* of private property. Easements provide an alternative to public ownership when the state lacks sufficient funds for an outright purchase or the landowner is unwilling to sell. In addition, easements may be especially useful for protecting sensitive areas (e.g., wetlands and bogs) without engendering the kind of visitor pressure that often accompanies public ownership. Conservation easements have helped Adirondack Park landowners keep marginal working landscapes economically viable by generating income from the sale of development rights.

Other market interventions used in concert with conservation easements to protect Adirondack working landscapes are: tax policies that assess farm and forest products lands at their "working landscape" value rather than their "developed" value; technical assistance from state agencies and other organizations (e.g., research on forestry conducted at Paul Smith's College and research on vegetable farming under Adirondack conditions conducted by Cornell University); and efforts to create new markets for goods produced on Adirondack working landscapes. It still is difficult to make a living off the land in the Adirondacks, but the preceding examples demonstrate that the economic value of marginal working landscapes can be strengthened by market interventions.

Landscape design has been used to protect biological diversity in some areas of the Adirondack Park. At Thirteenth Lake in the Town of Warrensburg, the state has retained ownership of the shoreline, except for a small private beach area, and motors (except for small electric ones) are prohibited on the lake. All of the homes around the lake are set well back from the roads and shoreline and screened from view with vegetation and conform to aesthetic standards that require "natural" building materials and/or colors and buried utility lines. As a result, early-morning anglers joined in their pursuit of Thirteenth Lake's abundant population of game fish by a resident family of loons, could be forgiven for thinking they were in the midst of a remote wilderness rather than a residential community.

The Adirondack Economic Development Corporation and the Adirondack North Country Association are two organizations that currently promote market interventions in the Park. Recently they created the Adirondack Community Development Loan Fund in conjunction with the Adirondack Council, the Adirondack Park Agency Economic Affairs Unit, and several banks that are active in the region. This fund will eventually grow to $1 million and will provide loans to small business, individuals, and not-for-profit organizations for projects that contribute to community revitalization within the Park. Similarly, the Northern Forest Alliance, which is made up of twenty-eight organizations (including the Adirondack Council) working to protect the 10.5-million-hectare forest that stretches from New York's Tug Hill region, through the Adirondack Park, and into northern Vermont, New Hampshire, and Maine, has begun to offer small grants to individuals and groups to help them protect wild lands, ensure well-managed forests, and build strong local economies and communities in this region.

The Adirondack Council is the Park's most prominent environmental "watchdog," and its participation in the Adirondack Community Development Loan Fund is significant, as in the past the Council mainly focused its efforts on the legal and political arenas. In a similar vein, the Council recently sponsored a series of Economic Renewal Workshops in the Adirondack community of Indian Lake. The workshops were conducted by the Rocky Mountain Institute to create teams of residents to develop and implement specific economic development and community conservation projects, and the Indian Lake Town Board's support of this effort marks a "sea change" for relationships between the Adirondack Council and Park communities.

Despite these efforts, much remains to be done. Family incomes in the Park are significantly lower, and unemployment rates significantly higher, than state averages. Residents often associate these hardships with the economic restrictions placed on private property by the Adirondack Park State Land Master Plan and the large areas of the park tied up in "unproductive" (in their view) wilderness. If state agencies and nongovernmental organizations such as The Nature Conservancy would divert a fraction of the funds they have spent on land acquisition in the park to programs that promote environmentally sound development, park residents' quality of life would improve, and their resistance to park regulations would probably diminish. These efforts might take the form of a series of development projects that provide for adequate setbacks from shorelines and roads, appropriate lot shapes and sizes, state-of-the-art waste treatment facilities, and designated "green spaces" and wildlife preserves, *and* incorporate some low-interest housing and opportunities for public recreation. Profits from these projects would be used to fund future developments or market interventions that would promote working landscapes, while the "invisible hand" of the market raises environmental standards in competing developments throughout the park.

It is sometimes possible to transform markets in a desirable manner simply by providing people with information. For example, research on nonpoint source lake pollution conducted by the Aquatic Institute at Paul Smith's College convinced the residents of one park hamlet to require a developer to scale back a proposed housing project pending the outcome of an extensive monitoring and water-quality modeling program.

Stewardship and Bioregions: Building the Tie That Binds

The final category of tools that emerges from a study of the Adirondack Park as a bioregion falls under the heading of stewardship. Stewardship is, in this context, an informed sense of responsibility that helps protect biological diversity by providing both the means and the motive to create and sustain bioregions in the face of economic, political, and social pressures. Without stewardship, the most elaborate arrangements for governing bioregions across boundaries may be ineffective. For example, violations of local zoning laws usually are brought to the attention of authorities by the violator's neighbors. This is not the case in the Adirondack Park, where residents' antipathy to the APA usually causes them to ignore regional zoning violations. The recent history of the Adirondack Park suggests that stewardship in bioregions must be fostered through two concepts that have been inexorably linked in democratic theory since the time of Plato: education and participation in the democratic process.

Given the dramatically different circumstances that have created the human boundaries that divide natural ecosystems, specific institutions and arrangements for governing bioregions must be developed on a case-by-case basis. However, some general principles that facilitate democratic participation in regional land-use planning can be derived from Mason (1995). Mason demonstrates that the success of the land-use planning process in British Columbia is based on the following factors: access to information, opportunities to be heard by public officials, a decision-making process that is open to all relevant interests, explicit legal bases for decision-making authority, public accountability, written reasons for significant decisions, and an independent appeal process.

Much of the controversy that has plagued the APA since its creation arose because one or more of the principles cited by Mason were ignored. The APA tended to

> act in the bureaucratic tradition, imposing its complex regulations on a confused public, and sometimes, according to the critics, changing the ground rules after the fact. . . . The agency seemed to take forever to process the simplest applications. . . . In this climate it was easy for those who had personal grievances to whip up popular hostility against the agency. Absurd rumors spread, including one that if a woman lived in a certain land use zone, the APA would restrict the number of children she could bear. (Graham 1978)

Writing as though he were anticipating the creation of the concept of bioregions, Graham (1978) concludes that:

> There were public relations blunders that ought to serve as warnings for regional planning groups in the future. To its capable staff of planners, lawyers, and ecologists, the agency might have added a community relations expert—and even a psychologist—who could have bridged the gap by interpreting the goals and techniques of the planning effort for local government officials, the press, the business community, and the public at large. Too often, the planners and the residents were not hearing what each other was saying.

Unfortunately, the Governor's Commission on the Adirondack Park in the 21st Century repeated many of the APA's mistakes. It did not provide adequate opportunities for residents to be heard, nor was it structured so that all relevant interests were allowed to participate in the decision-making process. As a result, none of the commission's 245 recommendations have been enacted by the state legislature to date, and the controversy generated by the commission and its recommendations contributed to the first-ever defeat of a New York State Environmental Quality Bond Act in 1991.

The problems spawned by the Governor's Commission seem to have convinced many of the environmentalists working in the park that they are prone to "a common failing among idealistic . . . men and women, full of good intentions and an eagerness to serve, to antagonize what they might unconsciously consider the ignorant wretches they have come to set straight" (Graham 1978). This realization probably is responsible for the recent community development initiatives sponsored by the Adirondack Council, and it is hoped that they signal the beginning of an era of improved relations between park residents and environmental groups.

Senegalese conservationist Baba Dioum reminds us that "In the end, we will conserve only what we love, we will love only what we understand, and we will understand only what we are taught" (Wilson 1992). There are three distinct, but overlapping, populations that must be educated about the Adirondack Park if it is to fulfill its promise as a model bioregion: park residents, other New York State residents, and park visitors. Because these populations have decidedly different relationships with the park, a multifaceted education strategy is required.

Two Visitors' Interpretive Centers run by the APA, the world-class Adirondack Museum, special-purpose educational centers such as the Sagamore Institute and SUNY Cortland's Huntington Outdoor Education Center, and a number of education programs sponsored by Adirondack schools and local governments currently teach residents and visitors about the Adirondack Park. Increasingly, these organizations are cooperating and developing innovative outreach efforts, and this trend should accelerate as they acquire distance learning technology. The Adirondack Research Consortium (ARC), recently established to promote and disseminate research about the Adirondack Park, is another promising educational development. The ARC draws its members from colleges, universities, and certified not-for-profit educational organizations and enjoys a symbiotic relationship with the interdisciplinary *Adirondack Journal of Environmental Studies*. The ARC's 1996 annual meeting and research symposium brought together more than one hundred participants, and featured more than fifty poster and panel presentations.

Despite these efforts, much remains to be done in terms of education for Adirondack Park stewardship. For example, recent surveys (Buerger and Pasquarello 1992, 1993) demonstrate that most park residents are not familiar with even the basic legal foundations and administrative arrangements that govern the Adirondack Park, and it seems safe to assume that New Yorkers who live outside the park and park visitors are equally uninformed. Drawing on the expertise and resources of educational organizations that focus on the Adirondacks, an extensive Adirondack unit should be added to the curriculum of schools located within or near the park, and a similar, but smaller, unit should be added to the curriculum for the rest of New York. These units should integrate the human and natural history of the Adirondacks with coverage of current issues and policies in a manner similar to the national parks units that are an important component of school curriculum in the United Kingdom.

Conclusion: The Adirondack Park and the Future of Bioregions

The Adirondack Park is a grand experiment in regional land-use planning, and the successes and failures of this experiment can help us create, manage, and govern bioregions across human boundaries. The model presented here is obviously not the complete set of tools we will need for this task, but it does illustrate four general categories of tools that can help reduce the inherent tension between the ecological principles that underlie the concept of bioregions and the political realities of defining, managing, and governing them. One hopes that an expanded version of this toolkit will one day help ensure that bioregions will achieve their true potential as a means of preserving biological diversity in a rapidly developing world.

REFERENCES

Brennan, A. 1988. *Thinking about nature*. University of Georgia Press, Athens.

Buerger, R., and T. Pasquarello. 1992. Residents' perceptions of recreation development and land use issues within the Adirondack Park. *Journal of Recreation and Leisure* 12:93–105.

Buerger, R., and T. Pasquarello. 1993. The Adirondack Park: changing perceptions of residents towards land use issues. *Journal of Recreation and Leisure* 13:86–95.

Cole, D.N., and P.B. Landres. 1996. Threats to wilderness ecosystems: impacts and research needs. *Ecological Applications* 6:168–184.

Dolan v. City of Tigard, 512 U.S., 374 (1994).

Graham, Frank. 1978. *The Adirondack Park: a political history*. Syracuse University Press, Syracuse.

Knight, R.L., G.W. Wallace, and W.E. Riebsame. 1995. Ranching the view: subdivisions versus agriculture. *Conservation Biology* 9:459–461.

Mason, M. 1995. Administrative fairness and forest land decision-making:

restructuring land use governance in British Columbia. Paper presented at the 20th Anniversary Conference of the British Association for Canadian Studies. University of Hull, Hull, England.

Nash, R. 1982. *Wilderness and the American mind*. Yale University Press, New Haven.

Newmark, W.D. 1985. Legal and biotic boundaries of western North American national parks: a problem of congruence. *Biological Conservation* 33:197–208.

New York State. 1991. *Conserving open space in New York State: a preliminary draft plan*. New York Department of Environmental Conservation, Albany, NY.

Sale, Kirkpatrick. 1985. *Dwellers in the land: the bioregional vision*. Sierra Club, San Francisco.

Tilman, D., R.M. May, C.L. Lehman, and M.A. Nowak. 1994. Habitat destruction and the extinction debt. *Nature* 371:65–67.

Wilson, E.O. 1992. *The diversity of life*. Belknap Press, Cambridge, MA.

PART IV

BUILDING BRIDGES ACROSS BOUNDARIES

In the concluding section of the book we make the strongest appeal to finding answers to cross-boundary challenges. The topics of the three concluding chapters are cooperation, the role of science and the humanities that seek to understand and explain boundaries, and last, an integration that offers a set of premises and actions on which stewardship across boundaries is based.

The first chapter by Steven Yaffee is titled "Cooperation: A Strategy for Achieving Stewardship across Boundaries." Yaffee opens his chapter by acknowledging the "fragmentation in our society between multiple agencies, levels of government, public and private sectors, diverse interest groups, and different disciplines and value structures. The benefits of a diverse, pluralistic society lie in its tremendous capacity for creativity and innovation, but the stability provided by fragmented decision making has been critical to America's continuous development. Yet the diversity that is so important as a source of raw materials for ideas and potential solutions makes it difficult for groups of people to bridge the perceptual and values-based differences that make them unique. Cooperation is necessary but problematic."

Ironically, Yaffee says, "we preach cooperation while we practice competition." Although cooperation is a great idea which everyone is for, it goes against the grain of incentives facing individuals in modern-day society. As Yaffee points out, the great economic, political, and biological ideas of our times—free market capitalism, pluralism, and evolution—rely on competition as a basic driving force for innovation and change. If these ideas stress the advantages of competition, why should anyone wish to cooperate? Yaffee addresses the popular misconception that people cooperate primarily for altruistic reasons. He counters that people cooperate because of strong, self-interested motives that can be achieved only through cooperation. People support each other because they know that they will benefit in turn.

Yaffee explains that cooperation in building working arrangements across boundaries can best be understood as a series of forces promoting and restraining appropriate behavior. His model envisions a center defined by the collective effort of goals, resources, and activities, surrounded by a periphery of individuals, groups, and organizations. Each of these groups and individuals is pulled by countervailing forces. Some, termed *centrifugal* because they pull away from the center, encourage individuals to act on their own in a way that restricts cooperation. Others, termed *centripetal* because they push the groups toward the center, promote cooperative interaction. The result is an ongoing tension between these forces, and the success of cooperative efforts depends on the centripetal forces outweighing the centrifugal forces.

Using examples from the book's case studies, Yaffee devotes the remainder of his chapter to exploring these different forces that promote and oppose effective cooperation across boundaries. He concludes by stressing that to promote cooperation across boundaries, managers can seek to foster the forces that facilitate cooperation or minimize those that oppose it. This may mean working with members of a group to promote effective interaction, as well as reforming elements of the institutional context so that cooperation can proceed.

The penultimate chapter by Curt Meine is titled "The Continent Indissoluble." Beginning with an excerpt from "For You O Democracy," Meine uses Walt Whitman's moving poem about America to explore whether Americans as a people are ready to integrate America's landscape with conservation, democracy, and community. Meine's theme is that the land not merely provides the setting and materials for our experiment in democracy, but is in fact the proving ground of democracy's success. Meine believes that in the process of becoming who and what we are, we have divided and bounded ourselves and the land in ways that now contain our ability to practice effective conservation. He asks the question: Can we look across these boundaries in the effort to live respectfully with the land, the creatures that share it, and the processes that characterize it? This question, Meine asserts, leads inevitably to a consideration of the oldest and most fundamental challenge that we as social creatures face:

Can we harmonize the self-interest of free individuals and the well-being of those entities within which the individual exists—the family, neighborhood, state, nation, watershed, flyway, atmosphere? If so, what will it take?

With this beginning, Meine weaves the connection between America, democracy, community, and boundaries. He states that we increasingly seek security not in "companionship" with our human and nonhuman neighbors, but in isolation, behind our boundaries (for example, locked-gate communities). Analogously, Meine believes, we have rested secure in the knowledge that, once the boundary of the park or forest or wildlife refuge is declared, the life within it will dwell forever in comfort. But is that the case? Meine believes otherwise.

Many environmentalists have proceeded on the assumption that wildness segregated is wildness saved. But how effective is the protection behind the administrative boundaries that formally designate public lands and other protected areas? And is this enough? Meine explores the concept that for us in our social lives, and also for our prized protected places, security cannot be found in simple sequestration, but only in good relations. He believes that there is no security for biodiversity, or in the long run for people, if our own interests—especially those spiritual and economic—are harshly segregated.

Meine goes on to explain that our boundaries, especially the boundaries of public lands, present a complex paradox. Many of our bounded lands were originally established to promote the possibility of better integration of the public and private spheres. Although we have protected the places, the task still awaits to strengthen linkages not only across the landscape, but also between the landscape and ourselves. Meine believes that to "secure nature's legacy of beauty and biodiversity for the future, we must address the impact not only of external boundaries, but also of our individual wants and desires."

Can we overcome boundaries in pursuit of the common good? However read, this question revolves around the same basic ecological fact of life: we are surrounded, and we are permeable. Self-interest and common interest are bound together in complicated ways, and in the long run we can be secure only to the degree that those bonds are respected. Meine concludes his chapter with eight prerequisites that must be met. These range from an awareness of human and land histories to the importance of science that better defines how to conserve and restore lands, waters, and biotas.

In ending his chapter Meine argues that the time is ready to reconnect people and landscapes. He says, "Why now? Because it is necessary for our own good and for the good of the life around us. Because both science and history are telling us that we need to think and plan in new ways for the future. Because many conservationists are weary and hope that the work of 'saving all the pieces' can be made more enjoyable, more humanizing, if we don't have to holler across the boundaries. Because we may, in the process, help to revive the neglected arts of democracy: reasoned debate, honed thought and open inquiry, tolerance for difference, resistance to demagoguery, and a living sense of history."

The final chapter is by Peter Landres and is titled "Integration: A Beginning for Landscape-Scale Stewardship." Landres provides a synopsis of the book's premises, the cross-cutting and underlying assumptions on which cross-boundary management depends. Each premise is then followed by one or more actions to implement and facilitate cross-boundary stewardship.

These nine premises and twenty-two actions are gleaned from the preceding fifteen chapters and attempt to encapsulate the tremendous diversity of thoughts and suggestions of the book's authors. Landres notes that none of these actions "by themselves overcome the barriers and solve the problems caused by boundaries, each is but one element of an overall strategy to be developed and applied in each, unique situation for improving cross-boundary stewardship. As the concept of stewardship across boundaries develops and matures, this discussion of premises and actions will also change." He concludes with a wish shared by all the authors: "A primary goal of stewardship across boundaries is to recognize these influences and learn to emphasize the positive ones and reduce the negative ones—in other words, to manage the land gracefully, with elegance, harmony, and a fluidity of action that bridge boundaries and diverse values."

Chapter 14

Cooperation: A Strategy for Achieving Stewardship Across Boundaries

Steven L. Yaffee

Preceding chapters have presented case studies in which diverse groups were able to bridge their differences and work cooperatively across administrative, political, and perceptual boundaries. In south Florida hunters, off-road vehicle users, landowners, environmentalists, and Native Americans came together to support the creation of the Big Cypress National Preserve. In Arizona environmental groups and developers found a way to protect viewsheds and ecological systems critical to the viability of the Saguaro National Park while allowing land development to proceed. In the Adirondacks conservation interests allied with business interests to convince the New York legislature to create one of the first administratively recognized bioregions in the United States. In Louisiana, a broad coalition of landowners, government agencies, environmental and agricultural interests, forest industry leaders, and academics is working to restore populations of Louisiana black bear (*Ursus americanus luteolus*). In the Greater Yellowstone ecosystem innovative groups are emerging to focus on common problems, including the Henry's Fork Watershed Council that brings together farmers, government personnel, and environmentalists in eastern Idaho.

Some of these efforts were initiated in response to a perceived crisis. Many were fostered through the work of dedicated champions of the cooperative effort. All seek to overcome the inherent fragmentation in our society between multiple agencies, levels of government, public and private sectors, diverse interest groups, and different disciplines and value structures. The benefits of a diverse, pluralistic society lie in its tremendous capacity for creativity and innovation, and the stability provided by fragmented decision making (for example, the checks and balances between branches and levels of government, and between public and private sectors) has been critical to America's continuous development. Yet the diversity that is so important as a source of raw materials for ideas and potential solutions makes it difficult for groups of people to bridge the perceptual and values-based differences that make them unique. Cooperation is necessary but problematic.

This chapter explores cooperation as a strategy for achieving stewardship across boundaries. It defines cooperation as a range of behaviors and explores the forces that promote and hinder cooperative behavior. A model is presented that views a cooperative effort as composed of a center (the collective objectives) and a periphery (the individual groups that contribute to the cooperative effort) and subject to a set of forces: some are centrifugal and lead individuals away from collaborative behavior; and some are centripetal and foster cooperation. The Greater Yellowstone Ecosystem case makes it clear that the forces that hinder cooperation are strong and longstanding. Nevertheless, an evolving set of parallel case studies of successful collaborations provide insight into ways to promote necessary cooperation (Wondolleck and Yaffee 1994, Yaffee et al. 1996). The final section of the chapter identifies several policy-level responses that can help support cooperative efforts.

Defining Cooperation

At times, cooperation appears much like the classic statement about pornography: hard to define, but easy to recognize. It seems clear that the term cooperation incorporates a wide variety of behaviors associated with the relationships between two or more individuals or organizations. The dictionary defines cooperation as the act of "jointly working with others to have an effect" (Collins-World Publishing 1975). The organizational management literature uses the term *collaboration* as a close synonym and defines it as "(1) the pooling of appreciations and/or tangible resources, e.g., information, money, labor, etc., (2) by two or more stakeholders, (3) to solve a set of problems which neither can solve individually" (Gray 1985). A recent article that examined collaborative management in environmental management states that: "Collaboration implies a joint decision-making approach to problem resolution where power is shared, and stakeholders take collective responsibility for their actions and subsequent outcomes from those actions" (Selin and Chavez 1995). Cooperation involves individuals or groups moving in concert where no party has the ability to command the behavior of the others.

Table 14.1. A rough taxonomy of cooperative behaviors

Behavior Type	Definition
Awareness	Being cognizant of others' interests and actions
Communication	Talking about goals and activities
Coordination	Actions of one party are carried out in a manner that supports (or does not conflict with) those of another
Collaboration	Active partnerships with resources being shared or work being done by multiple partners

As depicted in Table 14.1, cooperative interactions can be viewed as including at least four kinds of behaviors: awareness, communication, coordination, and collaboration. As one moves down this taxonomy, the level of effort and interaction increases. In addition, the level of deference of one party to another tends to increase. Hence, coordination and collaboration often involve compromises between the wishes and interests of different stakeholders. At the same time, in the best of cases, higher levels of interaction also result in synergies, so that "win–win" courses of action—those in which all parties do better—are possible (Fisher and Ury 1981).

These behaviors are organized through a variety of structures. Indeed, one recent study of cooperative working arrangements across agency boundaries defined twenty different kinds of "bridging" arrangements, including management partnerships, collaborative problem solving, joint research and fact-finding, and political linkages (Yaffee and Wondolleck 1997). Cooperative work takes the form of public–private partnerships, interagency memorandums of understanding, volunteer arrangements, and citizen councils. This structural diversity exists in part because there is no one right way to accomplish cooperative interactions, nor is there a single geographic or functional scale at which cooperation makes sense. Rather, effective cooperation in resource management involves a variety of types of interaction that are implemented at different scales. For some problems or issues, effective cooperation may come from the interactions of a scientist and a manager within a unit of a single agency. For other situations, complex, multiparty, public–private structures may be appropriate.

Cooperation As a Balance Among a Set of Forces

Ironically, we preach cooperation while we practice competition. As a concept, cooperation rates up there with motherhood and apple pie. *Sesame Street* and Mr. *Rogers* have long noted that "cooperation makes it happen." Everyone is for it. We are just not so good at doing it. Achieving cooperation in practice is partly difficult because it goes against the grain of many of the incentives facing individuals in modern-day society. The great economic, political, and biological ideas of our times— free market capitalism, pluralism, and evolution—rely on competition as a basic driving force for innovation and change. Much of our material and biological success has derived from the competitive forces that test ideas and hone fitness. Yet the stories contained in this book suggest some of the costs associated with excessive competition and inadequate cooperation: fragmented systems, decision-making impasses costing precious time in dealing with real problems, and a lack of innovation that can come from integration across diverse values, ideas, and capabilities.

So why do people cooperate? A popular misconception is that people cooperate primarily for altruistic reasons: that is, they do so to make others feel good or to promote the common good. In fact, most cooperative efforts develop and endure because of strong, self-interested motives that can be achieved only through cooperation (Axlerod 1984). The diverse groups involved in pushing for protection of the Big Cypress Swamp did not join hands and walk into the sunset because they wanted to make each other feel good, or they were all trying to "do good things" for the environment. Instead, they formed a coalition of interests because collectively they had a chance to protect their own individual interests, whereas individually, they were likely to fail: the classic "we can either hang together or surely we will hang separately" situation.

The experience in many of these cases is consistent with the general literature on cooperation, which argues that reciprocity underlies most cooperative behavior. Hence, people support each other because they know that they will benefit in return. Studies of voting behavior in the U.S. Congress (Mayhew 1974), trench warfare on the Western Front in World War I (Ashworth 1980), and computer simulations of two-party negotiations (Axlerod 1984) suggest that cooperative behaviors develop and are stable over time (that is, they resist efforts from competitors to change the pattern of behavior) because of the mutual benefit of establishing and maintaining norms of reciprocity. Hence, members of Congress agree to support another member's pet issue because of the support it buys for their own key issues. Similarly, the German and Allied soldiers in World War I evolved a "live and let live" set of behaviors and avoided killing each other because they would in turn have a lower risk of being killed (Ashworth 1980).

While it is very helpful to understand the possibilities for cooperation by understanding the potential costs and gains facing the individual parties to the cooperative effort, it seems clear that more is involved in determining whether a cooperative arrangement will succeed or not. Sometimes groups have a clear incentive to work together, but are unable to do so because of past relationships, ineffective mechanisms for interaction, laws, or institutional norms that preclude involvement and many other factors. At minimum, these variables influence how the groups' self-interest is perceived. In some cases, they go well beyond issues of self-interest. For example, people tend to get entrapped in past positions and behaviors even when they understand that their own interests would be best served by other modes of action (Bazerman 1986).

Cooperation in building working arrangements across boundaries can be understood best as a series of forces promoting and restraining appropriate behavior. Figure 14.1 depicts this model. It envisions a cooperative effort as consisting of a center (the collective effort, its goals, resources, and activities) and a periphery (the individuals, groups, and organizations that potentially contribute to the cooperative effort). Each of these groups is pulled by countervailing forces. Some (termed *centrifugal* because they pull away from the center) encourage individuals to act on their own in a way that restricts or opposes the efforts of the collective. Others (termed *centripetal* because they push the groups toward the center) promote cooperative interaction. There is an ongoing tension between these forces, and the success of cooperative efforts depends on the centripetal forces outweighing the often considerable centrifugal forces.

Figure 14.1 also suggests that these forces can be associated with the individual members of the collaborative effort or that they can be elements of the institutional and political environment in which these groups act. To promote cooperation across boundaries, managers can seek to foster the forces that facilitate cooperation or minimize those that oppose it. Often this means working with the members of the group to promote effective interaction, and sometimes it means reforming elements of the institutional context so that cooperation can proceed. Table 14.2 identifies nineteen different forces that promote and oppose effec-

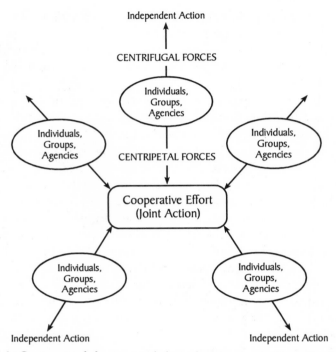

Figure 14.1. Cooperative behavior as a balance between a set of centrifugal and centripetal forces.

tive cooperation across boundaries, and clusters them by whether they are associated with the individual members of a potential collaboration (internal factors) or the environment in which the group functions (external factors). Much of the balance of this chapter discusses these forces and illustrates them with examples from the case studies presented in earlier chapters in this book.

Centrifugal Forces: Internal Factors That Hinder Cooperation

If cooperation is problematic, what factors consistently oppose effective interaction? Even creating new groups in a high-profile manner does not ensure that they will be successful. Forces intrinsic to the member groups, ranging from conflicting goals and norms to limited resources, and external conditions, such as public opposition and problematic policies, pull individuals away from joint action.

Table 14.2. Factors promoting and restricting cooperative behavior across boundaries

	CENTRIFUGAL FORCES (making cooperation less likely)	CENTRIPETAL FORCES (making cooperation more likely)
Internal factors (those relating to the actors/site)	Conflicting goals and missions Different traditions and norms Desire for autonomy and control Limited resources	Opportunities to gain through collective action Perception of common problems or threats Shared goals or sense of place Entrepreneurs and champions Relationships Effective processes and process management Innovative structures to maintain cooperative relationships
External factors (those relating to the external environment and context)	Public opposition, fear, and skepticism Preexisting allegiances and relationships Lack of agency support Government policies and procedures Opportunities to proceed independently	Opportunities, resources, and incentives Public pressure or interest Technology

Conflicting Goals and Missions

All organizations have formal and informal goals, and these often conflict with those of other organizations. In the Greater Yellowstone Ecosystem, the USDA Forest Service has a statutory and political need to promote timber harvest (among other objectives), the National Park Service is mandated to preserve Yellowstone's scenic and historic features while promoting access to them, the U.S. Fish and Wildlife Service is mandated to protect the endangered grizzly bear (*Ursus arctos horribilis*), and the state resource agencies seek an ample supply of hunting and fishing opportunities. Environmentalists seek to protect biological, recreational, and aesthetic values; industry is concerned with ensuring a good business environment; and local interests seek community economic growth. In the Saguaro National Monument case, development interests wanted to develop the lands adjacent to the protected area, while National Park Service managers wanted to protect viewsheds and ecosystem processes. These objectives conflict with each other. Without a good-faith and creative effort to bridge these diverse interests, these differences make it difficult for disparate groups to work together cooperatively across boundaries.

Different Traditions and Norms

Some of the forces that hinder cooperation have less to do with the stated goals of groups than with their organizational cultures and histories. Organizations develop different styles and ways of doing things that frustrate cooperative efforts even when their formal missions do not conflict. For example, the Forest Service has a statutory mission to protect native vertebrate species, yet its style of landscape manipulation in the Rockies and the Pacific Northwest diminished its commitment to protection of wide-ranging species such as the grizzly bear (Grumbine 1992) or interior-dwelling species such as the northern spotted owl (*Strix occidentalis caurina*) (Yaffee 1994). Agency managers steeped in concepts of multiple use honestly could not fathom the value of "setting aside" millions of acres of land to protect a bird or a bear. Similarly, the nontraditional nature of the Big Cypress Swamp Preserve made it problematic for old-line managers to understand and implement the preserve concept.

Often agency managers view cooperative efforts as "public involvement." While such activities are well established in law and agency operating procedures, longstanding norms of behavior resist them. Ever since Gifford Pinchot set down the principles of American conservation, agencies have viewed their roles as providing the "right answers" to management questions. As these questions have become more values-based, their solution relies more on choices made in consultation with affected groups. Yet the "we know best" perspective has frustrated efforts at effectively involving outside groups (Wondolleck 1988). In a recent study of cooperative arrangements involving the Forest Service and outside groups (hereafter referred to as the Building Bridges study), one agency employee commented that the agency does not "assign much importance to public opinion except when it bites us" (Wondolleck and Yaffee 1994). Another employee remarked that "in the past making linkages just hasn't been a big priority." A state natural resources agency official who has been involved in collaborative projects with the Forest Service noted that "there are still the old-timers who think the public is a nuisance." This impression was echoed by an environmental group representative: "They seem to have a sort of uneasiness about working with NGOs [nongovernmental organizations]. . . . They have an attitude of 'we know best and you don't.'" One assistant district ranger suggested personal constraints: "There are a lot of psychological barriers on my part. I've been in the practice of silviculture for 10 years. A lot of this goes against my training."

At times, these cultural and values-based differences translate into intergroup attitudes that are very hard to overcome. During research of the spotted owl case in the Pacific Northwest, an environmentalist described loggers as ignorant, crude, and unable to get along with other people, and a timber industry official described environmentalists as wanting to go back to the days when we lived in caves (Yaffee 1994). Such imagery helps groups mobilize resources to press for their interests and plays well in the media, but it makes it very difficult for the same groups to get past the yelling and screaming into a discussion of real interests and potential ways to solve common problems across large landscapes.

Desire for Autonomy and Control

Individuals and organizations also exhibit a strong desire to maintain a sense of autonomy and control over decisions that affect them. There are good psychological, bureaucratic, and political reasons for doing so. Independence allows individuals and groups to conserve energy and pursue objectives that are central to their own survival. Bureaucracies rarely are rewarded by their constituent groups or legislative contacts for helping out other interests. They fear the controversy that they feel may be triggered by nontraditional modes of action because controversy can consume scarce resources and delegitimize the agency's position of authority.

As statutory authority is defined agency by agency, program by program, and geographic unit by geographic unit, administrative agencies often feel that it is unlawful to provide even the perception that they are delegating authority to a multiparty or cross-boundary group. As one Forest Service respondent in the Building Bridges study noted, "at times a fear of taking risks hampers us from building linkages. We may feel that we are giving away power or authority." In fact, there are ways to maintain agency decision-making authority consistent with current statutes, and most members of cooperative groups use these groups as input into formal decision-making processes. Nevertheless, these strong forces encourage individuals and groups to act in ways that maintain independence, and that can, as a side effect, hamper the creation of cross-boundary relationships needed to deal with ecosystem-scale problems.

Limited Resources

Fostering and maintaining cooperative efforts also requires time and energy on the part of all the potential members of the collective group, and these kinds of individual and organizational resources are limited. In a recent study of 105 ecosystem management efforts nationwide (hereafter called the Michigan Ecosystem Management study), limited resources on the part of both public and private sector participants were cited as the second most frequent obstacle to achieving success at these cross-landscape efforts (Yaffee et al. 1996). In the Building Bridges study, resource constraints were cited most frequently by Forest Service personnel as an obstacle to achieving linkages across organizational boundaries. These constraints included organizational resources such as staff and funding, technical resources such as scientific data and effective models, and personal resources. Building and maintaining interpersonal relationships in situations that often are conflict-laden can lead to "burn-out" of participants.

Federal budget constraints have exacerbated these resource problems. As the federal work force has been down sized and discretionary spending is constrained by the growth in entitlement programs, agencies have tended to retrench into their core activities. Ironically, cooperative partnerships are lauded as a way to leverage added resources from nongovernmental sources, but it is clear that it takes resources to acquire resources. Cooperative arrangements require an ongoing investment of organizational resources, but this kind of investment is least likely to be made in times of tight budgets.

Centrifugal Forces: External Factors That Hinder Cooperation

Some of the factors that limit effective cooperation result from forces that arise from outside the meeting rooms in which cooperative activities are discussed. Public opposition and fear can dampen cooperative possibilities, as can preexisting alliances between member groups and the outside world. Limited support from agency superiors, conflicts with agency policies, constraints arising from federal law, and the existence of multiple decision points that allow potential cooperators the opportunity to pursue their interests elsewhere all pose problems for the development of cooperation across boundaries.

Public Opposition, Fear, and Skepticism

Any cooperative effort exists within a broader sociopolitical environment, and potential cooperators are influenced by the attitudes of the general public, members of their groups, and political officials. In the Michigan Ecosystem Management study, opposition by the public was cited most frequently as a barrier to the cooperative effort's successes. Opposition is manifest both at the site level and more generally. A generalized distrust of the federal government, government in general, and planning in particular dampens some cooperative efforts, particularly in areas where private property rights groups are active. A generalized fear of change and innovation also is a problem, particularly because the current situation often benefits the status quo pattern of economic and political power, even if the collective set of interests would be better off with change.

Landowners also fear that participation in a project might lead to additional government regulation or infringement on perceived private property rights. Although landowner participation on most projects is strictly voluntary, it can be difficult to convince the public that state or federal agencies are not involved for regulatory purposes or that cooperative efforts will not constrain their private property rights. For example, in the Adirondacks, protests, civil disobedience, and scattered acts of violence symbolized the fears of current residents when the Governor's Commission on the Adirondack Park in the 21st Century recommended a moratorium on new development, stricter regulations, and acquisition of additional parklands (see Chapter 13).

Although this kind of opposition takes many forms, as it moves into the political process, it raises another set of barriers to cooperative efforts. In the Adirondacks, the response by landowners led Governor Cuomo to back off his interest in the Commission and shut down the State Senate as a potential channel for action. In the Greater Yellowstone Ecosystem case, political forces overruled a creative visioning process in which the National Park Service and the Forest Service tried to articulate a future for the region that established goals and procedures across agency boundaries. A firestorm of local opposition resulted in members of Congress and the White House intervening to stop the effort. Some of the agency leaders who were involved in the innovative effort were punished by being transferred away from their leadership positions (Grumbine 1992).

Preexisting Allegiances and Relationships

Much human behavior rests on and is influenced by a network of interpersonal relationships and contacts. Although we can talk about laws and management regimes as if they are abstract beings that come to life without human form, in fact, their implementation largely is a process of humans interacting in a variety of ways—some supportive and some opposed to the policy directions. How the relationships between people play out has a great deal of influence over the success or failure of intended efforts. Some of these relationships act as centrifugal forces, pulling potential cooperators away from the center. Hence, the Forest Service's longstanding relationship with the timber industry has made it more difficult for the agency to participate effectively with other organizations in some cross-boundary interactions.

The influence created through relationships takes several forms. Perhaps the most straightforward of these are mutually beneficial constituency relationships, in which groups come to support each other. Hence, timber interests support the Forest Service budget and policy requests, and the Forest Service reciprocates by facilitating a considerable timber program. But the influence of relationships is more subtle. Through consistent interaction with one set of people, values and information are shared, influencing the decision-making outlook of each other. Because individuals draw conclusions based on personal experience much more than any other input, the stories and perspectives of those to whom they listen take on a prescriptive form of considerable influence. ("Sure your studies say that the Endangered Species Act hasn't had much effect on economic interests, but my neighbor Joe told me about his cousin Ed whose plans to develop a golf course were totally stymied by the heavy-handed Fish and Wildlife Service. I trust Joe's judgment because I have known him to be right for more than twenty years.") Indeed, psychologists know that people can get entrapped by their prior relationships, so that even when they know they should break the ties that bind them, it is very hard to do so (Bazerman 1986). As will be discussed, the power of relationships can be employed to assist cooperative efforts. But it is important to recognize that there are strong, preexisting forces that pull potential cooperators away from acting in line with the interests of the collective group.

Lack of Agency Support

Another barrier for government employees to participate in cooperative efforts lies in the response of their superiors and their agencies. For example, in the Building Bridges study, a "lack of support from upper levels of management" was a key barrier to bridging echoed by respondents from inside and outside the Forest Service. When the new park superintendent for the Big Cypress Preserve met with his regional director, it became clear that efforts to manage the region innovatively would be stymied by Park Service bureaucracy. Indeed, the situation improved considerably when the leadership situation changed (see Chapter 9).

Supporting cooperative efforts means being willing to put agency resources into them, rewarding employees who pioneer cross-boundary work, and following up on commitments made in the cooperative efforts. Sometimes agencies are enthusiastic about creating innovative public involvement structures, but fail to understand their responsibility to follow through on the decisions made through cooperation. For example, in a study that we have under way of the implementation of twenty national forest plan appeals settled through negotiation, success or failure could largely be attributed to the Forest Service's level of follow-through (Wondolleck and Yaffee 1996). In situations where the agency pursued its commitments, or changed direction in consultation with the affected interests, participants were satisfied with the processes. In others where agency leaders disavowed knowledge of the efforts or claimed no responsibility for them, participants left in a more antagonistic position than when they started.

Government Policies and Procedures

Sometimes this lack of agency follow-through is a result of specific government policies and operating procedures that make it difficult to live up to cooperative, cross-boundary agreements. These barriers include red tape that make it inconvenient for groups to be involved, inflexibility on the part of agencies that hamper cooperative interactions, and directives that actively prevent effective cooperation. Often cooperative efforts are stymied by government budgeting processes that emphasize one-year cycles and allocate funds to narrow line items and make it difficult to organize cross-agency efforts that require multi-year funding. In addition, efforts to collect a regionwide database often have been hampered by conflicting data-collection protocols and database technology.

Laws that regulate the relationship between agencies and the public also have been a problem. For example, the Federal Advisory Committee Act (FACA), a law framed to guard against excessive involvement by narrow interests in agency decision making, has created a considerable barrier to many cooperative efforts that seek to promote effective decision making. Similarly, antitrust laws are claimed to limit the involvement of private-sector groups with one another in cross-boundary activities. Fears that the Freedom of Information Act (FOIA) will force federal agencies to make private information public have caused some firms to avoid cooperating with the public sector. More fundamentally, agency mandates may directly conflict with one another, so that one agency may be poisoning predators, while another is attempting to reintroduce them. One might subsidize and promote agricultural production on marginal lands, while another seeks to protect these lands for habitat conservation purposes.

Personnel policies in some of the resource management agencies also have made it difficult to carry out cooperative working arrangements. Cooperative arrangements exist largely through the connection of individuals and the sense of understanding and trust that develops between them. But through personnel strategies such as transfers, agencies like the Forest Service have consciously broken up relationships at the ground level to foster allegiance to the agency and develop employee careers. These policies made sense in an era when we had to worry a great deal about the "capture" of agency personnel by local economic interests. In an information age characterized by fragmented political power, however, it is important that managers stay in place long enough to develop considerable knowledge of indigenous resources and maintain relationships across the ecosystem. Elsewhere we have described this as a need to develop "knowledge pools" and "relationsheds" (Yaffee and Wondolleck 1995). Both are damaged by excessive employee transfers.

Opportunities to Proceed Independently

Finally, the overall set of incentives that groups face influences the likelihood that they will pursue collective efforts, and often current incentives promote individual efforts at the expense of cooperative ones. For example, timber interests in the Pacific Northwest were successful in achieving their interests through longstanding political ties and influence with the Forest Service. Until the environmental groups battled them to a standstill in the late 1980s, there was little reason for timber to talk to other regional interests. In the jargon of negotiation, they had a good BATNA (best alternative to a negotiated agreement), so they had little incentive to cooperate (Fisher and Ury 1981).

The fragmentation of decision-making processes in American natural resource policy tends to promote individual efforts at the expense of cooperative solutions. In the case of forest management in the Pacific Northwest, multiple decision points made it possible for losers in one arena to "appeal" the decision to another arena (Yaffee 1994). Hence, decision making bounced from administrative decisions and appeals to congressional action to the courts to the executive office. At any one of these points, it might have been possible to promote a cooperative solution to the conflict. But the existence of multiple processes created incentives for individual groups to pursue their future elsewhere.

Centripetal Forces: Internal Factors That Facilitate Cooperation

In spite of forces that oppose cooperation, there are a considerable number of success stories in cross-boundary management. What characterized them and allowed them to overcome the centrifugal forces pulling away from cooperation? Some of these forces are intrinsic to the cooperative efforts, whereas others are a function of the overall environment in which cooperation flourishes or fails.

Opportunities to Gain Through Collective Action

One of the most straightforward answers to this question is that groups participated in a collective effort when their opportunities to gain from the collective activity were greater than those likely to be achieved individually. These efforts sometimes allow a group to acquire resources that are otherwise unattainable, as is the case in the use of volunteers in public land management. At times, they create political synergies that allow a coalition of interests to succeed where individually they could not. Or they may simply provide an opportunity for a set of interests to overcome a state of impasse that exists between them. Without acting, all parties are stuck. In negotiation jargon, they do not have a good BATNA and hence perceive a higher probability of success through cooperation.

In most of the cases of cross-boundary management described in this book, individual groups banded together to achieve things they could not achieve on their own. In the Adirondacks in the 1880s anglers and hunters, concerned about the loss of fish and game and business interests worried that an eroded landscape would harm the hydrology of the Erie Canal, joined forces to push for legislative protection of the region. In the Big Cimarron area, livestock interests and recreationists were able to agree to an interesting time-bounded management scheme to protect each of their interests.

In the Big Cypress, environmentalists sought ecological protection, hunters and off-road vehicle users wanted an area they could use, landowners wanted to protect their investments including the opportunity to develop oil and gas reserves, and Native American tribes wanted to continue subsistence and religious use of the resources of the region. Fearing that their individual efforts might fail, they united behind an innovative preservation regime. Similarly, preservationists and developers made for strange bedfellows in uniting behind the concepts underlying the Rincon Institute. None of these interests agreed to cooperate out of the goodness of their hearts. Rather, cooperation provided the means to achieve their individual interests more effectively than what they were likely to achieve on their own.

Perception of Common Problems or Threats

Having a shared sense of a problem or threat to an area sometimes motivates diverse individuals to overcome prior conflicts and work together. When faced with a common enemy, such as an economic downturn or the degradation of a valued public resource, people often pull together. For example, the Dade County jetport proposal created a sense of threat and prompted diverse stakeholders to view the Big Cypress Swamp and their own prospects differently. Similarly, fears of a development boom in the Adirondacks in the mid-1980s helped create a sense of crisis that propelled protection efforts forward. Such threats, particularly those to people's jobs or neighborhoods, are highly mobilizing. They create a sense of urgency and a common target that allow organizers to generate resources and the commitment of often disparate parties to face the common problem. The negotiation literature tells us that people are more risk-taking when faced with potential losses, rather than potential benefits (Bazerman 1986). Having a common threat draws on this psychological dynamic to foster cooperative action in response to a potential loss.

Shared Goals or Sense of Place

Similarly, having a shared set of goals, which often build on a feeling that an area or region is unique, sometimes motivates diverse individuals to overcome prior conflicts and work together. Many of the more successful cooperative efforts work hard at developing shared goals such as revitalizing local economies in an ecologically sustainable way. Sometimes to find shared goals, groups are forced to look for objectives above the current problem or conflict. That is, what started as a battle over a specific proposed action evolved into a broader look at a community's future. Fostering cooperation by articulating such "superordinate goals," goals above the current conflict, is consistent with classic research on cooperation (Sherif 1958).

The Black Bear Conservation Committee (BBCC) (Chapter 7, this volume) demonstrates the power of such overarching goals. Although the members of the BBCC had different opinions on the desirability of listing the Louisiana black bear under the Endangered Species Act, all members of the group shared a common interest in restoring bear populations, overcoming the state of impasse, and demonstrating that a cooperative management model was possible. Indeed, the group agreed to disagree on the listing question—each member could respond to the listing process as they wanted outside of the BBCC—while agreeing to work together on restoration activities.

A sense of place also is helpful to fostering a cooperative spirit. In discussing the concept of an environmental sense of place, Charles Foster notes that, even though we often think of place and space as synonymous, a sense of place is not purely a physical location (nor is it sometimes delimited by geography). According to Foster (1995), "places are considered to be physical locations imbued with human meaning constituting fields of genuine caring and concern. They display three primary characteristics: a landscape setting, a set of associated activities, and a significance to people. Thus, place involves both humans and nature, not the presence of one to the exclusion of the other." The importance of a sense of place for actions to protect it is well known. As Simonson (1989) has observed, "We pollute and plunder what is separate from us; we protect and cherish what we belong to."

Entrepreneurs and Champions

Many cross-boundary efforts owe a portion of their success to the motivation, dedication, and energies of key participants. In the policy literature these individuals have been called "fixers" (Bardach 1977). The organizational management literature refers to them as "maestros" (Westrum 1994) and highlights their importance to successful innovation. These roles include people such as Saguaro National Monument Superintendent Bill Paleck who put a lot of personal and organizational energy and commitment into an effort, motivated others to get involved, fostered trust among participants and support for the cooperative goals, and saw the efforts through. They also include private citizens, such as Janice Brown, conservationist and owner of a guest lodge on the Henry's Fork of the Snake River in the Yellowstone region, and Dale Swensen, executive director of the Fremont-Madison Irrigation District, who co-facilitate the Henry's Fork Watershed Council (Sherlock 1996). Project leaders, community leaders, agency field staff, natural resource managers, landowners, and elected officials all have played this role in various projects and at times keep cooperative efforts alive despite a lack of resources, political or public support, or agency direction.

What characterizes these individuals? They understand the benefits of cooperation and the importance of garnering broad stakeholder support. At the same time, they often try to downplay their own contributions so as not to dominate the process and demotivate other partners. Often they are willing to take risks and engage in entrepreneurial behavior within their organizations. They are not "superhuman." Rather, they put a lot of energy into moving projects forward. One respondent in the Michigan Ecosystem Management study put it well: "It always boils down to key talented people [who] are willing to invest themselves over and beyond the call of duty" (Yaffee et al. 1996).

Relationships

Preexisting allegiances and relationships were described as an example of a centrifugal force that can hamper cooperative efforts. But the power of relationships can work in the opposite way. Efforts that have been successful at bridging boundaries have usually worked quite hard at building relationships among key members of the cooperative effort. Such relationships allow groups to develop a better understanding of each others' concerns and motives, and personalize groups that are all too easy to demonize in the abstract. ("Joe's okay even though he is an environmentalist.") As relationships are built, problem definitions expand, so that the problems faced by cooperators are shared. In the best of situations, such relationships lay the groundwork for the development of trust that the others are acting in good faith and are going to follow through on commitments.

These kinds of relationships can help in dealing with specific resource problems that otherwise could boil into conflict. A good example comes from events that occurred during the summer of 1995 in the Henry's Fork case: "Normally by midsummer, farmers along the Henry's Fork are irrigating, thereby pulling cooler, deeper water from Henry's Lake into the river. But continual rain had made irrigation unnecessary, and by July, water in the Henry's Fork was heated to near-lethal levels for trout" (Sherlock 1996). The prior relationship established between Janice Brown and Dale Swenson facilitated a rapid response. Brown called Swenson and explained the situation. In response, the irrigation district and the Bureau of Reclamation "immediately sent 200 cubic-feet per second of cool water down the river, to be captured downstream. In the past such an action might have taken a week or two—and the lives of many fish—says Brown" (Sherlock 1996).

Effective Processes and Process Management

The importance of human relationships suggests the importance of processes that manage those relationships during problem solving. In both the Building Bridges and Michigan Ecosystem Management studies, the top-ranked factor promoting success was the fact that a different kind of process was used. In all cases, these processes were more open to real public involvement. In most, they evidenced shared decision making in which choices were made by consensus. All sought to develop ownership of the process and its outcomes by a full range of participants. From the Building Bridges study (Yaffee and Wondolleck 1997) come two illustrative quotes. According to one district ranger, "What makes this project different is that citizens have been involved from the beginning in the development of the plan. By working directly with citizens, managers are gaining greater insight into people's values and needs, and citizens are learning more about the complex issues." In the words of an environmental group representative, "The Forest Service was successful because its openness was not tokenism. It was sincere. Forest Service leaders were highly accessible to the people. Anyone could call them. They saw themselves as part of the citizenry."

The effectiveness of such processes is not just a matter of agencies becoming more open. Rather, skilled facilitation of meetings and processes is needed to foster the success of cooperative efforts. In some situations, facilitation is provided by independent meeting managers or mediators. In others, agency officials, interest group staff members, or individual citizens have played this role. They designed a sequence of interactions that enabled people with disparate knowledge, interests, and motives to focus on a common problem in a creative way. For example, individuals involved in the Black Bear Conservation Committee were asked at the outset to set aside their organizational biases and focus on the problem of bear restoration. The organizers also scheduled evening social events to build trust and relationships among the members of the committee (Chapter 7, this volume). In the best of cases, the creation of collaborative processes, skillfully organized and carried out, can help build a decision-making space that is inclusive and focuses energy on the concerns of the center, while defusing some of the centrifugal power of opposing forces.

Innovative Structures to Maintain Cooperative Effort

While some cooperative efforts are ad hoc and ebb and flow with the level of energy and interest of specific individuals, others have created innovative structures that continue to promote cooperative objectives over time. Some of these are institutional structures, such as the Adirondack Research Consortium that promotes research and fosters information flow about the Adirondacks, and the Adirondack Council that acts as a watchdog group. The creation of the Rincon Institute was an innovative way to ensure the long-term commitment of the new residential community to environmental objectives in the Saguaro region. Hiring a full-time coordinator, as was done in the Black Bear Conservation Committee case, can help support the cooperative effort and maintain impetus for its continued success. Funding mechanisms created to promote cooperative objectives, such as the Adirondack Community Development Loan Fund and the small grants program of the Northern Forest Alliance, also can help maintain centripetal forces.

Centripetal Forces: External Factors That Facilitate Cooperation

Forces that promote cooperation arise not only from the activities of the cooperators; they also are an outgrowth of outside programs, interests, or resources. Sometimes a favorable external environment simply allows a cooperative effort to move forward by not constraining it. Other times, external pressures or resources can actively promote interaction.

Opportunities, Resources, and Incentives for Cooperation

At times, preexisting government programs have provided an opportunity for cooperation to take place. For example, in the Michigan Ecosystem Management study, government programs provided the seedbed for more than half of the 105 projects analyzed in the study. In particular, the Forest Service's New Perspectives Program, the National Estuary Program (NEP) administered by the Environmental Protection Agency (EPA), and the North American Waterfowl Management Program administered by the Fish and Wildlife Service provided funding, personnel, and opportunities for cross-boundary management to take place. Similarly, tools provided by federal and state programs like the USDA Conservation Reserve Program were very helpful to facilitating the success of ecosystem-scale management.

Opportunities created in a more ad hoc and place-based way also can allow potential cooperators to move forward. For example, the Memorandum of Understanding signed between Beaverhead County, Montana, and a host of state and federal lands agencies, has created the opportunity for the exchange of resources, information, and perspectives to allow ecosystem-scale management in this northwest corner of the Greater Yellowstone Ecosystem. Creating regular meetings between managers and a county-wide "consensus council" has enabled cooperators to come together and manage across boundaries in nontraditional ways (see Chapter 11).

We also should note that these opportunities take place within an incentive structure that is defined by external political circumstances, statutes, and economic conditions. These forces can create incentives for different groups to attempt cooperation and participate in good faith. For example, the Endangered Species Act (ESA) has helped create an incentive structure that pushes groups to the negotiating table (Yaffee and Wondolleck 1994). Agencies and development interests have participated in habitat conservation planning and interagency consultations because of the fear of what might happen if they do not. Most of the time, the net effect has been changes in their proposals that accommodate the species concerns while allowing the projects to go forward. Such interactions, at times across boundaries, would not have occurred without the incentives provided by the ESA.

Statutory mechanisms that bind the parties to the collective objectives also can foster cooperation by acting as a disincentive to those who oppose the efforts of the cooperative group. For example, the "Forever Wild" clause of the New York State Constitution establishes a dominant objective for the Adirondacks Forest Preserve and is a very important governor on forces that would want to weaken protection efforts. To change the provision, two consecutive sessions of the state legislature need to approve changes, and they must be passed by referendum in a subsequent general election. The magnitude of these political acts and the amount of time it takes for them to happen make it unlikely that the protection goal accorded to the Adirondacks will be changed (see Chapter 13).

Public Pressure or Interest

Just as outside public interest and pressure can constrain cooperation, so, too, can public pressure promote collaborative efforts. Respondents in the Michigan Ecosystem Management study cited gaining public support for their cross-boundary management activities as the second most important factor when describing factors that facilitated their efforts (the top-ranked factor was the closely related item of following a collaborative approach). Many respondents emphasized the importance of identifying all stakeholder groups and involving them in planning and management decisions from a project's inception.

The Michigan Ecosystem Management study also suggests that projects that have roots in the local community are better received than those perceived as top-down agency directives or outsider initiatives. Gaining support from local community leaders and hiring project personnel from within the community were both cited repeatedly as important contributing factors. One respondent from a rural project area in the South explained: "The fact that I was a local boy, grew up here, knew lots of folks, and the fact that I didn't have a government uniform on, made all the difference in the world."

Such support also is needed as the cooperative efforts seek to acquire legitimacy and expanded resources from external sources. The Rincon Institute provides a good example. Its efforts at outreach, environmental education, and organization have built a strong constituency among private landowners, federal and state agencies, and other organizations. A coalition of these groups was instrumental in lobbying Congress to add 3,038 hectares to Saguaro and redesignate the monument as a national park. The broad-based support for the efforts of the Institute, along with its innovative vision and methods, have helped it secure funding from a variety of outside sources (see Chapter 12).

Technology

Finally, technical tools can help people and agencies bridge the physical, jurisdictional, and perceptual differences that separate them. The development of networked telecommunications systems that allow conference calls and electronic-mail networks can help bridge the physical distances that often separate people involved in ecosystem-scale management. The development of computer-based geographic information systems (GIS) has assisted collaborative groups with the process of combining information across boundaries. For example, GIS development is one of the strategies employed at the Big Cypress Preserve to foster the sharing of data between agencies. The managers there feel that, even if formal mandates and management objectives differ across landowners, the identification of critical resources will enable groups to work together better (see Chapter 9).

By providing descriptive images of an interconnected landscape as well as suitability and options maps, GIS can provide a remarkably effective focal point for a multi-party working group. It can help shift discussions from positional bargaining ("I need to do this" or "We cannot do that") to a focused discussion on the realities of one place. It also can provide the means for scenario building that can shatter preconceptions. In addition to its obvious benefits as a means of organizing data, GIS technology can be used as part of a process designed to build cooperators' perception of a sense of place with a shared set of problems and a potential for creative cross-cutting solutions.

Conclusions

It is clear that the forces promoting or hindering cooperation interact in interesting ways, and there are synergies between both centripetal and centrifugal forces that make cooperation either much more likely or much less so. Nevertheless, by all accounts, cooperation across boundaries is possible and more likely when interested parties work aggressively to minimize or overcome the centrifugal forces opposing cooperation, while maximizing the centripetal forces that help to encourage disparate individuals and groups to come together. None of this is easy, but neither is it impossible. And given the need to work across spatial, temporal, interest-based, and perceptual boundaries, there really is no choice but to try hard to do so.

There are ways for agencies, nongovernmental organizations, and public policy-makers to assist in this process. At an organizational level, several changes would be helpful. Training in negotiation, facilitation, and process management would expand the capabilities of staff members to participate and lead cooperative efforts. Developing the perspective-taking ability of potential cooperators by cross-disciplinary and cross-perspective training, such as exposing wildlife biologists to the decision-making parameters inherent in development decisions, also might help. Indeed, training sessions that cut across sectors and organizational lines might help forge relationships that will be beneficial in implementing a cooperative approach.

Organizations need to change the incentive structures facing their employees. At minimum, organizational leaders need to acknowledge the legitimacy of cross-boundary efforts and allow and encourage their staff members to participate in and champion them. Simply publicizing successful cooperative efforts can help provide imagery to employees and suggest that they are valued by organizational leaders. Agency leaders also need to understand the importance of commitment and follow-through. Mechanisms can be set up as firewalls between the statutory duties of agencies and the input provided by collaborative groups. But it is important to live up to the expectations created by participation in these groups, or all will be left worse off.

These efforts also need an adequate infusion of resources, and agency managers need to cut the champions of such efforts some slack. All should understand that cooperative efforts can leverage greater resources down the line, but it takes an investment on the part of most participants for these long-term synergies to occur. One kind of investment that can help is the development of effective GIS technology and data that can be accessed across agency and group lines. Although raising the funds for this development may not be highly problematic, the mind-set that leads to closed-wall information systems is much more difficult to overcome. Nevertheless, such technology can be very helpful in creating a knowledge pool that encourages decision making across boundaries.

Government policies and programs help seed and maintain cooperative efforts, and some programs, such as EPA's NEP effort, the Forest Service's ecosystem management efforts, and the Fish and Wildlife Service's habitat conservation planning activities, should be maintained and improved administratively. Critical to the success of these and other cooperative efforts is effective participation by all parties. Agency involvement in such processes should be funded adequately, or else they will bog down in frustration. Some government policies, such as FACA and inflexible and overspecified budget categories that constrain cross-jurisdictional efforts, need to be updated. More serious changes that would assist cooperative resource management efforts include changing the system of subsidies that discourage cooperative behavior, finding ways to reallocate public land jurisdiction to overcome administrative fragmentation, creating clearer outcome measures for agency performance that reward ends that are served through cross-boundary solutions, and changing the mandates of dominant-use agencies to facilitate their participation in collaborative efforts.

Fortunately, cooperative efforts often owe their success to the energies and ideas of specific individuals, which means that the centrifugal forces that frustrate cooperation are not impossible to overcome, even in the face of limited agency or policy responses. Individuals do make a difference in these processes. Their successes are exhilarating to those involved and motivating to those who observe them. Although cooperative behavior is resisted by many forces in our society, an evolving set of success stories suggests that an opposite set of forces can be employed to overcome them. Given the need for cross-boundary management expressed in this book, it is important to figure out how to cooperate in a future that will require cooperation to deal with its challenges.

REFERENCES

Ashworth, T. 1980. *Trench warfare, 1914–1918: the live and let live system.* Holmes & Meier, New York.

Axlerod, R. 1984. *The evolution of cooperation.* Basic Books, New York.

Bardach, E. 1977. *The implementation game: what happens after a bill becomes a law.* MIT Press, Cambridge.

Bazerman, M.H. 1986. *Judgment in managerial decision making.* Wiley, New York.

Collins-World Publishing. 1975. *Webster's new twentieth century dictionary of the English language*, 2nd edition. Collins-World, New York.

Fisher, R., and W. Ury. 1981. *Getting to yes: negotiating agreement without giving in.* Houghton Mifflin, Boston.

Foster, C.H.W. 1995. *The environmental sense of place: precepts for the environmental practitioner.* New England Natural Resources Center, Needham, MA.

Gray, B. 1985. Conditions facilitating interorganizational collaboration. *Human Relations* 38:912.

Grumbine, R.E. 1992. *Ghost bears: exploring the biodiversity crisis*. Island Press, Washington, DC.

Mayhew, D.R. 1974. *Congress: the electoral connection*. Yale University Press, New Haven.

Selin, S., and D. Chavez. 1995. Developing a collaborative model for environmental planning and management. *Environmental Management* 19:189–195.

Sherif, M. 1958. Superordinate goals in the reduction of intergroup conflicts. *American Journal of Sociology* 63:349–358.

Sherlock, P. 1996. Idaho learns to share two rivers. *High Country News*, May 13, 28:9–10.

Simonson, H.P. 1989. *Beyond the frontier: writers, western regionalism, and a sense of place*. Texas Christian University Press, Fort Worth, TX.

Westrum, R. 1994. An organizational perspective. Pages 327–349 in *Endangered species recovery: finding the lessons, improving the process* (T.W. Clark, R.P. Reading, and A.L. Clarke, editors). Island Press, Washington, DC.

Wondolleck, J.M. 1988. *Public lands conflict and resolution*. Plenum, New York.

Wondolleck, J.M., and S.L. Yaffee. 1994. *Building bridges across agency boundaries: in search of excellence in the U.S. Forest Service*. Research report to the USDA Forest Service Pacific Northwest Research Station. The University of Michigan, School of Natural Resources and Environment, Ann Arbor, MI.

Wondolleck, J.M., and S.L. Yaffee. 1996. The long term effects of negotiation in national forest planning. Paper presented at the International Social Science in Natural Resources Conference, May 21, State College, PA.

Yaffee, S.L. 1994. *The wisdom of the spotted owl: policy lessons for a new century*. Island Press, Washington, DC.

Yaffee, S.L., and J.M. Wondolleck, 1994. *Negotiating survival: an assessment of the potential use of alternative dispute resolution techniques for resolving conflicts between endangered species and development*. Research report to the Administrative Conference of the United States. School of Natural Resources and Environment, The University of Michigan, Ann Arbor, MI.

Yaffee, S.L., and J.M. Wondolleck. 1995. Building knowledge pools and relationsheds at the forest ecosystem level. *Journal of Forestry* 93:60.

Yaffee, S.L., and J.M. Wondolleck. 1997. Building bridges across agency boundaries. Pages 381–396 in *Creating a forestry for the 21st century: the science of ecosystem management* (K.A. Kohm and J.F. Franklin, editors). Island Press, Washington, DC.

Yaffee, S.L., A. Phillips, I. Frentz, P. Hardy, S. Maleki, and B. Thorpe. 1996. *Ecosystem management in the United States: an assessment of current experience*. Island Press, Washington, DC.

C h a p t e r   1 5

The Continent Indissoluble

Curt Meine

In one of the signature poems from *Leaves of Grass* (1892), "For You O Democracy," Walt Whitman bore witness to a land that in his day was both ripe with potential and riven with social discord:

"Come, I will make the continent indissoluble. . . ."
"I will make divine, magnetic lands. . . ."
"I will plant companionship thick as trees along all the rivers
  of America, and along the shores of the great
  lakes, and all over the prairies. . . ."

How, more than a century later, shall we read Whitman? Should we yearn nostalgically for the young republic, so full of promise, that he knew? Should we scoff knowingly and ironically at his naiveté, his happy vision of a land characterized by the civil "companionship" and self-governing capacity of its citizens? Should we dare hope that such a democracy might yet emerge so apparently late in the national ball game? We may question even the notion of a national or continental poet: who, we may ask, is *he* to speak for *me*?

If, however, notions of responsible citizenship, general welfare, and national vision retain any currency, we can turn again, for perspective, to Whitman's democratic vistas, the landscapes where he found a sense of the unity and shared adventure of America. In "Crossing Brooklyn Ferry," he gathered up the generations:

"It avails not, time nor place—distance avails not,
"I am with you, men and women of a generation, or ever
  so many generations hence. . . ."
"What is it then between us?"
"What is the count of the scores or hundreds of years between
  us?"

While "Facing West from California's Shores," he gathered up the globe, and the mystery of our undetermined destiny:

"Long having wander'd since, round the earth having wander'd,
Now I face home again, very pleas'd and joyous,
(But where is what I started for so long ago?
And why is it yet unfound?)"

Between the continental borders—the Atlantic and Pacific shores—Whitman saw a North America whose natural abundance was to give rise to a vigorous democracy. "All the vast materials of America" would produce a more robust body politic; the vivid landscapes of the New World would bring forth a "new society at last, proportionate to Nature." Those phrases come from "Song of the Redwood-Tree." In those preforestry, preconservation days, Whitman could rationalize the loss of the great redwoods under the "crackling blows of axes" and could accept the "Clearing of the ground for broad humanity, the true America, heir of the past so grand/To build a grander future."

Americans may still share (although seldom articulate) Whitman's perception that the vigor of this democracy is somehow tied to the state of the forests, waters, prairies. But they are no longer universally secure in their devotion to the formula: nature transformed = society fulfilled. Even as Whitman's great work was achieving its final form, that simplistic formula was coming into question. Whitman's last edition of *Leaves of Grass* was published in 1892, as President Benjamin Harrison was establishing the nation's first forest reserves. The century since has witnessed the transformation of the North American landscape on a scale Whitman could not have envisioned, and the emergence of a conservation movement that has served, in essence, as mediator between the body politic and the landscape from which it springs and on which it rests. Conservation, through all its phases of development, has elaborated a key insight that even the visionary Whitman may have undervalued: that the landscape does not merely provide the setting and materials for our experiment in democracy, but is in fact the proving ground of that democracy's success.

The American political adventure is embedded deeply within an ecological and evolutionary context. As dwellers in this land, Americans are, in Wallace Stegner's words, "the unfinished product of a long becoming" (Stegner and Stegner 1981). In the process of becoming who and what they are, they have divided and bounded themselves and the land in ways that reflect the epochs in their history, the conflicting values they have inherited, the varied goals to which they have aspired, the many forces that shape their individual and collective condition. The question we are now asking is: can we look across these boundaries in the effort to live respectfully with the land, the creatures that share it, and the processes that characterize it? That question leads inevitably to consideration of the oldest and most fundamental challenge that we as social creatures face: can we harmonize self-interest and the common good? Stated otherwise: can we successfully mesh the self-interest of free individuals and the well-being of those entities within which the individual exists—the family, tribe, neighborhood, town, state, nation, the salmon run, watershed, flyway, atmosphere? If so, what will it take?

Before seeking answers to such questions, we should try to define the core issue. Whitman wondered about this. What was it, he asked, that we "started for so long ago?" And "why is it yet unfound?"

Securing the Good

We would all frame our answers to those questions differently. But every answer revolves around, and sooner or later resolves itself in, matters of *security*. We draw boundaries to provide security and assume they will. But as doubts and contrary evidence grow, still more questions arise. What is it that we are trying to *secure*, in both senses of the word: what are we trying to gain, and what are we trying to safeguard? And how well have our boundaries served us in the effort?

A case study. My friend Thorsten lives in a neighborhood of tightly packed single-family homes in a midsize midwestern city. He enjoys city life, although he occasionally drops hints about a move to the country, where he might stretch out, indulge his aptitude for tinkering, and perhaps reconnect with his more rural childhood. That he has not yet felt the need to make such an ex-urban move is due in part to the glories of his backyard. Beneath the yard's dense tree canopy, the former owner of the house, a professor of botany at the nearby university, nurtured a rich mixture of native woodland wildflowers. For each of the twenty-odd years since he acquired the house, Thorsten has savored his seasonal inheritance of bluebells, trout lilies, dutchman's breeches, and trilliums.

One recent mid-winter day, Thorsten's neighbor removed several of the large trees whose shade he shared. The neighbor was building a new garage and widening the driveway between their houses. Having begun by removing just a couple trees, the neighbor eventually cleared the entire side of his lot. Thorsten immediately realized that the collateral damage from the project would include his endowment of shade- and moisture-loving plants.

As the winter days began to lengthen, and the sun's daily arc expanded, the ecological status quo shifted incrementally, inexorably. Faced with the dilemma, and no place to transplant, Thorsten sadly and reluctantly made the best of a bad situation. An electrician, he has long needed more garage storage space himself. He is now thinking of building out into the former garden plots, but extending the garage's eaves to provide at least a thin wedge of shaded refuge to a remnant of the threatened wildflowers.

The final tally: one new garage; one planned expansion; a boon for contractors; a diminished diversity of plants, colors, connections; the further dwindling of a forgotten professor's legacy; a shaken sense of certainty in the spring. Even as Thorsten improves his local infrastructure, he regrets the loss of a modest, but reliable, wonder.

Just one of myriad backyard dramas, but it suggests the magnitude of the larger dilemma. If a shared sense of place, value, and expectation is so elusive at home, how can we expect to find it at even larger geographic scales, where an even broader spectrum of values is involved? Difficult as it is to be stewards in our own backyards, how shall we be so in our watersheds, our greater ecosystems, our continent, our earth? Can we even hope to "make the continent indissoluble"? Is there any hope, in truth, of securing common goods across the boundaries? Can we even agree, in fact, on what the common good is?

Scaling the Garden Walls

Increasingly we seek security not in "companionship" with our human and non-human neighbors, but in isolation, behind our boundaries. Analogously, we have rested secure in the knowledge that once the boundary of the public park or forest or wildlife refuge is declared, the life within it will dwell forever in comfort. But history, ecology, island biogeography, and hierarchy theory tell us that there can be no such security. As the essays in this volume attest, we have come to recognize that boundaries, if not understood in terms of the content they internalize, the context they externalize, and the processes they affect, can undermine security in any lasting sense.

For proof that security is indeed a core modern concern, and that we understand it poorly, we need only look into the fearsome mirror of our television advertisements. Through a typical landscape of Western grandeur, a large and expensive four-wheel-drive vehicle successfully negotiates a series of obstacles—falling boulders, tumbling logs, slick waters—before arriving safe at home, behind the fence. Then the tag line: this vehicle provides "a little security in an insecure world." Hidden darkly beneath the modern words and images is the same old anxiety that Whitman identified: that despite our extravagant economic success (or maybe because of it), we are less secure than ever. The notion of security has shrunk to the mean dimensions of the sport utility vehicle's well-upholstered interior.

Modern though the expressions of anxiety are, our concern with security has deep biological roots, a long history, and a venerable place in our mythologies. In the Western tradition, we may trace it back to the expulsion from Eden, and the loss of security that came with self-awareness, curiosity, and the apprehension of mortality. There was security in that primeval paradise, but just one fruit from the wrong tree rendered it, one could say, unsustainable.

The word *paradise* derives from the ancient Persian term for the walled gardens of kings and noblemen—segregated islands of blessed and beautiful space, embedded within, but differentiated from, a wild and profane nature. In some connotations, the Oxford dictionary tells us, "paradise" referred to an oriental park or pleasure ground, "esp. one enclosing wild beasts for the chase" (Onions 1973). Within the garden walls, wild nature, from which the garden emerged, and upon which the garden yet depended, became symbol, separated from the larger reality yet intended to provide connection to it.

It is not so great a leap from the walled gardens of Persian estates, with their imported and impounded lions, oryx, and bustards, to the backyard plot of trilliums and bluebells. Expelled from paradise, bearing the burden of the original sin, Westerners have ventured forth seeking security and freedom in Edens new. The notion found literally fertile ground on the shores of the New World. In the democratic American context, the search for Eden has been, in historian Donald Worster's words (1993), "the key environmental idea, and at once the most destructive and most creative": "America, we have believed, is literally the Garden of Eden restored. It is the paradise once lost but now happily regained. . . . That mythic belief in Eden restored lies at the very core of our peculiar national identity. It is the primary source of our self-confidence and our legendary, indefatigable optimism. . . . We are still a people in love with our prolific Garden."

Love is all bound up in the matter of borders. Loving the Garden, but wanting a piece of it for their own, the latest settlers soon divided and bounded it, altering profoundly the landscape of the prior human and nonhuman inhabitants (H. Johnson 1976, Jackson 1994, Meine 1997). Much was gained—for some—in the process. The bounding of private property afforded the newly arrived owners security against the arbitrary authority of states and sovereigns. The land survey and distribution system offered an alternative to concentrated land ownership and the endowment of a land-rich elite. Corporations gained the opportunity to maximize private wealth. Conversely, the boundaries of reserved public lands provided at least temporary respite from the impacts of both unfettered greed and hubristic resource management.

Through it all, much has been sacrificed. The deprivation has fallen on not just the native people, but also on the newly arrived. In Worster's words, "Confident of having regained paradise, complacent and blissful in its midst, we have lost much of what we have most loved" (Worster 1993). And the search continues. Perhaps it began with Whitman, standing there at the far edge of the continent, asking on behalf of all those who "having wander'd since, round the earth having wander'd. . . . Where is what I started for so long ago? And why is it yet unfound?" Where might one finally find security, freedom, paradise—if not in California, then where?

A century later, many still seek paradise according to the old model. In the domestic spheres, we seek security by creating enclaves. The sign of our times may be the one that stands at the entrance to yet another "gated community" for those who can afford to purchase their share of freedom and refuge. Building walls against the profane and uncontrollable threats of crime, poverty, congestion, pollution, noise, ugliness, new ideas, and new realities, we flee not west into the Pacific, but back inward to the open land at the edge of town, the subdivision with a view, the planned community, the clean place of security "in an insecure world" (Rymer 1996, Knight 1997, Romme 1997).

What of the larger sphere of the natural? Many environmentalists have proceeded on the assumption that wildness segregated is wildness saved. Sometimes this strategy has been followed in full confidence of its effectiveness; sometimes because it was simply the best or only strategy available at the time; and sometimes because it was and remains neces-

sary. But (as other essays in this volume attest) there is no ultimate security for wild things and wild places behind boundaries. In a strictly biological sense, that illusion was suspect at least as long ago as the 1940s,
when Aldo Leopold in the essay "Wilderness" in *A Sand County Almanac*
(1949), noted that "many animal species, for reasons unknown, do not
seem to thrive as detached islands of population." We now have a better
grasp of the reasons why populations respond as they do to changes in
their ranges and habitats, and the assumption that the walls of the garden can provide sufficient security is no longer so widely accepted (Noss
and Cooperrider 1994, Quammen 1996).

So we have come to the time when both conservation biology and
sociology, as well as the testimony of our own eyes and ears, inform us of
a deficiency in the landscape. The age-old yearnings for security have
come up against modern ecological realities. Wendell Berry (1989) has
defined clearly these connections among security, conservation, and
community:

> There are two ways by which individual success and security can
> be made (within mortal limits) successful and secure: they must
> rest on a sound understanding and practice of economic justice;
> and they must involve and be involved in the success and
> security of the community. . . . If we were sincerely looking for a
> place of safety, for real security and success, then we would begin
> to turn to our communities—and not the communities simply of
> our human neighbors, but also of the water, earth, and air, the
> plants and animals, all the creatures with whom our local life is
> shared.

Ultimately, for us in our social lives, but also for our prized protected
places and for biodiversity generally, security cannot be found in simple
sequestration, but only in good relations. The *content* of all gardens, no
matter how well walled, no matter how successfully isolated, managed,
and fortified, is influenced by their *context*: obviously, by elemental
processes involving sunlight, temperature, topography, bedrock, soil, air,
fire, water, and plant, animal, and microbial life; but also by human political, economic, and demographic forces. There is no security for biodiversity or in the long run for people, if our own interests, especially our
spiritual and economic lives, are harshly segregated. In the words of Paul
Johnson, former chief of the U.S. Natural Resources Conservation Service, "a nation that ends up with urban islands on one side, and islands

of wildland on another side, and a vast sea of food and fiber factories in between, is not a geography of hope" (Johnson 1997).

Our boundaries, especially the boundaries of public lands, present a complex paradox. Many of our bounded lands were originally established to promote the possibility of better *integration* of the public and private spheres. As Donald Worster (1993) notes, "The conservation movement emerged out of discontent with an intensely private approach to land ownership and rights. It has been an effort to define and assert broader communitarian values, some idea of a public interest transcending the wants and desires of a strictly individualistic calculus." Americans as a democratic people chose to draw boundaries, to delineate public parks, forests, refuges, grasslands, and wilderness areas, to conserve their natural features and the opportunity to better integrate public and private interests and values.

Now, a century into the conservation movement, we are asked to resolve this paradox and to embark on a new conservation strategy. Boundaries have served historically (and still can serve) to conserve the wild; now, for different reasons but toward the same goal, we need to reconnect the spaces. We need to strengthen linkages not only in the landscape, but also between the landscape and ourselves. To secure nature's legacy of beauty and biodiversity for the future, we must address the impact of both external boundaries and of our individual "wants and desires."

Can we overcome boundaries in pursuit of the common good? We should first recognize that the question can be read in two diametrically opposite ways. On the one hand, it seems hopelessly idealistic to consider the possibility. The question might as well be rephrased: Can we become better people, more cooperative, more visionary, more considerate—better "companions" in Whitman's sense, better dwellers of the commons in Garrett Hardin's (1968) sense? On the other hand the question can be read as coldly realistic: given the fact that people will *always* be too short-sighted, too ornery and individualistic, too oblivious of nature's complexity, too unwilling to check self-interest, are there nonetheless steps we can take to minimize our unintended consequences and maximize our shared benefits?

However read, the question revolves around the same basic ecological fact of life: we, ourselves, are surrounded, and we are permeable. We exist in situ. Self-interest and common interest are bound together in complicated ways, and in the long run we can be secure only to the degree that those bonds are respected. Self and surrounding cannot be severed or reduced to base economics (Ayn Rand and her ilk notwithstanding). The clarification and definition of individuality not only does not negate, but positively requires, a *context*, a world with which to interact. Thoreau and Whitman, champions of American individualism, understood this. So did Aldo Leopold: "All ethics so far evolved rest upon a single premise: that the individual is a member of a community of interdependent parts. His instincts prompt him to compete for his place in the community, but his ethics prompt him also to cooperate (perhaps in order that there may be a place to compete for)" (Leopold 1949).

Prospects for Progress

How, then, do we proceed? The best answer may be: directly, but cautiously. The boundaries cannot be dimmed, however convincing the need, until several prerequisites are met. Many of these are obvious, but it is important to state them, to hear them, to weigh them, to roll the ideas around. A beginning list might include the following:

- An awareness of history, of the processes, forces, trends, pressures, events, people, and motives that have bounded the land. We cannot achieve any resolution of boundary issues without a more complete understanding of the "who, how, when, where, and why" of boundary establishment. If we are to build even a rudimentary sense of a common future, then we shall need basic consensus on at least some lessons from the past.

- Science that better defines how to conserve and restore lands and waters and biotas, and communicates its findings in a clear, relevant, and accessible manner to the public and its representatives.

- An increased degree of trust, slowly and steadily nurtured, that can begin to overcome an inherited and shared burden of distrust. Many of the most exciting and innovative experiments in conservation-land trusts, watershed restoration programs, community conservation projects, collaborative ecosystem management plans—can be seen as tentative steps toward this end.

- Development of new procedures and methods of cross-boundary communication to foster that trust. This presumes that we can span the boundaries which separate us only if we can strengthen the ties that bind us.

- A policy environment that supports cohesion and collaboration rather than speculation, contention, and desperation in land use. Altruism may motivate, but public policy must coordinate and reinforce. New policies, affecting both sides of boundaries, need to provide incentives, or at least remove existing disincentives.

- Revision of our economic philosophy and priorities. There is no ignoring this mega-issue. Conservation and economic justice are bound together in increasingly important ways. Greater concentrations of wealth will foster the illusion that security is just another consumer good, rather than something that can emerge only from individual conviction and community life.

- A strengthened general level of local responsibility (as opposed to mere local control). If boundaries are to become more flexible, the process must involve not relaxation toward the lowest common denominator of provincial self-interest, but steady movement toward the highest assumption locally of long-term responsibility.

- Greater opportunities in basic education and professional training to cross disciplinary lines. As we aspire to better cross-boundary stewardship on the landscape, we must support efforts to think through the boundaries separating the domains of knowledge.

In the end, the search for solutions comes around again to the question of our sense of ourselves, our sense of identity. We can come to *identify* not merely with the safe cultural spaces we build for ourselves, but also with all the places that provide us with our livelihood and our context, including especially the remnant, unwalled wild places. In this more expansive place we can seek not just security, but vitality for ourselves and for wildness, in ways of living that do not strain but strengthen connections and companionship.

Why now? Because it is necessary for our own good and for the good of the life around us. Because both science and history are telling us that we need to think and plan in new ways for the future. Because many conservationists are weary and hope that the work of "saving all the pieces" can be made more enjoyable, more humanizing, if we don't have to holler across the boundaries (or hire the lawyers to holler for us). Because we may, in the process, help to revive the neglected arts of democracy: fairness, reasoned debate, honed thought and open inquiry, tolerance for difference, built-in resistance to demagoguery, a living sense of history.

Conservation operates under both ecological and social mandates. We might once have accepted the fallacy that activities promoting the human good could be pursued and secured with no reference to context. But the garden walls no longer suffice, and the illusion is plain. We risk continuing losses of both biodiversity and community, and those losses are connected. When it comes to the good of life, and of people as a subset of life, we learn that we have a lot in common. In her novel *Ceremony* (1977) Leslie Marmon Silko bore witness to this confluence:

There was no end to it; it knew no boundaries; and he had arrived at the point of convergence where the fate of all living things, and even the earth, had been laid.

REFERENCES

Berry, W. 1989. *The hidden wound*. North Point Press, San Francisco.

Hardin, G. 1968. The tragedy of the commons. *Science* 162:1243-1248.

Jackson, J. B. 1994. *A sense of place, a sense of time*. Yale University Press, New Haven.

Johnson, H.B. 1976. *Order upon the land: the U.S. rectangular land survey and the Upper Mississippi Country*. Oxford University Press, New York.

Johnson, P. 1997. Statement at the symposium, *Preventing extinction: advances in biodiversity conservation*, American Museum of Natural History, 18 April 1997, New York.

Knight, R. L. 1997. Field report from the New American West. Pages 181–200 in *Wallace Stegner and the continental vision: essays on literature, history, and landscape* (C. Meine, editor). Island Press, Washington, DC.

Leopold, A. 1949. *A Sand County almanac and sketches here and there*. Oxford University Press, New York.

Meine, C. 1997. Inherit the grid. Pages 45–62 in *Placing nature: culture and landscape ecology* (J. Nassauer, editor). Island Press, Washington, DC.

Noss, R.F., and A.Y. Cooperrider. 1994. *Saving nature's legacy: protecting and restoring biodiversity*. Island Press, Washington, DC.

Onions, C.T., editor. 1973. *Shorter Oxford English Dictionary*, 3rd edition, vol. II. Oxford University Press, Oxford.

Quammen, D. 1996. *The song of the dodo: island biogeography in an age of extinction*. Simon and Schuster, New York.

Romme, W. H. 1997. Pseudo-rural landscapes in the mountain west. Pages 139–161 in *Placing nature: culture and landscape ecology* (J. Nassauer, editor). Island Press, Washington, DC.

Rymer, R. 1996. Back to the future: Disney reinvents the company town. *Harper's Magazine*, October 1996, 65–71, 75–78.

Silko, L. M. 1977. *Ceremony*. Viking Press, New York.

Stegner, W., and P. Stegner. 1981. *American places*. E. P. Dutton, New York.

Whitman, W. 1980 (original publication date 1892). *Leaves of grass*. New American Library, New York.

Worster, D. 1993. *The wealth of nature: environmental history and the ecological imagination*. Oxford University Press, New York.

Chapter 16

Integration: A Beginning for Landscape-Scale Stewardship

Peter B. Landres

This book has discussed the origins of boundaries from several different perspectives and pointed out the many ecological, social, and administrative problems caused by these boundaries. Many of the chapters also have discussed different solutions to these problems. In this concluding chapter, these various perspectives are integrated to begin establishing some general premises and required actions for achieving stewardship across boundaries.

It seems that all boundaries have dual and contrasting qualities, positive and negative effects. At their most general, boundaries both separate and bind: they separate one thing from another, but these entities also are linked by their common boundary. Boundaries have both positive and negative effects on ecological and social systems. Boundaries aid understanding by classifying and simplifying complex phenomena, but they prevent complete understanding by artificially fragmenting the whole. Boundaries define exclusive limits and responsibilities of individuals, while clearly showing the inclusive lines of the broader community to which the individual belongs. Because many boundaries have a long and rich history and are now relatively fixed, stewardship across landscapes requires working within the framework of existing boundaries to maximize their positive aspects while minimizing their negative effects.

Premises and Actions

The premises and actions that emerged from this book are summarized here. Premises are the cross-cutting and underlying assumptions on which stewardship across boundaries depends. Under each premise, one or more actions are listed that must be taken for effective cross-boundary management. Although each premise and action could be the subject of a whole book, the intent of this integration is to discuss each briefly. This is but a partial list, reflecting the concerns of the chapter authors and their experiences. None of the actions described here will by themselves overcome the barriers and solve the problems caused by boundaries, each is but one element of an overall strategy to be developed and applied in each unique situation for improving cross-boundary stewardship. As the concept of stewardship across boundaries develops and matures, this discussion of premises and actions also will change as new information and new and better ideas are developed.

Premise: A Democratic Society Supports Diverse Values

In our democratic society all values have merit, and as managers of public lands look beyond their boundaries they must now meld these values into the management process. Values are deeply held beliefs or attitudes forged from experience and social influences and reflect the enormous diversity within our society. Understanding diverse values and making them a respected part of the management process will be a significant challenge.

Actions to Understand and Meld Diverse Values

- Improve communication, cooperation, and coordination (the three Cs) among managers and stakeholders. Improving the three Cs within management agencies, among different agencies, and between these agencies and stakeholder groups clearly is necessary. But just as necessary is communication among stakeholder groups because any one of these groups can slow or defeat planning processes. Improving the three Cs will certainly take more time, cost more, and at first be difficult for both managers and the public because of a lack of experience with such endeavors. However, experiences presented throughout this book suggest many ways for bridging different values and different types of social and administrative boundaries.

- Relax traditional "command and control" attitudes common today within management agencies. This does not require managers to relax their legal and jurisdictional control and responsibility. It does require managers actively to seek and understand the values of others who affect and are affected by the outcomes of management decisions.

- Develop local support networks. The local community may be most affected by cross-boundary management decisions, and the local community makes these decisions difficult or easy to implement. Active efforts to engage the local community will allow the decision maker to understand local values and let the community understand the constraints under which decisions are made.

Premise: Decisions Are Influenced by Values

The values of our society, of the local area, and of the decision maker all play a role in the decision-making process, increasingly so as managers incorporate interests beyond their administrative borders. In nearly all cases these values influence the judgments that are required in making decisions. Especially in cases where little information is available about the potential consequences of different decisions, and in cases that are contentious, these value judgments may play a pivotal role.

Actions to Incorporate Values into Decision Making

- Make value judgments explicit. Value judgments cannot be avoided, nor should they be, but they can be made explicit, and by so doing their merits and impacts on the decision and on the land can be openly discussed among diverse people on both sides of a boundary.

- Clarify whether decisions are based on value judgments or technical merits. Failure to clearly distinguish data-driven technical issues from value judgments may seriously hamper the decision-making process and acceptance of decisions by the public.

Premise: Context and Content Are Equally Important

Both content and context are vital to understanding and resolving boundary-related problems. Content is the immediate cause of a problem and the mechanisms that influence it. Context is the broader relationship and interaction of the problem with the surrounding area and other forces that influence that problem. Content is understood by reductionist approaches that dissect a problem into its component parts, whereas context is understood by synthesis or holistic approaches that seek to understand how these disparate parts influence one another. Traditionally, both managers and scientists have relied almost solely on reductionist or content approaches to understanding and developing solutions to problems. Yet all problems also are embedded within a broader context of factors and forces, requiring synthesis approaches to fully understand and resolve these problems. Therefore, both reductionist and synthesis views, within an integrated framework, offer the greatest potential for mitigating cross-boundary impacts.

Actions to Understand Both Content and Context

- Recognize that both content and context affect all problems and issues.

- Use reductionist approaches to understand the content of a problem by consulting with experts and collecting new data on the problem or issue.

- Use synthesis approaches to understand the context of a problem or issue and cross-boundary influences. Tools such as computer-based geographic information systems (GIS) have been very effective at showing these broad-scale relationships. GIS maps also are a powerful tool for illustrating and educating people about the context of problems and issues and for discussing potential solutions.

- Develop management plans and goals for an area that complements those of adjoining lands. Within an agency, modifying land-use goals is relatively easy because authority lies within a single administrative entity. In contrast, developing complementary land-use goals among different agencies and other landowners may be much more difficult and require collaborative processes.

Premise: Every Problem and Issue Is Unique

Every problem or issue has a unique set of circumstances: the why, what, where, and how. Because these circumstances and cross-boundary influences are different in every case, the operating mechanisms and factors influencing the issue also are unique. For example, two different natural areas might both have a similar problem ranging from impacts of fire suppression outside the border of the area to impacts from dogs on wildlife, but because the terrain, vegetation, wildlife, legal and policy context, and values of the local communities are different, the definition and understanding of the problem, and the ultimate solution, will be different in the two areas.

Action to Deal with Unique Problems and Issues

- Develop specific understanding for each problem and issue. Without careful consideration, extrapolating knowledge from one area to another or from one problem to another can quickly lead to erroneous assumptions, data that do not address the problem or issue, analyses that are weak or inappropriate, and decisions that are easily contested.

Premise: Every Issue Is Scale-Dependent

Every issue has a geographic area and time frame that are appropriate for understanding the problem and proposing solutions. Recreation impacts along a trail, for example, occur within a relatively small area, and traditionally these impacts were considered primarily in the context of just the trail. But a cross-boundary perspective suggests that adjacent land uses may have a substantial impact on who uses this trail, as well as when and how this trail is used, thus broadening the traditional scope of analysis. Likewise, impacts of fire suppression occur over an area of hundreds or thousands of square kilometers and require data from a large area and a longer time frame as well. Yet here, too, a cross-boundary perspective enlarges the scale of analysis to include adjacent lands because the values and risks to these adjacent lands may strongly influence decisions about whether fires will be suppressed or not.

Action to Understand Appropriate Scale

- Delineate the geographic extent and time frame that defines and influences the problem or issue. A cross-boundary perspective will almost always broaden the area and time frame used in traditional management planning. Expert opinion will usually be needed in delineating these scales because this still is an area of active research and definitive guidelines do not exist.

Premise: Every Problem and Issue Is Fundamentally Gray

In our pluralistic society diverse values are supported, and stewardship across boundaries embraces this pluralism by transcending the traditional bounds that define issues. But as more people with diverse values become involved in the stewardship process, issues become increasingly complicated. Conflicts also arise between people with traditional and emerging views about the management of ecosystems. As a result, resolving conflicts becomes increasingly difficult as values and norms, rather than technical merits, influence management directions and there is no single correct or right decision.

Action to Resolve Complicated Issues

- Develop a shared understanding among all affected parties of the consequences, both positive and negative, from potential decisions. Shared understanding and collaborative problem solving will more likely lead to informed consent of these parties after decisions are rendered. Although not all participating parties may like the decision, they will at least have contributed to the process, understand why the decision was made, and be more likely to abide by it.

Premise: There Will Never Be Enough Information

Ecological and social systems are fantastically complex and our knowledge about these systems is clearly insufficient. This lack of knowledge and understanding is even more apparent in cross-boundary management, which expands the geographic area and time frame. Information comes in many different forms, varying from the relatively "hard" information of data collected on a particular site for a particular purpose, to the relatively "soft" information of expert opinion and judgment. In between these extremes are data collected at one location but used at another, and inferences and extrapolations from simulation models. Developing hard information is expensive in terms of time, funding, and personnel, but soft information is less precise and useful.

Actions to Use and Develop Information

- Use all types of information while recognizing the uses and limitations of each. For all types of information, but especially the softer types, make explicit the level of certainty and the assumptions this information is based on.

- Initiate data-collection programs when harder types of information are lacking and vital to the decision-making process.

- Establish networks of scientists and other people knowledgeable about a particular area, problem, or issue who are willing to provide their data (where available) or opinions.

Premise: Evaluating Decisions and Their Resulting Actions Improves Management

Managing ecological and social systems provides the opportunity and challenge to test our knowledge about these systems, how they function, and our impact on them. Critically evaluating how decisions are made, and if planned outcomes from those decisions are achieved, gives managers information that can be used to improve the decision-making process and land management.

Actions to Evaluate Management Decisions and Actions

- Recognize the limited knowledge we have about ecological and social systems and the impacts, especially in the long-term, of our management decisions and actions on these systems.

- Improve communication between scientists and managers so each can help the other: scientists can offer knowledge about ecological and social systems and techniques for developing new and better knowledge, and managers can offer the legal and policy context and practical experience of managing ecological and social systems.

- Develop research and monitoring programs to (1) develop new and better information, (2) test the current understanding about ecological and social systems, and (3) test our assumptions and inferences on which management decisions are made and actions taken.

- Develop formal strategies for incorporating this new and better information into decision-making and policy-setting processes.

Premise: Barriers to Cross-Boundary Stewardship Can Be Overcome

Barriers to cross-boundary stewardship are formidable and include legal, policy, and administrative barriers, social barriers in many forms, and a host of practical barriers. Given the lengthy time frame required to change most laws and policies, overcoming all these different types of barriers to cross-boundary stewardship will largely be done by creative individuals taking the initiative to work in unique ways within existing legal and administrative frameworks.

Actions to Overcome Cross-Boundary Barriers

- Recognize the barriers that prevent landscape-scale stewardship.

- Allow creative and risk-taking individuals to lead in forming innovative partnerships. Individuals can and do make a difference, especially in cross-boundary stewardship where there are few policies and no guidelines, every situation is unique, and the concepts and implementation frameworks are just now being developed.

- Improve laws, economic policies and tax incentives, and agency administrative policies to promote stewardship across boundaries. Laws can be interpreted and developed to minimize impacts to adjacent lands and lands managed in common along a border. Likewise, current economic policies and tax laws tend to externalize or shift impacts to adjacent lands and lands managed in common. This reduces or eliminates incentives for cross-boundary stewardship. And last, current agency administrative policies tend to support territorial notions that hinder cross-boundary stewardship. Administrative policy may be changed internally by an agency within a shorter time frame, offering the promise of policies that recognize and support cross-boundary stewardship.

Conclusion

Boundaries are everywhere, crossing and dividing the land in ways we usually are not aware of. Legal boundaries cannot be sensed, although their influence underlies everything. Administrative boundaries divide the land and sometimes are marked with signs and fences, sometimes not. Social boundaries define who we are and how we function in our society:

sometimes social boundaries are easy to see, sometimes they are not seen until encountered. Each of these boundaries influences the land and ourselves in obvious and subtle, positive and negative, ways. Legal, administrative, and social boundaries all reflect the values of our society, and these values change over time. As we become increasingly aware of the negative impacts caused by boundaries on the land and ourselves, the value of long-term stewardship across boundaries becomes increasingly clear. A primary goal of stewardship across boundaries is to recognize these influences and learn to emphasize the positive ones and reduce the negative ones—in other words, to manage the land gracefully, with elegance, harmony, and a fluidity of action that bridge boundaries and diverse values.

About the Contributors

MARK W. BRUNSON is an associate professor of forest resources and adjunct associate professor of rangeland resources at Utah State University, Logan, Utah. His research focuses on the human dimensions of natural resource management and policy, especially on the relationships among environmental attitudes, knowledge, and behaviors. He has studied ecosystem management and landscape-level collaborative processes in the Great Basin, Northern Rockies, Pacific Northwest, Midwest, and Southeast regions of the United States.

M. L. CADENASSO is a Ph.D. candidate in the Department of Ecology, Evolution, and Natural Resources at Rutgers University, New Jersey, and works at the Institute of Ecosystem Studies in Millbrook, New York, on how the structure of forest edges controls the exchange of organisms, materials, and energy between forest and nonforest habitats.

TIM W. CLARK is the president of the Northern Rockies Conservation Cooperative in Jackson, Wyoming, and an adjunct professor at Yale University where he teaches. He has authored or coedited five books, including: *Mammals in Wyoming; Tales of the Grizzly;* and *Greater Yellowstone's Future: Prospects for Ecosystem Science, Management, and Policy.*

FRED J. FAGERGREN is presently superintendent of Bryce Canyon National Park. Prior to this assignment he served as superintendent of Big Cypress National Preserve in Florida and of Mound City Group National Monument in Ohio. His National Park Service career has included assignments at Chiricahua, Saguaro, Florissant Fossil Beds, Grand Canyon, and the National Capitol Parks.

ERIC T. FREYFOGLE is the Max L. Rowe Professor of Law at the University of Illinois at Urbana-Champaign. He is the author of *Justice and the Earth* and more than three dozen scholarly and popular articles on property ownership, natural resources law, and environmental law and policy. A native of central Illinois, he has long been active in local land conservation projects and in Illinois-based environmental groups.

MARK D. GERSHMAN is a natural resource manager for the City of Boulder, Colorado, Open Space Program. He recently developed and implemented a Wetlands Protection Ordinance for the City of Boulder, Colorado.

DENNIS A. GLICK is director of the Greater Yellowstone Tomorrow project of The Greater Yellowstone Coalition. In this position he is responsible for developing and implementing a blueprint for sustaining the 18-million-acre Greater Yellowstone Ecosystem. Formerly he served as a member of the AID Ecuador SUBIR Project Evaluation Team, which focused on park protection, ecotourism, and research.

RICHARD L. KNIGHT is a professor of wildlife conservation at Colorado State University, Fort Collins, Colorado. He recently coedited two books published by Island Press, *A New Century for Natural Resources Management*, and *Wildlife and Recreationists: Coexistence through Research and Management*.

PETER B. LANDRES is a research ecologist at the USDA Forest Service's Aldo Leopold Wilderness Research Institute in Missoula, Montana, where he develops the knowledge needed to protect and preserve ecological systems throughout the National Wilderness Preservation System. Before working for the Forest Service, he was on the faculty of the University of Colorado at Boulder.

SUSAN MARSH is the Recreation and Wilderness staff officer on the Bridger-Teton National Forest, USDA Forest Service, in Jackson, Wyoming. She has worked on wilderness management issues in the Greater Yellowstone area since 1982. She is contributing coeditor of *Keeping It Wild: A Citizen's Guide to Wilderness Management* and author of *A Visitor Guide to the Wyoming Range*, as well as numerous other essays on wilderness and backcountry management.

ERROL E. MEIDINGER is a professor of Law and adjunct professor of Sociology at the State University of New York at Buffalo. His current research projects focus on the legal issues in ecosystem management, the changing roles of scientists in natural resources policy, and efforts to establish nongovernmental institutions for making and enforcing environmental policy.

CURT MEINE is a conservation writer and consultant and the author of *Aldo Leopold: His Life and Work*, published by University of Wisconsin Press. He is affiliated with the International Crane Foundation in Baraboo, Wisconsin.

LINDA MERIGLIANO is a natural resource specialist with the Bridger-Teton National Forest, in Jackson, Wyoming. Her current work focuses on wilderness stewardship and river management planning. She was a wilderness ranger for eleven years and spent many years working with the Limits of Acceptable Change process to develop wilderness management plans. She is particularly interested in engaging people in constructive dialog regarding wildland issues on public lands.

CLINTON K. MILLER is currently a land steward with the Nature Conservancy's Northern Tallgrass Prairie Ecoregion in Clear Lake, South Dakota. He is the former wildlife biologist/research coordinator for the City of Boulder Open Space/Real Estate Department in Boulder, Colorado.

JOHN E. MITCHELL is a range scientist with the USDA Forest Service, Rocky Mountain Forest and Range Experiment Station. His primary research interests include the inventory and monitoring of rangeland and the interactions between livestock grazing and recreational use of public lands.

ANDY NORMAN is the fuels specialist on the fire management staff of the Bridger-Teton National Forest, USDA Forest Service. His work focuses on prescribed fire planning and implementation with an emphasis on wilderness fire management.

WILLIAM F. PALECK is presently superintendent of the North Cascades National Park complex, which includes the North Cascades National Park, as well as Ross Lake and Lake Chelan National Recreation Areas. Formerly he was superintendent of Saguaro National Monument. His National Park Service career has included assignments at Sequoia, Kings Canyon, and Wrangell–St. Elias.

THOMAS PASQUARELLO is chair of the Center for Environmental and Outdoor Education at the State University of New York at Cortland. He is president of the Adirondack Research Consortium and author of numerous articles on the Adirondack Park.

STEWARD T. A. PICKETT is a scientist at the Institute of Ecosystem Studies, Millbrook, New York. He has edited or written six books, including *The Ecology of Natural Disturbance and Patch Dynamics*; *Humans As Components of Ecosystems: The Ecology of Subtle Human Effects and Populated Areas*; and *Ecological Understanding: The Nature of Theory and the Theory of Nature*.

LUTHER PROPST is executive director of the Sonoran Institute and the Rincon Institute in Tucson, Arizona. Formerly, he was an attorney in the Land Use Group with the Hartford, Connecticut, law firm of Robinson and Cole, where he represented landowners, local governments, and local environmental organizations in land-use matters. He coauthored *Creating Successful Communities: A Guidebook to Growth Management Strategies* and *Managing Development in Small Towns*.

DAN RITTER is a recreation and wilderness specialist with the USDA Forest Service Bitterroot National Forest in Montana. For five years he was the wilderness coordinator for the 526,000-hectare Selway-Bitterroot Wilderness that straddles the Idaho and Montana border and is administered by three national forests and six ranger districts.

LIZ ROSAN worked for the Urban Land Institute in Washington, DC, and served as Community Outreach Coordinator at the Sonoran Institute from 1995 to 1997. She now attends the Northwestern School of Law of Lewis and Clark College in Portland, Oregon.

WILLIAM A. WALL is the lead wildlife biologist in the Resource Department, Western Wood Product Division of the Potlatch Corporation. In this position he is in charge of developing an ecological approach to managing and monitoring wildlife across 700,000 acres of timberland in Idaho.

GEORGE WALLACE is associate professor of natural resource management at Colorado State University. He specializes in the management of wildlands and protected areas throughout the Western Hemisphere.

STEVEN L. YAFFEE is professor of natural resource and environmental policy at the University of Michigan's School of Natural Resources and Environment. His research focuses on environmental decision making and dispute resolution, endangered species and public lands policy, and ecosystem management. His recent publications include *The Wisdom of the Spotted Owl: Policy Lessons for a New Century* and *Ecosystem Management in the United States: An Assessment of Current Experience*.

Index

Labor theory of ownership, 28
Lacy, R. C., 54
Lande, R., 54
Land health, 19–21
Landowners, 90–92
  see also Public and private lands,
    boundary issues between
Landres, P. B., 1, 2, 120, 123, 279, 348
Landscape-scale planning and
    management, 59, 134–35, 179,
    288
Land trusts, 94
Land-use planning for bioregions,
    283–84
Lapping, M. B., 220
Larimer County (CO), 177
Larmer, P., 178, 182, 185, 226
Lassen Volcanic National Park (CA),
    122
Lasswell, H. D., 181
Laven, R. D., 180, 184
Lawns, 77
Laws and institutions in cross-boundary
    stewardship:
  common law, 93–94
  conclusions, 105–7
  defining boundaries, 87
  environmental law, 94–96
  generic problems with boundaries,
    87–88
  institutional patterns, fundamental,
    97–99
  landowners, 90–92
  nonenvironmental law, 96
  policy developments, current,
    100–105
  stewardship, defining, 88–89
  summary about cross-boundary laws,
    96–97
  see also Legislation
Leaves of Grass (Whitman), 325
Lee, K., 20
Lee, R. G., 68
Lee Metcalf Wilderness (MT), 127–28
Left-wing politics, 28
Legal boundaries, 344–45
Legal sociology, 71

Legislation:
  Antitrust Act, 166
  Endangered Species Act of 1973
    (ESA), 167, 241, 244, 245, 315, 319
  Environmental Quality Bond Act
    in 1991 (NY), 291
  Farm Bill of 1990, 222
  Federal Advisory Committee Act
    (FACA), 100, 106, 166, 312
  Federal Land Policy and Management
    Act of 1976, 222, 241
  Fish and Wildlife Act of 1956, 241
  Forest and Rangeland Renewable
    Resources Planning Act of 1974,
    222, 241
  Freedom of Information Act (FOIA),
    106, 166, 312
  Mining Law of 1872, 245
  Multiple Use–Sustained Yield Act
    of 1960, 130, 240–41
  National Environmental Policy Act
    (NEPA), 71, 91, 133, 166, 222
  National Forest Management Act
    of 1976, 222, 241
  National Park Service Organic Act
    of 1916, 240
  Negotiated Rulemaking Act of 1990,
    100
  Organic Administration Act of 1897,
    217, 240
  Public Law 93–440, 202–3
  Redwoods Act, 204
  Safe Drinking Water Act, 101, 105
  Wilderness Act of 1964, 129, 218,
    221, 232, 241
  Wilderness Act of 1980, 227
  see also Laws and institutions in
    cross-boundary stewardship
Lehman, C. L., 279
Lehmkuhl, J. F., 165
Length of administrative boundaries, 42
Leopold, A. S., 19, 106, 118, 159–61,
    258, 331, 333
Levenson, J. B., 50
Liberalism, 27–30, 102
Liberal order, 98
Light, S. S., 3

Visitors, wilderness, 232
Visual intrusion, 126–27

Wagar, J. A., 141
Walker, G. B., 71
Walker, L., 144
Wall, W. A., 161, 167, 172, 350
Wallace, G. N., 175, 178, 179, 224, 225, 228, 229, 233, 350
Wallace, G. W., 279
Walsh, R. G., 185, 225
Walters, K., 55
Warblers, 179
Ward, A. L., 53
Warren, R. P., 16
Waste, judicially created law of, 94
Watershed Integrity Review and Evaluation (WIRE), 250
Waters that cross a boundary, navigable, 128–29
Watson, A. E., 74, 155
Wear, D. N., 184
Weathers, K. C., 50
Weitzel, N. H., 51
Wells, M. D., 221, 229
West, cross-boundary stewardship in the, *see* Social dimensions of boundaries
Western, D., 33
Westra, L., 20
Westrum, R., 316
White, R., 185
"White Paper on Candidate Species Conservation Agreements," 173
Whitman, W., 325–27
Whittemore, D. G., 238
Whole and the parts, respecting the, 32–35
Wiens, J. A., 40, 47
Wilcove, D. S., 123, 175, 180, 181
Wilcox, B. A., 118, 150, 151, 155
Wilderness and other natural areas, boundary effects on, 117
  Big Cimarron watershed (CO), 227–31
  conclusions, 134–35
  ecological impacts of boundaries, 118–23

social impacts of boundaries, 124–28
visitors, wilderness, 232
wilderness similar/separate approaches, 129–34
  see also Adirondack Park (NY)
Wilkinson, C., 92, 245
Wilkinson, T., 178
Williams, D. R., 74
Williams-Linera, G., 50
Williamson, O., 88
Wilson, E. O., 66, 279, 283, 286, 292
Wondolleck, J. M., 71, 99, 101, 181, 300, 301, 306, 307, 311, 312, 317, 319
Wondzell, S. M., 47
Woodmaster, R. G., 217
World War I, 303
World Wildlife Fund (WWF), 265
Worley, C. A., 43, 179
Worster, D., 19, 329, 330, 332
Wright, B. A., 150
Wright, G. M., 53, 119
Wright, J., 178, 179
Wright, R. M., 33
Wrong, D., 66
Wuerthner, G., 243
Wyoming, 126–28

Xenobiotic chemicals, 123

Yaffee, S. L., 3, 99, 101, 176, 181–83, 300, 301, 306–8, 311–13, 316, 317, 319, 350–51
Yahner, R. H., 224
Yarrow, D. T., 78
Yellowstone National Park (WY, MT, ID), 53, 119
  see also Greater Yellowstone Ecosystem (GYE)
Yoakum, J., 258
Yonts-Shepard, S., 71

Zahniser, H., 284
Zaslowsky, D., 144
Zaunbrecher, D., 238
Zelle, M., 151
Zinn, H. C., 151
Zoning, 91, 262, 287